BUILDING INCLUSIVE COMMUNITIES IN RURAL CANADA

EDITED BY
CLARK BANACK AND DIONNE POHLER

UNIVERSITY *of* ALBERTA PRESS

PUBLISHED BY

University of Alberta Press
1-16 Rutherford Library South
11204 89 Avenue NW
Edmonton, Alberta, Canada T6G 2J4
amiskwacîwâskahikan | Treaty 6 |
Métis Territory
uap.ualberta.ca | uapress@ualberta.ca

Copyright © 2023 University of Alberta Press

Library and Archives Canada Cataloguing in Publication

Title: Building inclusive communities in rural Canada / edited by Clark Banack and Dionne Pohler.
Names: Banack, Clark, 1981- editor. | Pohler, Dionne, editor.
Description: Includes bibliographical references.
Identifiers: Canadiana (print) 20220260877 | Canadiana (ebook) 20220261024 | ISBN 9781772126334 (softcover) | ISBN 9781772126686 (EPUB) | ISBN 9781772126693 (PDF)
Subjects: LCSH: Social integration—Canada. | LCSH: Toleration—Canada. | LCSH: Cultural pluralism—Canada. | LCSH: Community life—Canada. | LCSH: Canada—Rural conditions.
Classification: LCC HN110.Z9 S64 2023 | DDC 307.720971—dc23

First edition, first printing, 2023.
First printed and bound in Canada by Blitzprint, Calgary, Alberta.
Copyediting and proofreading by Kay Rollans.

University of Alberta Press gratefully acknowledges the support received for its publishing program from the Government of Canada, the Canada Council for the Arts, and the Government of Alberta through the Alberta Media Fund.

This book has been published with the help of a grant from the Canadian Federation for the Humanities and Social Sciences, through the Awards to Scholarly Publications Program, using funds provided by the Social Sciences and Humanities Research Council of Canada.

University of Alberta Press is committed to protecting our natural environment. As part of our efforts, this book is printed on Enviro Paper: it contains 100% post-consumer recycled fibres and is acid- and chlorine-free.

University of Alberta Press to continue to publish books for every reader. You are supporting writers and allowing University of Alberta Press supports copyright. Copyright fuels creativity, encourages diverse voices, promotes free speech, and creates a vibrant culture. Thank you for buying an authorized edition of this book and for complying with the copyright laws by not reproducing, scanning, or distributing any part of it in any form without permission.

This publication is licensed under a Creative Commons licence, Attribution-Noncommercial–No Derivative Works 4.0 International: see www.creativecommons.org. The text may be reproduced for noncommercial purposes, provided that credit is given to the original author. To obtain permission for uses beyond those outlined in the Creative Commons licence, please contact the University of Alberta Press.

*For all rural people
striving to build inclusive communities
and be good neighbours.*

CONTENTS

ACKNOWLEDGEMENTS | ix

INTRODUCTION | xi
Clark Banack and Dionne Pohler

I   **RURAL DEMOGRAPHICS AND DIVERSITY** | 1

1   THE DEMOGRAPHIC CONTEXT OF RURAL CANADA | 3
    The Size of the Indigenous and Visible Minority Populations
    Ray D. Bollman

2   MAKING DIVERSITY IN RURAL AREAS VISIBLE | 47
    A Changing Perspective for Rural Schools in Québec
    Sivane Hirsch and Corina Borri-Anadon

II **UNDERSTANDING RURAL ATTITUDES TOWARD INCLUSIVITY** | 73

3   PARTISANSHIP, PATRIARCHY, AND PREJUDICE | 75
    Inclusivity among Evangelicals, Albertans, and Rural Canadians
    Samuel Reimer

4   UNDERSTANDING RURAL ATTITUDES TOWARD CULTURAL AND RELIGIOUS MINORITIES VIA POLITICAL ETHNOGRAPHY | 105
    The Case of Rural Alberta
    Clark Banack

5   DRIVING INTO NOWHERE | 129
    Refugee Resettlement and Integration in Rural Canada
    Stacey Haugen

III **PRACTICAL TOOLS FOR BUILDING INCLUSIVE RURAL COMMUNITIES** | 151

6   A NOISY SILENCE | 153
    Challenges for Rural Teacher Education
    Michael Corbett, Jennifer Tinkham, and Claudine Bonner

7   PROMOTING UNDERSTANDING AND EQUITY IN RURAL CANADA | 179
    The Role of Community Education
    Michelle Lam

8   CONTEXTUAL BIBLE STUDY | 199
    An Effective Practice to Promote Inclusivity in Rural Communities and Faith Groups
    Coleen Lynch

IV **A RURAL APPROACH TO ANTI-RACISM AND SETTLER-INDIGENOUS RELATIONS: CO-OPERATION AND NEIGHBOURLINESS** | 215

9   CO-OPERATIVE DEVELOPMENT POSSIBILITIES IN RURAL SETTLER AND INDIGENOUS COMMUNITIES | 217
    Lessons from the Co-operative Innovation Project and Co-operatives First
    Dionne Pohler, Jen Budney, Murray Fulton, Darcy Overland, Aasa Marshall, Trista Pewapisconias, and Kyle White

10 INCLUSION ON WHOSE GROUNDS? | 249
    Against Liberal Essentialisms and toward Radical Neighbourliness in Rural Anti-racism
    Phil Henderson

11 THE WORK OF NEIGHBOURS | 271
    A Rural Ethos for Reconciliation
    Roger Epp

CONCLUSION | 291
Clark Banack and Dionne Pohler

CONTRIBUTORS | 301

ACKNOWLEDGEMENTS

THE CONTRIBUTORS TO THIS VOLUME ARE GRATEFUL for the opportunity to live on the land across Turtle Island. The editors respectfully acknowledge that we both live and work on Treaty 6 territory, a traditional gathering place for diverse Indigenous peoples such as the Cree, Blackfoot, Métis, Nakota Sioux, Iroquois, Dene, Ojibway/Saulteaux/Anishinaabe, and Inuit.

We would like to extend our sincerest gratitude to everyone who contributed to the chapters included in this volume. Thank you for sharing your research, knowledge, and insights, and for your support, patience, and responsiveness throughout the many stages of the publishing process. We have learned so much from each one of you.

The seeds of this book grew out of a small workshop, "Enhancing Inclusivity in Rural Canada," held in 2018 at the University of Alberta Augustana Campus in Camrose. The workshop was supported by several people and centres at the Augustana Campus including Dr. Lars Hallström, then director of the Alberta Centre for Sustainable Rural Communities; Dr. Ian Wilson, then director of the Chester Ronning Centre for the Study of Religion and Public Life; Dr. Roxanne Harde, then associate dean of research at Augustana; and the SSHRC-funded Rural Policy Learning Commons, headed by the Rural Development Institute at

Brandon University in Manitoba. The open-access publication of this book has been supported by a grant from the Federation for the Humanities and Social Sciences through the Awards to Scholarly Publications Program using funds provided by the Social Sciences and Humanities Research Council of Canada, and by funding from the Chester Ronning Centre for the Study of Religion and Public life at the Augustana campus of the University of Alberta.

We must also acknowledge the work of Mat Buntin of the University of Alberta Press. Mat has been a consistent source of insightful commentary and editorial efficiency. Without him, this book would not have seen the light of day. We are also grateful to the book's two anonymous reviewers who identified many ways to improve the volume and pushed us to really capture the essence of its contributions, and to Kay Rollans who provided the essential finishing touches.

Finally, Clark would like to express his gratitude to his wife, Kendell, and to his children, Brynn and Everett, for their love and patience while we worked on this project. A thank-you also to his parents Larry and Linda, who grounded him with a wonderful rural Alberta upbringing, and to his rural neighbours in central Alberta, who continue to educate him on the beauty of rural community. Dionne would like to thank her partner, Kris Bratton, who helped her see how cities can also be small towns; her mom and dad, who were excellent role models for how to build community in different ways; and the rural people of Spalding, Saskatchewan, and surrounding communities, who taught her what it means to be a good neighbour.

INTRODUCTION

Clark Banack and Dionne Pohler

WE ARE LIVING IN AN AGE OF CULTURAL RECKONING. On one hand, the last decade has witnessed a surge in popularity of extreme right-wing movements, many inherently nativist and xenophobic, in parts of Europe and the United States (Akkerman, de Lange, and Rooduijn 2016; Hainsworth 2016). Although such movements have so far failed to gain a strong foothold in Canada, recent research does point to increasing occurrences of "hate group" activity (Perry and Scrivens 2016) and specific incidents of "hate crimes" across Canada (Leber 2017). Researchers have also noted weakening levels of popular support for immigrants and refugees (Donnelly 2017), including a growing suspicion of Muslim Canadians in particular (Sevunts 2016). Meanwhile, lack of sympathy for the historical and ongoing challenges faced by Indigenous peoples in settler-colonial Canada remains widespread, although this is beginning to change (Environics Institute for Survey Research 2016; Angus Reid Institute 2018).

On the other hand, mass protests across the United States in response to numerous instances of police brutality against Black Americans in the summer of 2020, coupled with the ongoing work of Canadian scholars like Marie Battiste (2011, 2017), Robyn Maynard (2017), and Rinaldo Walcott (2003), among many others, have seemingly awakened a parallel desire

to come to terms with, and address in authentic ways, racial injustice of all kinds here in Canada. Indeed, Indigenous sovereignty and Black Lives Matter protests have been generally well-supported across the country. An increasing number of politicians of all stripes have also enthusiastically voiced their own support, at least in principle. The ongoing debate over the existence of systemic racism aside, it does appear that we have reached a point wherein a large and growing contingent of Canadians are now calling for an end to racial injustice in our own society.

It is within this context—this seeming age of reckoning around issues of racial and cultural difference and Canadian belonging—that we consider the place of rural Canada. To what degree does cultural, racial, and/or religious intolerance exist in rural Canadian communities, what does it look like, and how does it manifest? How can intolerance be addressed in ways that account for the realities of rural life? What organizations and individuals are already working to counter intolerance and build more inclusive rural communities? What roles can institutions like schools, churches, co-operatives, and community groups, which are so fundamental to everyday life in rural communities, play in this work? And, more generally, what do more inclusive rural communities look like? These are the questions at the heart of this volume. We do not, to be sure, provide definitive answers to any of them. But this book provides a promising starting point for what will undoubtedly be a long academic and practical journey toward enhanced racial, cultural, and religious inclusivity in rural Canada.

As rural areas across Canada become increasingly diverse, and as momentum continues to grow toward a meaningful embrace of the recommendations of Canada's Truth and Reconciliation Commission at the level of local communities, the practical importance of these questions grows exponentially. Our interest in these issues is rooted in our deep belief that basic justice requires an authentic embrace of the principles of equity and inclusion for all residents of rural Canada.

Inclusivity is also essential to rural communities for practical reasons. The future of many rural communities is largely dependent on their ability to attract and retain immigrants (Caldwell et al. 2016; Carter, Morrish, and Amoyaw 2008; Ouattara and Tranchant 2007; Reimer 2007; Wiginton 2013; Yoshida and Ramos 2013). Furthermore, maximizing

opportunities for place-based rural economic development is related in important ways to a high degree of community-level social cohesion (Douglas and Annis 2010; Flora, Flora, and Gasteyer 2016; Reimer 2006; Ring, Peredo, and Chrisman 2010). Addressing issues of rural inclusivity in a meaningful way is required to meet each of these goals.

CONSIDERING INCLUSION IN RURAL COMMUNITIES

Urban stereotypes of rural Canada are well worn: Rural is White and Christian. It is proudly conservative and widely uneducated. It is backward and frequently bigoted, a bastion of cultural and religious intolerance and resentment, particularly toward Indigenous peoples. Media headlines that speak to these notions are burned into our nation's consciousness. Most Canadians of a certain age will recall the name Jim Keegstra, the rural Alberta school teacher who, in the 1980s, laced his social studies lessons with blatant anti-Semitic messaging. We collectively rolled our eyes in 2007 when Hérouxville, a small Québec hamlet whose population reportedly included a total of three non-White citizens, issued an Islamophobic code of conduct for immigrants that prohibited the stoning or burning of women. Much of Canada recoiled at the visceral anti-Indigenous language on display in rural Saskatchewan after the 2016 shooting of Colton Boushie, a 22-year-old Cree man, and the subsequent acquittal of the White farmer who shot him. As recently as 2020, the national media reported on the forced cancellation of a Black Lives Matter event in small-town Alberta, after the White organizer was bombarded with threats and racist taunts on social media. And much of the country stood by helplessly during the pandemic as the media reported on escalating confrontations and violence in rural southern Nova Scotia that included the destruction of fishing gear and the eventual burning of a Mi'kmaq lobster plant in late 2020.

Such stories seemingly leave little room for doubt with respect to rural Canadian attitudes toward cultural or religious minorities and Indigenous peoples. Research in both the United States and Europe supports this vision of the rural, regularly pointing to rural regions as geographies of intolerance (Ageyman and Spooner 1997; Blaschke and Torres 2002). Indeed, several studies that focus on intolerance and prejudice in rural communities in the United States speak in detail to

the presence of anti-immigration views (Fennelly and Federico 2008; Lay 2012) and broader displays of prejudice (Leitner 2012). These are often inflamed by older individuals from well-rooted rural families who express fear of cultural change (Gimpel and Lay 2008), and those from regions who have experienced significant economic decline (Kimmel and Ferber 2000).

Intolerant attitudes are often the product of a complex interaction of both systemic and case-specific factors (Cote and Erickson 2009; Palmer 1996). That being said, academic research commonly singles out certain factors for their particularly strong correlation with intolerant orientations. These factors include lower levels of education (Kingston, Matz, and Wood 2003; Schuman et al. 1997); older age (O'Rourke and Sinnett 2006); a commitment to a religious faith (Hall, Matz, and Wood 2010; Johnson, Rowatt, and LaBouff 2010); a sense of economic insecurity (Dustmann and Preston 2007; Kunovich 2004); heightened fears with respect to cultural loss (Scheve and Slaughter 2001); a general sense of having little control over one's circumstances (Harell, Soroka, and Iyengar 2017); and limited direct contact with individuals from minority groups (Dixon and Rosenbaum 2004; Erickson and Nosanchuk 1998). Of course, compared to those living in urban centres, rural individuals across the Western world tend to be older, are more likely to identify strongly with a (Christian) religious faith, possess less formal education, encounter a disproportionately high level of negative economic effects related to depopulation, globalization, and neoliberalism, and have less experience directly interacting with visible minorities compared to those residing in urban centres. Given what we know about the origins of intolerant attitudes, perhaps it ought not to surprise us that minorities may be more likely to encounter attitudes of intolerance in rural areas.

As Cramer (2016, 89) notes, however, such attitudes often play out within a broader context of a "rural consciousness" that is developed vis-à-vis the urban majority and in which rural citizens experience "a strong sense of identity as a rural person combined with a strong sense that rural areas are the victims of injustice." Research in the United States leaves little doubt as to the connection that exists today between rural citizens' sense of being "left behind" economically and culturally and the growing resentment aimed at minority populations (Hochschild

2016; Wuthnow 2018). This resentment increases the likelihood that rural citizens will join xenophobic and potentially violent hate groups, which maintain a striking presence in rural areas (Kimmel and Ferber 2000; Southern Poverty Law Centre 2021; Young 1990). The persistence of rural intolerance in this context, even if it does not lead to membership in a hate group, clearly increases feelings of insecurity for minorities living in rural communities who are often already in more vulnerable positions than urban-based minorities because of their heightened visibility, the lack of cultural competencies among public service providers in their communities, and a notable absence of victim support services.

Similar to economic trends in the rural United States (J. Adams 2003; Carr and Kefalas 2010; Wuthnow 2013), rural Canadian communities are experiencing losses of primary industries due to globalization, competitive pressures for economies of scale in agricultural production, and downturns in the fossil fuel industry, all of which are resulting in increasing exclusion of rural people from the labour market. In addition, government investments in education, health care, childcare, and infrastructure are declining in rural regions, and clear patterns of youth migration are apparent (Epp and Whitson 2001; Hallström et al. 2016; Parkins and Reed 2013). Such conditions contribute to an increasing sense of scarcity in rural communities (see Pohler et al., this volume), and a growing resentment of their economic and political position. As we saw above, similar developments have been shown to lead to increasing levels of intolerance and race-based scapegoating in the rural United States. Is the same true of rural Canada?

Banack (this volume) and Epp (2019) suggest it may be. However, it is crucial to consider this question within the Canadian context. For one thing, studies have routinely demonstrated that levels of tolerance toward minority groups are higher in Canada than in the United States or Europe (Adams 2007; Bloemraand 2006). For another, very little has been published that compares the attitudes of urban and rural Canadians towards minorities. There is little doubt that minority groups have experienced race-based discrimination in rural communities (Arora and Lauzon 2019; Lai and Huffey 2009; Nieguth and Lacassagne 2009). However, detailed scholarly work considering the nature of intolerance in rural communities in Canada is largely nonexistent. Interestingly, the limited survey data that does exist seems to show that attitudes in rural

Canada are much closer to those in urban Canada than often assumed (Angus Reid Institute 2019; McLay and Ramos 2019; Parkin 2019).

Consider, for example, Table 0.1, which presents the results of a 2019 Angus Reid survey about Canadians' attitudes towards immigration. The survey canvassed 1,500 people across the country. We've broken down responses to several of the survey's questions according to where the respondents lived: in urban or rural settings. While this data is drawn from only one survey, a few very interesting trends immediately stand out. First, it is true that rural respondents to this survey were more likely than urban respondents to agree that Canada accepts "too many" immigrants, that Canada ought to "stop immigration altogether," and that immigrants are a "burden on our country." However, with respect to the first two of those measures, the rural respondents differ from urban respondents by a mere two or three percentage points. Note, too, the relatively high number of respondents from rural areas who gave answers that could be interpreted positively with respect to immigration. For instance, exactly half of rural respondents are either content with the current level of immigrants or would welcome *more* immigrants, whereas less than 20% felt that immigration should be completely abandoned. Similarly, a solid majority (58%) of rural respondents felt that immigrants strengthen our country rather than burden it, and only 21% felt that immigrants needed to do more to "fit in better"—a number 10 points lower than urban respondents.

It would be a mistake to read too much into a single survey, but the results certainly throw a bit of cold water on the stereotype, so common in urban Canada, that rural communities are uniquely intolerant of immigrants. Indeed, we argue that this stereotype tells only one side of what is, in fact, a very complex reality. It ignores, for instance, the widespread efforts of municipalities, community groups, spiritual leaders, and schools across rural Canada to counter intolerance in their communities. It overlooks the fact that rural Canada is dotted with numerous Welcoming and Inclusive Community committees, Indigenous–settler friendship initiatives, and dozens upon dozens of other groups, religious and secular, dedicated to sponsoring and supporting the resettlement of refugee families from war-torn regions across the globe. The assumptions often made about rural Canada further disregard the deeply embedded

TABLE 0.1 Urban versus rural Canadian attitudes toward immigration, 2019

Survey statement	Urban respondent agreement	Rural respondent agreement
331,000 new permanent residents in 2019 is too many.	40%	43%
331,000 new permanent residents in 2019 is about right.	38%	44%
331,000 new permanent residents in 2019 is too few.	14%	6%
Canada should stop immigration altogether.	16%	18%
Minorities should do more to fit in better with mainstream Canadian society.	31%	21%
New immigrants take too many jobs away from Canadians.	71%	66%
Immigrants today strengthen our country.	66%	58%
Immigrants today are a burden on our country.	34%	42%

Source: Data compiled by authors from detailed data tables provided to authors by Shachi Kurl, president of Angus Reid Institute. For more information on this survey, see Angus Reid Institute (2019).

idea of neighbourliness, which forms a core part of rural consciousness and identity. We discuss the concept of neighbourliness in more detail later in this introduction.

DEFINING THE RURAL AND THE RELATIONSHIP BETWEEN RURAL AND URBAN

Urban people sometimes express surprise when they encounter sincere efforts in rural communities to welcome newcomers or to build bridges between Indigenous and settler peoples. They expect, in other words, that levels of inclusion will be dramatically lower in rural communities compared to urban ones. We suspect that these low expectations are partly rooted in a traditional understanding of the rural that no longer holds, if it ever did. In this volume, we problematize these stereotypes about the rural and try to provide a more complex picture of rural Canada.

What do we mean and who are we talking about when we talk about the rural? In one sense, rurality is a settler-colonial creation in North America. And as multiple scholars have noted, continuing to imagine rural communities as being largely isolated from urban centres (and the evolution of ideas and norms that occurs in cities) is, in most cases, significantly outdated (Hedberg and do Carmo 2012; Lichter and Brown

2011; Lichter and Ziliak 2017; Reimer 2013). Rather, over the past few decades, there has been an intensified movement of people, products, capital and, perhaps most importantly for our purposes, information and ideas between rural and urban communities. This back-and-forth speaks to the increasing interdependence of the rural-urban nexus and to a new complexity (and diversity) in rural areas, which has developed over a relatively short period of time.

Of course, the degree to which rural communities have become increasingly integrated with urban Canada has not unfolded in a uniform way. This highlights another way in which rural Canada is far from the homogeneous place many often assume—a point further emphasized in this volume by Bollman in Chapter 1 and by Hirsch and Borri-Anadon in Chapter 2. An emerging understanding of the interconnected relationship between urban and rural communities obviously complicates the idea of a basic rural-urban binary that is so common in popular culture. It also adds further complexity to attempts, already notoriously contested, to define the rural itself. The most common method of defining the rural adopts a descriptive approach, like that employed in Bollman's chapter. This type of approach relies on various indicators of population size, density, and distance to a major urban centre. However, Bollman rightly notes that attempts to be numerically precise in defining the rural are themselves heavily reliant on somewhat arbitrary cut-offs of density and remoteness indices.

Other scholars emphasize the economic aspects of distinguishing rural and urban areas—for instance, drawing rural/urban distinctions according to a region's economic base. Still others emphasize the socially constructed nature of understanding what constitutes the rural, arguing that this judgment is often rooted in a strong sense of "rural identity" (Parkins and Reed 2013, 11–13). Generally (but not exclusively), the contributions in this volume assume that communities with smaller populations that do not have an overly strong metropolitan influence are "rural." However, given the multitude of ways the rural can be conceived, we are somewhat agnostic about any strict definition of rural. In this sense, we strongly agree with Reimer's (2013, 100) observation that no matter how the rural is formally defined, "people develop a sense or vision of rural and urban that guides their behaviour." In other words,

people define these concepts for themselves in operative ways. This is the sense in which we are primarily interested in the rural in this volume. Specifically, we focus on contexts wherein residents understand themselves and their communities to be rural. When we speak about "rural people," we mean people who would self-identify as such.

RACISM AND ANTI-RACISM IN RURAL CANADA

There has until now been a lack of systematic research on issues of racial, cultural, and religious inclusion specifically focused on rural Canada. Knowing this, a group of 14 academics from across Canada met at an interdisciplinary workshop held in the middle of rural Alberta in the fall of 2018. The workshop was entitled "Enhancing Inclusivity in Rural Canada." It was here that the seeds of this volume were planted.

Not a single academic in the room could be counted as an "expert" on the topic of cultural, racial, or religious tolerance in rural Canada. Indeed, there are no experts in this field. Compared to the reams of scholarly work that address diversity and inclusivity in urban Canada, we know relatively little about inclusivity in rural Canada, the specific factors that contribute to and counter it, or the existing institutional and community efforts to overcome it. What we do know tends to come from media stories and anecdotes. We also know almost nothing about how rural people themselves perceive these issues or what they view as the best ways to address intolerance and build inclusive rural communities.

This lack of situated knowledge seems especially problematic given both the current social climate we find ourselves in and the fact that the demographics of rural Canada are changing. As Bollman's chapter in this volume makes clear, Indigenous populations are growing significantly across rural Canada (and indeed, Indigenous peoples have always been there, and throughout Turtle Island). Moreover, there are aggressive campaigns by various rural communities to attract immigrants. This is in addition to the extensive reliance of many rural Canadian industries on temporary foreign workers. We have also seen instances of so-called counterurbanization—a notable exodus of people from urban to rural areas—particularly since the pandemic. All of these factors have resulted in growing visible minority populations in rural areas. As rural Canada continues to diversify, and as tensions between different groups seem to

be rising more generally across the Western world, now is the precise time that work on the topic of inclusive rural communities is most needed.

Despite their lack of academic expertise in the areas of inclusion, the scholars at the "Enhancing Inclusivity" workshop entered into dialogue, motivated by a deep personal connection to some part of rural Canada. Each was also motivated by a collective desire to better understand the attitudes that exist in rural Canada, explore the factors that enable intolerant attitudes to manifest, and offer rural communities an array of practical inclusivity tools tailored to the realities of rural life. More specifically, we shared as a group the belief that rural Canada was not simply a bastion of intolerance that ought to be written off as hopelessly bigoted. While we acknowledged that more work needs to be done with respect to enhancing inclusivity in rural Canada, we also recognized and celebrated that there are already many, many individuals and groups doing this work. Our hope was to learn from this work and think about ways to share it more broadly across rural Canada.

Very broadly, then, this volume aims to make a rural-specific contribution to the topic of anti-racism, defined as "forms of thought and/or practice that seeks to confront, eradicate and/or ameliorate racism" (Bonnett 2000, 4). When we say that we seek to build inclusive rural communities across Canada, we are primarily referring to individual- and community-level processes that welcome, accept, and treat equally all individuals and groups, irrespective of race, culture, or religion. We understand that the language of inclusion is also used to consider the treatment of individuals and groups based on gender, sexual orientation, or disability. While we acknowledge that these identities all intersect with race, culture, and religion, they are beyond the scope of this book and are not explicitly addressed.

We also recognize that there are large and important bodies of work exploring broader issues of racism, inclusivity, and diversity in Canada more generally and elsewhere around the world. This volume does not engage deeply with these bodies of work, nor with ongoing and critical scholarly debates in the fields of race, racism, and anti-racism (see, e.g., Solomos 2020). This is simply because the bulk of our own expertise and that of our contributors lies outside of these fields of research and practice. This being the case, it is especially important that we situate our approach

to these subjects within our own practical knowledge, fields of study, and understandings of rural communities—something we turn to now.

NEIGHBOURLINESS AS THE LANGUAGE OF AND APPROACH TO RURAL ANTI-RACISM

We understand that language matters. So far, we've been talking about the issues at the heart of this book using words like *tolerance*, *diversity*, *inclusion*, and *anti-racism*. But central to our goals here is a desire to outline practical approaches to inclusivity work at the local level in rural Canada. This requires, we believe, meeting people where they are, both physically and conceptually: approaching them with terms, concepts, and language that are already woven into their communities and sense of identity. As Epp notes in Chapter 11, the language of anti-racism, diversity, and inclusion, and even the contested language of tolerance, are, in practice, unlikely to gain much traction in rural Canada. Not only does such terminology have the potential to put rural folks on the defensive, ready to guard the virtues of their community in the face of what must at times seem like a relentless onslaught from urban academics and other "elites," it also tends to miss the mark in terms of the ways in which rural residents think about their own moral obligations and daily practices. It thus becomes important to find language and concepts that can achieve the same goals but that speak to and are drawn from rural life.

We follow volume contributors Henderson and Epp in suggesting that the idea of the good neighbour, or more generally of neighbourliness, has tremendous potential with respect to generating welcoming and inclusive attitudes throughout rural communities. Drawing on neighbourliness— a concept that is already deeply engrained in rural life—could serve as a practical, rural-based way to broach issues of cultural, racial, and religious inclusivity in rural communities. While Henderson and Epp define neighbourliness in slightly different ways in their respective chapters, both use the concept to evoke a practical moral foundation that often governs relationships in everyday rural life. Stressing this "everyday" relational aspect of neighbourliness, especially as it pertains to building inclusive rural communities, is similar to what some anti-racism scholars have dubbed "everyday anti-racism" (Aquino 2016, 2020; Essed 1991): a

focus on the importance of the manner in which individuals respond to instances of racism that they witness or experience in their day-to-day lives. It also strongly aligns with Beaman's (2017, 13) conception of "deep equality," which she defines as

> a process, enacted and owned by so-called ordinary people in everyday life. Deep equality is a vision of equality that transcends law, politics and social policy, and that relocates equality as a process rather than a definition, and as lived rather than prescribed. It recognizes equality as an achievement of day-to-day interaction, and is traceable through agnostic respect, recognition of similarity, and a concomitant acceptance of difference, creation or community, and neighbourliness. It circulates through micro-processes of individual action and inaction and through group demonstrations of caring.

Beaman's deep equality is a relational conception of inclusion that pushes beyond a goal of mere "tolerance" of the other. It moves, rather, toward a genuine embrace of equality, acceptance of meaningful difference, and, above all, a desire to be in community together, much like good neighbours. This, in our view, is what a truly inclusive community looks like. By associating inclusivity in rural Canada with concepts of neighbourliness, everyday anti-racism, and deep equality, we are largely focusing our attention within this volume at the actionable level of rural individuals and how they interact with and treat their diverse neighbours.

That being said, the concept of neighbourliness is obviously not a silver bullet when it comes to addressing racial or cultural intolerance. As Reimer (2013, 100) notes, "people form attachments to place" in ways that can both include and exclude. This is precisely why the notion that neighbourliness can be an antidote to issues of racial, cultural, and religious intolerance across rural Canada must be approached with care. As this volume will demonstrate, neighbourliness has always moved in both directions in rural Canada, defining local community membership in both inclusive and exclusive ways.

The broad goals of this book are, therefore, to (1) understand what drives intolerant or exclusionary racial, cultural, and religious attitudes

among rural citizens; (2) provide a variety of starting points for addressing such attitudes; and (3) encourage the use of language and approaches that grow out of the well-accepted rural idea of the "good neighbour" and that aim toward the outcome of deep equality within the everyday interactions of rural residents.

By focusing on the everyday interactions of individuals, we do not aim to dismiss the very real ways in which racism and cultural and religious exclusion are often structural problems of unequal relations of power that may require broader legal and policy changes in any given community or state. But it is our contention that, in much of rural Canada, the most promising approaches towards building inclusive communities must work with individuals from the ground up, rather than from the top down. For this reason, we focus on rural individuals and groups, in addition to local institutions such as rural schools, churches, co-operatives, and other community-embedded organizations.

ORGANIZATION OF THE CHAPTERS

The contributors to this volume come from different academic disciplines and community perspectives. Some employ quantitative, others qualitative approaches, considering various facets of the issues of inclusivity, neighbourliness, and deep equality in rural communities. We have organized these diverse contributions into four sections.

The first section considers the changing demographics of rural Canada and makes visible the diversity that already exists there, outlining both challenges and opportunities for rural communities. The section opens with a very detailed, descriptive chapter by Ray Bollman, former head of the Rural Research Group at Statistics Canada. Bollman helpfully dissects the descriptive challenges involved in defining what constitutes the "rural" in the Canadian context before providing an overview of the population trends and demographic composition of rural Canada. Central to this analysis is Bollman's emphasis on the growth in proportion of both Indigenous people and visible minorities in rural populations, demonstrating the already present and increasing diversity that exists in these regions.

Chapter 2 attempts to make the diversity in rural areas of Québec more visible while considering the implications of this diversity in

terms of our perceptions of where diversity exists in the province. It also explores the broader challenges and opportunities this rural diversity presents for Québec schools and education curriculum when it comes to enhancing inclusivity beyond metro Québec. Education scholars Sivane Hirsch and Corina Borri-Anadon clearly illuminate the ethnocultural, religious, and linguistic diversity that exists outside of the metro regions of *la belle province* and note the challenges of both the overvisibilization and invisibilization of different forms of diversity. An important outcome of their analysis is a new categorization of diversity in Québec. They convincingly argue that understanding the unique mix of diversity in different regions beyond the major urban centres is important for schools and educational policy. While particular to Québec, Hirsch and Borri-Anadon's general argument can easily be extended throughout Canada, as rural regions across the country experience the changing demographics outlined by Bollman.

The second section in the volume broadens the scope of the book beyond an acknowledgement of diversity in rural areas by considering, from different perspectives, the various attitudes one finds across rural Canada toward racial, cultural, and religious inclusivity. In Chapter 3, Samuel Reimer, a sociologist and scholar of Protestant evangelicalism, uses survey data to explore the question: Are evangelicals—who are well represented throughout rural regions in Canada and the United States and who are often assumed to be less open to people of different races or religions—a threat to inclusivity? Comparing evangelicals in rural Alberta to other Canadians, as well as to evangelicals in the United States, Reimer concludes that rural evangelicals are not, in fact, distinct from other Canadians in their acceptance of religious and racial diversity or immigration (although they do rank as less open to both interfaith and same-sex marriages). Importantly, Reimer notes that political alignment, particularly alignment with conservatism, appears to be a much more meaningful factor in predicting a negative individual orientation to immigrants and minority groups. This is an important finding given the conservative political slant of many rural areas across the country.

The relationship between political conservatism and diversity intolerance reemerges in Chapter 4, but from a different angle. Clark Banack, a political scientist, approaches the attitudes of rural citizens

not through survey data, but through an ethnographic study. In an attempt to better understand the ways in which negative attitudes towards minority groups or Indigenous peoples manifest in rural areas, Banack immersed himself in a series of regularly occurring conversational coffee groups across rural Alberta, an area that is among the most conservative in the country. In this chapter, Banack demonstrates an important link between rural Albertans' sense of identity—which he ties to their growing sense of multilayered alienation more than their conservative political persuasion—and a broader anger they experience when witnessing what they feel to be government attention and sympathy being given to "other groups" instead of themselves. These results strongly echo findings in rural, conservative-leaning regions in the United States. There, researchers have shown a strong connection between the support for someone like Donald Trump, including his penchant for fomenting nativism and xenophobia, and a broader sense of being "left behind" while "newcomers" and "special interests" seemingly get ahead (Cramer 2016; Hochschild 2016; Wuthnow 2018).

In Chapter 5, Stacey Haugen, also a political scientist, considers the experiences of Syrian refugees who have settled in rural communities across Canada, as well as the attitudes of existing community members toward them. Identifying both the benefits and potential challenges that can arise when refugees are settled in rural Canada, Haugen highlights the warmth and hospitality exhibited by rural citizens in these circumstances, as well as the potential limits of this hospitality. These limits are often related to the assumptions and expectations that rural citizens sometimes hold with respect to newcomers. Directly addressing such expectations, Haugen concludes, can go a long way toward ensuring the successful integration of refugees based on equal relationships between newcomers and community members in rural Canada. Taken together, the work of Reimer, Banack, and Haugen provides much insight into the forces that tend to drive (or dispel) intolerant attitudes in rural communities, while also pointing to some new and hopeful ways to think about this issue.

The third section of the volume expands the conversation to include practical ways of addressing intolerant attitudes in rural educational settings. Michael Corbett, Jennifer Tinkham, and Claudine Bonner, all education scholars who train students to become teachers in rural

Atlantic Canada, offer a unique approach to the topic in Chapter 6. By interrogating their own experiences as university educators, including how their students respond to discussions about race and Indigeneity in the context of rural Nova Scotia, they note that most of their rural undergraduate students tend to imagine their communities and their lives as largely disconnected from the issues of racialization. The authors conclude that more must be done to ensure that teachers in training receive a strong grounding in the social scientific and humanities literatures on the realities of racism. They also emphasize that the curricula of largely rural teacher education programs must do more to challenge the well-worn notion of the allegedly "close-knit" character of rural life.

In Chapter 7, Michelle Lam, also an education scholar, notes that issues in rural diversity and inclusion may be linked to the fact that many individuals in rural communities simply lack knowledge about the cultural, linguistic, and religious diversity of newcomers. She points to the need for well-designed, community-based education programming in rural Canada. These programs, she stresses, must be "two-way"—that is, they must be aimed at both the increasing number of newcomers arriving in rural communities and the existing rural citizens who have often never received much formal education on issues related to cultural, racial, or religious diversity, or the lived realities of minority groups. Moving from the abstract to the practical, Lam convincingly depicts the effectiveness of specific experiential learning activities in this regard, documenting her experiences leading groups of rural Manitoba citizens in playing a board game she developed called *Refugee Journeys*. As she shows, the game can successfully encourage complicated conversations about the realities faced by newcomers after their arrival in rural Canada. She points out that while discussions at the intersection of education and integration often focus on the educational needs of newcomers, it is important to consider the context into which they arrive, and to also direct educational efforts toward the broader community. Lam's approach to community education, as well as her practical educational tool, provide a way to address the challenges Haugen highlights in Chapter 5: the assumptions and expectations rural citizens may hold with respect to refugees before they arrive in their community.

Coleen Lynch, a former Anglican priest with over four decades of experience ministering in rural communities, provides a second powerful example of an experiential learning tool in Chapter 8, this time aimed at changing individual attitudes towards both newcomers and Indigenous peoples in rural Canada. Given the continuing role played by Christian churches in rural communities across Canada (as highlighted by Reimer in Chapter 3), Lynch notes the opportunity that church leaders have to influence the attitudes of church members in general. She describes her own positive experiences facilitating group-based Contextual Bible Studies: interactive sessions of interpreting Biblical and religious stories in ways that, as she says in her chapter, bring "the perspectives of both the context of the reader and the context of the Bible into dialogue, for the purpose of transformation." Her case study highlights the experience of a group of rural churchgoers and neighbours who come together to read and discuss some well-known Christian texts. Lynch documents how the participants' experience in these Contextual Bible Studies can lead them to consider the difficulties facing both newcomers to Canada and Indigenous peoples, which they had previously overlooked.

The final section of the volume continues exploring uniquely rural approaches to everyday anti-racism, but with a focus on settler–Indigenous relations and their challenges. All three chapters in this section provide unique and thoughtful examples of possible solutions to these challenges— solutions that demand much attention and engagement given the negative history of colonization and ongoing reality of settler–Indigenous relations, a growing Indigenous population in rural regions, and well-documented instances of ongoing conflict between Indigenous and settler peoples and communities across rural Canada. Chapter 9 considers the issue of inclusivity through an economic and social development lens, exploring how community needs, the notion of scarcity in rural settler and Indigenous communities, and barriers to collaboration can all contribute to high levels of distrust among rural settlers and Indigenous peoples and communities. Dionne Pohler, Jen Budney, Murray Fulton, Darcy Overland, Aasa Marshall, Trista Pewapisconias, and Kyle White—a set of Saskatchewan academics and rural community and co-operative development workers— outline how the co-operative community development model employed by organizations such as Co-operatives First can be used to address the

self-defined socioeconomic needs of both settlers and Indigenous people living in rural areas. They highlight the way this model also works to build resilience and trust by creating opportunities for people to work together within and across their communities.

Finally, Philip Henderson (Chapter 10) and Roger Epp (Chapter 11) draw out the concept of rural neighbourliness, which grounds this volume and its anti-racist approach, in the context of rural reconciliation. Henderson, a scholar of politics and Indigenous Nationhood, uses recent examples of White supremacist vandalism and corresponding reactions of elected officials in Owen Sound, Ontario, as a window to explore and strongly challenge the liberal underpinnings of much existing analysis on the issue of racism in rural communities across North America. Writing from a critical perspective, Henderson argues that a much more radical conceptualization of neighbourliness is key to moving issues of inclusivity forward in rural Canada.

Epp, also a political scientist, argues that the most important work of reconciliation between settlers and Indigenous peoples in rural areas is the work undertaken at the local level. He suggests, however, that the language of diversity and inclusion typically used in such work is not as likely to gain traction in rural areas as that of "the neighbour"—an idea that already deeply resonates with rural community members. Anchoring his analysis in a thoughtful exploration of the well-known Christian story of the Good Samaritan (a story that, like the idea of neighbourliness, will resonate strongly with many rural Canadians), Epp argues that neighbourliness could provide a compelling moral ethos for reconciliation in rural areas, partly because it is deeply embedded in rural consciousness and partly because it has very practical implications for the responsibilities rural settlers have toward their Indigenous neighbours.

Overall, each of the chapters in this volume is written in a way that speaks directly to the realities of rural life in Canada. Firmly undergirding our approach is a collective belief that rural Canada can be and is distinct from urban Canada, not just demographically or economically, but also socially and culturally. For better or worse, rural Canada is not the same as urban Canada. We think it is important for this uniqueness to be taken seriously when considering issues of inclusion, especially when it comes to recommending practical tools that could provide meaningful

assistance to rural groups and communities who desire to work toward building inclusive communities. Taken together, we believe the contributions in this volume represent a necessary starting point from which additional research can take place and new practices can form. Just as importantly, we see these contributions as necessary to and helpful for moving in the direction of an enhanced inclusivity across rural Canada that is rooted in the familiar concept of neighbourliness and strives for something akin to deep equality among neighbours in these communities.

Finally, we as editors feel it important to acknowledge our position as White settlers. We do not claim to speak from the perspective of Indigenous peoples, nor from that of racialized, religious, or cultural minority settlers. We do not suggest that we can fully understand the experiences of members of these groups in rural Canada. Our perspectives are rooted in the fact that we were both raised on the rural prairie and understand ourselves as people who intimately know and love the places that we call rural Canada. From these perspectives, we desire to work as allies with people who seek to achieve deep equality and build good relations with all their neighbours. In addition to encouraging more scholarly work in this area, we sincerely hope that this edited volume will help rural people think about ways to work with each other toward these goals in the context of their own communities.

REFERENCES

Adams, Jane. 2003. *Fighting for the Farm: Rural America Transformed*. Philadelphia: University of Pennsylvania Press.

Adams, Michael. 2007. *Unlikely Utopia: The Surprising Triumph of Canadian Pluralism*. Toronto: Viking Canada.

Ageyman, Julian, and Rachel Spooner. 1997. "Ethnicity and the Rural Environment." In *Contested Countryside Cultures*, edited by P. Cloke and J. Little, 197–217. London: Routledge.

Akkerman, Tjitske, Sarah de Lange, and Matthijs Rooduijn, eds. 2016. *Radical Right-Wing Populist Parties in Western Europe: Into the Mainstream?* London: Routledge.

Angus Reid Institute. 2018. "Truths of Reconciliation: Canadians Are Deeply Divided on How to Best Address Indigenous Issues." *Angus Reid Institute Data Digest*, June 7, 2018. https://angusreid.org/indigenous-canada/.

Angus Reid Institute. 2019. "Immigration: Half Back Current Targets, But Colossal Misperceptions, Pushback over Refugees Cloud Debate." *Angus Reid Institute Data Digest*, October 7, 2019. https://angusreid.org/election-2019-immigration/.

Aquino, Kristine. 2016. "Anti-racism 'From Below': Exploring Repertoires of Everyday Anti-racism." *Ethnic and Racial Studies* 39 (1): 105–22.

Aquino, Kristine. 2020. "Anti-racism and Everyday Life." In *Routledge International Handbook of Contemporary Racisms*, edited by John Solomos, 216–29. London: Routledge.

Arora, Pallak, and Al C. Lauzon. 2019. "Through Their Eyes: Experiences of Rural Immigrants." *The Journal of Community Development* 14 (2): 24–41.

Battiste, Marie. 2011. *Reclaiming Indigenous Voice and Vision*. Vancouver: UBC Press.

Battiste, Marie. 2017. *Decolonizing Education: Nourishing the Learning Spirit*. Vancouver: UBC Press.

Beaman, Lori. 2017. *Deep Equality in an Era of Religious Diversity*. Oxford: Oxford University Press.

Blaschke, Jochen, and Guillermo Torres. 2002. *Racism in Rural Areas*. Vienna: European Monitoring Centre on Racism and Xenophobia.

Bloemraad, Irene. 2006. *Becoming a Citizen: Incorporating Immigrants and Refugees in the United States and Canada*. Berkeley: University of California Press.

Bonnett, Alastair. 2000. *Anti-racism*. London: Routledge.

Caldwell, Wayne, Brianne Labute, Bakhtawar Kwan, and Natasha D'Souza Rea. 2016. *Attracting and Retaining Newcomers in Rural Communities and Small Towns*. St. Catharines, ON: Crabtree Publishers.

Carr, Patrick J., and Maria J. Kefalas. 2010. *Hollowing Out the Middle: The Rural Brain Drain and What It Means for America*. Boston: Beacon Press.

Carter, Tom, Margot Morrish, and Benjamin Amoyaw. 2008. "Attracting Immigrants to Smaller Urban and Rural Communities: Lessons Learned from the Manitoba Provincial Nominee Program." *Journal of International Migration and Integration* 9 (2): 161–83.

Cote, Rochelle, and Bonnie Erickson. 2009. "Untangling the Roots of Tolerance: How Forms of Social Capital Shape Attitudes Toward Ethnic Minorities." *American Behavioral Scientist* 52 (12): 1664–89.

Cramer, Katherine. 2016. *The Politics of Resentment: Rural Consciousness in Wisconsin and the Rise of Scott Walker*. Chicago: University of Chicago Press.

Dixon, Jeffrey C., and Michael S. Rosenbaum. 2004. "Nice to Know You? Testing Contact, Cultural and Group Threat Theories of Anti-Black and Anti-Hispanic Stereotypes." *Social Science Quarterly* 85 (2): 257–80.

Donnelly, Michael. 2017. *Canadian Exceptionalism: Are We Good or Are We Lucky? A Survey of Canadian Attitudes in Comparative Perspective.* Montréal: McGill Institute for the Study of Canada.

Douglas, David J.A., and Bob Annis. 2010. "Community Development: A Cornerstone of Rural Planning and Development." In *Rural Planning and Development in Canada*, edited by David J.A. Douglas, 281–327. Toronto: Nelson.

Dustmann, Christian, and Ian Preston. 2007. "Racial and Economic Factors in Attitudes to Immigration." *The B.E. Journal of Economic Analysis and Policy* 7 (1): 1–41.

Environics Institute for Survey Research. 2016. *Final Report: Canadian Public Opinion on Aboriginal Peoples.* Toronto: Environics Institute for Survey Research.

Epp, Roger, and Dave Whitson, eds. 2001. *Writing Off the Rural West: Globalization, Governments, and the Transformation of Rural Communities.* Edmonton: University of Alberta Press.

Epp, Roger. 2019. "The End of Exceptionalism: Post-rural Politics in Alberta." In *Orange Chinook: Politics in the New Alberta*, edited by Duane Bratt, Keith Brownsey, Richard Sutherland, and David Taras, 293–315. Calgary: University of Calgary Press.

Erickson, Bonnie H., and T.A. Nosanchuk. 1998. "Contact and Stereotyping in a Voluntary Association." *Bulletin de Méthodologie Sociologique* 60, 5–33.

Essed, Philomena. 1991. *Understanding Everyday Racism: An Interdisciplinary Theory.* Newbury Park, CA: SAGE.

Fennelly, Katherine, and Christopher Federico. 2008. "Rural Residence as a Determinant of Attitudes Toward US Immigration Policy." *International Migration* 46 (1): 151–90.

Flora, Cornelia Butler, Jan L. Flora, and Stephen P. Gasteyer. 2016. *Rural Communities: Legacy and Change.* 5th ed. Boulder, CO: Westview Press.

Gimpel, James, and Celeste Lay. 2008. "Political Socialization and Reactions to Immigration- Related Diversity in Rural America." *Rural Sociology* 73 (2): 180–204.

Hainsworth, Paul, ed. 2016. *Politics of the Extreme Right: From the Margins to the Mainstream.* London: Bloomsbury Academic.

Hall, Deborah, David C. Matz, and Wendy Wood. 2010. "Why Don't We Practice What We Preach? A Meta-analytic Review of Religious Racism." *Personality and Social Psychology Review* 14 (1): 126–39.

Hallström, Lars, Mary A. Beckie, Glen T. Hvenegaard, and Karsten Mündel, eds. 2016. *Sustainability Planning and Collaboration in Rural Canada*. Edmonton: University of Alberta Press.

Harell, Allison, Stuart Soroka, and Shanto Iyengar. 2017. "Locus of Control and Anti-immigrant Sentiment in Canada, the United States, and the United Kingdom." *Political Psychology* 38 (2): 245–60.

Hedburg, Charlotta, and Renato Miguel do Carmo, eds. 2012. *Translocal Ruralism: Mobility and Connectivity in European Rural Spaces*. New York: Springer.

Hochschild, Arlie Russell. 2016. *Strangers in Their Own Land: Anger and Mourning on the American Right*. New York: The New Press.

Johnson, Megan, Wade Rowatt, and Jordan LaBouff. 2010. "Priming Christian Religious Concepts Increases Racial Prejudice." *Social Psychological and Personality Science* 1 (1): 19–126.

Kimmel, Michael, and Abbey Ferber. 2000. "Right-Wing Militias and the Restoration of Rural American Masculinity." *Rural Sociology* 65 (4): 582–604.

Kingston, Paul W., Ryan Hubbard, Brent Lapp, Paul Schroeder, and Julia Wilson. 2003. "Why Education Matters." *Sociology of Education* 76 (1): 53–70.

Kunovich, Robert. 2004. "Social Structural Position and Prejudice: An Exploration of Cross-National Differences in Regression Slopes." *Social Science Research* 33 (1): 20–44.

Lai, Daniel, and Nedra Huffey. 2009. "Experience of Discrimination by Visible Minorities in Small Communities." *Our Diverse Cities* 6: 124–29.

Lay, J. Celeste. 2012. *A Midwestern Mosaic: Immigration and Political Socialization in Rural America*. Philadelphia: Temple University Press.

Leber, Ben. 2017. "Police Reported Hate Crime in Canada, 2015." Statistics Canada, *The Daily*, June 13, 2017. https://www150.statcan.gc.ca/n1/pub/85-002-x/2017001/article/14832-eng.htm.

Leitner, Helga. 2012. "Spaces of Encounters: Immigration, Race, Class, and the Politics of Belonging in Small-Town America." *Annals of the Association of American Geographers* 102 (4), 828–46.

Lichter, Daniel T., and David L. Brown. 2011. "Rural America in an Urban Society: Changing Spatial and Social Boundaries." *Annual Review of Sociology* 37: 565–92.

Lichter, Daniel T., and James P. Zilliak. 2017. "Interface: New Patterns of Spatial Interdependence and Inequality in America." *The Annals of the American Academy of Political and Social Science* 672 (1): 6–25.

Maynard, Robyn. 2017. *Policing Black Lives: State Violence in Canada From Slavery to the Present*. Halifax: Fernwood Publishing.

McLay, Rachel, and Howard Ramos. 2019. "Urban-Rural Divide in Atlantic Canada is a Myth." *Policy Options*, June 3, 2019. https://policyoptions.irpp.org/magazines/june-2019/urban-rural-divide-atlantic-canada-myth/.

Nieguth, Tim, and Aurelie Lacassagne. 2009. "Contesting the Nation: Reasonable Accommodation in Rural Quebec." *Canadian Political Science Review* 3 (1): 1–16.

O'Rourke, Kevin, and Richard Sinnot. 2006. "The Determinants of Individual Attitudes Towards Immigration." *European Journal of Political Economy* 22 (4): 838–61.

Ouattara, Ibrahim, and Carole C. Tranchant. 2007. "Immigration to Rural Communities: A Distinctive and Distinctly Promising Phenomenon." In "Rural Communities," edited by Bill Reimer, special issue, *Our Diverse Cities* 3 (Summer): 97–103.

Palmer, Douglas L. 1996. "Determinants of Canadian Attitudes Toward Immigration: More Than Just Racism?" *Canadian Journal of Behavioural Science* 28 (3): 180–92.

Parkin, Andrew. 2019. "Is There an Urban-Rural Divide in Canada?" *Policy Options*, October 16, 2019. https://policyoptions.irpp.org/magazines/october-2019/is-there-an-urban-rural-divide-in-canada/.

Parkins, John R., and Maureen G. Reed. 2013. *Social Transformation in Rural Canada: Community, Cultures, and Collective Action*. Vancouver: University of British Columbia Press.

Perry, Barbara, and Ryan Scrivens. 2016. *Right Wing Extremism in Canada: An Environmental Scan*. Public Safety Canada.

Reimer, Bill. 2006. "The Rural Context of Community Development in Canada." *Journal of Rural and Community Development* 1, 155–75.

Reimer, Bill. 2007. "Immigration in the New Rural Economy." In "Rural Communities," edited by Bill Reimer, special issue, *Our Diverse Cities* 3 (Summer): 3–8.

Reimer, Bill. 2013. "Rural-Urban Interdependence: Understanding Our Common Interests." In *Social Transformation in Rural Canada: Community, Cultures, and Collective Action*, edited by John R. Parkins and Maureen G. Reed, 91–109. Vancouver: UBC Press.

Ring, J. Kirk, Ana Maria Peredo, and James J. Chrisman. 2010. "Business Networks and Economic Development in Rural Communities in the United States." *Entrepreneurship Theory and Practice* 34 (1): 171–95.

Scheve, Kenneth F., and Matthew J. Slaughter. 2001. "Labour Market Competition and Individual Preferences over Immigration Policy." *Review of Economics and Statistics* 83 (1): 133–45.

Schuman, Howard, Charlotte Steeh, Lawrence Bobo, and Maria Krysan. 1997. *Racial Attitudes in America: Trends and Interpretations*. Cambridge, MA: Harvard University Press.

Sevunts, Levon. 2016. "Majority of Canadians Have Negative Views of Muslims: Survey." *Radio-Canada International*, March 21, 2016. https://www.rcinet.ca/en/2016/03/21/majority-of-canadians-have-negative-views-of-muslims-survey/.

Solomos, John, ed. 2020. *Routledge International Handbook of Contemporary Racisms*. London: Routledge.

Southern Poverty Law Centre. 2021. "Hate Map 2021." Accessed March 10, 2022. https://www.splcenter.org/hate-map.

Walcott, Rinaldo. 2003. *Black Like Who? Writing Black Canada*. London, ON: Insomniac Press.

Wiginton, Lindsay. 2013. *Canada's Decentralized Immigration Policy Through a Local Lens: How Small Communities Are Attracting and Welcoming Immigrants*. Brandon, MB: Rural Development Institute. https://www.brandonu.ca/rdi/files/2015/09/Canadas_Decentralized_Immigration_Policy_How_Small_Communities_are_attracting_and-welcoming_Immigrants.pdf.

Wuthnow, Robert. 2013. *Small-Town America Finding Community, Shaping the Future*. Princeton: Princeton University Press.

Wuthnow, Robert. 2018. *The Left Behind: Decline and Rage in Rural America*. Princeton: Princeton University Press.

Yoshida, Yoko, and Howard Ramos. 2013. "Destination Rural Canada: An Overview of Recent Immigrants to Rural Small Towns." In *Social Transformation in Rural Canada: Community, Cultures, and Collective Action*, edited by John R. Parkins and Maureen G. Reed, 67–87. Vancouver: UBC Press.

Young, Thomas J. 1990. "Violent Hate Groups in Rural America." *International Journal of Offender Therapy and Comparative Criminology* 34 (1): 15–21.

RURAL DEMOGRAPHICS AND DIVERSITY

THE DEMOGRAPHIC CONTEXT OF RURAL CANADA

The Size of the Indigenous and Visible Minority Populations

Ray D. Bollman

THE CENTRAL NORMATIVE PROJECT IN THIS VOLUME is understanding how to build inclusive communities in rural Canada, where people of all racial, cultural, and religious backgrounds feel at home among neighbours. This is an important goal because rural Canada is more racially diverse than many people realize.

Building inclusive communities in rural Canada requires, first and foremost, an understanding of who lives in these communities and who is settling there. My aim in this chapter is to paint a picture of the racial composition of rural peoples and communities across Canada, focusing on the size and growth of Indigenous and visible minority populations. As I will show, rural diversity looks much different than urban diversity in Canada. Rural communities also look very different from each other, particularly when comparing communities across regions and provinces. Those working in areas of diversity and inclusion in rural communities need to take the specific demography into account when developing their approaches. As the ol' saying goes, "When you have seen one rural community, you have seen one rural community."

FIGURE 1.1 The two dimensions of the rurality of localities: density and distance-to-density

	Degree of rurality in the *density* dimension								
Degree of rurality in the *distance-to-density* **dimension**	Low rurality, high density →								High rurality, low density
Low rurality, short distance									
↓									
High rurality, long distance									

WHAT DOES IT MEAN TO BE "RURAL"?

Rurality is commonly described in terms of two geospatial dimensions: density (or population size) and distance-to-density (or distance to an urban centre) (World Bank 2009; Bollman and Reimer 2019). These two dimensions of rurality are depicted as continuums in Figure 1.1, with density along the horizontal axis and distance-to-density along the vertical axis. Communities in the upper-right corner of Figure 1.1 are smaller (i.e., more rural in the density dimension) but located relatively close to a larger centre (i.e., are less rural on the distance-to-density dimension). Communities in the lower-left corner are larger (i.e., less rural in the density dimension) but are located further from a larger centre (i.e., more rural in the distance-to-density dimension). The closer you get in either or both dimensions to the lower-right corner, the higher the overall rurality of the community.

The degree of rurality along these two dimensions determines many features of the lived experience of rural residents. For instance, smaller communities may have few available and/or quality services; however, if a smaller community is close to a larger centre, then commuting to the larger centre would enable access to more and better-quality services. Similarly, businesses in smaller communities are limited in the range of goods and services they can sell locally. However, if the community is close to a larger centre, then it is easier to sell into the nearby larger

market and it is easier for individuals to access the types of jobs available in a larger centre.

The dimensions of density and distance-to-density offer a straightforward, geospatial way of defining the rurality of the resident population. Working with such a definition separates the concept of the rural from the demographic characteristics—such as age structure, degree of poverty, or ethnic mix—of the individuals and organizations who live or operate in rural communities. The degree to which a community can be called rural depends only on where it falls along the density and distance-to-density axes, not on who lives there. That being said, a community's demographic composition may be correlated with these dimensions of rurality. The degree of diversity of communities might be expected to differ across the rurality dimensions of density and distance-to-density. For instance, the rurality of a community may impact its attractiveness to recent immigrants looking for a place to settle.

THE SIZE OF CANADA'S RURAL POPULATION

This chapter uses statistical thresholds to describe and define the rurality of a community. Almost every classification of rural populations in countries around the world will use a density (or population size) threshold and a threshold of distance-to-density or adjacency. Different thresholds will provide different perspectives on the size and location of the populations and communities that we classify as rural.

Table 1.1 shows Canadian communities organized along the two dimensions of rurality. For the purposes of this table, a community is defined as a census subdivision (CSD)—the general term used by Statistics Canada (2016) for "incorporated towns or incorporated municipalities (as determined by provincial/territorial legislation) or for areas treated as municipal equivalents for statistical purposes (e.g., Indian reserves, Indian settlements and unorganized territories)." The Group A and Group B labels in Table 1.1 illustrate alternative thresholds for population size and distance-to-density. Group A represents communities that I will call "small and remote"; Group B, communities that I will call "smaller and more remote." Using these two (somewhat arbitrary) thresholds and adding up the CSDs in each group, we see that there are 1877 small and remote communities in Canada (36% of all communities). Of these, 527 are smaller and more remote (10% of all communities).

TABLE 1.1 Distribution of census subdivisions (CSDs) by density and distance to density in 2011, Canada

CSD remoteness index (distance-to-density dimension)	500,000 and over	100,000 to 499,999	50,000 to 99,999	25,000 to 49,999	10,000 to 24,999	5,000 to 9,999	2,500 to 5,000	1,000 to 2,499	750 to 999	500 to 749	100 to 499	Less than 100	All CSDs
					Number of CSDs								
Less than 0.09	6	19	15	24	49	30	19	13	3	3	3	2	186
0.1 to 0.19	5	13	18	24	79	106	114	202	64	65	99	40	829
0.2 to 0.29		7	9	9	60	96	124	204	63	94	168	89	923
0.3 to 0.39			5	11	34	39	82	269	131	176	462	229	1,438
0.4 to 0.49					10	39	68	137	78	115	311	158	916
0.5 to 0.59					3	2	25	60	20	41	166	117	434
0.6 to 0.69							4	21	15	19	77	112	248
0.7 to 0.79			GROUP A				1	14	12	17	53	59	156
0.8 to 0.89							1	9	13	11	22	10	66
0.9 to 1.0					GROUP B		1	4	3	2	5		15
No population												42	42
All CSDs	11	39	47	68	235	312	439	933	402	543	1,366	858	5,253
					Percent distribution of number of CSDs								
Less than 0.09	0	0	0	0	1	1	0	0	0	0	0	0	4
0.1 to 0.19	0	0	0	0	2	2	2	4	1	1	2	1	16
0.2 to 0.29		0	0	0	1	2	2	4	1	2	3	2	18
0.3 to 0.39			0	0	1	1	2	5	2	3	9	4	27
0.4 to 0.49					0	1	1	3	1	2	6	3	17
0.5 to 0.59					0	0	0	1	0	1	3	2	8
0.6 to 0.69							0	0	0	0	1	2	5
0.7 to 0.79			GROUP A				0	0	0	0	1	1	3
0.8 to 0.89							0	0	0	0	0	0	1
0.9 to 1.0					GROUP B		0	0	0	0	0		0
No population												1	1
All CSDs	0	1	1	1	4	6	8	18	8	10	26	16	100

Sources: Statistics Canada, 2011 Census of Population, catalogue no. 98-311-XCB2011006, https://www12.statcan.gc.ca/datasets/Index-eng.cfm; Alessandro Alasia, Frédéric Bédard, Julie Bélanger, Eric Guimond, and Cristopher Penney, *Measuring Remoteness and Accessibility: A Set of Indices for Canadian Communities* (Ottawa: Statistics Canada, 2017).

Notes: Group A: small and remote (population <25,000 and remoteness index ≥0.4); number of communities: 1,877; percent of all CSDs: 36%. Group B: smaller and more remote (population <5,000 and remoteness index ≥0.6); number of communities: 527; percent of all CSDs: 10%. See chapter glossary for definitions of other terms and abbreviations. Numbers in this table are rounded to the nearest whole number. Sums may not add exactly to the totals shown.

The distribution of the Canadian population by the density and the distance-to-density dimensions of rurality is shown in Table 1.2. Using the same thresholds as Table 1.1, we see 1,584,000 inhabitants in small and remote communities (Group A; just under 5% of the Canadian population) and 205,000 inhabitants in smaller and more remote communities (Group B; just under 1% of the Canadian population).

Of course, my Group A and Group B thresholds are just one way of looking at rurality. Another set of thresholds could highlight rurality by grouping CSDs into, on the one hand, rural and small town (RST) populations and, on the other, census agglomerations (CAs) and census metropolitan areas (CMAs) (du Plessis et al. 2001, 2002). RST populations reside outside of both CMAs and CAs and have fewer than 10,000 inhabitants. CMAs have total populations of 100,000 or more (with at least 50,000 in the urban core) and CAs have populations of 10,000 to 99,999. Both CMAs and CAs include residents of neighbouring towns and municipalities where 50% or more of employed residents commute to the CMA or CA. In 2016, Canada's RST population was 5,918,771, representing 17% of all Canadians (see Table 1.3). Within each province or territory, the RST population ranged from a low of 10% in Ontario to a high of 100% in Nunavut (as the population of the largest centre, Iqaluit, is less than 10,000).

Yet another set of thresholds could break down CSDs into "metro" and "non-metro" populations, with metro areas being defined as CMAs and non-metro areas being defined as all non-CMA areas. In other words, non-metro areas include both CAs and RSTs. The density thresholds used to define non-metro areas is, thus, much higher than that of RSTs: less than 100,000 for non-metro areas versus less than 10,000 for RSTs. As well, the distance-to-density threshold for non-metro areas is based on residents' commuting patterns to a CMA.

In 2016, Canada's non-metro population was 10,206,605, representing 29% of Canadians (Table 1.3). Across the provinces, the non-metro population ranged from a low of 19% in Ontario to a high of 100% in Prince Edward Island and in each of the northern territories. Although Ontario is the province with the lowest shares of both RST population (10%) and non-metro population (19%), it has the highest absolute number of non-metro residents and trails Québec in the absolute number of RST residents.

TABLE 1.2 Distribution of population of census subdivisions (CSDs) by density and distance to density 2011, Canada

CSD remoteness index (distance-to-density dimension)	500,000 and over	100,000 to 499,999	50,000 to 99,999	25,000 to 49,999	10,000 to 24,999	5,000 to 9,999	2,500 to 5,000	1,000 to 2,499	750 to 999	500 to 749	100 to 499	Less than 100	All CSDs
					Population (× 1,000)								
Less than 0.09	6,905	4,047	1,134	822	828	209	66	25	3	2	0	0	14,041
0.1 to 0.19	3,693	2,182	1,308	866	1,165	760	394	332	56	41	33	1	10,832
0.2 to 0.29		1,052	642	292	895	679	450	317	55	59	49	4	4,493
0.3 to 0.39			365	378	499	254	290	425	113	108	137	8	2,578
0.4 to 0.49					123	258	227	209	68	71	90	5	1,050
0.5 to 0.59					38	13	87	99	17	26	45	3	329
0.6 to 0.69							13	30	13	12	20	2	91
0.7 to 0.79			GROUP A				3	21	10	10	14	1	59
0.8 to 0.89							3	13	11	7	7	0	41
0.9 to 1.0						GROUP B	3	6	3	1	1		14
No population													0
All CSDs	10,598	7,281	3,449	2,358	3,548	2,173	1,538	1,477	348	336	397	24	33,528
					Percent distribution of number of CSDs								
Less than 0.09	21	12	3	2	2	1	0	0	0	0	0	0	42
0.1 to 0.19	11	7	4	3	3	2	1	1	0	0	0	0	32
0.2 to 0.29		3	2	1	3	2	1	1	0	0	0	0	13
0.3 to 0.39			1	1	1	1	1	1	0	0	0	0	8
0.4 to 0.49					0	1	1	1	0	0	0	0	3
0.5 to 0.59					0	0	0	0	0	0	0	0	1
0.6 to 0.69							0	0	0	0	0	0	0
0.7 to 0.79			GROUP A				0	0	0	0	0	0	0
0.8 to 0.89							0	0	0	0	0	0	0
0.9 to 1.0						GROUP B	0	0	0	0	0		0
No population													0
All CSDs	32	22	10	7	11	6	5	4	1	1	1	0	100

Sources: Statistics Canada, 2011 Census of Population, catalogue no. 98-311-XCB2011006, https://www12.statcan.gc.ca/datasets/Index-eng.cfm; Alessandro Alasia, Frédéric Bédard, Julie Bélanger, Eric Guimond, and Cristopher Penney, *Measuring Remoteness and Accessibility: A Set of Indices for Canadian Communities* (Ottawa: Statistics Canada, 2017).

Notes: Group A: Small and remote communities (population <25,000 and remoteness index ≥0.4); population (× 1,000): 1,584; percent of Canadian population: 5%. Group B: Smaller and more remote (population <5,000 and remoteness index ≥0.6); population (× 1,000): 205; percent of Canadian population: 1%. See chapter glossary for definitions of other terms and abbreviations. Numbers in this table are rounded to the nearest whole number. Sums may not add exactly to the totals shown.

The RST population can also be broken down in different ways—for instance, according to measures of distance-to-density that take commuting patterns into account. Table 1.3 shows this kind of disaggregation using a measure called the metropolitan influenced zone (MIZ), which classifies CSDs according to the share of the population that commutes to a centre of 10,000 or more. A CSD is classified as a strong MIZ if 30% or more of employed residents commute to a centre of 10,000 or more; a moderate MIZ if 5% to 29% commute; a weak MIZ if less than 5% but more than 0% commute; and no MIZ if there is no commuting to a CMA or CA.[1] Because some RSTs in the northern territories outside of Whitehorse and Yellowknife are particularly remote, they are not classified under the MIZ system, and are instead called RST territories. In 2016, 6% of Canadians lived in strong MIZ CSDs, 7% in moderate MIZ CSDs, 4% in weak MIZ CSDs, and 1% in no MIZ CSDs.

Our thresholds would change yet again if we changed the basic geographic unit we are seeking to define. One may, for instance, use census divisions rather than CSDs as the basic geographic units for classifying the population. Statistics Canada (2016) defines census divisions as "provincially legislated areas (such as a county, a *municipalité régionale de comté*, or a regional district) or their equivalents...Census divisions are intermediate geographic areas between the province/territory and the municipality (census subdivision)." Data for each census division includes all embedded (incorporated and unincorporated) localities in the census division. Like CMAs and CAs, census divisions are composed of CSDs, but the boundaries are different, making it possible or even likely that some CSDs in a given census division could be delineated as part of a CMA while others could not be delineated as part of a CMA. Table 1.4 illustrates one approach of this kind—my own—in which the population of a census division is classified as "metro" if all component CSDs are delineated as part of a CMA; "partially non-metro" if some component CSDs are part of a CMA (thus a partially non-metro census division may also be viewed as a "metro-adjacent" census division); and "non-metro" if no component CSDs are part of a CMA.[2] Using this classification, Table 1.4 shows that 25% of Canadians reside in non-metro census divisions, ranging from a low of 15% of the Ontario population to 100% in Prince Edward Island and each of the territories.

TABLE 1.3 Metro and non-metro populations in 2016, Canada, provinces, and territories

	Total metro (CMA)	Non-metro (non-CMA)								Total
		Total non-metro	CAs	RST areas						
				Total RST areas	Strong MIZ	Moderate MIZ	Weak MIZ	No MIZ	RST territories	
Total population, 2016										
Newfoundland & Labrador	205,955	313,761	70,405	243,356	36,172	121,079	60,285	25,820	n.a.	519,716
Prince Edward Island	0	142,907	85,912	56,995	25,323	30,395	460	817	n.a.	142,907
Nova Scotia	403,390	520,208	205,184	315,024	71,638	117,933	124,264	1,189	n.a.	923,598
New Brunswick	271,012	476,089	197,031	279,058	74,455	128,374	73,315	2,914	n.a.	747,101
Quebec	5,760,407	2,403,954	864,450	1,539,504	635,631	653,473	218,326	32,074	n.a.	8,164,361
Ontario	10,956,264	2,492,230	1,106,057	1,386,173	708,869	451,442	189,085	36,777	n.a.	13,448,494
Manitoba	778,489	499,876	131,111	368,765	86,189	127,464	129,490	25,622	n.a.	1,278,365
Saskatchewan	531,576	566,776	175,700	391,076	44,468	145,602	140,600	60,406	n.a.	1,098,352
Alberta	2,831,429	1,235,746	502,663	733,083	174,320	308,929	220,275	29,559	n.a.	4,067,175
British Columbia	3,206,601	1,441,454	901,527	539,927	136,640	227,912	151,751	23,624	n.a.	4,648,055
Yukon	0	35,874	28,225	7,649	-	-	-	-	7,649	35,874
Northwest Territories	0	41,786	19,569	22,217	-	-	-	-	22,217	41,786
Nunavut	0	35,944	0	35,944	-	-	-	-	35,944	35,944
Canada	24,945,123	10,206,605	4,287,834	5,918,771	1,993,705	2,312,603	1,307,851	238,802	65,810	35,151,728
Percent distribution of population (row percent)										
Newfoundland & Labrador	40	60	14	47	7	23	12	5	n.a.	100
Prince Edward Island	0	100	60	40	18	21	0	1	n.a.	100
Nova Scotia	44	56	22	34	8	13	13	0	n.a.	100
New Brunswick	36	64	26	37	10	17	10	0	n.a.	100
Quebec	71	29	11	19	8	8	3	0	n.a.	100
Ontario	81	19	8	10	5	3	1	0	n.a.	100
Manitoba	61	39	10	29	7	10	10	2	n.a.	100
Saskatchewan	48	52	16	36	4	13	13	5	n.a.	100
Alberta	70	30	12	18	4	8	5	1	n.a.	100
British Columbia	69	31	19	12	3	5	3	1	n.a.	100
Yukon	0	100	79	21	n.a.	n.a.	n.a.	n.a.	21	100
Northwest Territories	0	100	47	53	n.a.	n.a.	n.a.	n.a.	53	100
Nunavut	0	100	0	100	n.a.	n.a.	n.a.	n.a.	100	100
Canada	71	29	12	17	6	7	4	1	0	100

| | Total metro (CMA) | Total non-metro | CAs | Non-metro (non-CMA) ||||||| Total |
| | | | | RST areas ||||||| |
				Total RST areas	Strong MIZ	Moderate MIZ	Weak MIZ	No MIZ	RST territories	
	Percent distribution of population (column percent)										
Newfoundland and Labrador	1	3	2	4	2	5	5	11	n.a.	1
Prince Edward Island	0	1	2	1	1	1	0	0	n.a.	0
Nova Scotia	2	5	5	5	4	5	10	0	n.a.	3
New Brunswick	1	5	5	5	4	6	6	1	n.a.	2
Quebec	23	24	20	26	32	28	17	13	n.a.	23
Ontario	44	24	26	23	36	20	14	15	n.a.	38
Manitoba	3	5	3	6	4	6	10	11	n.a.	4
Saskatchewan	2	6	4	7	2	6	11	25	n.a.	3
Alberta	11	12	12	12	9	13	17	12	n.a.	12
British Columbia	13	14	21	9	7	10	12	10	n.a.	13
Yukon	0	0	1	0	n.a.	n.a.	n.a.	n.a.	12	0
Northwest Territories	0	0	0	0	n.a.	n.a.	n.a.	n.a.	34	0
Nunavut	0	0	0	1	n.a.	n.a.	n.a.	n.a.	55	0
Canada	100	100	100	100	100	100	100	100	100	100

Sources: Statistics Canada, 2016 Census of the Population GeoSuite, https://geosuite.statcan.gc.ca/geosuite/en/index.

Notes: See chapter glossary for definitions of terms and abbreviations. The percentages in this table are rounded to the nearest one percent. Row and column sums may not add exactly to the totals shown.

In other words, there are many ways to break down and describe rurality. The thresholds we choose affect who we consider "rural" versus "urban." Importantly, the demographics of rural communities change depending on where we draw those borders. It is also important to note that any approach to defining a rural community has limitations. Just as different thresholds change which communities are classified as rural, they may also change how we assess diversity, or lack thereof, in rural Canada. Moreover, statistical approaches like this one may not be a good proxy for whether residents in the communities identified as "rural" would view their own communities in the same way. They do, however, provide a starting point for classifying and describing the racial composition of rural communities across Canada.

TABLE 1.4 Distribution of population by metro, partially non-metro, and non-metro census divisions in 2019, Canada, provinces, and territories

Province / territory	Type of census division			
	Metro CDs	Partially non-metro CDs	Non-metro CDs	Total
Total population, 2019				
Newfoundland and Labrador		276,020	245,522	521,542
Prince Edward Island			156,947	156,947
Nova Scotia	440,332		531,063	971,395
New Brunswick	77,484	272,273	427,070	776,827
Quebec	5,028,081	1,377,643	2,079,241	8,484,965
Ontario	8,207,176	4,242,023	2,117,348	14,566,547
Manitoba	768,185	192,307	408,973	1,369,465
Saskatchewan		651,562	522,900	1,174,462
Alberta		3,116,152	1,255,164	4,371,316
British Columbia	2,908,572	750,044	1,412,720	5,071,336
Yukon			40,854	40,854
Northwest Territories			44,826	44,826
Nunavut			38,780	38,780
Canada	17,429,830	10,878,024	9,281,408	37,589,262
Percent distribution of the population within each province (row percent)				
Newfoundland and Labrador	0	53	47	100
Prince Edward Island	0	0	100	100
Nova Scotia	45	0	55	100
New Brunswick	10	35	55	100
Quebec	59	16	25	100
Ontario	56	29	15	100
Manitoba	56	14	30	100
Saskatchewan	0	55	45	100
Alberta	0	71	29	100
British Columbia	57	15	28	100
Yukon	0	0	100	100
Northwest Territories	0	0	100	100
Nunavut	0	0	100	100
Canada	46	29	25	100

	Type of census division			
Province / territory	Metro CDs	Partially non-metro CDs	Non-metro CDs	Total
Percent distribution of the population within each type of region (column percent)				
Newfoundland and Labrador	0	3	3	1
Prince Edward Island	0	0	2	0
Nova Scotia	3	0	6	3
New Brunswick	0	3	5	2
Quebec	29	13	22	23
Ontario	47	39	23	39
Manitoba	4	2	4	4
Saskatchewan	0	6	6	3
Alberta	0	29	14	12
British Columbia	17	7	15	13
Yukon	0	0	0	0
Northwest Territories	0	0	0	0
Nunavut	0	0	0	0
Canada	100	100	100	100

Source: Statistics Canada, Table 17-10-0139-01, https://doi.org/10.25318/1710013901.

Notes: This table uses 2016 Census boundaries for census divisions. See chapter glossary for definitions of terms. The percentages in this table are rounded to the nearest one percent. Row and column sums may not add exactly to the totals shown.

POPULATION GROWTH IN RURAL CANADA

As shown in Figure 1.2, the overall population of rural Canada has been growing since 2003, but population growth has not occurred everywhere in rural Canada (Mendelson and Bollman 1989; Bollman and Clemenson 2008; Bollman 2017a), and rural Canada is not growing as fast as urban Canada. Thus, the share of the population residing in rural areas is declining.[3] This statement of averages does not, however, represent the reality of every rural community, each of which has unique factors that affect their growth. For instance, growth is concentrated near cities, in cottage country, and, due in part to higher fertility rates among Indigenous peoples, in the north.[4]

Density also matters for growth. As shown in Figure 1.3, only communities with a population size of 10,000 or more grew more than the Canadian average (when averaged over the 1981–2016 period). However, there are some communities within each population size group that grew

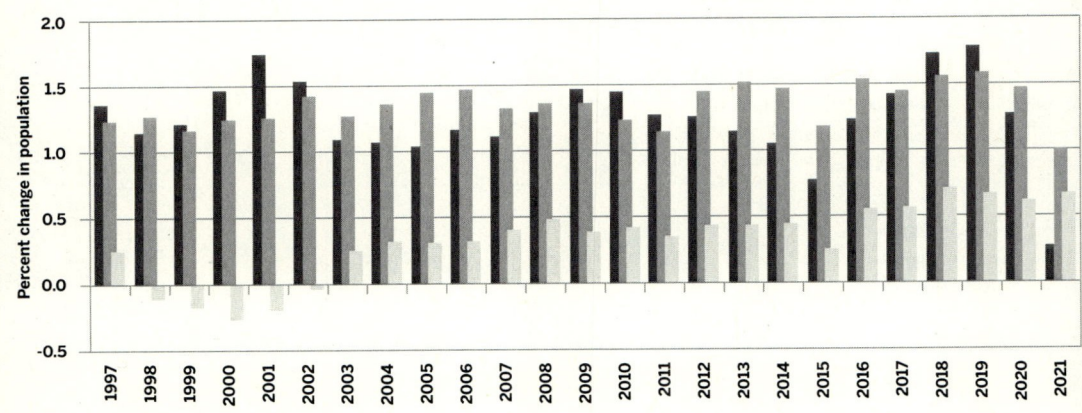

FIGURE 1.2 Canada's population in non-metro census divisions has been growing since 2003

■ Metro census divisions
■ Partially non-metro census divisions
□ Non-metro census divisions

Sources: Statistics Canada, Table 17-10-0139-01, https://doi.org/10.25318/1710013901;
Table 17-10-0140-01, https://doi.org/10.25318/1710014001-eng.

*Notes: This figure uses 2016 Census boundaries for census divisions for the entire 1997–2021 period.
See chapter glossary for definitions of terms.*

in each five-year period from 1981 to 2016. There are also communities that failed to grow in the same periods (Bollman 2018). Thus, while it is generally true that larger communities grow more quickly, being small is not necessarily a constraint and being large is not necessarily an advantage in terms of growth.

When it comes to distance-to-density, the data show that communities that are farther from urban centres are less likely to grow. As shown in Figure 1.4, on average over the 1981–2016 period, only communities within 50 kilometres of a metro centre reported population growth greater than the Canadian average. Within each distance-to-density group, however, some communities saw population growth and others saw population decline in each five-year period from 1981 to 2016 (Bollman 2018). Thus, a shorter distance-to-density does not necessarily guarantee population growth and a longer distance-to-density does not necessarily constrain it.

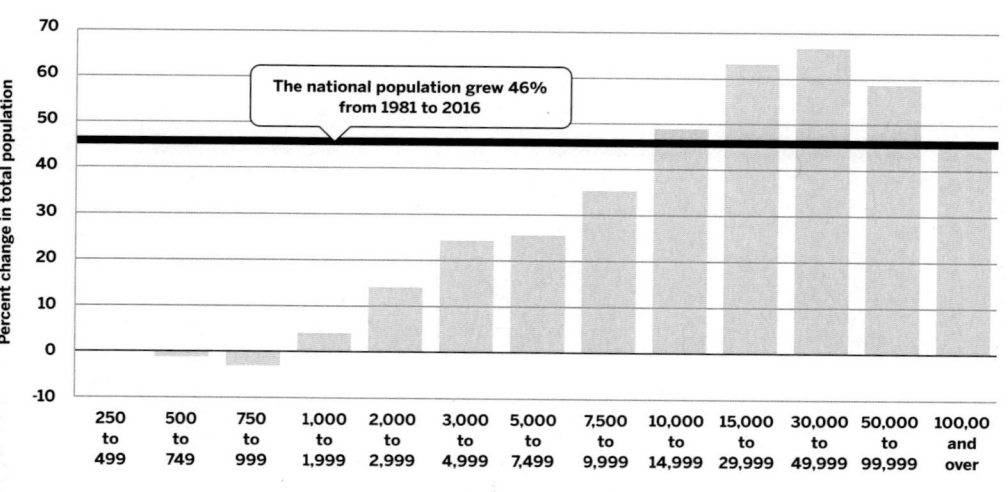

FIGURE 1.3 Nationally, the larger the community in 1981, the greater the rate of population growth from 1981 to 2016, Canada

Source: Data used in this table represent custom tabulations of Statistics Canada census data from 1981 and 2016.

Notes: Communities in this graph are represented by census consolidated subdivisions, or groups of adjacent CSDs. This figure uses the 1996 Census boundaries for CSDs. See chapter glossary for definitions of terms and abbreviations.

Population growth rates have an impact on the availability of labour. In general, Canada is in an era of labour shortages (see Figure 1.5). At the national level, there are now fewer potential labour market entrants (i.e., individuals between 10 and 19 years of age) than potential labour market exiters (i.e., individuals between 55 and 64 years of age). In the early 1970s, there were 250 potential entrants to the labour market for every 100 potential retirees. By the mid-2000s, potential entrants had dropped below 100. On average nationally, there are now (at the beginning of the 2020s) only about 80 potential entrants to the labour market for every 100 potential retirees. Projections suggest that not until about 2029 will Canada be entering a decade where labour market entrants may be about equal to labour market exiters. In the meantime, the bright lights of city wages may draw more and more rural folks to the city. To avoid excessive depopulation of rural areas, proactive campaigns are needed to entice city folks and immigrants to rural areas.

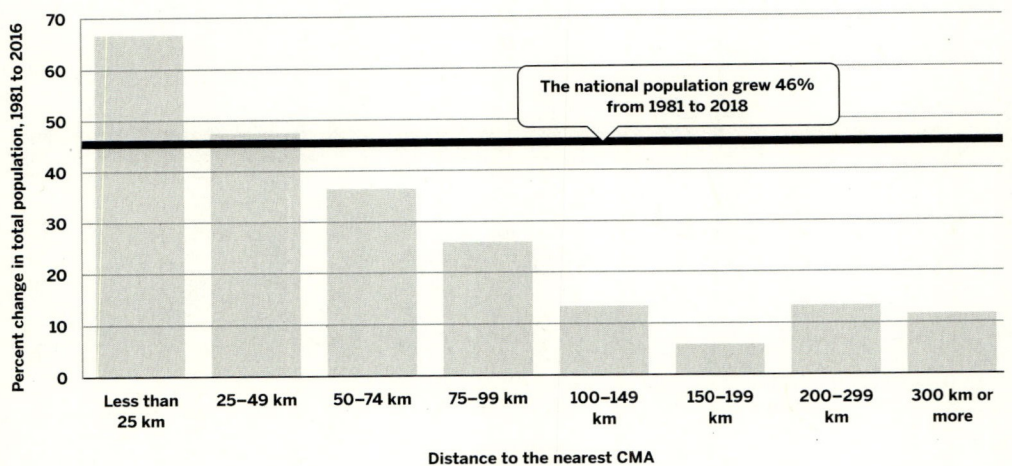

FIGURE 1.4 The greater the distance from a metro centre, the lower the rate of population growth from 1981 to 2016, Canada

Source: Data used in this table represent custom tabulations of Statistics Canada census data from 1981 and 2016.

Notes: This figure uses the 1996 Census boundaries. The growth pattern highlighted in this chart was not present in regional service centres 200 km or more from a CMA, for which greater distance to density was not correlated with lower population growth rates. See chapter glossary for definitions of terms and abbreviations.

The situation is more extreme in non-metro labour markets. In 2021, there were about 70 potential entrants to the non-metro labour market for every 100 potential retirees. Compare this to about 85 potential entrants to the labour market in metro areas (see Figure 1.6). Because of this, there has been an increasing urgency in rural communities to attract in-migrants from urban communities and/or to attract immigrants to settle in rural communities.

There is also a different composition and demand for skills among the rural workforce relative to the urban workforce. While the demand for skilled workers is increasing everywhere, rural Canada is more specialized in sectors that require fewer skilled workers. Still, the share of skilled workers within each sector in rural Canada is increasing—it's just not increasing at the same pace as the share of skilled workers in the same sectors in urban Canada (Bollman 2019a–2019h; Magnusson and Alasia 2004; Alasia and Magnusson 2005). The greater demand for

FIGURE 1.5 Canada's labour market shortage may continue to 2029

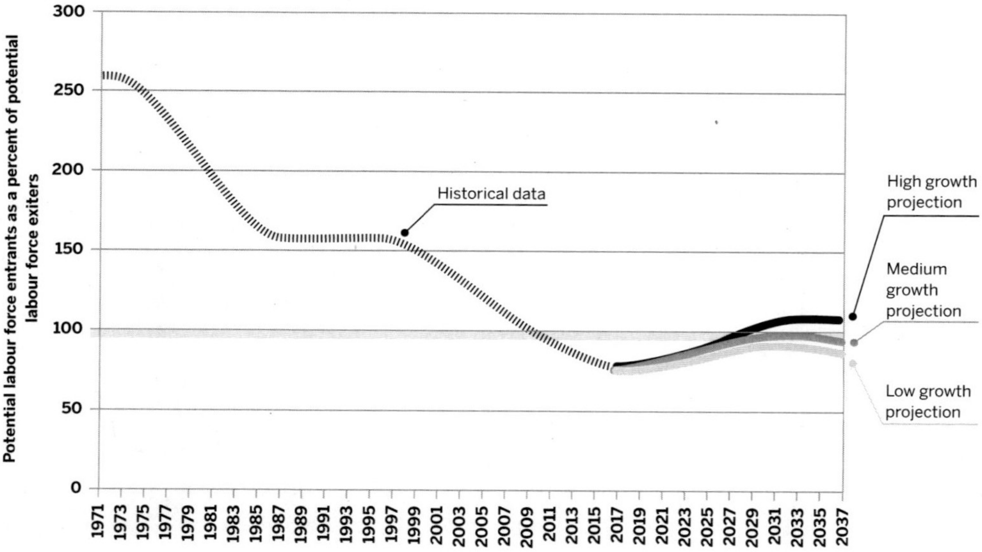

Source: Statistics Canada, Table 17-01-0005-01, https://doi.org/10.25318/1710000501-eng; Table 17-10-0057-01, https://doi.org/10.25318/1710005701-eng.

Notes: Potential labour market entrants are defined as the population between 10 and 19 years of age. Potential labour market exiters are defined as the population between 55 and 64 years of age. The medium growth projection scenario assumes a continuation of the trends during the 1992–2011 period.

so-called lower-skilled workers in rural Canada appears in the increasing reliance on temporary foreign workers, particularly in the agricultural sector. This same demand may reduce the attractiveness of rural locations for recent immigrants with so-called higher skills.

INDIGENOUS PEOPLES IN RURAL CANADA

Rural Canadians are aware of the Indigenous peoples in Canada—arguably more so than urban Canadians. The Indigenous population in Canada is rural intensive and rural Canada is Indigenous intensive.

In step with the Constitution Act of 1982, the Canadian Census of the Population uses the term *Aboriginal* rather than *Indigenous* to describe those who self-identify as First Nations, Inuit, or Métis, who are legally registered under the Indian Act, or who have membership in a First Nations band. In this section, for precision, I use the terms *Aboriginal*

FIGURE 1.6 Demographic replacement of the working-age population fell below 100% in non-metro Canada in 2008

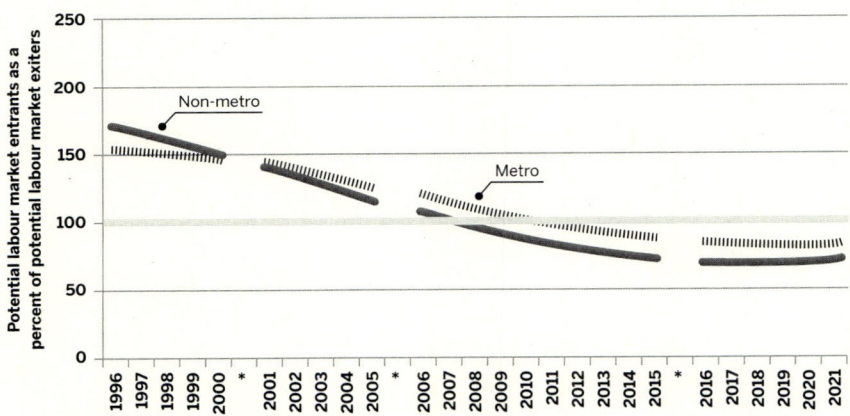

Source: Statistics Canada, Table 17-01-0005-01, https://doi.org/10.25318/1710000501-eng; Table 17-10-0078-01, https://doi.org/10.25318/1710007801-eng; Table 17-10-0135-01, https://doi.org/10.25318/1710013501-eng.

Notes: Potential labour market entrants are defined as the population between 10 and 19 years of age. Potential labour market exiters are defined as the population between 55 and 64 years of age. See chapter glossary for definitions of other terms and abbreviations.

* Signifies a change in the size of the metro and non-metro population because of a change in CMA boundaries due to changes in commuting patterns and/or the addition of another locality that met the criteria to be classified as a CMA.

and *Aboriginal identity* when I am speaking specifically about census demographic data. In all other instances, I use *Indigenous*.

Bollman, Beshiri, and Clemenson (2007) note that diversity and inclusiveness are very different issues in rural and urban Canada. In this regard, it is important to note that in Canadian census data, Aboriginal people are counted separately from "visible minorities." The latter are defined by the Employment Equality Act as "persons, other than Aboriginal peoples, who are non-Caucasian in race or non-white in colour." When it comes to comparing diversity and inclusiveness in rural and urban areas, this distinction matters. In rural Canada, Indigenous people are the most "visible" minority; in urban Canada, visible minorities, in the legal sense of the term, are more prominent.

For instance, 10.2% of the population (all ages) in non-metro areas reported an Aboriginal identity on the 2016 Census compared to 2.7% of the metro population (see Table 1.5).[5] In 2016, 12.2% of the metro population in Manitoba (where Winnipeg is the sole metro area) reported an Aboriginal identity compared to 27.2% of the non-metro population. The proportions in Saskatchewan are almost as high: the Aboriginal-identified population represents 10.2% of the population in the metro areas of Regina and Saskatoon and 22.2% in the non-metro areas outside Regina and Saskatoon.

When we look at the share of youth who reported an Aboriginal identity at the national level, we see that 16.9% of non-metro youth reported an Aboriginal identity (Figure 1.7 and Table 1.5). This means that one-sixth of future entrants to the non-metro labour market will be Aboriginal.

Within non-metro areas, the share of the youth population that is Aboriginal varies across the provinces and territories. In most provinces and territories, 10% or more of the non-metro youth population report an Aboriginal identity. Nunavut and the Northwest Territories rank the highest (Figure 1.8). These territories are followed by Manitoba and Saskatchewan. In fact, 40.6% of the youth population in non-metro Manitoba reported an Aboriginal identity in 2016 (Figure 1.7). Importantly, this means that within a few years, 4 in 10 labour market entrants in non-metro Manitoba will be Aboriginal. Again, the proportion in Saskatchewan is nearly as high. Within the next few years, over one-third of entrants to the non-metro labour market in Saskatchewan will have an Aboriginal identity.

Not surprisingly, the absolute size of the non-metro Aboriginal youth population also differs across the provinces. In 2016, the province with the highest absolute number of Aboriginal youth was British Columbia (Figure 1.9) followed by Ontario and the three prairie provinces.

In provinces with high non-metro Aboriginal youth populations, successful job creation for Aboriginal workers will drive successful rural development. The relatively higher share of Aboriginal workers in the non-metro labour market in the next few years in each province needs to be addressed in the context of high school noncompletion rates being

TABLE 1.5 Percent of population who report an Aboriginal identity by age and metro/non-metro residence in 2016, Canada, provinces, and territories

	0–14 years		15–24 years		25–34 years		35–44 years		45–54 years		55–64 years		65 years and over		All age groups	
	Metro	Non-metro	Metro	Non-metro	Metro	Non-metro	Metro	Non-metro	Metro	Non-metro	Metro	Non-metro	Metro	Non-metro	Metro	Non-metro
Newfoundland & Labrador	4.7	18.9	5.4	18.8	3.8	15.4	3.5	13.4	2.8	11.8	1.6	10.1	1.2	7.2	3.3	12.6
Prince Edward Island	-	3.3	-	3.2	-	2.7	-	1.8	-	1.7	-	1.0	-	0.6	-	2.0
Nova Scotia	5.8	11.0	5.1	10.9	4.2	8.5	4.3	7.5	3.8	6.6	2.8	5.1	2.0	3.3	4.0	7.0
New Brunswick	2.9	8.3	3.1	7.1	2.5	5.7	2.4	5.0	1.9	4.6	1.9	4.0	1.1	2.6	2.2	5.1
Quebec	1.3	7.4	1.5	6.8	1.3	5.4	1.2	5.1	1.3	4.5	1.3	3.5	1.0	2.6	1.3	4.8
Ontario	2.5	11.3	2.4	10.5	2.0	8.5	1.8	8.1	1.7	6.7	1.5	5.2	0.9	3.1	1.8	7.2
Manitoba	19.8	40.6	16.3	36.5	12.7	29.5	11.2	25.6	10.4	24.0	8.2	16.9	4.8	10.2	12.2	27.2
Saskatchewan	17.0	35.9	14.4	33.1	10.3	25.2	9.1	21.1	8.3	18.7	5.3	12.3	2.9	7.3	10.2	22.2
Alberta	6.4	16.9	6.4	16.0	4.6	11.6	4.0	9.8	3.8	9.5	2.9	7.0	2.0	5.0	4.5	11.3
British Columbia	2.5	20.8	4.4	18.7	3.5	14.4	2.9	12.4	2.8	11.3	2.3	8.0	1.3	4.8	3.2	12.1
Yukon	-	30.7	-	32.6	-	22.3	-	20.6	-	23.3	-	17.5	-	16.0	-	23.3
Northwest Territories	-	60.2	-	62.6	-	44.7	-	41.6	-	46.0	-	42.5	-	54.6	-	50.7
Nunavut	-	94.4	-	94.7	-	80.9	-	75.8	-	77.0	-	67.2	-	84.4	-	85.9
Canada	4.0	16.9	3.7	15.2	3.0	11.9	2.6	10.2	2.4	8.9	2.0	6.4	1.2	4.1	2.7	10.2

Source: Statistics Canada, 2016 Census of Population, catalogue no. 98-400-X2016155, https://www12.statcan.gc.ca/datasets/Index-eng.cfm.

Note: See chapter glossary for definitions of terms.

considerably higher among Aboriginal students (Looker and Bollman 2020). Specifically, high school noncompletion rates are overall higher for Aboriginal students than for non-Aboriginal students (Bollman and Looker 2020, slides 415 to 468). Notably, the high school noncompletion rates for non-Aboriginal students are low, and are equally low across the urban-to-rural spectrum in each province. Thus, rural schools are not failing in their ability to graduate non-Aboriginal students. However, the high school noncompletion rates are higher for Aboriginal students in each degree of rurality in each province. A policy focus is required to encourage and to support Aboriginal students to acquire a high school diploma in schools across the urban-to-rural spectrum. The same

FIGURE 1.7 Over 16% of non-metro Canadians under 15 years of age reported an Aboriginal Identity in 2016

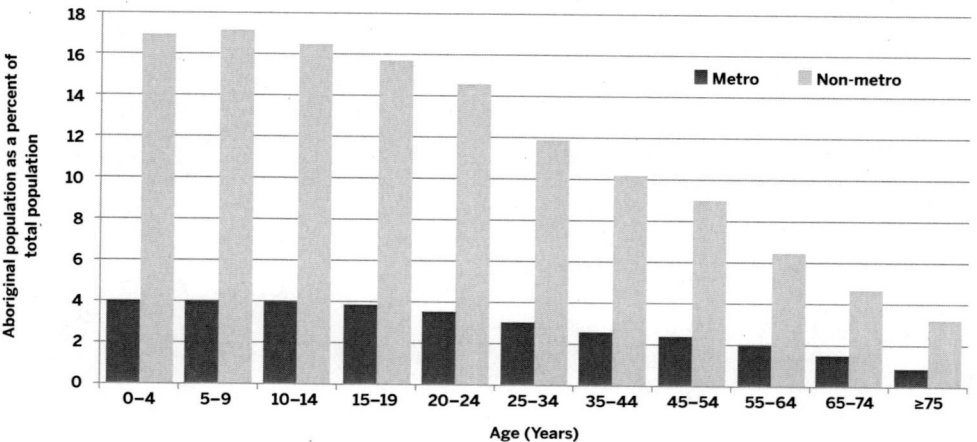

Source: Statistics Canada, Table 98-400X2016155, https://www150.statcan.gc.ca/n1/en/catalogue/98-400-X2016155.

Notes: This chart presents data for Canada as a whole. Detailed charts for each province are given in Bollman and Looker (2020), and can be downloaded from http://crrf.ca/ruraleducation. See chapter glossary for definitions of terms.

observation was also starkly evident in 2001 (Bollman and Looker 2020, slides 470 to 483).

The failure of the federal, provincial, and territorial governments to graduate Aboriginal high school students means that an increasing share of non-metro workforce entrants may be lacking essential skills for workforce participation (Angus 2017). Aboriginal individuals have experienced a systemically lower labour utilization rate over the period 1976 to 2021 (Bollman 2021, figures 4 and 5). The increasing demographic impact of Aboriginal youth among labour market entrants represents the major challenge, in my view, for policy development and program delivery for rural development across Canada. This also has major implications for building communities of inclusion, where everyone has equal access to the available economic opportunities.

FIGURE 1.8 In Nunavut, 95% of the non-metro population under 20 years of age reported an Aboriginal identity in 2016

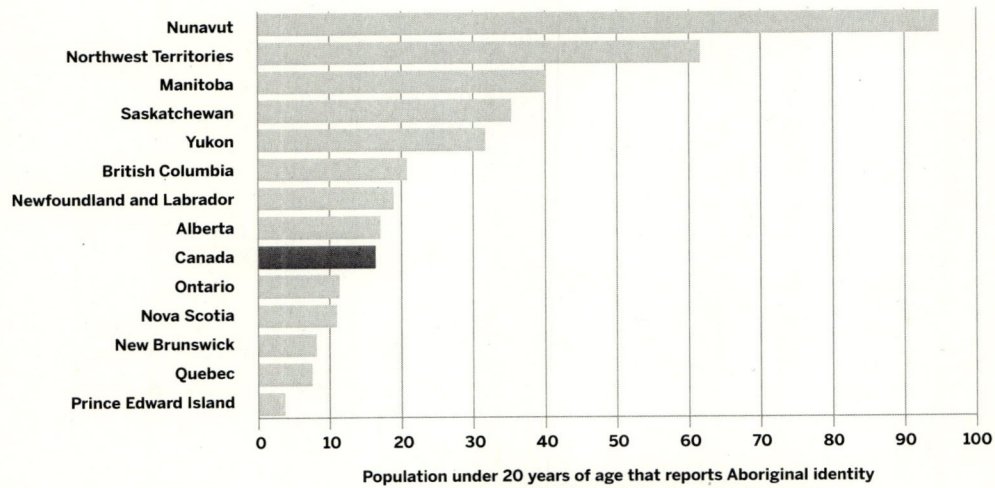

Population under 20 years of age that reports Aboriginal identity as a percent of total population in non-metro areas

Source: Statistics Canada, Table 98-400-X2016155, https://www150.statcan.gc.ca/n1/en/catalogue/98-400-X2016155.

MIGRATION AND VISIBLE MINORITY PRESENCE IN RURAL CANADA

In contrast with Indigenous peoples, visible minorities have a generally lower presence in most of rural Canada, particularly when compared to the urban centres, but there is still substantial variation across rural Canada. In general, the migration of Canadian residents from more racially diverse urban areas to less racially diverse rural areas is minimal and the arrival of new immigrants into rural areas is also minimal.

Recall from Figure 1.2 that the population of non-metro census divisions has been growing since 2003, but at about one-half the pace of partially non-metro and metro census divisions—about or below 0.5% compared to more than 1% per year. Traditionally, a major component of population growth has been the natural balance—the number of births minus the number of deaths. However, as Figure 1.10 shows, the natural balance was negative (i.e., there were fewer births than deaths) in non-metro census divisions in 2020 and 2021. The contribution of natural

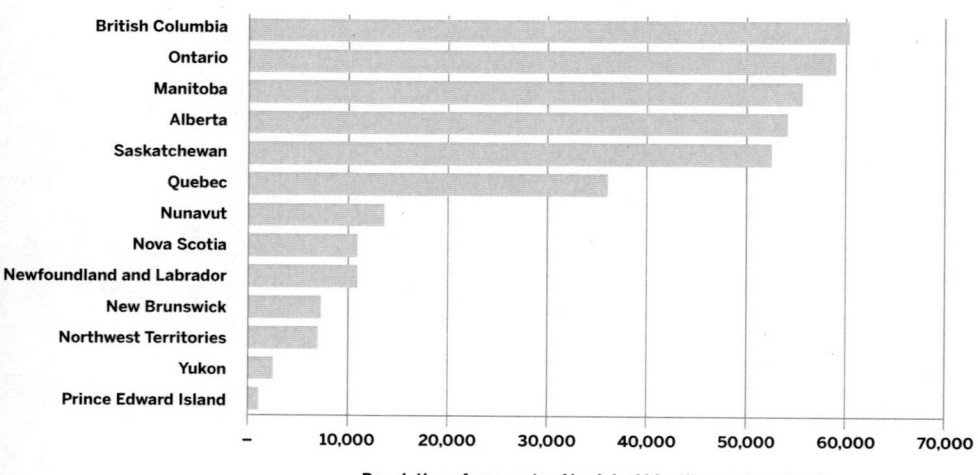

FIGURE 1.9 British Columbia had the largest absolute number of non-metro Aboriginal youth under 20 years of age in 2016

Source: Statistics Canada, Table 98-400X2016155, https://www150.statcan.gc.ca/n1/en/catalogue/98-400-X2016155.

balance to population change has been declining since 2009. This fact has been one reason for the increased attention in rural communities toward attracting migrants—both in-migrants from urban areas in Canada and immigrants from other countries.

Migration from one area in Canada to another is called internal migration. Traditionally, there has been net internal migration out of cities (i.e., the metro census divisions in Figure 1.11) and net internal migration into metro-adjacent census divisions (i.e., the partially non-metro census divisions in Figure 1.11). There has been a small rate of net internal migration out of non-metro census divisions. However, as shown in Figure 1.11, starting in 2017, we see a small net internal migration into non-metro areas. The net flow contributed 0.6% to non-metro population change in 2021.

As noted by Clemenson and Pitblado, a small net migration into or out of RST areas in Canada is the result of a relatively small difference in the size of the gross flow into and out of these areas. In the seven intercensal periods from 1966 to 2001, the net flow ranged from –6.5% of the RST

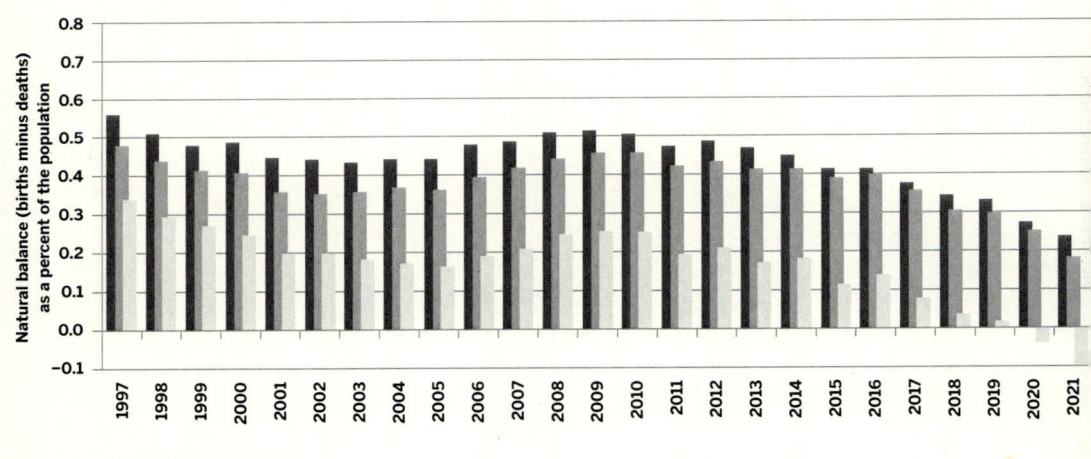

FIGURE 1.10 Births were fewer than deaths in Canada's non-metro census divisions in 2020 and 2021

■ Metro census divisions
■ Partially non-metro census divisions
□ Non-metro census divisions

Sources: Statistics Canada, Table 17-10-0139-01, https://doi.org/10.25318/1710013901; Table 17-10-0140-01, https://doi.org/10.25318/1710014001-eng.

Notes: The 2016 Census classification of census divisions as metro, partially non-metro, and non-metro was used in the classification of all census divisions in this figure for the 1996–2021 period. See chapter glossary for definitions of terms and abbreviations.

population in the 1966–1971 period to 1.4% of the RST population in the 1991–1996 period. Between 1966 and 1971, the gross inflow was 6.2% and the gross outflow was 12.7%. Between 1991 and 1996, the gross inflow was 10.1% and the gross outflow was 8.7% (Clemenson and Pitbaldo 2007, 26, table 1). On average, over these seven intercensal periods, they show that there was a net gain of population for each five-year age group between 25 and 69 years of age. However, there was a net loss in populations between 15 and 24 years of age, and in those 70 or older (28, figure 2).

In addition to migration within Canada, attention has turned to the ability of rural areas to attract immigrants. As Figure 1.12 shows, in each year since 1997, immigrants to metro census divisions have contributed 1% or more to population change. Since 2010, immigrants to partially

FIGURE 1.11 Net internal migration contributed 0.6% to population change in Canada's non-metro census divisions in 2021

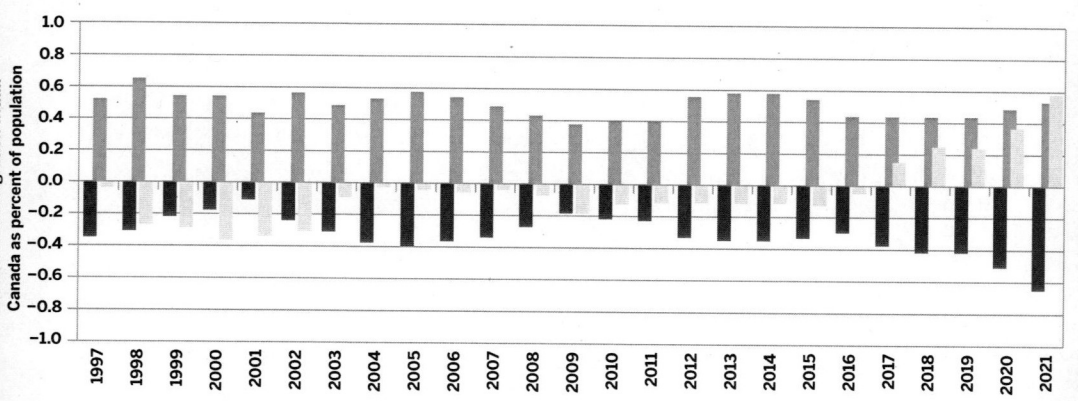

■ Metro census divisions
■ Partially non-metro census divisions
□ Non-metro census divisions

Sources: Statistics Canada, Table 17-10-0139-01, https://doi.org/10.25318/1710013901; Table 17-10-0140-01, https://doi.org/10.25318/1710014001-eng.

Notes: The 2016 Census delineations of CSDs to CMAs was used in the classification of all census divisions in this figure for the 1996–2021 period. See chapter glossary for definitions of terms and abbreviations.

non-metro census divisions have contributed 0.5% or more to annual population change. Immigrant arrivals to non-metro census divisions have made a comparatively small contribution to population change. Until 2015, immigrant arrivals contributed no more than 0.20% to population change. Since 2016, however, this contribution has been 0.28% or more. While 0.28% remains a small contribution, it is 40% more than 0.20%. Since 2016, then, there have been significantly more immigrants arriving in non-metro census divisions. In 2011, there were 23 communities in Canada where recent immigrants represented more than 10% of the total population: 17 of these were in the prairie provinces, 19 were in non-metro regions, and almost all were located in "regions with a relatively low share of their population being recent immigrants" and thus "regions with less experience in welcoming new immigrants" (Bollman 2015, 10).

The top destinations for immigrants to non-metro census divisions, shown in Table 1.6, are well known among rural development analysts. Prince Edward Island has had an active immigrant recruitment program over the past decade, and thus Charlottetown ranks as the top non-metro destination in terms of immigrants as a percent of the resident population (averaging 2% per year over the 10-year period between 2010 and 2019). Both Neepawa and Brandon in Manitoba have pork processing plants that have been continuously recruiting immigrants to staff the second shift. Fort McMurray is the home of the oil sands industry in Alberta. A few decades ago, community leaders in Winkler, a largely Mennonite community in Manitoba, resolved to create the same number of jobs in their community as there were high school graduates. This generated a focus on local manufacturing, which then led to a focus on recruiting immigrants from the Mennonite diaspora in many countries. In both rural Alberta and rural Saskatchewan, the oil industry has created jobs in drilling and pipeline maintenance as well as the associated service sector (e.g., retail, accommodation, and food services). As Table 1.6 shows, some places—including, Peel, Charlottetown, and Winkler—had a faster pace of immigrant arrivals in the last four years of the 2010–2019 period than their average for the entire 10-year period.

Houle (2007) documents that secondary migration of new immigrants is higher for those who first settle outside a centre of 500,000 or more; for those who first settle in the Atlantic provinces; for those with a higher level of education at the time of arrival; and for those not working after 6, 12, or 24 months of being in Canada. As Houle notes, "the very high internal migration intensity that takes place immediately after arrival could be explained by the fact that secondary migration constitutes the completion of an unfinished journey between a given origin abroad and a final destination within Canada. A significant number of new immigrants clearly did not land where they wished to settle, and decided to move to a place they feel is a better suited destination for them" (23).

Table 1.7 shows that in 2016, 6.5% of Canadian residents were "recent" immigrants. Recent immigrants are defined as having arrived in the past 10 years. In 2016, then, recent immigrants were those immigrants who had arrived between 2006 and 2016. Across the Canadian provinces and

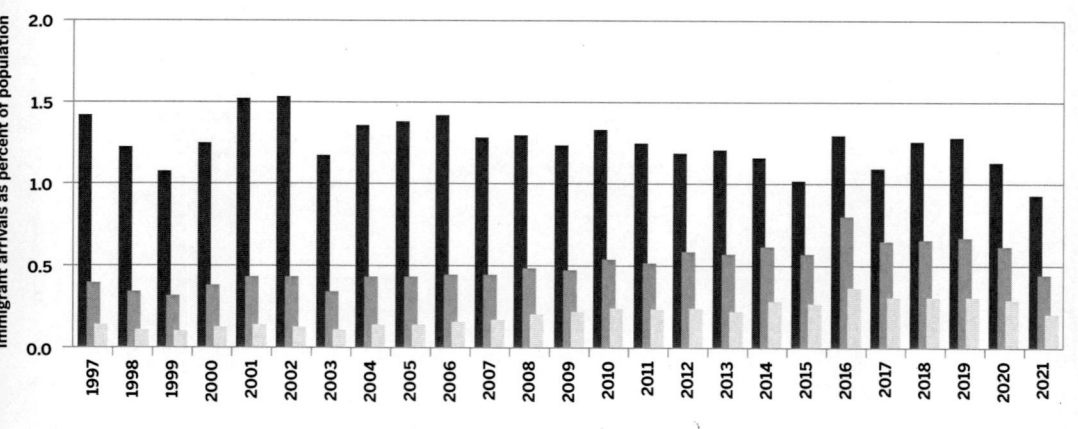

FIGURE 1.12 Immigrant arrivals contributed 0.2% to population change in Canada's non-metro census divisions in 2021

■ Metro census divisions
■ Partially non-metro census divisions
□ Non-metro census divisions

Sources: Statistics Canada, Table 17-10-0139-01, https://doi.org/10.25318/1710013901; Table 17-10-0140-01, https://doi.org/10.25318/1710014001-eng.

Notes: The 2016 Census classification of census divisions as metro, partially non-metro, and non-metro was used in the classification of all census divisions in this figure for the 1996–2021 period. See chapter glossary for definitions of terms and abbreviations.

territories, the share of the population classified as recent immigrants ranged from a high of 8.7% in Manitoba and Alberta to a low of 0.9% in Nunavut. At the national level, the predominant regions of birth of recent immigrants were Asian, with 18% coming from Southern Asia, 16% from Southeast Asia, 15% from Eastern Asia, and 11% from West Central Asia and the Middle East.[6] Asian regions were also the modal place of birth of recent immigrants in each province and territory, with the exception of Québec where the modal region was Northern Africa (21% of recent immigrants).

Not surprisingly, there is a wide range across Canada's census divisions in terms of the share of the population born outside Canada who arrived in the 10-years prior to 2016. As Table 1.8 shows, the metro census divisions ranking highest in this measure were Peel, Ontario (14% of the population);

TABLE 1.6 Immigrants as a percent of total population in metro, partially non-metro, and non-metro census divisions in the 2010–2019 and 2016–2019 periods

Census Division ID#	Name of census division	Total immigrant arrivals as a percent of average total population, 2010 to 2019	Total immigrant arrivals as a percent of average total population, 2016 to 2019
Top 5 metro census divisions			
3521	Peel, Ontario	1.85	2.12
2466	Montréal, Quebec	1.80	1.69
4611	Man. Div. 11 (Winnipeg)	1.72	1.70
3520	Toronto, Ontario	1.61	1.62
5915	Greater Vancouver, British Columbia	1.27	1.25
Top 5 partially non-metro census divisions			
4711	Sask. Div. 11 (incl. Saskatoon)	1.60	1.89
4706	Sask. Div. 6 (incl. Regina)	1.57	1.84
4806	Alta. Div. 6 (incl. Calgary)	1.27	1.31
4811	Alta. Div. 11 (incl. Edmonton)	1.08	1.22
4802	Alta. Div. 2 (incl. Lethbridge & Brooks)	0.71	0.73
Top 20 non-metro census divisions			
1102	Queens (incl. Charlottetown), Prince Edward Island	2.00	2.21
4615	Man. Div. 15 (incl. Minnedosa & Neepawa)	1.52	1.89
4816	Alta. Div. 16 (incl. Fort McMurray)	1.35	1.46
4815	Alta. Div. 15 (incl. Canmore)	1.25	1.19
4607	Man. Div. 7 (incl. Brandon)	1.19	1.09
4603	Man. Div. 3 (incl. Winkler, Morden, Altona)	1.11	1.25
5931	Squamish-Lillooet (incl. Squamish & Whistler), British Columbia	1.08	1.23
1310	York (incl. Fredericton), New Brunswick	0.93	1.25
4701	Sask. Div. 1 (incl. Estevan)	0.90	1.00
6001	Yukon, Yukon	0.75	0.68
6106	NWT Region 6 (incl. Yellowknife)	0.75	0.95
4702	Sask. Div. 2 (incl. Weyburn)	0.74	0.80
4717	Sask. Div. 17 (incl. Lloydminster & Meadow Lake)	0.70	0.67
4709	Sask. Div. 9 (incl. Yorkton)	0.65	0.75
4708	Sask. Div. 8 (incl. Swift Current)	0.64	0.83
5959	Northern Rockies (incl. Fort Nelson), British Columbia	0.64	0.81
4716	Sask. Div. 16 (incl. North Battleford)	0.58	0.71
4705	Sask. Div. 5 (incl. Melville)	0.58	0.72
4713	Sask. Div. 13 (incl. Kindersley)	0.55	0.71
4808	Alta. Div. 8 (incl. Red Deer)	0.53	0.56

Source: Statistics Canada, Table 17-10-0139-01, https://doi.org/10.25318/1710013901; Table 17-10-0140-01, https://doi.org/10.25318/1710014001-eng.

Notes: This table uses 2016 Census boundaries for census divisions. Census divisions are ranked by the number of immigrant arrivals across the 2010–2019 period as a percent of the average population over the 2010–2019 period. See chapter glossary for definitions of terms.

Toronto, Ontario (13% of the population); and Montréal, Québec (12.6% of the population). Top ranking non-metro census divisions were Alberta census division #16, which includes Fort McMurray (12.3%); Manitoba census division #3, which includes Winkler, Morden, and Altona (9.4%); Manitoba census division #12, which includes Brandon (8.7%); and Manitoba census division #15, which includes Minnedosa and Neepawa (7.7%).

We also see differences in terms of where recent immigrants to different census divisions tended to come from in 2016. Following the 2016 provincial and territorial mode, the recent immigrants to the Peel and Toronto census divisions at the time were largely from Asian countries. In step with its own province, the Montréal census division's largest single source of recent immigrants was Northern Africa (23%). Looking at the non-metro census divisions, Asia was the birth region of many recent immigrants to Alberta census division #16, which includes Fort McMurray (57%), but Western Europe was the birth region of many immigrants to Winkler (26%). Central America was a major source of immigrants to Brandon (24%), whereas Southeast Asia was a large source of immigrants for Neepawa (81%).

It is important to note that not all recent immigrants are visible minorities, and not all visible minorities are recent immigrants. Consequently, the percent of a region's population that is made up of recent immigrants does not necessarily correlate with its visible minority population. Table 1.9 shows the presence of all visible minorities in Canada and various cities (i.e., CMAs and CAs), regardless of whether or not they were born outside Canada. The columns in Table 1.9 are sorted by intensity of each visible minority group at the national level.

In 2016, visible minority residents of Canada represented 22% of all residents in Canada. Three provinces ranked above the Canadian average: British Columbia (39%); Ontario (29%); and Alberta (23%). Ten cities had more than the Canadian average share of visible minority population: Toronto (51%); Vancouver (49%); Calgary (34%); Abbotsford-Mission (29%); Edmonton (28%); Wood Buffalo (Fort McMurray) (26%); Winnipeg (26%); the Ontario part of Ottawa-Gatineau (25%); Brooks (23%); and Montréal (23%). Among the cities ranked in Table 1.9, the Filipino visible minority group was the modal group in 17 cities, and the South Asian group in another 16 cities.

TABLE 1.7 Percent distribution by region of birth for immigrants who arrived in Canada, provinces, and territories between 2006 and 2016

Name of province / territory	Immigrants (2006–2016 arrival) as percent of total population, 2016	Total immigrant population (2006–2016 arrival)	North America	Central America	Caribbean and Bermuda	South America	Western Europe	Eastern Europe	Northern Europe	Southern Europe	Western Africa	Eastern Africa	Northern Africa	Central Africa	Southern Africa	West Central Asia & the Middle East	Eastern Asia	South-east Asia	Southern Asia	Oceania
Newfoundland & Labrador	1.1	100	6	1	3	3	3	4	7	3	4	5	4	1	2	15	8	13	16	1
Prince Edward Island	3.3	100	5	1	1	1	3	3	7	2	1	1	1	0	0	12	40	11	9	0
Nova Scotia	2.2	100	7	1	3	2	4	3	13	1	2	2	3	1	1	19	12	11	12	1
New Brunswick	1.9	100	8	1	2	2	7	5	6	1	3	2	4	3	1	17	22	13	5	1
Quebec	4.9	100	2	3	9	8	10	7	1	1	6	3	21	5	0	10	6	4	4	0
Ontario	7.0	100	3	2	5	4	1	5	2	2	2	3	2	1	0	15	15	12	25	0
Manitoba	8.7	100	2	3	1	2	4	6	1	1	4	4	1	1	0	6	8	38	18	0
Saskatchewan	6.6	100	2	2	1	1	1	6	3	2	3	3	1	1	2	6	8	37	21	0
Alberta	8.7	100	3	3	2	4	2	4	4	1	4	6	2	1	1	7	9	27	20	1
British Columbia	7.5	100	4	2	1	2	2	4	5	1	1	1	1	0	1	8	32	17	17	2
Yukon	5.1	100	4	2	1	1	12	2	3	1	1	1	1	0	2	5	9	50	5	2
Northwest Territories	3.4	100	2	0	4	2	1	1	4	1	2	9	3	0	1	4	11	40	12	1
Nunavut	0.9	100	6	6	7	3	3	0	4	0	10	7	0	6	3	6	3	31	9	3
Canada	**6.5**	**100**	**3**	**2**	**4**	**4**	**3**	**5**	**3**	**2**	**3**	**3**	**5**	**1**	**1**	**11**	**15**	**16**	**18**	**1**

Source: Statistics Canada, 2016 Census of Population, catalogue no. 98-400-X2016185, https://www12.statcan.gc.ca/datasets/Index-eng.cfm.

Note: Percentages in this table are rounded to the nearest one percentage point. Sums may not add exactly to the totals shown.

TABLE 1.8 Percent distribution by region of birth for immigrants to Canada who arrived in metro, partially non-metro, and non-metro census divisions between 2006 and 2016

Rank	ID#	Name of census division	Immigrants (2006–2016 arrival) as percent of total population, 2016	Total immigrant population (2006–2016 arrival)	North America	Central America	Caribbean and Bermuda	South America	Western Europe	Eastern Europe	Northern Europe	Southern Europe	Western Africa	Eastern Africa	Northern Africa	Central Africa	Southern Africa	West Central Asia & the Middle East	Eastern Asia	South-east Asia	Southern Asia	Oceania
									Top 5 metro census divisions													
1	3521	Peel, Ontario	14.0	100	2	1	5	4	0	3	1	1	2	2	3	0	0	11	5	9	50	0
2	3520	Toronto, Ontario	13.0	100	2	2	5	5	1	5	2	3	2	3	1	1	0	14	16	18	21	0
3	2466	Montréal, Quebec	12.6	100	2	3	10	6	9	7	0	1	5	2	23	4	0	10	7	5	4	0
4	4611	Man. Div. 11 (Winnipeg)	12.5	100	1	1	1	1	1	5	1	1	4	5	1	1	0	5	8	43	20	0
6	5915	Greater Vancouver, British Columbia	11.6	100	3	2	0	2	1	3	4	1	0	1	1	0	1	9	36	17	16	1
									Top 10 partially non-metro census divisions													
7	4806	Alta. Div. 6 (incl. Calgary)	11.4	100	2	3	1	5	1	5	5	1	5	4	2	1	1	8	11	23	21	1
9	4711	Sask. Div. 11 (incl. Saskatoon)	9.6	100	1	2	1	2	1	6	4	1	2	3	1	1	1	7	10	32	23	0
10	4811	Alta. Div. 11 (incl. Edmonton)	9.6	100	2	2	2	3	1	4	3	1	3	7	3	1	1	7	8	26	23	1
12	4706	Sask. Div. 6 (incl. Regina)	9.2	100	1	1	1	1	1	5	3	2	4	5	1	1	1	7	10	32	26	0
18	4802	Alta. Div. 2 (incl. Lethbridge & Brooks)	6.4	100	4	18	0	5	3	2	5	1	2	12	2	1	1	3	4	24	13	1
21	4602	Man. Div. 2 (incl. Steinbach)	6.1	100	4	4	0	11	30	13	3	0	0	1	1	0	1	10	1	20	2	0
24	3530	Waterloo, Ontario	5.4	100	4	2	3	6	1	6	3	3	1	7	3	0	0	18	12	8	20	0
31	5909	Fraser Valley, British Columbia	5.0	100	4	2	1	2	2	3	5	1	1	1	1	0	1	3	9	10	53	1
32	3537	Essex, Ontario	5.0	100	10	5	3	2	1	4	2	4	2	3	2	2	0	32	8	8	14	0
34	3539	Middlesex, Ontario	4.9	100	5	3	3	10	1	4	3	2	1	3	4	1	0	26	13	6	14	0

Rank	ID#	Name of census division	Immigrants (2006–2016 arrival) as percent of total population, 2016	Total immigrant population (2006–2016 arrival)	Region of birth (row percent distribution)																	
					North America	Central America	Caribbean and Bermuda	South America	Western Europe	Eastern Europe	Northern Europe	Southern Europe	Western Africa	Eastern Africa	Northern Africa	Central Africa	Southern Africa	West Central Asia & the Middle East	Eastern Asia	South-east Asia	Southern Asia	Oceania
		Top 20 non-metro census divisions																				
5	4816	Alta. Div. 16 (incl. Fort McMurray)	12.3	100	2	1	2	5	1	2	2	1	4	11	2	1	2	5	4	32	21	2
11	4603	Man. Div. 3 (incl. Winkler, Morden, Altona)	9.4	100	3	17	1	6	26	16	1	1	0	1	0	0	1	17	1	6	3	0
13	4607	Man. Div. 7 (incl. Brandon)	8.7	100	1	24	1	7	2	6	2	0	2	6	1	0	2	1	22	7	14	0
14	4615	Man. Div. 15 (incl. Minnedosa & Neepawa)	7.7	100	1	1	1	0	2	3	6	0	0	2	0	0	0	2	3	81	1	0
19	5931	Squamish-Lillooet, British Columbia	6.4	100	6	3	0	3	6	5	26	2	0	1	1	0	3	0	6	18	8	13
22	4815	Alta. Div. 15 (incl. Canmore)	5.9	100	7	1	2	2	6	3	14	1	0	0	0	0	2	0	12	37	7	6
23	6106	NWT Region 5 (incl. Hay River & Fort Simpson)	5.8	100	1	0	3	1	1	1	5	0	2	11	3	0	2	5	12	41	12	0
25	4701	Sask. Div. 1 (incl. Estevan)	5.4	100	3	1	3	1	4	8	3	1	1	1	1	1	1	3	1	61	8	0
26	4717	Sask. Div. 17 (incl. Lloydminster & Meadow Lake)	5.2	100	2	1	0	0	0	7	2	0	1	3	1	0	1	2	1	68	10	0
27	6001	Yukon, Yukon	5.1	100	4	2	1	1	13	2	4	1	1	1	1	0	2	5	9	50	5	2
28	1102	Queens, Prince Edward Island	5.1	100	4	1	2	1	3	3	6	3	1	1	1	1	0	13	44	7	10	0
29	4808	Alta. Div. 8 (incl. Red Deer)	5.0	100	3	5	1	3	3	7	4	0	2	2	1	1	2	6	4	49	7	
35	4702	Sask. Div. 2 (incl. Weyburn)	4.3	100	4	2	2	0	2	7	3	0	1	5	0	0	0	1	0	46	26	
36	5959	Northern Rockies, British Columbia	4.3	100	4	0	6	0	4	4	4	4	0	0	0	0	0	0	0	73	0	
37	4709	Sask. Div. 9 (incl. Yorkton)	4.3	100	3	0	1	0	3	11	2	1	5	1	3	1	2	1	6	52	11	0

Rank	ID#	Name of census division	Immigrants (2006–2016 arrival) as percent of total population, 2016	Total immigrant population (2006–2016 arrival)	North America	Central America	Caribbean and Bermuda	South America	Western Europe	Eastern Europe	Northern Europe	Southern Europe	Western Africa	Eastern Africa	Northern Africa	Central Africa	Southern Africa	West Central Asia & the Middle East	Eastern Asia	South-east Asia	Southern Asia	Oceania
											Region of birth (row percent distribution)											
38	4704	Sask. Div. 4 (incl. Maple Creek)	4.1	100	8	10	0	0	0	7	2	0	0	0	0	0	2	2	7	61	2	4
39	4819	Alta. Div. 19 (incl. Grande Prairie)	4.1	100	3	5	2	2	3	4	2	0	4	4	2	1	2	4	3	46	10	2
40	4716	Sask. Div. 16 (incl. North Battleford)	4.1	100	2	3	0	1	2	5	5	14	0	1	0	0	3	1	4	46	13	1
41	1310	York, New Brunswick	3.9	100	4	1	1	1	3	4	6	1	3	4	2	1	0	26	25	10	8	0

Source: Statistics Canada, 2016 Census of Population, catalogue no. 98-400-X2016185. https://www12.statcan.gc.ca/datasets/Index-eng.cfm.

Notes: This table uses 2016 Census boundaries for census divisions. Census divisions are ranked by the number of immigrant arrivals across the 2006–2016 period as a percent percent of the average total population over the 2006–2016 period. Percentages in this table are rounded to the nearest one percent. Sums may not add exactly to the totals shown. See chapter glossary for definitions of terms.

Table 1.10 also looks at the shares of visible minorities in different areas, this time comparing the metro and non-metro populations in each province and territory. Again, the visible minority population in Canada represented 22% of Canadian residents at the national level in 2016. As Table 1.10 shows, however, visible minorities accounted for only 4% of non-metro residents. A higher visible minority population is seen in non-metro Alberta (8%) and non-metro British Columbia (6%).

Within the umbrella category of "visible minority," the modal visible minority groups in provincial non-metro areas were South Asian (28% of the visible minority population) in British Columbia; Chinese (39%) in Prince Edward Island (which is entirely non-metro); and Black in Nova Scotia (51%), Québec (34%), and New Brunswick (25%). In the non-metro areas of all other provinces and territories, the Filipino visible minority group comprised the modal group, representing 24% or more of the visible minority population.

TABLE 1.9 Percent distribution of the visible minority population in 2016, Canadian CMAs and CAs

Name of CMA or CA sorted by visible minority population as a percent of total population	Visible minority population as a percent of total population	Visible minority population (row percent distribution)												
		Total visible minority population	South Asian	Chinese	Black	Filipino	Latin American	Arab	Southeast Asian	West Asian	Korean	Japanese	Visible minority, n.i.e.*	Multiple visible minorities
Toronto, Ontario	51	100	32	21	15	8	4	4	3	4	2	1	3	3
Vancouver, British Columbia	49	100	25	40	3	10	3	1	4	4	4	3	1	3
Calgary, Alberta	34	100	27	19	12	15	6	6	5	3	2	1	1	3
British Columbia (province)	30	100	26	37	3	10	3	1	4	4	4	3	1	3
Ontario (province)	29	100	30	19	16	8	5	5	3	4	2	1	3	3
Abbotsford - Mission, British Columbia	29	100	75	5	3	4	3	1	3	0	3	1	1	2
Edmonton, Alberta	28	100	25	17	16	17	5	7	5	2	2	1	1	3
Wood Buffalo (Fort McMurray), Alberta	26	100	26	5	22	26	5	9	2	1	1	1	1	1
Winnipeg, Manitoba	26	100	20	10	14	38	3	2	4	1	2	1	1	3
Ottawa - Gatineau (Ontario part)	25	100	16	17	25	5	5	17	5	4	1	1	1	3
Alberta (province)	23	100	25	17	14	18	6	6	5	2	2	1	1	3
Brooks, Alberta	23	100	6	6	37	27	12	1	3	1	1	2	1	2
Montréal, Quebec	23	100	9	10	30	4	12	21	6	3	1	0	1	2
Canada	**22**	**100**	**25**	**21**	**16**	**10**	**6**	**7**	**4**	**3**	**2**	**1**	**2**	**3**
Ottawa - Gatineau (Ontario & Quebec)	22	100	14	16	28	5	6	18	5	4	1	1	1	3
Windsor, Ontario	20	100	18	13	19	6	5	27	5	2	1	0	2	3
Kitchener - Cambridge - Waterloo, Ontario	19	100	27	16	15	4	9	7	8	4	2	1	3	3
Lloydminster (Saskatchewan part)	18	100	18	1	5	68	2	1	2	0	1	0	1	2
Hamilton, Ontario	18	100	24	11	19	8	8	10	6	5	2	1	3	4
Regina, Saskatchewan	18	100	30	14	16	21	3	4	6	2	1	1	1	2
Manitoba (province)	17	100	19	10	14	37	5	2	4	1	2	1	1	3
Oshawa, Ontario	17	100	25	9	33	8	5	3	2	3	1	1	4	5
Saskatoon, Saskatchewan	17	100	28	16	11	23	4	5	5	2	1	1	1	3
Guelph, Ontario	17	100	27	17	12	11	5	3	10	6	1	1	1	5
Yellowknife, Northwest Territories	17	100	16	7	19	33	3	2	7	1	3	4	3	2

Name of CMA or CA sorted by visible minority population as a percent of total population	Visible minority population as a percent of total population	Visible minority population (row percent distribution)												
		Total visible minority population	South Asian	Chinese	Black	Filipino	Latin American	Arab	Southeast Asian	West Asian	Korean	Japanese	Visible minority, n.i.e.*	Multiple visible minorities
London, Ontario	16	100	15	14	15	5	12	18	6	4	4	1	2	3
Red Deer, Alberta	15	100	11	9	11	41	12	3	4	3	2	1	1	2
Lloydminster (Alberta & Saskatchewan)	15	100	23	3	10	49	3	3	4	0	1	0	1	2
Squamish, British Columbia	14	100	46	7	4	20	4	1	2	1	3	9	0	2
Victoria, British Columbia	14	100	20	32	7	12	5	3	5	2	4	5	1	3
Brandon, Manitoba	14	100	18	23	13	7	30	2	1	0	2	1	1	2
Quebec City, Quebec	13	100	9	10	31	3	13	21	6	3	1	0	1	2
Thompson, Manitoba	13	100	60	6	17	7	1	1	1	0	2	1	2	1
Lloydminster (Alberta part)	12	100	28	6	16	27	5	7	5	1	2	1	1	2
High River, Alberta	12	100	9	4	8	55	9	6	4	1	1	1	1	3
Prince Rupert, British Columbia	12	100	27	16	5	14	1	0	29	1	1	4	1	2
Grande Prairie, Alberta	12	100	16	6	18	42	5	4	1	1	1	1	1	2
Steinbach, Manitoba	12	100	9	4	11	56	6	0	8	0	2	0	2	3
Estevan, Saskatchewan	12	100	16	3	9	62	2	0	2	0	2	1	1	2
Ottawa - Gatineau (Quebec part)	12	100	3	7	45	2	11	22	3	2	1	0	1	2
Halifax, Nova Scotia	11	100	14	15	33	6	3	16	2	3	3	1	1	2
Wetaskiwin, Alberta	11	100	13	5	12	48	6	10	0	0	1	2	2	1
Cold Lake, Alberta	11	100	12	11	16	37	6	4	3	2	2	3	3	4
Lethbridge, Alberta	11	100	17	10	16	15	13	2	5	4	2	12	1	2
Saskatchewan (province)	11	100	26	13	13	28	4	4	5	2	2	1	1	2
Dawson Creek, British Columbia	10	100	29	3	13	39	3	1	4	3	2	0	1	1
Whitehorse, Yukon	10	100	18	14	8	39	4	0	6	1	3	2	1	4
Northwest Territories (territory)	10	100	16	8	19	33	3	3	6	1	3	4	2	2

Source: Statistics Canada, 2016 Census of Population, catalogue no. 98-400-X2016190, https://www12.statcan.gc.ca/datasets/Index-eng.cfm.

Notes: Table only include CMAs and CAs with visible minority population greater than or equal to 10% of total population. Modal visibility group for each city is shown in italic text.

*n.i.e.: not indicated elsewhere. See chapter glossary for definitions of other terms and abbreviations.

TABLE 1.10 Percent distribution of the visible minority population in metro and non-metro areas in 2016, Canada, provinces, and territories

Metro and non-metro areas by each province or territory	Visible minority population as a percent of total population, 2016	Visible minority population (row percent distribution)												
		Total visible minority population	South Asian	Chinese	Black	Filipino	Latin American	Arab	Southeast Asian	West Asian	Korean	Japanese	Visible minority, n.i.e.*	Multiple visible minorities
Newfoundland and Labrador														
Metro	4	100	22	21	21	7	6	12	3	2	1	1	1	2
Non-metro	1	100	23	15	18	24	3	9	2	0	0	0	2	2
Total	2	100	22	20	20	12	5	12	3	2	1	1	1	2
Prince Edward Island														
Metro	..	..	..	..	..	..	..	..	..	..	..	..	..	..
Non-metro	5	100	14	39	12	10	4	9	2	3	3	2	1	1
Total	5	100	14	39	12	10	4	9	2	3	3	2	1	1
Nova Scotia														
Metro	11	100	14	15	33	6	3	16	2	3	3	1	1	2
Non-metro	3	100	10	13	51	6	4	6	2	1	2	2	1	2
Total	6	100	13	15	37	6	3	14	2	3	3	1	1	2
New Brunswick														
Metro	5	100	9	16	32	6	4	13	5	3	8	1	1	2
Non-metro	3	100	12	16	25	10	7	11	5	3	5	1	2	3
Total	3	100	10	16	29	8	5	12	5	3	7	1	1	3
Quebec														
Metro	18	100	9	10	31	3	13	21	6	3	1	0	1	2
Non-metro	1	100	3	11	34	3	23	13	6	2	1	1	2	3
Total	13	100	9	10	31	3	13	21	6	3	1	0	1	2
Ontario														
Metro	35	100	30	20	16	8	5	5	3	4	2	1	3	3
Non-metro	3	100	20	13	24	10	8	5	6	2	3	2	3	3
Total	29	100	30	19	16	8	5	5	3	4	2	1	3	3
Manitoba														
Metro	26	100	20	10	14	38	3	2	4	1	2	1	1	3
Non-metro	4	100	18	12	14	28	14	2	3	1	3	1	2	2
Total	17	100	19	10	14	37	5	2	4	1	2	1	1	3
Saskatchewan														
Metro	17	100	29	15	13	22	4	4	5	2	1	1	1	3
Non-metro	5	100	15	8	11	49	4	2	3	1	3	1	1	2
Total	11	100	26	13	13	28	4	4	5	2	2	1	1	2

Metro and non-metro areas by each province or territory	Visible minority population as a percent of total population, 2016	Visible minority population (row percent distribution)												
		Total visible minority population	South Asian	Chinese	Black	Filipino	Latin American	Arab	Southeast Asian	West Asian	Korean	Japanese	Visible minority, n.i.e.*	Multiple visible minorities
Alberta														
Metro	30	100	26	18	14	16	6	6	5	2	2	1	1	3
Non-metro	8	100	16	8	17	*35*	7	5	3	1	3	3	1	2
Total	23	100	25	17	14	18	6	6	5	2	2	1	1	3
Britsih Columba														
Metro	41	100	26	38	3	10	3	1	4	4	4	3	1	3
Non-metro	6	100	28	16	9	15	5	2	6	1	4	8	2	3
Total	30	100	26	37	3	10	3	1	4	4	4	3	1	3
Yukon														
Metro	..	..	..	..	..	..	..	..	..	..	..	..	..	..
Non-metro	9	100	17	14	9	*40*	4	0	6	1	2	2	1	4
Total	9	100	17	14	9	40	4	0	6	1	2	2	1	4
Northwest Territories														
Metro	..	..	..	..	..	..	..	..	..	..	..	..	..	..
Non-metro	10	100	16	8	19	*33*	3	3	6	1	3	4	2	2
Total	10	100	16	8	19	33	3	3	6	1	3	4	2	2
Nunavut														
Metro	..	..	..	..	..	..	..	..	..	..	..	..	..	..
Non-metro	3	100	13	8	*36*	25	4	4	3	1	1	0	2	2
Total	3	100	13	8	36	25	4	4	3	1	1	0	2	2
Canada														
Metro	30	100	25	21	15	10	6	7	4	4	2	1	2	3
Non-metro	4	100	18	12	19	*21*	8	5	5	1	3	3	2	3
Total	22	100	25	21	16	10	6	7	4	3	2	1	2	3

Source: Statistics Canada, 2016 Census of Population, catalogue no. 98-400-X2016190, https://www12.statcan.gc.ca/datasets/Index-eng.cfm.

Notes: Modal visibility group for each non-metro area is shown with italic text.

*n.i.e.: not indicated elsewhere. See chapter glossary for definitions of other terms and abbreviations.

THE BOTTOM LINE

Building inclusive rural communities in Canada requires a strong understanding of who actually lives in these communities, who is moving to them, and what factors contribute to different settlement patterns. I have sought to highlight the racial diversity of rural Canada by making comparisons to urban Canada and across different rural communities, and by looking at different ways of defining rurality.

Rural Canada is, in general, growing, but not everywhere. The density and distance-to-density dimensions of rurality matter for growth and for decline. Smaller and/or more remote communities grow more slowly than the national average. At the same time, successful rural development in some areas means rural communities become reclassified as urban over time. Both of these factors contribute to the fact that the rural share of the total population in Canada is declining.

Meanwhile, a declining birth rate has generated a demographic labour market shortage in rural communities, which is fueling an increased focus on attracting migrants to rural communities. Annual immigrant arrivals still contribute only a small amount to the population change in rural areas, but that contribution is growing. As well, while recent immigrants and visible minorities represent a smaller share of the rural population than the urban population, that share is growing. These factors are contributing to the increasing diversity of rural communities and people over time.

The importance of understanding the nature of the changing demographic diversity in rural Canada, including how it differs from urban areas and also by province or region, is highlighted by the changing demographics of Indigenous peoples. Indigenous peoples represent the largest and growing minority group in rural Canada. Within non-metro Canada, young Indigenous residents now represent 16% of expected labour market entrants. In some provinces, Indigenous labour market entrants in non-metro areas are a much higher share of all labour market entrants (Manitoba, 36%; Saskatchewan, 33%). Thus, in building inclusive rural communities, special efforts must be made to recognize and respond to the trends we are seeing in terms of rural diversity. This means, for one thing, responding to the still small but steadily increasing demand for immigrant services. It also means

creating policies and community practices that will foster reconciliation and neighbourliness between settlers and Indigenous peoples who have always been here and whose presence is quickly growing. In short, it means seeing and responding to the specific diversity demographics on a community-by-community basis.

NOTES

1. The MIZ delineation is part of Statistics Canada's statistical area classification, outlined in the dictionary of the 2016 Census of Population (Statistics Canada 2016). Note that even in weak and no MIZ areas, there is certainly commuting to other destinations within rural Canada (Green and Meyer 1997; Persson, Westholm, and Fuller 1997; Harris, Alasia, and Bollman 2008).
2. For the case of Ontario, the 2016 classification of metro, partially-non-metro, and non-metro census divisions is shown in table 2 of Bollman (2017b, 13).
3. The rural share of Canada's population is also declining due to successful rural development causing the reclassification over time of rural communities to urban communities. See slides 6 and 40 in Bollman (2017a).
4. For tables and charts of population trends by province and territory, see Bollman (2017a). See also Dupuy, Mayer, and Morissette (2000), Alasia (2004), Mwansa and Bollman (2005), Caron-Malenfant et al. (2007), and Bollman (2017b).
5. An increasing number of individuals are reporting an Aboriginal identity in recent intercensal periods at the time of writing. Specifically, the number of individuals reporting an Aboriginal identity has increased by more than the number of births of children with an Aboriginal identity (Caron-Malenfant et al. 2014; O'Donnell and LaPointe 2019). Interestingly, this increase in the reporting of an Aboriginal identity occurs in each age group in each province *except* among youth in the western provinces as they move from the 15–19 years of age bracket in one census to the 20–24 years of age bracket in the subsequent census (Bollman 2020).
6. The countries assigned to each region and the number of immigrants from each country are shown in Statistics Canada (2017).

GLOSSARY

All definitions are based on Statistics Canada's (2016) *Dictionary, Census of Population 2016* unless otherwise stated.

Aboriginal identity: Census data on Aboriginal identity is based on respondents to the Census of Population self-identifying as Aboriginal in response to the following question:

> Is this person an Aboriginal person, that is, First Nations (North American Indian), Métis or Inuk (Inuit)?
> Note: First Nations (North American Indian) includes Status and Non-Status Indians.
> If "Yes," mark the [answer(s)] that best describe(s) this person now.
> 1: No, not an Aboriginal person. Continue with the next question.
> 2: Yes, First Nations (North American Indian).
> 3: Yes, Métis.
> 4: Yes, Inuk (Inuit).

As stated in Statistics Canada (2016), Aboriginal individuals include "those who are First Nations (North American Indian), Métis or Inuk (Inuit) and/or those who are Registered or Treaty Indians (that is, registered under the *Indian Act* of Canada), and/or those who have membership in a First Nation or Indian band. Aboriginal peoples of Canada are defined in the *Constitution Act, 1982*, Section 35 (2) as including the Indian, Inuit and Métis peoples of Canada."

Census agglomeration (CA): A CA has a total population of 10,000 to 99,999, with 10,000 or more residents in the urban core. Specifically, according to Statistics Canada (2016), a CA is formed by "one or more adjacent municipalities [CSDs] centred on a population centre (known as the core) of 10,000 or more...based on adjusted data from the previous Census of Population Program." To be included in the CA, "other adjacent [CSDs] must have a high degree of integration with the core, as measured by commuting flows derived from data on place of work from

the previous Census Program." Generally, in the adjacent CSDs, there is 50% or more of the workforce that commutes to the CA. In some cases, a reverse-commuting rule and/or a contiguity rule may apply. For the exact delineation rules, see the Statistics Canada (2016) entry "Census Metropolitan Area (CMA) and Census Agglomeration (CA)."

Census division: According to Statistics Canada (2016), a census division is a group of CSDs that are "provincially legislated areas (such as a county, a *municipalité régionale de comté*, or a regional district) or their equivalents. In...provinces and the territories where laws do not provide for such areas, Statistics Canada defines equivalent areas for statistical reporting purposes in co-operation with these provinces and territories. Census divisions are intermediate geographic areas between the province/territory level and the municipality (census subdivision)."

In this chapter, the term *metro census division* describes a census division with all its component CSDs classified as part of a CMA. A *partially non-metro census division* has some of its component CSDs classified as part of a CMA and others classified as being outside a CMA. A *non-metro census division* has all its component CSDs classified as being outside a CMA.

Census metropolitan area (CMA): A CMA has a total population of 100,000 or more, with 50,000 or more residents in the urban core. Specifically, a CMA is formed by one or more CSDs centred on a population centre (known as the core) of 50,000 or more, based on adjusted data from the previous Census of Population Program. As noted in Statistics Canada (2016), to be included in a CMA, "other adjacent CSDs must have a high degree of integration with the core, as measured by commuting flows derived from data on place of work from the previous Census Program." Generally, in the adjacent CSDs, there is 50% or more of the workforce that commutes to the CMA. In some cases, a reverse-commuting rule and/or a contiguity rule may apply. For the exact delineation rules, see the Statistics Canada (2016) entry "Census Metropolitan Area (CMA) and Census Agglomeration (CA)."

In this chapter, the term *metro* is used interchangeably with CMA. The term *non-metro* is used interchangeably with non-CMA.

Census subdivision (CSD): According to Statistics Canada (2016), a CSD is "an incorporated town or incorporated municipality (or equivalent for statistical purposes). Specifically, a CSD is the general term for municipalities (as determined by provincial/territorial legislation) or areas treated as municipal equivalents for statistical purposes (e.g., Indian reserves, Indian settlements and unorganized territories). Municipal status is defined by laws in effect in each province and territory in Canada."

Metropolitan influenced zone (MIZ): An MIZ is an RST area in which a given share of the workforce commutes to any CMA or CA. An area is a *strong* MIZ if 30% or more of employed residents commute to CA or CMA; a *moderate* MIZ if 5% to 29% commute; a *weak* MIZ if less than 5% but more than 0% commute; and *no* MIZ if there is no commuting to a CMA or CA. The CSDs outside the CAs of Whitehorse and Yellowknife are designated as RST *territories*. For the detailed delineation rules, see the Statistics Canada (2016) entry "Census Metropolitan Influenced Zone (MIZ)."

Rural and small town (RST) area: RST areas include all CSDs that are outside CMAs and CAs. In other words, RST areas are non-CMA/CA areas.

Visible minority population: According to Statistics Canada (2016), "'visible minority' refers to whether a person belongs to a visible minority group as defined by the *Employment Equity Act* and, if so, the visible minority group to which the person belongs. The *Employment Equity Act* defines visible minorities as 'persons, other than Aboriginal peoples, who are non-Caucasian in race or non-white in colour.' The visible minority population consists mainly of the following groups: South Asian, Chinese, Black, Filipino, Latin American, Arab, Southeast Asian, West Asian, Korean and Japanese."

REFERENCES

Alasia, Alessandro. 2004. "Mapping the Socio-economic Diversity of Rural Canada." *Rural and Small Town Canada Analysis Bulletin* 5, no. 2 (March): 1–36. https://www150.statcan.gc.ca/n1/en/catalogue/21-006-X2003002.

Alasia, Alessandro, and Erik Magnusson. 2005. "Occupational Skill Level: The Divide Between Rural and Urban Canada." *Rural and Small Town Canada Analysis Bulletin* 6, no. 2 (February): 1–30. https://www150.statcan.gc.ca/n1/en/catalogue/21-006-X2005002.

Angus, Charlie. 2017. *Children of the Broken Treaty*. 2nd ed. Regina: University of Regina Press.

Bollman, Ray D. 2015. "Factsheet: Hot Spots of Recent Immigrant Arrivals at the Community Level in Canada." *Pathways to Prosperity Bulletin*, January 2015. http://p2pcanada.ca/wp-content/blogs.dir/1/files/2015/01/eBulletin-January-2015.pdf.

Bollman, Ray D. 2017a. *Rural Demography Update: 2016*. Guelph: Rural Ontario Institute. Available from https://www.ruralontarioinstitute.ca/knowledge-centre/focus-on-rural-ontario.

Bollman, Ray D. 2017b. *Rural Ontario's Demography: Census Update 2016*. Guelph: Rural Ontario Institute. Available from https://www.ruralontarioinstitute.ca/knowledge-centre/focus-on-rural-ontario.

Bollman, Ray D. 2018. "Rural Youth Out-Migration: A Look at Some Numbers." Presentation at book launch for *Finding a Place in the World: Understanding Youth Outmigration from Shrinking Rural Communities* by Karen Foster and Hannah Main, Dalhousie University, Halifax, April 30, 2018. Available from https://rfrc.ca/sites/default/files/2020-05/Bollman%20Youth%20Outmigration%20April%2030%202018.pdf.

Bollman, Ray D. 2019a. "Change in Occupation Mix: All Sectors, 2006–2016." *Focus on Rural Ontario* 7 (1). Available from https://www.ruralontarioinstitute.ca/knowledge-centre/focus-on-rural-ontario.

Bollman, Ray D. 2019b. "Change in Occupation Mix: Overview by Sector." *Focus on Rural Ontario* 7 (2). Available from https://www.ruralontarioinstitute.ca/knowledge-centre/focus-on-rural-ontario.

Bollman, Ray D. 2019c. "Change in Occupation Mix: Agriculture, Forestry, Fishing and Hunting." *Focus on Rural Ontario* 7 (3). Available from https://www.ruralontarioinstitute.ca/knowledge-centre/focus-on-rural-ontario.

Bollman, Ray D. 2019d. "Change in Occupation Mix: Construction Sector, 2006–2016." *Focus on Rural Ontario* 7 (4). Available from https://www.ruralontarioinstitute.ca/knowledge-centre/focus-on-rural-ontario.

Bollman, Ray D. 2019e. "Change in Occupation Mix: Manufacturing Sector, 2006–2016." *Focus on Rural Ontario* 7 (5). Available from https://www.ruralontarioinstitute.ca/knowledge-centre/focus-on-rural-ontario.

Bollman, Ray D. 2019f. "Change in Occupation Mix: Wholesale Trade Sector, 2006–2016." *Focus on Rural Ontario* 7 (6). Available from https://www.ruralontarioinstitute.ca/knowledge-centre/focus-on-rural-ontario.

Bollman, Ray D. 2019g. "Change in Occupation Mix: Professional, Scientific and Technical Services, 2006–2016." *Focus on Rural Ontario* 7 (7). Available from https://www.ruralontarioinstitute.ca/knowledge-centre/focus-on-rural-ontario.

Bollman, Ray D. 2019h. "Change in Occupation Mix: Health Care and Social Assistance, 2006–2016." *Focus on Rural Ontario* 7 (8). Available from https://www.ruralontarioinstitute.ca/knowledge-centre/focus-on-rural-ontario.

Bollman, Ray D. 2020. "Change in Reporting an Aboriginal Identity: Age Matters." *Journal of Rural and Community Development* 15 (2): 114–21. https://journals.brandonu.ca/jrcd/article/view/1778.

Bollman, Ray D. 2021. "COVID-19 and the Differential Impacts on the Rural and Urban Economies." *The Journal of Rural and Community Development*. 16 (4): 245–49. https://journals.brandonu.ca/jrcd/article/view/2063/557.

Bollman, Ray D., Roland Beshiri, and Heather Clemenson. 2007. "Immigrants in Rural Canada." In "Rural Communities," edited by Bill Reimer, special issue, *Our Diverse Cities* 3 (Summer): 9–15. https://publications.gc.ca/collections/collection_2008/cic/Ci2-1-3-2007E.pdf.

Bollman, Ray D., and Heather A. Clemenson. 2008. "Structure and Change in Canada's Rural Demography: An Update to 2006 with Provincial Detail." Agriculture and Rural Working Paper Series, December 2008. Statistics Canada (catalogue no. 21-601-M — no. 90). https://www150.statcan.gc.ca/n1/en/catalogue/21-601-M2008090.

Bollman, Ray D., and E. Dianne Looker. 2020. "Demography, Time Trends and Rural-Urban Differences Relating to Educational Issues in Canada, Provinces and Territories." PowerPoint presentation containing supplementary charts for Looker and Bollman (2020). Available from http://crrf.ca/ruraleducation/.

Bollman, Ray D., and Bill Reimer. 2019. "What Is Rural? What Is Rural Policy? What Is Rural Development Policy?" In *The Routledge Handbook of Comparative Rural Policy*, edited by M. Vittuari, J. Devlin, M. Pagani, and T.G. Johnson, 9–26. London: Routledge.

Caron-Malenfant, Éric, Simon Coulombe, Eric Guimond, Chantal Grondin, and André Lebel. 2014. "Ethnic Mobility of Aboriginal Peoples in Canada Between the 2001 and 2006 Censuses." *Population* 69 (1): 29–54.

Caron-Malenfant, Éric, Anne Milan, Mathieu Charron, and Alain Bélanger. 2007. "Demographic Changes in Canada from 1971 to 2001 across an Urban-to-Rural Gradient." Research Paper, Demographic Documents, April 2007. Statistics Canada (catalogue no. 91F0015MIE — no. 008).

Clemenson, Heather A., and J. Roger Pitblado. 2007. "Recent Trends in Rural-Urban Migration." In "Rural Communities," edited by Bill Reimer, special issue, *Our Diverse Cities* 3 (Summer): 25–29. https://publications.gc.ca/collections/collection_2008/cic/Ci2-1-3-2007E.pdf.

du Plessis, Valerie, Roland Beshiri, Ray D. Bollman, and Heather Clemenson. 2001. "Definitions of Rural." *Rural and Small Town Canada Analysis Bulletin* 3, no. 3 (November): 1–17. https://www150.statcan.gc.ca/n1/en/catalogue/21-006-X2001003.

du Plessis, Valerie, Roland Beshiri, Ray D. Bollman, and Heather Clemenson. 2002. "Definitions of Rural with Provincial Detail." Agriculture and Rural Working Paper Series, December 2002. Statistics Canada (catalogue no. 21-601-MIE — no. 61). https://www150.statcan.gc.ca/n1/en/catalogue/21-601-M2002061.

Dupuy, Richard, Francine Mayer, and René Morissette. 2000. "Rural Youth: Stayers, Leavers and Return Migrants." Analytic Studies Branch Research Paper Series, September 2000. Statistics Canada (catalogue no. 11F0019MPE — no. 152). https://www150.statcan.gc.ca/n1/en/catalogue/11F0019M2000152.

Green, Milford B., and Stephen P. Meyer. 1997. "Occupational Stratification of Rural Commuting." In *Rural Employment: An International Perspective*, edited by Ray D. Bollman and John M. Bryden, 225–38. Brandon: Brandon University for the Canadian Rural Revitalization Foundation; Wallingford, UK: CAB International.

Harris, Spencer, Alessandro Alasia, and Ray D. Bollman. 2008. "Rural Commuting: Its Relevance to Rural and Urban Labour Markets." *Rural and Small Town Canada Analysis Bulletin* 7, no. 6 (September): 1–23. https://www150.statcan.gc.ca/n1/en/catalogue/21-006-X2007006.

Houle, René. 2007. "Secondary Migration of New Immigrants to Canada." In "Rural Communities," edited by Bill Reimer, special issue, *Our Diverse Cities* 3 (Summer): 25–29. https://publications.gc.ca/collections/collection_2008/cic/Ci2-1-3-2007E.pdf.

Looker, E. Dianne, and Ray D. Bollman. 2020. "Setting the Stage: Overview of Data on Teachers and Students in Rural and Urban Canada." In *Rural Teacher Education: Connecting Land and People*, edited by Michael Corbett and Dianne Gereluk, 21–73. Toronto: Springer.

Magnusson, Erik, and Alessandro Alasia. 2004. "Occupational Patterns Within Industry Groups: A Rural-Urban Comparison." *Rural and Small Town Canada Analysis Bulletin* 5, no. 6 (November): 1–16. https://www150.statcan.gc.ca/n1/en/catalogue/21-006-X2004006.

Mendelson, Robert, and Ray D. Bollman. 1998. "Rural and Small Town Population is Growing in the 1990s." *Rural and Small Town Canada Analysis Bulletin* 1, no. 1 (October): 1–12. https://www150.statcan.gc.ca/n1/en/catalogue/21-006-X1998001.

Mwansa, Pius, and Ray D. Bollman. 2005. "Community Demographic Trends within Their Regional Context." *Rural and Small Town Canada Analysis Bulletin* 6, no. 3 (May): 1–36. https://www150.statcan.gc.ca/n1/en/catalogue/21-006-X2005003.

O'Donnell, Vivian, and Russell LaPointe. 2019. "Response Mobility and the Growth of the Aboriginal Identity Population, 2006–2011 and 2011–2016." National Household Survey: Aboriginal Peoples, October 29, 2019. Statistics Canada (catalogue no. 99-011-X201902). https://www150.statcan.gc.ca/n1/en/catalogue/99-011-X2019002.

Persson, Lars Olaf, Erik Westholm, and Tony Fuller. 1997. "Two Contexts, One Outcome: The Importance of Lifestyle Choice in Creating Rural Jobs in Canada and Sweden." In *Rural Employment: An International Perspective*, edited by Ray D. Bollman and John M. Bryden, 136–63. Brandon: Brandon University for the Canadian Rural Revitalization Foundation; Wallingford, UK: CAB International.

Statistics Canada. 2016. *Dictionary, Census of Population, 2016* (catalogue no. 98-301-X). https://www12.statcan.gc.ca/census-recensement/2016/ref/dict/index-eng.cfm.

Statistics Canada. 2017. *Table 98-400-x2016185 Immigrant Status and Period of Immigration, Place of Birth, Age and Sex for the Population in Private Households of Canada, Provinces and Territories, Census Divisions and Census subdivisions, 2016 Census – 25% Sample Data*. https://www150.statcan.gc.ca/n1/en/catalogue/98-400-X2016185.

World Bank. 2009. *World Development Report: Reshaping Economic Geography*. Washington, DC: World Bank. http://hdl.handle.net/10986/5991.

MAKING DIVERSITY IN RURAL AREAS VISIBLE

A Changing Perspective for Rural Schools in Québec

Sivane Hirsch and Corina Borri-Anadon

THIS CHAPTER REPORTS ON A TYPOLOGICAL APPROACH used in the project "Keys for a Better Understanding of the Ethnocultural, Religious, and Linguistic Diversity in Schools."[1] The project and its typology bring to the forefront the different forms of diversity that exist within and across the 17 administrative regions of Québec.[2] Research on ethnocultural, religious, and linguistic diversity in Québec too often focuses only on the province's metropolitan regions—Montréal in particular—forgetting how, or even that, diversity manifests across the province. In this way, the diversity of metropolitan Québec is overvisibilized, while the diversity of nonmetropolitan Québec is invisibilized. The typology of the "Keys for a Better Understanding" project is worthwhile in that it investigates diversity in all of Québec's administrative regions, across the rural-urban spectrum.

The "Keys for a Better Understanding" project is focused on diversity in the context of education. The typology reported here thus focuses on student-specific indicators of diversity, though it also looks at some indicators that are applicable to many contexts in Québec society. Because of its school-centred focus, however, we see this typology as a valuable tool in encouraging schools to take stock of their local diversity profiles as they design and deliver educational programs. It contributes to research

on ethnic relations in education in Québec by offering a detailed and nuanced understanding of diversity across the province and in its schools, and ultimately supporting the development of educational policies that are better adapted to region-specific needs in Québec and elsewhere.

It should be understood, however, that typologies such as this one are snapshots of data from particular times and places and are susceptible to change. Still, this snapshot serves as a milestone in understanding the regional particularities of diversity across Québec—an understanding that has, until now, been largely neglected in the research.

RURALITY AND DIVERSITY IN AND ACROSS QUÉBEC

It is generally acknowledged that Montréal and the greater metropolitan region of Québec are highly ethnoculturally, religiously, and linguistically diverse, and that this diversity is due to large waves of immigrant settlement.[3] Recognition of the diversity within and throughout other regions of Québec is, however, more recent. This recognition and the associated exploration of the challenges of living together in a diverse society across the province are now becoming more prominent in both the public debate and within academic research. Indeed, throughout all regions of Québec, the historically diverse mix of Indigenous nations, majority French-speaking communities, English-speaking communities, and long-established racialized minorities has been amplified by more recent immigration. The long-standing and increasing diversity throughout Québec creates different opportunities and challenges across the province that cannot be overlooked.[4] Yet in discussions of Québec's diversity, we continue to think in terms of a divide, frequently expressed in public opinion, between Greater Montréal and Québec's other regions. This divide is a result of the common assumption that diversity is a phenomenon that is exclusive to metropolitan areas, and that all other (more rural) regions are ethnically, religiously, and linguistically homogenous. The presumed divide between metropolitan and other regions fails to acknowledge the diversity inherent within and the challenges unique to nonmetropolitan areas, which are too often simplistically considered homogenously "rural."

Research often treats everything that is not urban as rural (Mc Andrew and L'Équipe du Griés 2015), not considering the variety

of local realities, such as urban centres located outside metropolitan areas. Using the term *rural* therefore carries the risk of homogenization and reduces the possibility of contextualizing diversity, which is more necessary now than ever. We do not understand rurality in this simplistic way. For us, the notion of rurality must be apprehended in a complex way that takes into account the unique sociocultural profiles of each individual "rural" region. In this chapter, when we talk about the "regional context" or "regional level," we are talking about the different realities of Québec's regions in all of their complexity, and thus go beyond the simplistic rural-urban binary and nuance the general understanding of "regional" in the Québec context. Nuancing the rural in this way will allow us to consider how regions' unique diversity profiles impact school settings—the focus of the "Keys for a Better Understanding" project. By increasing the visibility of the unique profiles of cultural, religious, and linguistic diversity in rural or nonmetropolitan regions, we can encourage more inclusive approaches to education for diverse rural students, and in the process build a more deeply equal society.

In Québec's school system, the effects of the presumed urban-rural divide are observed in at least three areas. First, public policy, based on a notion of "critical mass" diversity (Vatz-Laaroussi 2005), adopts a vocabulary that mostly describes diversity within the context of Montréal, thus ignoring the diversity across the province. Second, research shows that there are important differences in the practices adopted by and sometimes between schools in Québec's administrative regions—such as the kinds of support given to newly arrived immigrant students to further their educational, social, and linguistic integration (De Koninck and Armand 2012). However, these local initiatives have yet to be documented, especially in the areas outside of Montréal (Mc Andrew and L'Équipe du Griés 2015). Finally, diversity as a theme is weakly anchored in preservice and in-service teacher training in the regional context. This is not due to the lack of diversity in schools, but to the fact that only a few researchers study these issues and almost no courses address them (Larochelle-Audet et al. 2013; Borri-Anadon et al. 2018; Hirsch and Mc Andrew 2016).

As we see it, the biggest challenge to recognizing the particularities of diversity at the regional level across the regions of Québec are

the phenomena of, first, overvisibilization of the presence and needs of certain diverse groups in certain areas and, second, invisibilization of the presence and needs of other diverse groups in other areas. These phenomena impede the recognition of diversity as it actually exists across Québec.

Overvisibilization occurs through the instrumentalization of diversity both in the media and in politics (Potvin 2008, 2010). According to Potvin (2017, 50), these instrumentalizations have led to narratives that "have repetitively, spectacularly and mimetically spun various anecdotal news stories by priming, agenda setting and contentiously framing diversity." In the context of our project, overvisibilization works to frame diversity as something that, for all intents and purposes, exists almost exclusively in metropolitan zones. This is problematic not only in that it neglects the fact that diverse populations live throughout Québec, but in that it narrowly limits diversity to the kinds of diversity that we see in metropolitan areas. That is, it doesn't allow for the diversity of diversity itself.

Invisibilization is the other side of the same coin, perhaps embodied most obviously in the status of Indigenous Nations in Québec, where the majority francophone group takes precedence. Indigenous Nations are not included in any consideration of interculturalism in Québec, and are thereby relegated to the status of a cultural minority like other cultural minorities in the province. This negates any possibility of nation-to-nation relationships, rendering Indigenous Peoples invisible in analyses of diversity within Québec society (Bouchard and Taylor 2008; Frozzini 2014). The Gouvernement du Québec's (2019) report on relations between Indigenous Peoples and certain public services in Québec highlighted the tensions that exist in some regions of the province between Indigenous peoples and the rest of the Québec population.

The impacts of over- and invisibilization are felt province-wide, though some regions feel it more intensely than others (Gouvernement du Québec 2019; Potvin 2017). As the "regionalization" of immigration—that is, the encouraging of immigration to nonmetropolitan regions of Québec—becomes a frequent political talking point, the need to understand how these phenomena impact and function within the province's different regions and their school systems becomes more urgent.[5]

To address the need for region- and school-specific information around diversity, we began the "Keys for a Better Understanding of the Ethnocultural, Religious, and Linguistic Diversity in Schools" project in 2017. This project collects diversity data from each of Québec's 17 administrative regions, and organizes it according to four categories: (1) a historical portrait of the region's diversity from its historical and colonial past up to contemporary waves of migration; (2) an analysis of how the media have portrayed diversity; (3) the key current demographic characteristics of each region; and (4) the implications of this diversity for schools by means of a statistical portrait and an overview of some of the relevant and promising initiatives already in place (Borri-Anadon and Hirsch 2019). This chapter focuses primarily on categories 3 and 4, which we will refer to simply as "the databases" in this chapter.

Using data from the "Keys for a Better Understanding" project, this chapter aims to make the range and particularities of diversity across Québec visible without setting them in stone. We start by presenting the theoretical and methodological choices we made to extract from the data the differences and similarities in diversity within and between Québec's administrative regions. We then offer a typology that regroups the 17 administrative regions of Québec into six groupings based on their particular diversity profiles. We conclude by discussing the particular, diverse makeups of these new groupings, the unique needs and challenges they imply, and the impacts they have on schools.

THEORETICAL AND METHODOLOGICAL CONSIDERATIONS
Adopting a Constructivist Perspective
Like Juteau (2018), we use a constructivist approach that understands diversity as a social construct—a result of the mobilization of certain social boundaries, or markers. Juteau understands these markers as "lines of demarcation" that denote the existence of distinct social relationships systems and the mechanisms designed to maintain them (30). These socially constructed boundaries are two sided. One side is "internal": the relationship a specific group has towards the markers of its own diversity. The other side is "external": the categories of diversity attributed to a specific group by other, often majority, groups.

It should, however, be made clear from the outset that operationalizing these markers using the available data has certain limits. For one, data often only focuses on one or the other of these two-sided boundaries. On the one hand, fact-based or so-called objective data[6]—which includes, for instance, information gathered by Statistics Canada about place of birth, age, and sex—involves externally assigning people to particular categories. On the other hand, self-reported data—for instance, data about Indigenous identity and gender—are often internally categorized; people assign themselves to certain categories through self-reports.

Other limits follow from this. For instance, from a deliberately constructivist perspective on otherness (Mc Andrew 2011), using solely statistical and fact-based analyses runs the risk of essentializing a given group by implying that the data describe inherent characteristics of the group, leaving no room for how group characteristics are socially defined and may therefore shift and change over time. (Juteau 2018). Using solely self-reported data comes with its own challenges. Because these data often reflect broad societal changes, they pose interpretative challenges.[7]

Recognizing Particularities and Establishing Groupings:
Using Typological Analysis to Move Towards Mapping
With the goal of portraying the ethnocultural, religious, and linguistic particularities of diversity for each of the regions of Québec, we use Demazière's (2013) typological method, an inductive and descriptive multistage approach. For Demazière, the challenge is to use the typology efficiently by extracting and comparing individual cases to identify similarities without losing the richness of the corpus. This approach helps sociologists (and, by extension, their public) to understand the diversity that exists within a general class of phenomena (Ragin 1987, 149; Demazière 2013). It serves to put things in order—that is, to reduce the complexity without destroying it (Demazière 2013, 334).

In the context of our study, we extracted cases from our databases and the variety of data collected there. We used data from three main sources: federal data from the 2011 and 2016 censuses; provincial data from the Ministère de l'Immigration, de la Diversité et de l'Inclusion (MIDI 2016); and school data from the Ministère de l'Éducation et de l'Enseignement supérieur (MEES 2017). A first step in selecting and

condensing relevant and pertinent information was to identify indicators of diversity that captured the diversity that was characteristic of the different regions of Québec.

The data on which these indicators were based are self-reported in some cases and fact based in others. Sometimes, self-reported data was included because it was the only data available. This is true of, for instance, religious affiliation. While religious affiliation was not one of our primary indicators, it did, in some regions, offer insight into diversity. This data allowed us to build an interesting portrait of religious diversity in Québec, which includes those who declare Catholic affiliation (still a clear majority in all regions of Québec); those who declare being nonreligious (ranging from less than 1% to 17%); and those who declare affiliation to other religions, including various branches of Protestantism, Islam, Judaism, Buddhism, and so on (Statistics Canada 2017). Even though the numbers were too low in many regions to be used as significant diversity indicators for our categories, they enabled us to take religious diversity into account in our general cartography by documenting the importance of the Catholic majority within religious diversity.

Other times, self-reported data provided a better portrait of certain aspects of diversity than fact-based data. This was particularly true with regard to Indigenous identity. To establish the proportion of Indigenous people in Québec's different regions, we used self-declared data on Indigenous identity as opposed to fact-based data on the number of people with treaty and Indian status because this latter data has excluded some Indigenous people for historical and political reasons that are often not accepted by Indigenous Peoples.[8]

Fact-based data were the bases of the other indicators, which describe regional immigrant populations.[9] This data was important to understanding the proportion of recent immigrants, notably refugees, admitted to Québec between 2005 and 2014, many of whom had been settled in nonmetropolitan regions by the state.[10] The data on students from immigrant backgrounds, based principally on the students' and their parents' countries of birth and mother tongues, were also considered for analysis purposes. We analyzed the proportion of first- and second-generation students from immigrant backgrounds; the growth of these populations between 2013/14 and 2016/17; the number of mother-tongue languages

declared by parents; and the proportions of francophones, anglophones, and allophones.[11]

The next steps in the process were to compare the different regions using our primary indicators, to group broadly similar regions together, and to identify regions with differences in certain indicators. The goal of grouping and differentiating regions in this way was, as mentioned already, to overcome the urban-rural dichotomy. As it turned out, however, the groupings varied enormously depending on the indicator selected—a finding that brings to mind the implications of over- and invisibilization in data analysis. Because of this variability, we opted for a typology of the different regions that was based on a selection of indicators that researchers have found to be particularly relevant for better understanding school diversity, and which were subsequently categorized as core units (Demazière 2013, 336). We settled on seven primary indicators:

- Proportion of Indigenous people in the total population
- Proportion of immigrants in the total population
- Proportion of refugees among first-generation immigrants
- Proportion of student population from immigrant backgrounds
- Proportion of second-generation students among immigrant background students
- Growth in number of students from immigrant backgrounds
- Proportion of student population that is anglophone or allophone

The collected data clearly demonstrate the importance of cross-referencing the various indicators to make all existing data meaningful.

RESULTS
A Typology of the Ethnocultural, Religious, and Linguistic Diversity in the Regions of Québec

Having used the same types of data for all regions, we grouped Québec's administrative regions according to their common characteristics in order to have a better understanding of the similarities and differences in their unique diversity profiles. These groupings are illustrated and summarized in Figure 2.1. For each grouping, we focus on describing

the different primary indicators selected. These primary indicators are listed in Table 2.1. We then provide information on the characteristics of each of the six groupings of our typology based on these indicators.

Detailed Presentation of Regional Groupings in the Typology

Group A in our typology corresponded to the metropolitan administrative regions of Montréal (06) and Laval (13). These two regions stood out from the other regions of Québec as they had the highest number of immigrants, particularly from the economic and family unification admission categories.[12] Together, they account for more than 25% of the immigrant population. These administrative regions also had a large proportion of students compared to other regions. Around 50% or more of these students were from immigrant backgrounds, and most of these students were second generation. Some schools in these administrative regions were attended almost entirely by students from immigrant backgrounds. Growth in the proportion of students from immigrant backgrounds has begun to slow, especially in Montréal. Still, it comes as no surprise that these two administrative regions had the highest number of mother tongues in the province (more than 110 languages). Less than 50% of parents in Montréal and Laval declared French as a mother tongue. These administrative regions also had the highest proportion of English speakers (10%–20%) and allophones (around 40%) in Québec. Religious diversity was also a salient feature. Compared to all other regional groupings, Montréal and Laval had the lowest proportion of people declaring Catholic affiliation (50%–65%) and the highest proportion of people declaring other religious affiliations in the province. Group A also had the lowest proportion of people identifying as Indigenous. On the basis of all our indicators, the data showed that these two regions are extremely diverse and that this diversity could be mainly attributed to the migratory movements that have marked Québec's past and present.

Group B included the administrative regions that surround the Group A metropolitan areas: Lanaudière (14), the Laurentides (15), and Montérégie (16). These administrative regions had similar diversity profiles, though the similarity was less pronounced than Group A. The average proportion of immigrants to these regions ranged from 5%–10%. The distribution of these people among the immigration admission

FIGURE 2.1 Groupings of Québec administrative regions according to typology of diversity

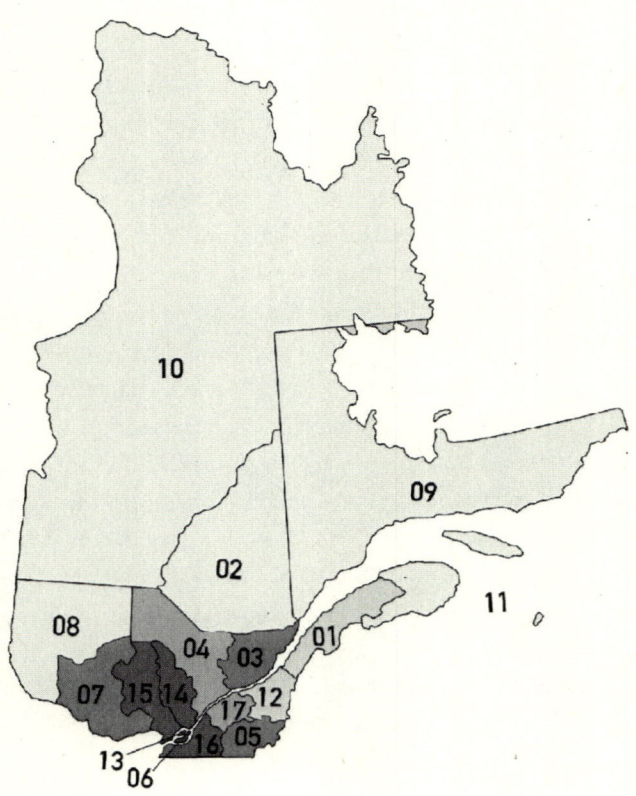

■ **Group A**
Metropolitan regions
13   Laval
06   Montréal

■ **Group B**
Areas surrounding metropolitan regions
14   Lanaudière
15   Laurentides
16   Montérégie

■ **Group C**
Medium-sized urban agglomerations
03   Capitale-Nationale
05   Estrie
07   Outaouais

■ **Group D**
Central regions
04   Mauricie
17   Centre-du-Québec

■ **Group E**
Semi-remote regions
01   Bas-Saint-Laurent
12   Chaudière-Appalaches

■ **Group F**
Most remote regions
02   Saguenay-Lac-Saint-Jean
08   Abitibi-Témiscamingue
09   Côte-Nord
11   Gaspésie-Îles-de-la-Madeleine
10   Nord-du-Québec

categories, including refugees, are the same as for Group A. Group B schools welcomed a high proportion of students from immigrant backgrounds (10%–25%). This proportion is set to rise as Group B regions have seen a significant increase in the numbers of students from immigrant backgrounds, especially those who are second generation, since the early 2010s. The majority of the population in Group B declared French as their mother tongue, including more than 75% of students in these regions. Nonetheless, more than 60 other languages were declared, and the proportion of allophone students was average compared to other regional groupings (4%–9%). The proportion of anglophone students varied largely across the three regions in Group B, ranging from around 1% in Lanaudière to almost 8% in Montérégie. This wide variation can be explained by the migrational history of each of these regions, notably the settlement of anglophone communities and more recent immigration. The majority of people in Group B regions, as in all Québec's regions, declared Catholic affiliation, but some religious diversity was observed: between 5% and 10% professed another religious affiliation. Thus, as concerns the ethnocultural, religious, and linguistic markers, the selected indicators revealed that the level of diversity in Group B was qualitatively similar to, albeit quantitatively much less significant than, that of metropolitan Group A.

Group C in our typology gathered together the administrative regions that have sizeable urban agglomerations: Capitale-Nationale (03), Estrie (05), and Outaouais (07). Even though the immigration rate in these regions was comparable to other regional groupings (5%–10%), there were considerably more refugees in the Group C immigrant population than in other groupings (16%–30%). The proportion of students from immigrant backgrounds varied between 10% and 25% and was similarly distributed across the first- and second-generational statuses. Group C regions have seen an overall increase in the number of students from immigrant backgrounds since the early 2010s, due largely to an increase in first-generation students. More than 75% of the students in Group C regions declared French as their mother tongue. Still, as in Group B, more than 60 languages were declared. The proportion of allophone students was average, ranging from 4% to 10%. There was considerable variation among the three administrative regions in Group C

with regard to those whose first language was English: 1% of respondents in Capitale-Nationale were anglophone, compared to almost 16% in the Outaouais region. The proportion of anglophones in Outaouais can be at least partly explained by this region's geographical location bordering Ontario, more specifically Ottawa. The portrait of religious diversity in Group C was very similar to that of Group B. The proportionately large number of refugees in the urban agglomerations of Group C made this grouping distinct from others in our typology. This finding also leads to the conclusion that diversity in Group C is a relatively recent phenomenon in the social fabric of these regions.

The two central regions—Mauricie (04) and Centre-du-Québec (17)—comprise Group D. This group was characterized by low immigrant population (around 2%). As state-sponsored refugees had been settled in the towns in these administrative regions, however, the regions represented 22% and 40% of all immigrants welcomed between 2005 and 2014, respectively—the highest proportions in the province. The proportion of students from immigrant backgrounds in Group D schools corresponded to the provincial median (7%–8%) and was equitably divided between the generational statuses, but was showing a rapid increase. This increase was largely due to a growing number of second-generation students from immigrant backgrounds, which suggests that the diversity in Group D is not exclusively from recent immigration. Linguistic diversity was similar in the two regions in Group D: 44 mother tongues in Mauricie and 48 in Centre-du-Québec. The proportion of allophone students was around 2%; anglophones sat at just under 1%. Although a very high proportion of the population (more than 95%) spoke French at home, Group D is approximately within the average of all six regional groupings in our typology in terms of language diversity. Group D stands out for the proportion of refugees among recent immigrants to its regions. Still, it shares several characteristics of diversity with Group E.

Group E was composed of two semi-remote regions—Chaudière-Appalaches (12) and Bas-Saint-Laurent (01)—that both had a very low proportion of immigrants (less than 2%). The number of students from immigrant backgrounds was also very low (around 5%) and predominantly second generation. Unlike the other groups, the numbers of

students from immigrant backgrounds in Group E showed very little growth. It is therefore not surprising that French was the mother tongue for more than 95% of students in these regions and that there was only a tiny percentage of anglophones and allophones (less than 1%). The actual numbers of languages spoken varied between the two administrative regions: 27 languages were declared in Bas-Saint-Laurent versus 41 in Chaudières-Appalaches. The proximity of the latter region to Capitale-Nationale partly explains this difference.

Group F, the last grouping in our typology, incorporated the five most remote regions: Saguenay-Lac-Saint-Jean (02), Abitibi-Témiscamingue (08), Côte-Nord (09), Nord-du-Québec (10), and Gaspésie-Îles-de-la-Madeleine (11). The Indigenous population was larger here compared to any of the other regional groupings. Still, it was difficult to compare the diversity profiles of the regions in this group. Whereas the majority of the population in Nord-du-Québec declared Indigenous identity (almost 66%), the proportions were substantially lower in the other administrative regions. Only 5% of the populations in Saguenay-Lac-Saint-Jean and Abitibi-Témiscamingue, and 18% in Côte-Nord. Immigrants made up a very low proportion of the population in Group F, and recent immigration stemmed mainly from economic immigrants and family reunification. Indeed, three of the administrative regions in Group F had no refugees at all between 2005 and 2014. In the school context, given the small number of students from immigrant backgrounds, no common characteristics could be determined regarding either generational status or change in immigrant presence in Group F schools. It was also difficult to compare the linguistic diversity of the administrative regions in Group F. Although Nord-du-Québec declared only 19 mother tongues, it was here that we found the lowest proportion of francophone students of any administrative region (18%). In the other Group F regions, French was the predominant mother tongue (more than 85%). Overall, Group F was characterized by its Indigenous population and the diversity among the different Indigenous Nations present.

Still, the one thing all regional groupings had in common was the low proportion of people declaring Indigenous identity (1%–3%). The Outaouais region, where Indigenous peoples made up more than 5% of

the population, was an exception to this rule. Despite this, all regions contained one or more traditional and usually unceded territory of the eleven Indigenous nations in Québec. The regional groupings differed, however, in terms of where Indigenous populations were largely located. In Group C, which had sizeable urban agglomerations such as Québec City, Sherbrooke, and Gatineau, Indigenous communities lived close to or in these urban zones. In other groupings, Indigenous communities were remote. In some of the groupings, contact between Indigenous populations and other populations was frequent, especially in school settings. In others, mostly Groups E and F, contact was relatively infrequent.

The profile for each of our six regional groupings based on our primary indicators is summarized in Table 2.1.

TABLE 2.1 Selected diversity indicators by diversity group

	Group					
	A	B	C	D	E	F
Proportion of Indigenous people in total population (%)	≤1	1–3	1–3*	1–3	1–3	≥5
Proportion of immigrants in total population (%)	≥25	5–10	5–10	~2	≤2	≤2
Proportion of refugees among first-generation immigrants (%)	9–13	9–13	≥15	≥15	3–8	≤4
Proportion of student population from immigrant background (%)	≥50	10–25	10–25	~7	~5	≤4
Proportion of second-generation students among immigrant background students (%)	60–75*	60–75	50–60*	50–60	50–60	Variable
Growth in number of students from immigrant background (%)	10–15	15–30	15–30	15–30	5–10	Variable
Proportion of English-speaking and allophone students (%)	10–20 ≤40	1–8 4–10	1–8* 4–10	~1 ~2	~1 <1	1–8 <1

Sources: Data on total Indigenous and immigrant populations is from Statistics Canada census profile data for the 2016 Census of Population. Data on proportion of refugees among recent immigrants is from MIDI (2017). All other data is from MEES (2017).

* Intragroup variation not considered by the typology. These nuances are discussed in the detailed presentation and discussion.

DISCUSSION AND CONTRIBUTIONS OF THE TYPOLOGY
Support for a Detailed and Nuanced Understanding of Diversity across Québec's Regions

Our typology of the ethnocultural, religious, and linguistic diversity across the 17 administrative regions of Québec begins to lay bare the shortcomings of such a widespread dichotomy between Montréal and the province's other regions. A map is beginning to emerge from this typological analysis, charting the extent and nature of diversity across the different groupings.

In effect, our typology aims to "explore the differences, describe them more fully, explain how they break down, combine, and connect, and identify borderline categories" (Demazière 2013, 340). As our typology shows, the rural-urban binary does not hold, or at least not in an uncomplicated way, when it comes to diversity. Indeed, even our six-pronged typology has its limitations in displaying the complexity of diversity across Québec's regions. For one, it is important to group the administrative regions of Laval and Montréal together as "metropolitan regions" (as we have done), even though the growth rate of students from immigrant backgrounds in Laval plays out differently than it does in Montréal, which, since the early 2000s, has received fewer and fewer of these students to the benefit of the other Québec regions (MELS 2014). In other words, the diversity of Montréal's student population is no longer growing as quickly as it once was. Our typology also brings to light the fact that regions in different groupings share diversity indicators with one another.

It is, for instance, clear that, even though the extent of the diversity in the metropolitan regions generally sets it apart from the other typology groupings, it shares some of the dynamics found in other groupings. For example, the number of anglophone students in Outaouais, a Group C region, is comparable to that of Group A. Group B regions also share indicators with the metropolitan zone. In particular, the numbers of second-generation students from immigrant backgrounds in the Montérégie region are similar to those of Laval and Montréal. In terms of linguistic diversity, Montérégie has the second highest number of mother tongues in the province (148), after Montréal (193). Furthermore, the administrative regions in Group B receive as many refugees as the metropolitan regions (9%–13%).

Our analysis also shows that, although the five nonmetropolitan groupings rank lower than Group A on most diversity indicators, there are some telling exceptions—notably, the Indigenous population in Group F. Without going into detail on the plurality of realities that shape the entire territory, our typology helps shed light on what we call the diversity of diversity. It has thus been important for the groupings that have emerged from our analysis to be sufficiently adaptable to allow for variation not only in the selected indicators, but also in the political, economic, and social contexts in Québec's regions. This is particularly true of the Bas-Saint-Laurent region, which, although it is part of the semi-remote Group E, is likely to shift into another grouping in the future, given that Rimouski, its largest city, has been designated as a major area to receive refugees (MIDI 2017).

Support for Schools

It seems to us that this mapping is essential to acquiring a better understanding of how the phenomena of overvisibilization and invisibilization of diversity work in Québec, including in education. Indeed, just as there is variation in the indicators themselves, the impact of these indicators on schools varies among the different diversity groupings. The typology can thus contribute to the schools' tripartite mission of instruction, socialization, and qualification (MEQ 1997), and help guide Québec's schools on the best ways of adapting their teaching methods to the reality of the diversity in their schools.

With regard to the mission of instruction, our typology may inspire schools in the various groupings to use teaching practices that respond to their particular diversity realities and experiences in order to support the academic progress of students. The Québec Education Program supports this differentiated teaching by suggesting that Ethics and Religious Culture teachers address local issues according to their area's "own characteristics" (MEQ 2001). Knowing the diversity portrait of each specific region and understanding the possible similarities and differences with other regions will allow teachers to *truly* adapt their teaching to the actual diversity characteristics of their area rather than to the image they have of this diversity. This is particularly important as this false image is often tainted by the prevailing narratives and stereotypes about

certain regions, including, in no small part, the imagined divide between Montréal and the other regions. The current revision of the Ethics and Religious Culture program can also make use of a typology like ours to better identify the markers of diversity observable throughout Québec rather than focusing—as they did in this program—specifically on religion as a marker of diversity.

With respect to educational qualification, the typology sheds light on the importance of schools adopting initiatives that prepare students to enter the workforce of Québec's society. This is particularly important when taking into consideration the elevated high school dropout and nongraduation rates affecting some communities and racialized groups. For example, research has shown that Indigenous students in particular face challenges regarding educational success (CSE 2010; Presseau, Martineau, and Bergevin 2006). Our typology indicates which regions have higher proportions of Indigenous and racialized students and can be used to support projects that increase these students' sense of equality, belonging, inclusion, and well-being at school. Creating information and awareness-raising tools that are crafted for specific student populations and parents to educate them about the Québec school system and its pathways to qualification could be a promising starting point. Ultimately, we hope such projects improve retention and graduation rates.

To encourage socialization, schools can start to promote intercultural education and "living together" by preparing students to recognize the diversity in their own regional context. This knowledge of diversity can then be expanded and adapted to other contexts. The implementation of practices aimed at establishing an equitable intercultural climate is especially important in schools that belong to groupings with mainly second-generation students from immigrant backgrounds, given that some research suggests that these students perceive greater inequities within their schools (Archambault et al. 2019). More concretely, over and above the practices that aim to welcome new arrivals or to celebrate the diverse origins of students, schools would benefit from creating opportunities to promote discussion about diversity and to act on the processes that exclude minority groups, at both the regional and provincial levels.

Contributions to Rural Inclusivity

This analysis contributes to the reflection on rural inclusivity in several ways. First, the typology allows us to recognize, appreciate, and take advantage of the presence of ethnocultural, religious, and linguistic diversity in all regions of Québec, including the rural and remote regions. By regrouping the regions according to different criteria, the schools in these areas find themselves united around common realities. This provides an opportunity to share spaces for reflection and for learning from one another, and to gain inspiration from the experiences that have already been documented by some schools. In addition, the "Keys for a Better Understanding of the Ethnocultural, Religious, and Linguistic Diversity in Schools" project from which this typology emanates has already identified promising initiatives from across the regions of Québec.

The typology also allows schools from groupings with similarities—for instance, in smaller urban agglomerations and central regions, which both welcome a high proportion of refugee students—to connect, share, and collaborate on their initiatives. As one example, these areas could collaborate on initiatives aimed at students that are more at risk academically and who are more likely to drop out. The significant proportion of refugees among immigrants in the central regions increases the probability that schools in these regions will welcome students who have experienced a more difficult migratory journey and have had to interrupt their schooling. The challenges of linguistic, educational, and social integration are all the more salient in these contexts, and call for differentiated support practices (Papazian-Zohrabian et al. 2018). Thus, schools must encourage collaboration with refugee families' host organizations and implement services that respond to the needs of refugee students who are critically behind in their schooling or who have experienced traumatic situations and bereavement.

A second way in which the typology contributes to rural inclusivity is by making a case for the inclusion of the regions themselves in the updating and implementing of educational policies and training practices, which are currently largely thought about in terms of the urban-rural divide. Our typology clearly shows that policies cannot be based solely on the notion of "critical mass." Some rural and remote administrative

regions, for example, are confronted with challenges relating to the recognition of diversity and the building of inclusion, in the sense of deep equality (Banack and Pohler, introduction to this volume), into their schools given the fact that the numbers of diverse students in their schools may not be as quantitatively significant as in other regions. Our typology also shows the diversity of our groupings' diversity portraits, leading to an understanding of the similarities and differences in the diversity of administrative regions near and far. By illustrating ethnocultural, religious, and linguistic markers across the province, the door is opened to a wider study of diversity within Québec society. This is an invaluable tool for intercultural education as it offers schools opportunities for developing awareness and discussing the different aspects and manifestations of this diversity (MEES 2019, 14). Neglecting the plurality of Québec's diversity has real policy- and budget-related consequences for schools. For example, the subsidies provided under the budgetary support measure for intercultural education are based on the number of first-generation students in schools (MEES 2019), but as our typology shows, this is only one indicator of diversity in schools. Budgetary support is highly relevant to the development of awareness around issues of ethnocultural, religious, and linguistic diversity among students, but the current means of financing schools fails to provide the support needed by some regional groups, like those in the semi-remote regions.

Our typology will also be a critical tool for improving preservice and in-service teacher training practices around diversity. These practices must be adapted to illustrate a local reality or be used to present a more detailed picture of schools across Québec, given that schools must each respond to different kinds of challenges, each just as important as the next. This is also the case for university-led initiatives that partner with Indigenous communities on their territory to provide training to help those working in the remotest regions to understand Indigenous realities.

The particularities of Québec's regional diversity profiles have consequences for education. These particularities need to be taken into account not only by teaching, nonteaching, and administrative school staff, but also by those working on education-related research, policies, and programs, and those training to enter the educational workforce.

NOTES

1. This is an English translation of the project's original French title "Des clés pour miex comprendre la diversite ethnoculturelle, religieuse et linguistique en milieu scolaire." This project was made possible through the support of the Direction de l'intégration linguistique et de l'éducation interculturelle of the Ministère de l'Éducation du Québec. The project is availabe in French through the Laboratoire éducation et diversité en région at www.uqtr.ca/ledir/fichesregionales.
2. The province of Québec is divided into 17 administrative regions for the purposes of organizing government services. Each region is identified by a number in official documents; these same numbers are used on the map in Figure 2.1. Statistics Canada data used in this chapter also largely corresponds to these administrative region divisions, though it is technically organized by economic regions.
3. The expression *ethnocultural, religious, and linguistic diversity* is currently used in Québec (notably in *A School for the Future: Policy Statement on Educational Integration and Intercultural Education* [MEQ 1998]), to refer to the multiethnic character of Québec's society and the relationship between the majority and the minority populations (Potvin et al. 2015). When we use the term *diversity* in this chapter, we are referring to ethnocultural, religious, and linguistic diversity in this sense.
4. Take for example the Gouvernement du Québec (2019) report *Public Inquiry Commission on Relations Between Indigenous Peoples and Certain Public Services in Québec: Listening, Reconciliation and Progress*, which highlighted the current tensions that exist in some regions of the province between Indigenous Peoples and the rest of the Québec population. In addition, headlines have been made in the last few years by the endless debate on visible religious symbols, the attack on the Québec City mosque in January 2017, the Muslim community's search for land for a cemetery in the Capitale-Nationale region, and the attempts by various Muslim communities (including those of Shawinigan and Trois-Rivières) to find meeting places, among other issues.
5. In fact, since the 1990s, when the *Policy Statement on Immigration and Integration* was adopted, Québec has been regionalizing its immigration (MICC 1990). That is, its immigration policies have encouraged the settlement of as many immigrants as possible in its different regions and have emphasized the importance of welcoming and supporting them. According to the policy statement, "the imbalance in the regional distribution of immigrants in Québec raises important issues that must

be addressed. First, the level of urban concentration [i.e., in Montréal]—the highest of any of the Canadian cities—deprives many of Québec's regions of the economic, demographic, and sociocultural benefits of immigration…Moreover, without a balanced regional distribution of immigrants, the responsibility integrating new arrivals falls solely on Montréal and its institutions…Finally, this imbalance could create an important gap over the long term between the metropolitan region and the rest of the province" (MICC 1990, 73; our translation).

6. This data is often designated as "objective." However, constructivist approaches to data analysis, because of their focus on the social factors at play, problematize the conventional understanding of objectivity. For this reason, we prefer the term *fact-based*.

7. Take, for example, the data on religious affiliations. For several years now, these data have presented somewhat of a conundrum. There has been a significant drop in Catholic religious practices—for instance, the number of marriages fell by 51% between 1968 and 2001—yet the drop in those self-identifying as Catholic during the same period has been much less significant (Meunier and Wilkins-Laflamme 2011). The way in which these various data have been interpreted has given rise to criticism. This has led Statistics Canada to promise changes to the way the questions are asked to ensure that a clearer picture of religious and ethnic diversity in Canada emerges from the 2021 census (Statistics Canada 2019).

8. Statistics Canada (2018) uses the term *Aboriginal identity* to refer to those who are First Nations, Métis, or Inuit, and/or are status or treaty Indians, and/or are members of a First Nation or an Indian band (under the terms of Canada's Indian Act). This usage is based on Section 35 of the Constitution Act, 1982, which states that "Aboriginal peoples of Canada" include Indians, Inuit, and Métis people. It should be noted that the available data collected in this way are subject to criticism by Indigenous Peoples themselves (APN 2019), which may impact some communities' willingness to participate in surveys (Guimond 2009). Indigenous identity may thus be much higher than conveyed by national statistics based on household surveys, and self-identification data may present a better portrait of the size of Indigenous populations.

9. The term *immigrant population* refers to persons who are, or have at any time been, landed immigrants or permanent residents. Such persons have been granted the right to permanently live in Canada by immigration authorities. Immigrants who have obtained Canadian citizenship are also included in this category (Statistics Canada 2018).

10. Refugees, including those admitted to Québec between 2005 and 2014, are categorized as follows: "Refugees and persons in a similar situation are subdivided into five subgroups: government-assisted refugees, sponsored refugees, locally recognized refugees, family members of locally recognized refugees, and other refugees" (MIDI 2018, 26; our translation).
11. In our research, we define allophone students as follows: "allophone students are all students who declare a mother tongue other than French, English, or an Indigenous language" (MELS 2013, 2; our translation). This notion, even though it has been much criticized on conceptual and methodological grounds, is widely used to understand linguistic diversity (Boisvert et al. 2020).
12. These admission categories refer to "the immigration program or group of programs under which an immigrant has been granted for the first time the right to live in Canada permanently by immigration authorities" (Statistics Canada 2018). The economic category refers to the ability of the immigrant to contribute to Canada's economy. The family unification category refers to those who are sponsored by family members who are already Canadian citizens. Immigrants may also be admitted under the refugee category. Refugees are granted permanent resident status on the basis of a well-founded fear for their life and well-being should they return to their home country. For more information, see the Statistics Canada (2018) entry on admission categories.

REFERENCES

APN (Assemblée des Premières Nations). 2019. *Renforcer la disponibilité des données sur les premières nations*. Available from https://www.afn.ca.

Archambault, Isabelle, Geneviève Audet, Corina Borri-Anadon, Sivane Hirsch, Marie Mc Andrew, and Kristel Tardif-Grenier. 2019. *L'Impact du climat interculturel des établissements sur la réussite éducative des élèves issus de l'immigration*. Québec: Ministère de l'Éducation et de l'Enseignement. Available from frq.gouv.qc.ca.

Boisvert, Marilyne, Eve Lemaire, and Corina Borri-Anadon. 2020. "Nommer la diversité linguistique: Un premier pas vers sa prise en compte." *Cahiers de l'AQPF* 11 (1): 20–22.

Borri-Anadon, Corina, and Sivane Hirsch. 2019. "La Diversité ethnoculturelle, religieuse et linguistique à l'école: Un outil pour prendre en compte les spécificités régionales." *Éducation Canada* 59 (3). Available from https://www.edcan.ca/magazine/fall-2019/?lang=fr.

Borri-Anadon, Corina, Maryse Potvin, Tania Longpré, and Luciana Pereira Braga. 2018. *La Formation du personnel scolaire sur la diversité ethnoculturelle, religieuse et linguistique dans les universités québécoises: Portrait quantitatif et qualitatif de l'offre de cours de deuxième cycle en éducation.* Montréal: Observatoire sur la Formation à la Diversité et à l'Équité.

Bouchard, Gérard, and Charles Taylor. 2008. *Fonder l'avenir, le temps de la conciliation.* Québec: Commission de Consultation sur les Pratiques d'Accommodement reliées aux Différences culturelles.

CSE (Conseil supérieur de l'éducation). 2010. *Rapport sur l'état et les besoins de l'éducation 2008–2010.* Québec: Gouvernement du Québec.

De Koninck, Zita, and Françoise Armand. 2012. *Portrait des services d'accueil et d'intégration scolaire des élèves issus de l'immigration.* Québec: Direction des Services aux Communautés culturelles du Ministère de l'Éducation, du Loisir et du Sport.

Demazière, Didier. 2013. "Typologie et description: À propos de l'intelligibilité des expériences vécues." *Sociologie* 4 (3): 333–47. https://doi.org/10.3917/socio.043.0333.

Frozzini, Jorge. 2014. "L'Interculturalisme et la Commission Bouchard-Taylor." In *L'Interculturel au Québec: Rencontres historiques et enjeux politiques*, edited by Lomomba Emongo and Bob W. White, 45–62. Montréal: Presses de l'Université de Montréal.

Gouvernement du Québec. 2019. *Public Inquiry Commission on Relations Between Indigenous Peoples and Certain Public Services in Québec: Listening, Reconciliation and Progress.* Québec: Gouvernement du Québec.

Guimond, Éric. 2009. *L'Explosion démographique des populations autochtones du Canada de 1986 à 2011.* PhD diss., Université de Montréal. Papyrus. http://hdl.handle.net/1866/6827.

Hirsch, Sivane, and Marie Mc Andrew. 2016. "L'Enseignement de l'histoire des communautés juives au Québec: Le Traitement curriculaire et les besoins des enseignants." In *Judaïsme et éducation: Enjeux et défis pédagogiques*, edited by Sivane Hirsch, Marie Mc Andrew, Geneviève Audet, and Julia Ipgrave, 9–25. Québec: Presses de l'Université Laval.

Juteau, Danielle. 2018. "Au Cœur des dynamiques sociales: L'Ethnicité." In *L'Immigration et l'ethnicité dans le Québec contemporain*, edited by Deirdre Meintel, Annick Germain, Danielle Juteau, Victor Piché, and Jean Renaud, 13–40. Montréal: Presses de l'Université de Montréal.

Larochelle-Audet, Julie, Corina Borri-Anadon, Marie Mc Andrew, and Maryse Potvin. 2013. *La Formation initiale du personnel scolaire sur la diversité ethnoculturelle, religieuse et linguistique dans les universités québécoises:*

    Portrait quantitatif et qualitatif. Montréal: CEETUM/Chaire de Recherche du Canada sur l'Éducation et les Rapports Ethniques. Available from http://ofde.ca.

Mc Andrew, Marie. 2011. "Le Débat sur le voile à l'école à la lumière des diverses conceptions de l'ethnicité et des rapports ethniques." *Alterstice* 1 (1): 19–34. https://doi.org/10.7202/1077588ar.

Mc Andrew, Marie, and l'Équipe du Griés. 2015. *La Réussite éducative des élèves issus de l'immigration: Dix ans de recherche et d'intervention au Québec.* Montréal: Presses de l'Université de Montréal.

MEES (Ministère de l'Éducation et de l'Enseignement supérieur). 2017. *Portail informationnel, système Charlemagne: Direction de l'intégration linguistique et de l'éducation interculturelle (DILEI).* Québec: Gouvernement du Québec.

MEES (Ministère de l'Éducation et de l'Enseignement supérieur). 2019. *Soutien au milieu scolaire 2019–2020: Intégration et réussite des élèves issus de l'immigration et éducation interculturelle.* Québec: Gouvernement du Québec.

MELS (Ministère de l'Éducation, du Loisir et du Sport). 2013. *Indicateurs linguistiques dans le secteur de l'éducation.* Québec: Gouvernement du Québec. Available from http://www.education.gouv.qc.ca/.

MELS (Ministère de l'Éducation, du Loisir et du Sport). 2014. *Portrait des élèves.* Vol. 1, *Cadre de référence: Accueil et intégration des élèves issus de l'immigration au Québec.* Québec: Direction des Services aux Communautés culturelles.

MEQ (Ministère de l'Éducation du Québec). 1997. *L'École, tout un programme: Énoncé de politique educative.* Québec: Gouvernement du Québec.

MEQ (Ministère de l'Éducation du Québec). 1998. *A School for the Future: Policy Statement on Educational Integration and Intercultural Education.* Québec: Gouvernement du Québec.

MEQ (Ministère de l'Éducation du Québec). 2001. *Programme de formation de l'école québécoise.* Québec: Gouvernement du Québec.

Meunier, E.-Martin, and Sarah Wilkins-Laflamme. 2011. "Sécularisation, catholicisme et transformation du régime de religiosité au Québec: Étude comparative avec le catholicisme au Canada (1968–2007)." *Recherches sociographiques* 52 (3): 683–729.

MICC (Ministère des Communautés culturelles et de l'Immigration). 1990. *Let's Build Québec Together: A Policy Statement on Immigration and Integration.* Québec: Gouvernement du Québec.

MIDI (Ministère de l'Immigration, de la Diversité et de l'Inclusion). 2016. *Portraits régionaux 2005–2014: Caractéristiques des immigrants établis au Québec et dans les régions en 2016.* Québec: Gouvernement du Québec. Available from http://www.midi.gouv.qc.ca/.

MIDI (Ministère de l'Immigration, de la Diversité et de l'Inclusion). 2017. "Rimouski devient la 14e ville d'accueil des personnes réfugiées prises en charge par l'État," news release, January 11, 2017. http://www.mifi.gouv.qc.ca/fr/presse/communiques/com20170111.html?vi=1.

MIDI (Ministère de l'Immigration, de la Diversité et de l'Inclusion). 2018. *Portrait de l'immigration permanente au Québec selon les catégories l'immigration 2013–2017.* Québec: Gouvernement du Québec.

Papazian-Zohrabian, Garine, Caterina Mamprin, Vanessa Lemire, Alyssa Turpin-Samson, Ghayda Hassan, Cécile Rousseau, and Ray Aoun. 2018. "Le Milieu scolaire québécois face aux défis de l'accueil des élèves réfugiés: Quels enjeux pour la gouvernance scolaire et la formation des intervenants scolaires?" *Éducation et francophonie* 46 (2): 208–29. https://doi.org/10.7202/1055569ar.

Potvin, Maryse. 2008. "Racisme et discours public commun au Québec." In *De tricoté serré à métissé serré? La Culture publique commune en débats*, edited by Stephan Gervais, Dimitrios Karmis, and Diane Lamoureux, 227–48. Québec: Presses de l'Université Laval.

Potvin, Maryse. 2010. "Discours sociaux et médiatiques dans le débat sur les accommodements raisonnables." In "Le Québec," edited by Annick Germain, special issue, *Nos diverses cités* 7 (Spring): 83–89.

Potvin, Maryse. 2017. "Discours racistes et propagande haineuse: Trois groupes populistes identitaires au Québec." *Diversité urbaine* 17: 49–72. https://doi.org/10.7202/1047977ar.

Potvin, Maryse, Corina Borri-Anadon, Julie Larochelle-Audet, Françoise Armand, Monica Cividini, Zita De Koninck, David Lefrançois, et al. 2015. *Rapport du Groupe de Travail sur les Compétences interculturelles et inclusives dans les Orientations et Compétences professionnelles en Formation à l'Enseignement.* Montréal: Observatoire sur la Formation à la Diversité et à l'Équité. http://collections.banq.qc.ca/ark:/52327/bs2482627.

Presseau, Annie, Stéphane Martineau, and Christine Bergevin. 2006. *Contribution à la compréhension du cheminement et de l'expérience scolaires de jeunes autochtones à risque ou en difficulté en vue de soutenir leur réussite et leur persévérance scolaires: Rapport de recherche final soumis au Fonds québécois de recherche sur la société et la culture (FQRSC).* Trois-Rivières: Centre de Recherche interuniversitaire sur la Formation et la Profession enseignante.

Ragin, Charles C. 1987. *The Comparative Method: Moving Beyond Qualitative and Quantitative Strategies*. Berkeley: University of California Press.

Statistics Canada. 2016. *Dictionary, Census of Population, 2016* (catalogue no. 98-301-X). https://www12.statcan.gc.ca/census-recensement/2016/ref/dict/index-eng.cfm.

Statistics Canada. 2019. "Ethnic origin, population groups and religion." Accessed March 1, 2022. https://www12.statcan.gc.ca/census-recensement/2021/road2021-chemin2021/fs-fi/ethnic-origin-population-groups-and-religion.cfm.

Vatz-Laaroussi, Michele. 2011. "Les Collaborations familles immigrantes-école dans les régions du Québec." PowerPoint presentation at the international seminar Rethinking Equity in Quebec and India: Towards Inclusive Societies, Montreal, QC, November 2011. http://chereum.umontreal.ca/activites_pdf/Pr%C3%A9sentations%20Colloque%205-6%20nov%202009en%20PDF/Laaroussi.pdf.

11

UNDERSTANDING RURAL ATTITUDES TOWARD INCLUSIVITY

PARTISANSHIP, PATRIARCHY, AND PREJUDICE

Inclusivity among Evangelicals, Albertans, and Rural Canadians

Samuel Reimer

The role of religion is paradoxical. It makes and unmakes prejudice. While the creeds of the great religions are universalistic, all stressing brotherhood; the practices of these creeds are frequently divisive and brutal.
(Allport 1954, 444)

NEARLY ALL WORLD RELIGIONS promote love and acceptance of all people, yet they also seem to create division and intolerance. If anyone has a bad rap for intolerance in the West, it is the conservative Protestants or evangelical Christians.[1] These evangelicals are perceived to be narrow-minded, right-wing authoritarians who tend to inhabit the rural, "backwater" regions of North America, especially the southern United States. In fact, there are sizable numbers of religious conservatives across the rural Canadian prairies. Alberta has a disproportionately high numbers of American-style evangelicals, and at least one-third of their churches are in rural areas. In regions where there are high numbers of evangelicals, their conservatism seems to spread to nonevangelicals, increasing the general conservatism of the region (Olson and Li 2015; Marshall and Olson 2018). Are evangelicals undermining inclusivity and thus impeding neighbourliness and deep

equality in rural Canada (Banack and Pohler, introduction to this volume)?

Recent events and considerable research have furthered this perception. Upwards of 80% of American evangelicals voted for Donald Trump in 2016 and 2020, a president known for his xenophobia and anti-immigration policies. Canadian evangelicals are often thought to have a similar conservative political alignment. The fear that a Christian Right has emerged in Canada is ongoing (McDonald 2010; Gagné 2019). Conservative Christians are considered the backbone of the resistance to same-sex marriage and LGBTQ+ rights in both the United States and Canada (Hooghe et al. 2010; Schulte and Battle 2004; Hoffarth, Hodson, and Molnar 2018). Further, decades of research has confirmed that conservative Christians in the United States are less politically tolerant than most Americans (Nunn, Crockett, and Williams 1978; Eisenstein 2006, 2008; Schwadel and Garneau 2019). Patriarchal attitudes, like submission of wives to their husbands and domestic roles for women, are also common among conservative Christians, even though views of gender roles are changing toward egalitarianism (Gallagher 2003; Bartkowski 2001). Add to this the political and social conservatism in Alberta and rural Canada (Banack 2016), and my focus on the partisanship, patriarchy, and prejudice among rural and Albertan evangelicals is justified.

Not surprisingly, most of the research on conservative Protestants has been done in the United States, where their sheer numbers and political influence put them in the spotlight regularly. As a result, we do not know much about evangelicals in Canada in relation to inclusivity. In Canada, evangelicals form a much smaller proportion of the population—5% to 10%, compared to 20% to 30% in the United States—and are more irenic and subdued than their American co-religionists (Rawlyk 1996; Reimer 2003). In spite of some differences and a lack of Canadian-specific data, evangelicals in Canada are often painted with the same brush as American evangelicals, whether rightly or wrongly. What is presumed to be true of evangelicals in Canada is in fact often based on news about their southern neighbours.

In this chapter, I examine Canadian conservative Protestants' political alignment, tolerance of racial/ethnic minorities and LGBTQ+ rights,

and attitudes toward women. Special attention will be paid to evangelicals in Alberta where possible. Albertans have long been conservative, both socially and politically (Banack 2016; see also Banack, this volume), which may undermine inclusivity. I also attend to rural-urban differences among evangelical Canadians. Research has shown that community size, concentration, and contact with minorities all influence attitudes toward minority groups (see, e.g., Ray and Preston 2013), especially toward Indigenous populations in Canada (e.g., Denis 2015). Overall, I seek to answer this research question: Are evangelical Canadians (and/or Albertans and rural Canadians) a threat to inclusivity because of their partisanship, patriarchy, and prejudice?

DEFINITIONAL ISSUES

Evangelicals or conservative Protestants have been defined in a variety of ways, including self-identification (they identify as evangelicals); denominational affiliation (they identify with one of over one hundred conservative Protestant denominations, including most Baptist, Pentecostal, Mennonite, Wesleyan, Nazarene, Christian and Missionary Alliance, and Christian Reformed churches, among others); and belief (they hold conservative beliefs about the Bible, believe in salvation through Jesus Christ alone, and place an emphasis on evangelism and conversion experiences). Different measurement strategies give different results. Self-identified evangelicals show high tolerance and lower conservatism (see, e.g., Smith 1998; Woodberry and Smith 1998), whereas denominational and belief measures are often correlated with lower levels of tolerance and low socio-economic status (Hunter 1983, 1987).[2] The data for this chapter use either belief or denominational strategies.

Equally complex are definitional issues related to tolerance and prejudice. Prejudice can be defined as an inappropriate negative valuation of a category of people (Allport 1950). Allport (1954) found that religion seems to both "make and unmake" prejudice. This led him to distinguish between what he called intrinsic and extrinsic religious orientations, the former being a more mature, committed, "sincere" faith that reduced prejudice and the latter being an immature, consensual, externalized faith that increased prejudice (Allport and Ross 1967). This division has been criticized for its lack of empirical support

(see, e.g., Hunsberger 1995), which has resulted in more detailed explorations of the mechanisms within religion that may promote or inhibit prejudice. Altemeyer and Hunsberger (1992) found, on the one hand, that religious fundamentalism (characterized by closed-mindedness, certainty of religious beliefs, and belief in absolute truth) and right-wing authoritarianism (characterized by authoritarian submission, aggression, and conventionalism) increased prejudice (see also Hunsberger 1995; Wylie and Forest 1992). On the other hand, a quest religious orientation (characterized by an open, questioning, flexible religiosity) reduces prejudice (Batson and Ventis 1982).

The relationship between tolerance and religion is not straightforward either. Since John Stuart Mill, tolerance has been seen as necessary for the preservation of liberty in diverse societies. Much research on tolerance stems from the work of Samuel Stouffer (1955) that looks at an individual's willingness to grant civil liberties to unpopular groups. Stouffer's survey explored tolerance toward widely varied, preselected outgroup items such as "gays/lesbians," "communists," "anti-religionists and atheists," "racists," and "militarists." Stouffer's method of measuring tolerance using these outgroup items has been used over the years in the popular American General Social Survey. Based on these items, the religiously committed, particularly those who are conservative Protestants, have consistently been found to be more intolerant than their nonreligious peers (Nunn et al. 1978; Reimer and Park 2001; Burdette et al. 2005; Schwadel and Garneau 2019).

Stouffer's items have, however, been critiqued for their liberal bias and their inability to distinguish between permissiveness and tolerance (Smidt and Penning 1982; Woodberry and Smith 1998). Sullivan and colleagues (1982) argue that, by definition, tolerance requires that a person dislike the group they are tolerating; if they didn't, they wouldn't have to "put up with" or "tolerate" it (see also Marcus et al. 1995; Busch 1998). Since Stouffer does not measure dislike for the groups he studies, a person who is tolerant by Stouffer's measures may simply be apathetic or permissive. Scholars critical of Stouffer's measures insist that measures of tolerance should ask respondents to choose (from an extensive list) the group(s) that they like the least. Based on this "least-liked" strategy, Sullivan and colleagues found that Americans have not become more

tolerant over time as the Stouffer tolerance items have consistently shown. More important, those religious measures that are commonly associated with intolerance—fundamentalism, orthodoxy, biblical literalism, and so on—were not significant once demographic controls were added (Green et al. 1994). In fact, Beverly Busch (1998, ii) argues that religion is neither "related to political tolerance" nor to "the predispositions which do affect political tolerance," which are primarily "psychological traits and political attitudes." For Busch, the purported intolerance of conservative and committed Christians is simply an artifact of Stouffer's measures. Similarly, Eisenstein (2008) argues that religious belief and practice are, in fact, positively correlated with political tolerance.

TOLERANCE, INTOLERANCE, AND EVANGELICAL AFFILIATION

Focusing on Stouffer-like studies for a moment, there is considerable evidence of conservative Protestant intolerance and prejudice, especially toward groups like atheists, communists, and the LGBTQ+ community. Why? One explanation is the "in-group effect," which focuses on how members in one group communicate with one another and form social networks that promote certain beliefs and attitudes among members. Researchers of Protestant churches in the United States have found subtle cues among parishioners that promote politically conservative attitudes. Bean (2014), for example, found (pro-Republican) political cues among parishioners in American churches; there were, however, no partisan political cues in the Canadian churches she studied. Similarly, Djupe and Calfano (2013) found that certain values and perceived threats were communicated that increased intolerance. Rhodes (2012) further found that the tendency of evangelicals to have fairly insular and homophilous social networks increases both the degree to which in-group members perceive outgroups to be different, and the tensions between these groups.

Another explanation for conservative Protestant intolerance arises from the idea of exclusive beliefs. Exclusive beliefs, like assumptions that one's religious beliefs are uniquely right, undermine the legitimacy of other views and decrease tolerance for difference (Wilcox and Jelen 1990). Views of Christian nationalism or fundamentalist beliefs, like belief in a literal Bible, correlate positively with dogmatism and right-wing authoritarianism

(McDaniel, Nooruddin, and Shortle 2011). These psychological traits are, in turn, correlated with intolerance (Eisenstein 2006, 2008; Eisenstein, Clark, and Jelen 2017).

Again, research findings on evangelical tolerance and intolerance are based on the measures of tolerance used. If the "least-liked" strategy is used, then conservative Protestants are not more prejudiced or intolerant than other groups. In fact, even if Stouffer-like tolerance items are used, evidence of conservative Protestant intolerance is not conclusive.

For our purposes, three conclusions from research on evangelicals and tolerance or prejudice are important. First, it is not Christian orthodoxy—that is, it is not the actual *content* of conservative beliefs—that leads to increased prejudice. Instead, it seems to be right-wing authoritarianism—that is, the *way* the beliefs are held—that increases prejudice. For example, Christians who hold religious views in an all-or-nothing, dogmatic way will demonstrate prejudice while those who hold the same religious views but in more open, less dogmatic ways will not. Parsing out the effects of orthodoxy and authoritarianism is confusing because they are both positively correlated with prejudice. However, once authoritarianism is controlled for in regression analysis, the effect of orthodoxy actually reduces prejudice in some studies (Kirkpatrick 1993; Laythe, Finkel, and Kirkpatrick 2002; Jonathan 2008). This should not surprise since orthodox doctrine normally promotes love to all. Yet if the beliefs are held militantly, as captured by measures of fundamentalism and authoritarianism, they promote prejudice.

Second, it is not religious commitment per se that decreases tolerance. That is, attending church and praying are not, on their own, correlated with decreased tolerance. Contrary to early research (Stouffer 1955; Nunn et al. 1978; McClosky and Brill 1983), more recent, sophisticated models show that Christian commitment is, in fact, positively correlated with tolerance (although with important indirect effects; see Eisenstein 2006).[3] Even when analyzing American evangelicals specifically, orthodox belief, church attendance, and prayer had no effect on tolerance, while factors like perceived threat, commitment to democratic values, and having a secure personality are important predictors of tolerance and intolerance (Eisenstein 2006; see also Eisenstein 2008).

Third, even with Stouffer's traditional measure of tolerance in which outgroups are preselected, research shows conservative Christians are not intolerant of all groups. Even when authoritarianism is controlled for, intolerance toward the "gays/lesbians" outgroup is significantly higher among conservative Christians, but racism and ethnic prejudice is not (Laythe et al. 2002). It follows that religious groups may promote positive views of certain groups and negative views of others (Jackson and Hunsberger 1999).

These conclusions give us many reasons to hope that conservative Christianity and cultural and/or racial tolerance can co-exist, but it also points to areas of concern. Political conservatism, which is highly correlated with conservative Protestantism, at least in the United States, seems to breed intolerance. Prejudice against LGBTQ+ persons and women persist in conservative Protestant communities. Yet nearly all this research has been done in the United States. What do we know about Canadians generally, or Albertans and rural Canadians specifically?

ALBERTA EVANGELICALISM AND POLITICAL INFLUENCE
If there is a place in Canada that resembles the (political) conservatism of the United States, it is Alberta. In *God's Province: Evangelical Christianity, Political Thought, and Conservatism in Alberta*, Banack (2016) points to the influence of American fundamentalist premillennialism on the political views of eminent, conservative political leaders in Alberta—notably, Social Credit founder William "Bible Bill" Aberhart, along with Ernest Manning and his son Preston. This influence has broadened to create a political ethos in present-day Alberta that is anti-statist: it promotes small government as a way to maximize individual freedoms (see also Banack, this volume). As a result, politically conservative parties (in their various forms) held power in Alberta for 44 years before Rachel Notley's (left-leaning) New Democratic Party formed government in 2015. Banack (2016) notes that this short swing away from conservative government likely had more to do with a divided conservative wing (between the Progressive Conservatives and Wildrose) than a province-wide move to the political left—a prophetic analysis borne out by Jason Kenney's United Conservative Party victory in 2019.

The history of immigration from the United States to Alberta is well known, as is the influence of American evangelicals on their Albertan co-religionists. Stackhouse (1993), for example, notes that American influences helped create a "sectish" evangelicalism in Alberta and the Canadian Prairies that stands out against the more "churchish" evangelicalism of Ontario and British Columbia.

Alberta's history of American immigration continues to leave its mark, both politically and religiously. There are approximately 11,000 evangelical churches in Canada, and about 1,400 of those are in Alberta. Roughly one-third of these are located in rural areas of the province, suggesting a definite overrepresentation of rural citizens among evangelical churchgoers. Overall, there are approximately 225,000 weekly attendees of evangelical churches in Alberta.[4] This is not disproportionately high for Alberta's population. What is disproportionately high, however, is the percentage of these churches with strong ties to the United States. Table 3.1 looks at evangelical denominations in Alberta with over 10 churches. Such denominations are more concentrated in Alberta than in other provinces. Specifically, these denominations have 20% or more of their Canadian churches in Alberta, even though Alberta contains only about 11.5% of the Canadian population (Statistics Canada 2019). The third column of Table 3.1 shows the percentage of churches in each denomination that are in Alberta; the fourth column gives the estimated number of churches that this percentage represents. For example, the North American Baptists, a predominately American denomination, has nearly half (47.5%) of its Canadian churches in Alberta, or an estimated 48 of its roughly 100 churches. The North American Baptist, Nazarene, Church of God (Anderson, IN), Christian Reformed, and Church of God of Prophecy denominations have their headquarters in the United States, whereas the Canadian bodies of the Christian and Missionary Alliance, Baptist General Conference, and Evangelical Free became independent from the United States in the 1970s and 1980s. All these denominations are overrepresented in Alberta—evidence of a strong American flavour to the evangelicalism in the province.

The American evangelical influence in Alberta, quantified in Table 3.1, may add to the province's political and economic conservatism. At the national level, Hoover and colleagues (2002) found that a key difference

TABLE 3.1 The concentration of evangelical churches in Alberta

Denomination	Location of headquarters	% CA churches located in AB	Number of CA churches located in AB
North American Baptist	United States	47.5	48
Christian and Missionary Alliance	Canada, became independent in 1980	26.2	106
Evangelical Missionary Church of Canada	Canada	23.8	29
Baptist General Conference	Canada, became independent in 1979	24.1	20
Nazarene	United States	20.9	27
Church of God (Anderson, IN)	United States	34.2	13
Fellowship of Christian Assemblies in Canada	Canada and United States	41.3	31
Christian Reformed Church of North America	United States	20.0	48
Nondenominational	N/A	25.4	15
Evangelical Free	Canada, became independent in 1984	38.8	52
Church of God of Prophesy	United States	26.1	12
Church of God in Christ (Mennonite)	Canada and United States	30.4	14
Apostolic Church of Pentecost	Canada	20.6	22
Redeemed Christian Church of God	Nigeria	21.1	12

Source: Data collected by Rick Hiemstra, Evangelical Fellowship Canada.

between American and Canadian evangelicals is that the latter do not embrace the economic conservatism of their American co-religionists, even while they agree on social-moral issues like the rejection of same-sex marriage. This national difference is less evident in Alberta. Similarly, Lydia Bean's (2014) ethnographic research matching American and Canadian evangelical churches in Buffalo, New York, and Hamilton, Ontario, found similar moral views and programs, such as helping the poor, on both sides of the border. But she also found important national differences. One difference was that there was an implicit understanding among American evangelical churchgoers that liberals (whether political or social) were the cause of the moral decline in the United States and therefore support for the Republican party was assumed. For American evangelicals, the government is suspect; thus, they desire small government that minimally interferes in their lives. In Canada, Bean found no subtle cues toward a partisan vote, nor any indications that political liberalism was part of the problem. Instead, Canadian evangelicals saw the government as part of the solution to issues such as poverty and other

social woes. For Canadian evangelicals, moral decline was more about the failure of the churches themselves.

These national differences in political and economic conservatism are, however, less evident at the provincial level in Alberta. This can be illustrated, at least in part, by looking at how Albertan evangelicals cast votes compared to others in the country. Figure 3.1 shows the percentages of all Albertans, all residents in the rest of English Canada (excluding Alberta), Canadian evangelicals, and Albertan evangelicals who voted conservative in elections between 2004 and 2019. Note that the sample sizes for Albertan evangelicals are small in 2004, 2008, and 2015, and are prone to sampling error.

In 2015 and 2019, just over 50% of evangelicals in English Canada voted conservative. Between 60% and 70% of all Albertans voted conservative over these same years. With some fluctuation, the general pattern is that evangelical Albertans have similar levels of conservative support as nonevangelicals in the province. That is, there does not seem to be an evangelical in-group effect that increases their likelihood of voting conservative above that of other Albertans. This is true in election years in which the Liberals won a majority (2004 and 2015) or minority government (2019), and in years when Stephen Harper's Conservatives won a minority (2006 and 2008) or majority government (2011). However, if evangelicals do talk politics in the parking lot after church services, the in-group effect that this creates does seem to strengthen their partisanship in the rest of English Canada. In provinces other than Alberta, evangelical voting patterns also tend to parallel provincial voting patterns, although evangelicals are more likely to vote conservative (Hutchinson and Hiemstra 2009). Evangelicals outside of Alberta are about 20% more likely to vote conservative than the rest of English Canadians. This gap was quite stable over the six elections between 2004 and 2019.

Conservative support among Albertans (73.2%) and Albertan evangelicals (62.5%) in 2015 did not reach the levels of American evangelical Republican support in 2016 (80%) (though such a comparison ignores significant differences between Canadian and American conservative parties). As others have argued, the religious conservative–political conservative link is not as strong in Canada as it is in the United States (Malloy 2009; Reimer 2003). As well, one's reasons for voting

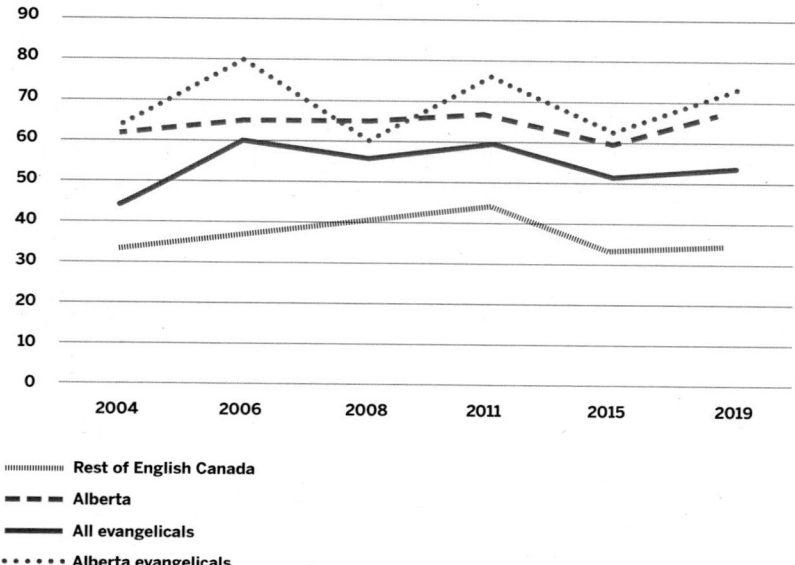

FIGURE 3.1 Conservative vote in Canadian federal elections, 2004 to 2019

⋯⋯⋯ **Rest of English Canada**
— — — **Alberta**
———— **All evangelicals**
• • • • • **Alberta evangelicals**

Sources: Data for Canada and Alberta from Elections Canada, open data for past elections, available from https://www.elections.ca. Data for evangelicals from survey data shared with author: 2004 Angus Reid Institute pre-election poll (n=2,000); 2006 Angus Reid Institute / CanWest online exit poll (n=36,000); 2008 Angus Reid Strategies pre-election poll (n=3,000); 2011 Angus Reid Strategies online poll (n=39,000); 2015 Angus Reid Forum online exit poll (n=2,004); 2019 Evangelical Fellowship Canada / Maru pre-election poll (n=5,014).

Note: This figure is based on preelection polling. Preelection polls indicate voting intentions, which can change by the time votes are cast. The sample sizes for Albertan evangelicals are small in 2004, 2008, and 2015, and are prone to sampling error. My thanks to Rick Hiemstra for help with data for this figure.

conservative do not, in and of themselves, threaten tolerance and inclusivity in Canada. Of course, one could argue that if Trump-style conservative politics came to Canada, inclusivity would be threatened.

On March 11, 2020, Maru/Matchbox ran an online panel survey in both the United States and Canada, including a series of questions related to politics, tolerance, and religiosity.[5] The survey for each country had a nationally representative sample size of roughly 1,500 respondents. The data from these surveys include area codes in Canada, which allowed me to create a rural-urban variable.[6] They also included a religious group variable, which allowed me to select out evangelicals.[7]

One question asked, "Regarding your political views, where would you place yourself?" Respondents could answer on a seven-point scale from "extremely liberal" to "extremely conservative."[8] All questions reported on in this chapter were identical in the Canadian and American surveys. The Maru/Matchbox survey data showed that evangelicals in Canada and the United States are more likely than nonevangelicals to consider themselves, politically speaking, either conservative or extremely conservative. The same is generally true of Albertans and of rural Canadians. Specifically, this survey data showed the following percentages of people who considered themselves either politically conservative or extremely conservative:

- Canadian evangelicals: 50.0%
- American evangelicals: 42.1%
- American nonevangelicals: 22.6%
- Residents of rural Canada: 37.0%
- Residents of urban Canada: 27.9%
- Residents of Alberta: 39.5%
- Residents of the rest of English Canada (excludes Québec and Alberta): 22.0%

These data on political alignment confirm the voting behaviour shown in Figure 3.1: evangelicals regardless of country and Albertans regardless of religious affiliation were more likely to identify as conservative.

ATTITUDES TOWARD RACIAL AND RELIGIOUS MINORITIES

Using the 2015 Canadian Elections Study (CES) data,[9] I created a rough denominational measure of evangelicalism, distinguishing evangelicals from mainline Protestants (e.g., Anglican, Lutheran, United Church, and Presbyterian), and from Catholics.[10] The CES does not allow for a strong measure of evangelicalism, and the sample was not large enough to extract out Alberta evangelicals specifically. These data also do not have a measure of rural/urban location. Nonetheless, the data do provide some good questions related to patriarchy and prejudice. I use these, alongside further Maru/Matchbox survey data, to compare evangelicals with mainline Protestants and Catholics on attitudes toward

other races and religions, and on issues related to traditional views of the family, including gender roles.

The first three rows of Table 3.2 show issue positions related to immigrants or racial minorities. The four bottom rows give results for "feeling thermometer" questions, where respondents are asked to rank their warmness toward certain groups from 0 to 100 degrees. Higher scores correspond to more positive rankings. In general, evangelicals do not distinguish themselves from other religious groups or from Albertans in general on questions related to racial groups. This is true even in their feelings toward Muslims. This supports previous research that shows that Canadian evangelicals are not less tolerant of immigrants and visible minorities than non-evangelical Canadians (Reimer 2011).

In Table 3.3, I use the 2020 Maru/Matchbox data to examine how accepting Canadians and Americans are of their child marrying someone from a certain religion, a recent immigrant, or an LGBTQ+ person. It is well known that evangelicals are protective of traditional marriage, so this question set provides a particularly rigorous test for inclusivity. The question set asks, "Would it be acceptable or unacceptable to you if one of your children were to marry a person who is..." with separate items for various religions. It also asks if they would accept their child marrying "a recent immigrant from an African country like Nigeria," "a recent immigrant from an Asian country like India," or "a gay, lesbian, bisexual or transgendered person." Respondents could choose one of three responses: acceptable, unacceptable, or not sure. Table 3.3 shows the percentage of respondents who answered "acceptable" to each item.

Unsurprisingly, the data show that evangelicals are more supportive of their children marrying a Christian (98.3% in Canada and 93% in the United States) and much less supportive of their children marrying followers of non-Christian religions. For Canadian evangelicals, acceptance ranged between a low of 10.9% for Muslims and a high of 35.8% for Jews. Unexpectedly, evangelicals in the United States showed higher support for outgroup marriages than Canadian evangelicals. I am not sure why this is, but a reasonable explanation may be that evangelicals are more culturally distinctive in Canada, and thus their religious identity is more salient to them than it is for many evangelicals in the United States. One can imagine, for instance, that being a Baptist or Pentecostal

TABLE 3.2 Attitudes toward race and religion among all Canadians, all Albertans, and Canadians of different religious affiliations in 2015

	Evangelicals	Mainline Protestants	Catholics	AB residents	CA residents
Agree or strongly agree that Canada should admit fewer immigrants	21.8%	19.2%	19.3%	26.1%	18.3%
Somewhat less or much less should be done for racial minorities	12.6%	12.2%	8.7%	17.7%	9.5%
Agree or strongly agree that immigrants take jobs from other Canadians	34.2%	33.9%	28.9%	28.0%	27.8%
Degree of warmth towards racial minorities (0–100)	79.7	80.2	77.9	75.1	80.4
Degree of warmth towards immigrants (0–100)	77.0	77.9	75.7	73.6	78.1
Degree of warmth towards Muslims living in Canada (0–100)	69.2	72.3	68.5	66.6	72.2
Degree of warmth towards Indigenous* people (0–100)	79.0	79.6	77.8	73.1	79.5

Source: Fournier, Patrick, Fred Cutler, Stuart Soroka, and Dietlind Stolle, *The 2015 Canadian Election Study* (dataset), 2015, http://ces-eec.arts.ubc.ca/english-section/surveys/.

* *The 2015 Canadian Election Study* used the term *aboriginal*.

in the southeastern United States is not very distinctive—that is, it does not set you apart from the general population. I say more on this in the next section.

Looking to other respondents and survey items in Canada, we find that Albertans and rural Canadians are somewhat less accepting of their child marrying followers of non-Christian religions than urban Canadians and respondents across the rest of English Canada. Regarding marrying an African or Asian immigrant, Canadian evangelicals, rural Canadians, and Albertans are approximately on par with other Canadian respondents. Regarding LGBTQ+ marriages, however, Canadian evangelicals are much less accepting than any other Canadian group.

The data support the contention that, compared to other populations in Canada, evangelicals are less accepting of interfaith marriages and marriages to LGBTQ+ groups. This lack of acceptance does not, however, include racial minorities. But the picture is more complex than

TABLE 3.3 Respondents who would accept a child marrying someone from religious, immigrant, and LGBTQ+ outgroups, 2020 (%)

	CA evangelicals	US evangelicals	US non-evangelicals	CA rural residents	CA urban residents	AB residents	English CA (excluding QC, AB)
Christian	98.3	93.0	85.7	82.0	80.9	81.9	84.5
Muslim	10.9	31.8	43.2	37.4	44.8	40.0	48.8
Hindu	20.0	33.9	51.9	53.9	56.3	54.7	59.6
Sikh	19.6	28.2	41.6	40.4	49.6	48.6	52.6
Buddhist	21.4	39.2	56.6	59.9	65.6	63.8	67.1
Jewish	35.8	47.9	62.0	62.0	64.3	65.9	68.3
African immigrant	60.7	53.2	51.9	57.5	56.3	59.6	58.5
Asian im-migrant	63.2	51.0	58.4	62.8	61.7	63.1	63.7
LGBTQ+	21.2	35.7	57.6	63.1	66.1	60.6	66.8
Average acceptance overall	**39.0**	**46.0**	**56.5**	**57.7**	**60.6**	**59.8**	**63.3**

Source: Maru/Matchbox Omni online panel survey, March 11–12, 2020.

it first seems. Using regression analysis (not shown), I found that political alignment is a more powerful predictor of all the items in Table 3.3 than is evangelical affiliation. In fact, in the case of Sikhs and Jews, the evangelical effect was insignificant once I controlled for political alignment. Where the evangelical effect does remain strong, however, is on the Christian and LGBTQ+ questions. This indicates that political views do not account for the higher acceptance of Christian marriages and the lower acceptance of marriages with LGBTQ+ persons among evangelicals. Finally, the regression analysis showed that rural, urban, and Alberta residency were not significant predictors of any items.

Table 3.4 again looks at Maru/Matchbox data, this time on whether respondents strongly agree, agree, disagree, or strongly disagree on two items: (1) that Canada or the United States (depending on the respondent's country of residence) "should admit fewer immigrants" and (2) that their country "would be better off if fewer women worked outside the home." Albertans and rural Canadians are more likely than the rest of English Canada to agree that fewer immigrants should be admitted to Canada, while Canadian evangelicals are slightly less likely to agree with the statement. Regression analysis confirms that the rural-urban distinction

TABLE 3.4 Respondents who agree their country should admit fewer immigrants and there should be fewer women working outside the home, 2020 (%)

	CA evangelicals	US evangelicals	US non-evangelicals	CA rural residents	CA urban residents	AB residents	English CA (excluding QC, AB)
Fewer immigrants	48.6	66.2	54.2	61.7	50.3	55.0	51.7
Fewer women work outside home	31.9	34.5	24.9	22.3	17.2	20.1	17.5

Source: Maru/Matchbox Omni online panel survey, March 11–12, 2020.

is a robust predictor of anti-immigration views in Canada, while evangelical affiliation is not. American evangelicals, however, are more likely to be anti-immigration than nonevangelicals. Regarding women working outside the home, evangelicals in Canada and the United States both show their traditional view of the family, preferring traditional gender roles. Other differences on this item are negligible.

Table 3.5 shows similar findings about traditional family values in 2015 Canadian Election Study survey data. Evangelicals differ somewhat from the majority of Canadians in attitudes toward women working outside the home in that they are slightly more likely to support traditional family values. This is consistent with other research (Wilkins-Laflamme and Reimer 2019). Evangelicals also feel less warm toward gays/lesbians and feminists than most Canadians, but these differences are not large. The area of major difference is views of same-sex marriage, where three times as many evangelicals oppose same-sex marriage as other Canadians. However, like Canadians in general, very few evangelicals think that less should be done for women. Albertans are somewhat more conservative than most Canadians on all of these issues. Regression analysis (not shown) supports these conclusions: evangelical affiliation is not a significant predictor of attitudes toward Muslims, immigrants, or racial minorities, but is a significant predictor of attitudes toward feminists, gays/lesbians, and same-sex marriage.

TABLE 3.5 Attitudes related to the traditional family among all Canadians, all Albertans, and Canadians of different religious affiliations, 2015

	Evangelicals	Mainline Protestants	Catholics	AB residents	CA residents
Agree or strongly agree that there would be fewer problems if more emphasis were placed on traditional family values	71.1%	58.7%	61.1%	66.6%	54.3%
Oppose same-sex marriage	60.4%	22.8%	18.5%	29.0%	20.5%
Agree or strongly agree society would be better if fewer women worked outside the home	34.1%	20.3%	19.3%	31.8%	19.9%
Somewhat less or much less should be done for women	2.1%	1.7%	1.6%	3.2%	1.8%
Degree of warmth toward gays/lesbians (0–100)	66.3	79.9	79.3	74.6	79.6
Degree of warmth toward feminists (0–100)	65.7	76.8	74.2	69.4	75.9

Source: Fournier, Patrick, Fred Cutler, Stuart Soroka, and Dietlind Stolle, The 2015 Canadian Election Study (dataset), 2015, http://ces-eec.arts.ubc.ca/english-section/surveys/.

ARE EVANGELICALS INTOLERANT OR PREJUDICED?

This chapter has analyzed the partisanship, patriarchy, and prejudice among groups often perceived to be less inclusive: evangelicals, Albertans, and rural Canadians. While the measures of tolerance and prejudice used in this chapter are important indicators of inclusivity in Canada, "putting up with" or avoiding "negative valuations" falls short of the deep equality envisioned for true inclusivity (Beaman 2017; see also Banack and Pohler, introduction to this volume). Yet, tolerance and nonprejudicial attitudes are foundational to creating a more inclusive Canada.

Overall, we can conclude from the data that evangelicals are less accepting than other Canadians of interfaith marriages (for their children) and are particularly unaccepting of same-sex marriage. They are somewhat more politically conservative, and somewhat more conservative in their views of women working outside the home. These differences relate to their emphasis on traditional family values. Evangelicals are not distinct from other Canadians in their acceptance of religious

and racial diversity, or of immigration. Albertans are more politically conservative than other English Canadians, but this does not translate into major differences in patriarchal or prejudiced views.[11] Based on the data presented, Alberta and rural residence are not important predictors of any items except desiring fewer immigrants.

The Importance of Political Conservatism

The importance of political conservatism seems to be a recurring theme. As indicated above, political alignment is the most powerful predictor in regression equations of all items in Tables 3.3 and 3.4; it is more powerful than evangelical affiliation, age, gender, education, rural/urban location, and church attendance. Of course, conservative political alignment in itself does not necessarily lead to patriarchy or prejudice, so this finding probably points toward some other trait that is strongly correlated with political conservatism. Based on the theory and literature presented in this chapter, it may be that political conservatism—which is correlated with evangelicalism, Alberta residence, and (sometimes) rural location—is picking up a kind of conservatism that perceives diversity of various kinds as a threat, at least for some respondents. This type of conservatism may include concern about immigrants taking their jobs (Ray and Preston 2013), or about those of other religions or sexual orientations undermining the traditional family and their conservative values. Plenty of research points to perceived threat as a significant cause of intolerance (e.g., Djupe and Calfano 2013; Eisenstein 2006, 2008). Perceived threat is likely one explanation for these findings, but certainly not the only one.

While it is true that American evangelicals disproportionately supported Donald Trump during his presidency, and have continued to support him afterward, the data in this chapter show that it is not necessarily true that American evangelicals are as right wing and xenophobic as some might expect. In fact, they were more accepting of interfaith marriages and less politically conservative than Canadian evangelicals. This surprising finding may be related to a different religious ethos in each country. Canadian evangelicals represent a small and declining percentage of Canadians in our samples (about 6%), as many who were raised as evangelicals disaffiliate, becoming religious "nones" (Hiemstra 2020). Comparatively, the percentage of evangelicals in the American

sample is 21.5%, and the decline in affiliation is less. As a result, those evangelicals in Canada who have not disaffiliated (the "remnant") are more distinctive in their views than evangelicals in the American sample.[12] It seems reasonable to theorize that those who maintain their affiliation to evangelical denominations in Canada do so because they are committed to that identity in a national context where evangelical identity is not supported. In general, there are still more cultural supports for evangelical affiliation in the United States than in Canada (Reimer 2003).

The Future of Evangelical Inclusivity

Do evangelicals undermine inclusivity in rural Canada? The results presented here are mixed. In areas related to the traditional family, they seem to. In areas of ethnic or religious diversity, they do not. With regard to partisanship, patriarchy, and prejudice, should we be hopeful or doubtful about the possibility of greater inclusivity among evangelicals in Canada, especially in Alberta and rural Canada?

Let's start with reasons to doubt. First, we know that evangelicals tend to be conservative on issues like divorce, same-sex marriage, and abortion. They also tend to be politically conservative. We also know that conservative networks spread conservatism (Olson and Li 2015; Marshall and Olson 2018). It may be that Albertan evangelicals, who are heavily influenced by American conservative Protestantism, will continue to influence the political and social culture of Albertans in general. The 49th parallel is not impervious to such cultural influences, which more often travel from the south up than the north down (Kauffman 2009).

Second, while attitudes toward women's roles are becoming more egalitarian among both Canadians in general and evangelicals in particular, a minority of evangelical denominations hold complementarian views and reject women's ordination. Although a growing number of evangelical denominations are changing their positions, allowing women full access to all roles in the church, women are still marginalized, holding few lead pastor positions and are mostly relegated to small, struggling churches (Reimer and Wilkinson 2015).

Third, evangelicalism's disproportionate rejection of same-sex marriage is unlikely to change any time soon. Even though support for

same-sex marriage is growing among younger conservative Protestants (Bean and Martinez 2014), the support gap with the rest of Canada will not close in the near future.

There are, however, also many reasons to hope for increased inclusivity. First, Canada is not the United States, even though Alberta's conservatism resembles American conservatism. Further, Canadian evangelicals are not American evangelicals, even if their similarities outweigh their differences (Bean 2014; Reimer 2003). National differences are substantial, including less political and economic conservatism (Malloy 2009; Bean 2014; Bean, Gonzalez, and Kaufman 2008; Hoover et al. 2002) and a more irenic, accommodating spirit (Rawlyk 1996; Noll 1997a, 1997b, 2006) in Canada than the United States.

Second, there is a clear difference between positions on issues and attitudes toward persons. That is, while many conservative Protestants hold fast to a conservative position on same-sex marriage, their general attitudes toward LGBTQ+ persons are not as distinctive (as Table 3.5 shows). Few reported being uncomfortable meeting gay or lesbian persons, even if they are against sexual relations outside heterosexual marriage (Reimer 2011). As noted, attitudes are changing quickly, particularly among younger evangelicals in both countries, who are egalitarians on gender roles and sexual identity and are increasingly supportive of same-sex marriage (Bean and Martinez 2014; Smith and Johnson 2010).

Third, regarding women and feminists, there is increasing inclusivity. For all the talk about "women's submission" and "male headship," we have known since at least the 1990s that decision-making is usually egalitarian among evangelical couples, even among those who embrace male headship rhetoric (Gallagher 2003; Bartkowski 2001). As noted above, however, not all evangelical churches and denominations practice egalitarianism.

Fourth, fundamentalism—the intolerant, exclusive orientation toward one's beliefs—is rare in Canada (at least in comparison to the United States). In a study of Canadian evangelical churches, pastors in only 14 of 139 churches (10%) thought the term *fundamentalist* described their church very well, while the majority (65%) said it did not describe

their church well at all (Reimer and Wilkinson 2015). This aligns with historical findings that fundamentalism marked southern evangelicalism more than its Canadian counterpart (Noll 1992).

Finally, good research reminds us that appearances (or what we hear in the news) are not always reality. Rural dwellers and Albertans are not more patriarchal or prejudiced than most Canadians on many of the questions discussed above, even if they are more politically conservative. Regarding evangelicalism, once the precise mechanisms that explain the link between conservative religiosity and intolerance are exposed, concerns about evangelicals and exclusivity are mediated, although not fully negated. As political scientist Marie Eisenstein (2006, 343) states, "the results here for the direct influence of religious commitment and doctrinal orthodoxy on political tolerance suggests [sic] that religion is not inherently incompatible with liberal democratic values. In rethinking the link between religious commitment and doctrinal orthodoxy and political tolerance, the evidence here suggests that there is no direct link between them."

Whatever the legacy of evangelicals in Canada, there is reason to hope for—even expect—increasing inclusivity. The broader cultural milieu in Canada is moving in that direction, and evangelicals are not immune to cultural currents, even though they resist some trends. Further, accommodating influences need not be external to conservative churches. Maureen Miner Bridges (2018) suggests that evangelical church leaders can combat prejudice by minimizing ideological authoritarianism and promoting secure relational attachment. The former can be minimized by encouraging a more narrative, open reading of the Bible as opposed to a closed, propositional reading. The latter is strengthened by secure attachments to God or co-religionists. This promotes a more open and questing spirituality, which in turn is negatively correlated to prejudice. As Bridges states, "Christian churches can form less prejudiced hearts and minds by emphasizing theologies that nuance truth claims and by supporting secure attachment bonds that provide alternative sources of internal coherence and significance" (372).

NOTES

1. I use the terms *evangelical* and *conservative Protestant* interchangeably in this chapter. Both categories include fundamentalists, who are a smaller subgroup of the most conservative evangelicals, and are rarer in Canada than in the United States.
2. For example, if adherence to conservative beliefs is used to define evangelicals, and one of the measures used is belief that the Bible should be interpreted "literally" (as opposed to belief that the Bible is "inspired" or "authoritative"), then evangelicals will appear intolerant (Eisenstein 2006, 2008; Wilcox and Jelen 1990). As Ammerman (1982) and others have noted, many evangelicals do not believe in a literal Bible (which is a more fitting definitional strategy for fundamentalists). Biblical literalism is highly correlated with (low) education in the United States. For an overview on definitional strategies and their effects, see Hackett and Lindsay (2008) and Woodberry and Smith (1998) in the United States. In Canada, see Stackhouse (2007).
3. Eisenstein (2006, 338) found that "while there is no direct negative effect that either religious commitment or doctrinal orthodoxy has on political tolerance, the results do show that for both of these variables, there is an indirect negative effect on political tolerance, which is due to the influence of doctrinal orthodoxy on threat perception, the influence of doctrinal orthodoxy on religious commitment, and the influence of religious commitment on a secure personality."
4. My thanks to Rick Hiemstra at the Evangelical Fellowship of Canada for these data. Rick maintains a large, private database of Christian churches, particularly evangelical churches. At time of writing, this is the best data available in Canada. See Reimer and Wilkinson (2015) for more on this database.
5. Special thanks to Andrew Grenville, Chief Research Officer for Maru/Matchbox, for adding these questions to their Canadian and American surveys. In an email exchange with me, Grenville described the Canadian Maru/Matchbox data as follows: "From March 11th to March 12th, 2020 an online survey of 1,512 randomly selected Canadian adults who are Maru Voice Canada (https://www.maruvoice.ca/) panelists was executed by Maru/Blue (https://www.marublue.com/). For comparison purposes, a probability sample of this size has an estimated margin of error (which measures sampling variability) of ±2.5%, 19 times out of 20. The results have been weighted by education, age, gender and region (and in Quebec, language) to match the population, according to Census data." Grenville

described the American data as follows: "From March 11th to March 12th, 2020, an online survey of 1,509 randomly selected American adults who are Maru Springboard America Community (https://www.springboardamerica.com) panel members was executed by Maru/Blue. For comparison purposes, a probability sample of this size has an estimated margin of error (which measures sampling variability) of ±2.5%, 19 times out of 20. The results have been weighted by education, age, gender and region to match the population, according to Census data."

6. For the purposes of this chapter, the rural-urban distinction was based on the second character of the area code. If it was a zero, it was considered a rural area. Area codes with any other second character were considered urban. In New Brunswick, some zero area codes have been urbanized; these were coded rural or urban based on population size, with a population of 10,000 or more being considered urban. My thanks to Rick Hiemstra for his help creating this variable.

7. To measure religious affiliation, respondents selected from the following categories: Catholic, mainline Protestant, other Protestant, Orthodox Christian, and other Christian, as well as several non-Christian religious categories. The other Protestant (i.e., Baptist, Pentecostal, Alliance, Salvation Army) category captured most of the evangelicals, but some were coded evangelical based on written-in responses which included non-denominational, Christian, born-again Christian, and so on. In the United States, specific denominational affiliations were listed and coded into Catholic, Orthodox, mainline Protestant, and evangelical, accordingly. For greater comparability across countries, I excluded those from the evangelical category who claimed affiliation with an evangelical denomination but never attended church. I did this because maintaining affiliation without participation is more common in the United States than Canada, as nonattending Canadians are more likely say they have no affiliation. Recall that denominational measures tend to show higher intolerance as compared to those who self-identify as evangelical.

8. Respondents could choose among the following descriptors: extremely liberal, liberal, slightly liberal, moderate, slightly conservative, conservative, and extremely conservative. Those who responded "don't know" were removed from the analysis.

9. The CES polls are run each time there is a federal election in Canada. In more recent years, these surveys have taken a three-wave format: a series of questions asked by means of telephone interviews (1) during the election campaign period and (2) just after election day, then (3) through

a self-completion mail-back questionnaire (turned online questionnaire in 2011). The cross-sectional probability sample in the 2015 CES includes 9,982 respondents (web and phone combined file).

10. Categorizing religious traditions is always difficult, especially with imprecise denominational codes like those used in the CES. I coded those who identified as Baptist, Pentecostal/Fundamentalist/Born Again/Evangelical, Christian Reformed, Mennonite, or Salvation Army, as well as those in the generic Christian category, as evangelicals (N=395, or 9.5% of the sample). I coded Anglicans, Lutherans, Presbyterians, United Church, and those in the generic Protestant category as mainline Protestants (N=928, 22.1%). There are 1,408 Catholics (33.5%) in the sample. I did some analysis of the generic Protestant and Christian categories. Although differences were not extreme, the Christian category is more conservative than the Protestant category on issues like same-sex marriage, literal Bible interpretation, traditional family values, and other issues.

11. The same data sources used in this chapter in fact show that Québec was more distinctive than Alberta in terms of prejudiced views, with Québecois being less open to ethnic and religious diversity than Albertans.

12. The argument for a more distinctive evangelicalism in Canada is not due to higher church attendance rates in the Canadian evangelical sample. In fact, about 54% of American evangelicals claim to attend church weekly or more, while the same is true for 51% of Canadian evangelicals. Still, research has shown that American evangelicals tend to overreport their church attendance more than Canadians (Reimer, 2003). As stated in note 7, I removed those who never attend from the evangelical category in both countries.

REFERENCES

Allport, Gordon W. 1950. *The Individual and His Religion*. New York: Macmillan.

Allport, Gordon W. 1954. *The Nature of Prejudice*. Reading, MA: Addison-Wesley.

Allport, Gordon W., and J. Michael Ross. 1967. "Personal Religious Orientation and Prejudice." *Journal of Personality and Social Psychology* 5 (4): 432–43.

Altemeyer, Bob, and Bruce Hunsberger. 1992. "Authoritarianism, Religious Fundamentalism, Quest, and Prejudice." *International Journal of the Psychology of Religion* 2 (2): 113–33.

Ammerman, Nancy. 1982. "Operationalizing Evangelicalism: An Amendment." *Sociological Analysis* 43 (2): 170–71.

Banack, Clark. 2016. *God's Province: Evangelical Christianity, Political Thought, and Conservatism in Alberta*. Montréal: McGill-Queen's University Press.

Bartkowski, John P. 2001. *Remaking the Godly Marriage: Gender Negotiation in Evangelical Families*. New Brunswick, NJ: Rutgers University Press.

Batson, Charles D., and W. Larry Ventis. 1982. *The Religious Experience: A Social-Psychological Perspective*. New York: Oxford University Press.

Beaman, Lori. 2017. *Deep Equality in an Era of Religious Diversity*. Oxford: Oxford University Press.

Bean, Lydia. 2014. *The Politics of Evangelical Identity: Local Churches and Partisan Divides in the United States and Canada*. Princeton and Oxford: Princeton University Press.

Bean, Lydia, Marco J. Gonzalez, and Jason Kaufman. 2008. "Why Doesn't Canada Have an American-Style Christian Right? A Comparative Framework for Analyzing the Political Effects of Evangelical Subcultural Identity." *Canadian Journal of Sociology* 33 (4): 899–943.

Bean, Lydia, and Brandon C. Martinez. 2014. "Evangelical Ambivalence toward Gays and Lesbians." *Sociology of Religion* 75 (3): 395–417.

Bridges, Maureen Miner. 2018. "Psychological Contributions to Understanding Prejudice and the Evangelical Mind." *Christian Scholar's Review* 47 (4): 363–72.

Burdette, Amy M., Christopher G. Ellison, and Terrence D. Hill. 2005. "Conservative Protestantism and Tolerance toward Homosexuals: An Examination of Potential Mechanisms." *Sociological Inquiry* 75 (2): 177–96.

Busch, Beverly G. 1998. "Faith, Truth, and Tolerance: Religion and Political Tolerance in the United States." PhD diss., University of Nebraska.

Denis, Jeffrey S. 2015. "Contact Theory in a Small-Town Settler-Colonial Context: The Reproduction of Laissez-Fair Racism in Indigenous-White Canadian Relations." *American Journal of Sociology* 80 (1): 218–42.

Djupe, Paul A., and Brian R. Calfano. 2013. "Religious Value Priming, Threat, and Political Tolerance." *Political Research Quarterly* 66 (4): 768–80.

Eisenstein, Marie A. 2006. "Rethinking the Relationship between Religion and Political Tolerance in the US" *Political Behavior* 28 (4): 327–48.

Eisenstein, Marie A. 2008. *Religion and the Politics of Tolerance: How Christianity Builds Democracy*. Waco, TX: Baylor University Press.

Eisenstein, Marie A., April K. Clark, and Ted G. Jelen. 2017. "Political Tolerance and Religion: An Age-Period-Cohort Analysis, 1984–2014." *Review of Religious Research* 59 (3): 395–418.

Gagné, André. 2019. "The Christian Right's Efforts to Transform Society." *The Conversation*, July 24, 2019. https://theconversation.com/the-christian-rights-efforts-to-transform-society-120878.

Gallagher, Sally K. 2003. *Evangelical Identity and Gendered Family Life*. New Brunswick, NJ: Rutgers University Press.

Green, John C., James L. Guth, Lymon A. Kellstedt, and Corwin E. Smidt. 1994. "Uncivil Challenges? Support for Civil Liberties among Religious Activists." *Journal of Political Science* 22 (1): 25–49.

Hackett, Conrad, and D. Michael Lindsay. 2008. "Measuring Evangelicalism: Consequences of Different Operationalization Strategies." *Journal for the Scientific Study of Religion* 47 (3): 499–514.

Hiemstra, Rick. 2020. "Not Christian Anymore." *Faith Today*, January/February 2020.

Hoffarth, Mark R., Gordon Hodson, and Danielle S. Molnar. 2018. "When and Why Is Religious Attendance Associated with Antigay Bias and Gay Rights Opposition? A Justification-Suppression Model Approach." *Journal of Personality and Social Psychology* 115 (3): 526–63.

Hooghe, Marc, Ellen Clases, Allison Harrell, Ellen Quintelier, and Yves Dejaeghere. 2010. "Anti-Gay Sentiment Among Adolescents in Belgium and Canada: A Comparative Investigation into the Role of Gender and Religion." *Journal of Homosexuality* 57 (3): 384–400.

Hoover, Dennis R., Michael D. Martinez, Samuel H. Reimer, and Kenneth D. Wald. 2002. "Evangelicalism Meets the Continental Divide: Moral and Economic Conservatism in the United States and Canada." *Political Research Quarterly* 55 (2): 351–74.

Hunsberger, Bruce. 1995. "Religion and Prejudice: The Role of Religious Fundamentalism, Quest and Right Wing Authoritarianism." *Journal of Social Issues* 51 (2): 113–29.

Hunter, James D. 1983. *American Evangelicalism: Conservative Religion and the Quandary of Modernity*. New Brunswick, NJ: Rutgers University Press.

Hunter, James, D. 1987. *Evangelicalism: The Coming Generation*. Chicago: University of Chicago Press.

Hutchinson, Don, and Rick Hiemstra. 2009. "Canadian Evangelical Voting Trends by Region, 1996–2008." *Church and Faith Trends* 2 (2): 1–10.

Jackson, Lynne M., and Bruce Hunsberger. 1999. "An Intergroup Perspective on Religion and Prejudice." *Journal for the Scientific Study of Religion* 38 (4): 509–23.

Jonathan, Eunike. 2008. "The Influence of Religious Fundamentalism, Right-Wing Authoritarianism, and Christian Orthodoxy and Explicit and Implicit Attitudes toward Homosexuals." *The International Journal for the Psychology of Religion* 18 (4): 316–29.

Kaufman, Jason A. 2009. *The Origins of Canadian and American Political Differences.* Cambridge, MA: Harvard University Press.

Kirkpatrick, Lee A. 1993. "Fundamentalism, Christian Orthodoxy and Intrinsic Religious Orientation as Predictors of Discriminatory Attitudes." *Journal for the Scientific Study of Religion* 32 (3): 256–68.

Laythe, Brian, Deborah Finkel, and Lee A. Kirkpatrick. 2002. "Predicting Prejudice from Religious Fundamentalism and Right-Wing Authoritarianism: A Multiple-Regression Approach." *Journal for the Scientific Study of Religion* 41 (4): 623–35.

Malloy, Jonathan. 2009. "Bush/Harper? Canadian and American Evangelical Politics Compared." *American Review of Canadian Studies* 39 (4): 352–63.

Marcus, George E., John L. Sullivan, Elizabeth Theiss-Morse, and Sandra L. Wood. 1995. *With Malice Toward Some: How People Make Civil Liberties Judgments.* Cambridge: Cambridge University Press.

Marshall, Joey, and Daniel V. A. Olson. 2018. "Local Religious Subcultures and Generalized Social Trust in the United States." *Journal for the Scientific Study of Religion* 57 (1): 473–94.

McClosky, Herbert, and Alida Brill. 1983. *Dimensions of Tolerance.* New York: Russell Sage.

McDaniel, Eric Leon, Irfan Nooruddin, and Allyson Faith Shortle. 2011. "Divine Boundaries: How Religion Shapes Citizens' Attitudes toward Immigrants." *American Politics Research* 39 (1): 205–33.

McDonald, Marci. 2010. *The Armageddon Factor: The Rise of Christian Nationalism in Canada.* Toronto: Random House.

Noll, Mark. 1992. *A History of Christianity in the United States and Canada.* Grand Rapids, MI: Eerdmans.

Noll, Mark. 1997a. "Canadian Evangelicalism: A View from the United States." In *Aspects of the Canadian Evangelical Experience*, edited by George A. Rawlyk. Montréal: McGill-Queen's University Press, 3–20.

Noll, Mark. 1997b. *Turning Points: Decisive Moments in the History of Christianity.* Grand Rapids, MI: Baker.

Noll, Mark. 2006. "What Happened to Christian Canada?" *Church History* 75 (2): 245–73.

Nunn, Clyde Z., Harry J. Crockett, Jr., and J. Allan Williams, Jr. 1978. *Tolerance for Nonconformity.* San Francisco: Jossey-Bass.

Olson, Daniel V.A., and Miao Li. 2015. "Does a Nation's Religious Composition Affect Generalized Trust? The Role of Religious Heterogeneity and The Percent Religious." *Journal for the Scientific Study of Religion* 54 (4): 756–73.

Rawlyk, George A. 1996. *Is Jesus Your Personal Saviour? In Search of Canadian Evangelicalism in the 1990s.* Montréal: McGill-Queen's University Press.

Ray, Brian, and Valerie Preston. 2013. "Experiences of Discrimination and Discomfort: A Comparison of Metropolitan and Non-metropolitan Location." *The Canadian Geographer* 57 (2): 233–54.

Reimer, Samuel. 2003. *Evangelicals and the Continental Divide.* Montréal: McGill-Queen's University Press.

Reimer, Samuel. 2011. "'Civility without Compromise': Evangelical Attitudes toward Same-Sex Issues in Comparative Context." In *Faith, Politics, and Sexual Diversity in Canada and the United States,* edited by David Rayside and Clyde Wilcox, 71–86. Vancouver: UBC Press.

Reimer, Samuel, and Jerry Park. 2001. "Tolerant (In)Civility? A Longitudinal Analysis of White Conservative Protestants' Willingness to Grant Civil Liberties." *Journal for the Scientific Study of Religion* 40: 735–45.

Reimer, Samuel, and Michael Wilkinson. 2015. *A Culture of Faith: Evangelical Congregations in Canada.* Montréal: McGill-Queen's University Press.

Rhodes, Jeremy. 2012. "The Ties that Divide: Bonding Social Capital, Religious Friendship Networks, and Political Tolerance among Evangelicals." *Sociological Inquiry* 82 (2): 163–86.

Schulte, Lisa, and Juan Battle. 2004. "The Relative Importance of Ethnicity and Religion in Predicting Attitudes toward Gays and Lesbians." *Journal of Homosexuality* 47 (2): 127–42.

Schwadel, Philip, and Christopher R.H. Garneau. 2019. "Sectarian Religion and Political Tolerance in the United States." *Sociology of Religion* 80 (2): 168–93.

Smidt, Corwin E., and James M. Penning. 1982. "Religious Commitment, Political Conservatism, and Political and Social Tolerance in the United States: A Longitudinal Analysis." *Sociological Analysis* 43 (3): 231–45.

Smith, Buster G., and Byron Johnson. 2010. "The Liberalization of Young Evangelicals: A Research Note." *Journal for the Scientific Study of Religion* 49 (2): 351–60.

Smith, Christian. 1998. *American Evangelicals: Embattled and Thriving.* Chicago: University of Chicago Press.

Stackhouse, John G. Jr. 1993. *Canadian Evangelicalism in the Twentieth Century.* Toronto: University of Toronto Press.

Stackhouse, John G. Jr. 2007. "Defining 'Evangelical.'" *Church and Faith Trends* 1 (1): 1–5.

Statistics Canada. 2019. *Table 17-10-0009-01 Population Estimates, Quarterly.* https://doi.org/10.25318/1710000901-eng.

Stouffer, Samuel. 1955. *Communism, Conformity, and Civil Liberties.* Garden City, NY: Doubleday.

Sullivan, John L., James Piereson, and George E. Marcus. 1982. *Political Tolerance and American Democracy.* Chicago: University of Chicago Press.

Wilcox, Clyde, and Ted Jelen. 1990. "Evangelicals and Political Tolerance." *American Politics Quarterly* 18 (1): 25–46.

Wilkins-Laflamme, Sarah, and Samuel Reimer. 2019. "Religion and Grassroots Social Conservatism in Canada." *Canadian Journal of Political Science* 52 (4): 865–81.

Woodberry, Robert D., and Christian Smith. 1998. "Fundamentalism et al.: Conservative Protestants in America." *Annual Review of Sociology* 24 (1): 25–56.

Wylie, Linda, and James Forest. 1992. "Religious Fundamentalism, Right Wing Authoritarianism and Prejudice." *Psychological Reports* 71 (3): 1291–98.

4

UNDERSTANDING RURAL ATTITUDES TOWARD CULTURAL AND RELIGIOUS MINORITIES VIA POLITICAL ETHNOGRAPHY

The Case of Rural Alberta

Clark Banack

AS WAS HIGHLIGHTED in the introduction to this volume, factors that are known to be strongly correlated with negative attitudes toward cultural, racial, and religious minorities are especially prevalent in rural areas. These include lower levels of education, older age, a commitment to a religious faith, a sense of economic insecurity, heightened fears with respect to cultural loss, and especially limited direct contact with individuals from minority groups. It is thus unsurprising that rural Canadians tend to hold more negative attitudes toward minorities. No doubt there exist a number of examples wherein rural citizens have belied these trends and exhibited all manners of warmth and welcome to newcomers, Indigenous people, and other minority groups, but the data clearly highlight the fact that more work needs to be done to ensure rural communities are centres of inclusion and are moving in the direction of deep equality (see Banack and Pohler, introduction to this volume).

Although survey data such as that used by Reimer (this volume) can tell us much about the factors that correlate with negative attitudes towards these groups, it is generally unable to pinpoint the precise causes of such views. This in turn can make it difficult to design appropriate community-level interventions aimed at reducing these negative attitudes and ultimately building more inclusive rural communities

erected upon the principle of being a "good neighbour" (Banack and Pohler, introduction to this volume). Survey data can absolutely provide helpful hints with respect to potential countermeasures (the importance of "additional education" or "intercultural dialogue," for instance) but I am not convinced we can always use such data to narrow in on the most appropriate method of designing such "education" or "dialogue" in ways that speak directly to the lived experience of rural citizens and thus lead to the meaningful outcomes we seek with respect to the goal of achieving deep equality. Indeed, ground-level anti-racism interventions must be designed in a manner that is sensitive to the circumstances and overarching culture of the communities in which they are being implemented, lest such efforts fail to generate changed attitudes (Vrij, Schie, and Cherryman 1996; Vrij, Akehurst, and Smith 2003), or perhaps even lead to "white backlash" (Thomas 2007). With this in mind, I argue that, as a necessary complement to survey data, researchers must make a more thorough, ground-level commitment to grasping the manners in which people living in rural areas in Canada come to hold their particular views toward cultural, racial, and religious minorities and Indigenous peoples.

This volume contains many excellent examples of such qualitative ground-level approaches, from Haugen's community interviews in Chapter 5, to Corbett, Tinkham, and Bonner's personal reflections in Chapter 6, to Lam's and Lynch's group interventions in Chapters 7 and 8, respectively. Mimicking Katherine Cramer's (2016) path-breaking study *The Politics of Resentment* (see also Cramer-Walsh 2012), this chapter provides a different example of a qualitative ground-level approach by documenting an ethnographic case study designed to provide deeper insight into the ways in which political opinion manifest in rural areas of Alberta.

Over the course of the spring and summer of 2019, I immersed myself in the regularly occurring political conversations of 23 different groups of acquaintances in 16 rural communities across Alberta. The aim of this work was not simply to ascertain where rural Albertans stood on particular issues. Rather, the goal was to employ what Cramer (2016) has labelled "a method of listening," with the intent of better understanding *how* the people in these groups came to hold the opinions they held. Indeed, this is the essence of ethnography: the self-immersion of the researcher into the subjects' world, with the explicit goal of

seeking a deeper grasp of not just what they think, but how they come to think these things. What better way to do this then to spend time with people "as unobtrusively as possible, to listen to what individuals say and how members of groups interact with one another, in the settings in which they normally meet, under the conditions they set for themselves" (Cramer-Walsh 2009, 170)? I have done just that, and in this chapter provide a deeper consideration of how political opinions are currently formulated in rural Alberta, especially as they pertain to views toward cultural and religious minorities and Indigenous peoples.

After providing a more thorough overview of the ethnographic approach, this chapter will unpack my study and its central findings: that rural Albertans are feeling politically alienated and angry in ways that go beyond ideological preference, age, and income level. In fact, each of the grievances unveiled in this study are instead directly connected to key aspects of rural Albertans' social identity: their sense of belonging in particular groups. Two sources of this alienation have deep historical roots in the province. The first is related specifically to their provincial social identity: rural Albertans currently feel a strong sense of what has traditionally been referred to in Canada as "western alienation"—the feeling that the western provinces are largely not taken into consideration in federal politics. The second is connected to their self-identification as "ordinary people": rural Albertans feel an even broader political alienation centred on the notion that politicians "do not listen to ordinary people." This is a populist and anti-party sentiment that has long been embedded within the province's political culture. More recently, rural Albertans have begun to feel a third source of alienation: a specific rural alienation related to their sense of "rural identity," and a corresponding belief in the idea that rural communities and citizens in Alberta are often treated unfairly, overlooked, and even looked down upon by governments and urbanites in general.

Importantly, these forms of alienation are not always experienced as distinct irritations. Instead, they are layered experiences, frequently melting into each other, especially when citizens are working to make sense of other, seemingly unrelated, political issues. In particular, this sense of layered alienation frequently informs the manner in which rural Albertans are interpreting the plight of both racialized or cultural

minorities and Indigenous peoples. In fact, I argue that it is largely impossible to truly make sense of the views rural Albertans currently hold on these issues without grasping how this layered sense of alienation—which is connected to their social identities as Albertans, ordinary people, and rural—is animating their thinking. As the remainder of this chapter will illustrate, there is a certain logic at work in terms of the formulation of these views, however distasteful we may find them. Without fully grasping this logic, any efforts by policy-makers and community educators to counter such views in the interest of building inclusive communities will most likely meet significant resistance from the citizens themselves.

THE ETHNOGRAPHIC APPROACH

Ethnographic approaches have a long and unique history, especially in the fields of anthropology and sociology. Although the method has become somewhat of a contested concept, being both defined and employed in a number of ways, I will rely here on a well-established definition of the term. In its basic formulation, ethnography involves "social research based on the close-up, on-the-ground observation of people and institutions in real time and space, in which the investigator embeds herself near (or within) the phenomenon so as to detect how and why agents on the scene act, think and feel the way they do" (Wacquant 2003, 5).

Schatz (2009, 5) has further elaborated on an "ethnographic sensibility" that uses direct observation or immersion in a community or group with the specific aim of gleaning "the meanings that the people under study attribute to their social and political reality." This search for underlying meaning often leads to a distinct mode of social inquiry, frequently labelled "interpretivism," which begins from the premise that humans are embodied beings whose actions are dependent upon their interpretations of the moral frameworks within which they live. The task of interpretive social inquiry is thus to understand and make clear these frameworks and thereby provide an accurate explanation of *what* the subject is doing by grasping *why* they are doing it (Bauman 1992, 12).

Central to interpretive inquiry are "intersubjective" or communally shared understandings, and thus a recognition that a proper accounting of a particular action requires a more culturally bound answer than some

modern researchers are prepared to allow. The interpretive inquirer accepts that those in similar situations may have unique backgrounds and can thus hold distinct reasons for doing the same action. This notion can problematize the explanatory power of large-N survey research that attempts to demonstrate correlations between personal attributes and particular behaviour. Correlation of this sort can clearly point to valuable connections, but it is not always capable of uncovering the particular causes of individual actions. It may, thus, promote general causal theories that do not necessarily correspond to what is actually occurring for human beings in their day-to-day life. As Geertz (2003, 27) has noted, the interpretive researcher does not seek to correlate behaviour but rather works like a detective trying to get "a meaning frame to provide an understanding of what is going on. You want to understand what it is that is motivating people."

Ethnography, in the sense that it has been employed in this study, is precisely this type of interpretive enterprise (Wedeen 2009). This approach typically does not begin with independent or dependent variables nor does it propose a hypothesis. This is because, as Yanow (2006, 71–72) has argued, the researcher does not know what "meanings" will emerge in their interaction with the subjects. It is through their interaction with the subjects that understanding eventually emerges. This difference in layout between this approach and one based on survey research does not imply that ethnographic interpretivism is not a rigorous form of research. Rather, it approaches rigor by a different standard. It does not borrow standards such as validity, reliability, or generalizability from the natural science model. Instead, it relies on logical argumentation, backed up by detailed, thick descriptions. It offers, in other words, a new "interpretation" of why a subject thinks or acts in a particular way, and it uses thick description to demonstrate why this interpretation makes sense.

In general, the ethnographic approach stands well outside the norms of political science, especially as it pertains to the study of public opinion (Auyero 2006, 258). However, given that dedicated ethnographic immersion is so well suited to unearthing an individual's own understanding of the political, a variety of scholars of politics are now pointing to the potential of the ethnographic approach to problematize several traditional assumptions of political science and thus lead to opportunities for

significant theorization, especially with respect to opinion formation (Bayard de Volo and Scatz 2004; Benzecry and Baiocchi 2017; Boswell et al. 2019; Kumar 2014).

Cramer's (2016) *The Politics of Resentment* is perhaps the preeminent model of this newly emerging trend. Seeking to penetrate the web within which people make sense of their political world and subsequently form political opinions, Cramer immersed herself in several political conversations among acquaintances in regularly occurring coffee groups across urban and rural Wisconsin. In a way that traditional survey research missed, Cramer came to understand the manner in which a particular social identity—in this case, a rural consciousness—shaped the political attitudes for rural citizens in Wisconsin. This consciousness, Cramer demonstrates, acts as the central lens through which most rural citizens make sense of politics, ultimately generating a strong anti-government sentiment. Importantly, this sentiment is not rooted in a straightforward acceptance of the logic of a neoliberal or anti-government ideology. Instead, it is rooted in a sense of resentment against urbanites and the politicians who seemingly act in their own interests rather than in the interests of rural citizens. Having unearthed the role played by this consciousness, the seeming paradox of citizens from lower-income regions of Wisconsin stridently supporting anti-government politicians begins to dissolve. It is in both the ethnographic approach employed and the specific conclusions drawn that Cramer's work has served as a guide to this study of political opinion in rural Alberta.

THE STUDY

Replicating Cramer's approach, I met with 23 groups of acquaintances across 16 communities throughout rural Alberta (see Table 4.1). Although ethnographic work of this sort precludes traditional random sampling, care was taken to ensure groups represented a wide cross-section of the population. Following Cramer (2016, 29–30), communities were chosen via a stratified, purposeful approach beginning with a geographic breakdown of the province. This was followed by a purposeful identification of communities to ensure variation in socioeconomic background, including factors such as total population, population density, distance from a major urban centre, median household income, and central economic drivers.

TABLE 4.1 Breakdown of groups in study by location and by participant age and gender

Group	Date (2019)	Location	Region	Total participants	Women under 45	Men under 45	Women over 45	Men over 45	Distance (km) from major urban centre
1	March 16	Camrose	Central	5	0	0	0	5	94 / Edmonton
2	April 30	Tofield	Central	12	2	0	10	0	68 / Edmonton
3	May 6	Camrose	Central	5	0	0	0	5	94 / Edmonton
4	May 8	Tofield	Central	4	0	0	0	4	68 / Edmonton
5	May 14	Tofield	Central	7	0	0	0	7	68 / Edmonton
6	June 11	Wetaskiwin	Central	4	0	0	0	4	71 / Edmonton
7	June 13	Vegreville	East	5	0	0	0	5	103 / Edmonton
8	June 13	Vegreville	East	4	0	0	0	4	103 / Edmonton
9	June 18	Round Hill	Central	9	0	9	0	0	90 / Edmonton
10	June 27	Killam	East	7	0	1	0	6	172 / Edmonton
11	July 3	Sundre	West	7	3	4	0	0	115 / Calgary
12	July 4	Carstairs	West	5	0	0	0	5	65 / Calgary
13	July 10	Drayton Valley	West	8	0	0	3	5	144 / Edmonton
14	July 10	Drayton Valley	West	4	0	0	0	4	144 / Edmonton
15	July 17	Barrhead	North	7	0	2	0	5	120 / Edmonton
16	July 17	Westlock	North	8	0	0	3	5	90 / Edmonton
17	July 29	Fort Macleod	South	7	0	0	2	5	49 / Lethbridge
18	July 29	Pincher Creek	South	4	0	2	0	2	99 / Lethbridge
19	July 29	Picture Butte	South	4	1	3	0	0	29 / Lethbridge
20	July 30	Vulcan	South	8	0	0	3	5	128 / Calgary
21	August 1	Wetaskiwin	Central	2	0	0	0	2	71 / Edmonton
22	August 23	Kingman	Central	6	2	2	1	1	79 / Edmonton
23	Sept 4	Camrose	Central	6	0	0	6	0	94 / Edmonton
Total				138	8	23	28	79	

Once the communities were identified, I planned to simply show up unannounced at coffee shops and restaurants and ask to join groups who happened to be chatting over coffee. It quickly became apparent, however, that such an approach was going to result in a group of participants that were almost exclusively men over the age of 45. In order to widen the scope of participants, I had to be more deliberate in finding groups that included both women and people under the age of 45. This involved reaching out to preexisting contacts in the communities to access a wider array of regularly meeting groups. Although men over the age of 45 are still overrepresented in this study, these steps allowed access to more women and younger people.

In each case, I began by introducing myself as a political scientist from the University of Alberta who was studying political attitudes in rural Alberta and asked permission to join their group. Although there was some groaning, every group except one welcomed me to sit down. It was clear that my association with academia made a number of participants uneasy—universities were not viewed in a very positive light in many of the groups. However, one significant aspect of my background undoubtedly opened avenues to me that may not have been open to others: I grew up in a rural community and admitted early on in the conversation that my interest in rural public opinion was due partly to my own rural background. This admission noticeably eased some tension around the table, and some participants referred to my background during their conversation in ways that signaled to me that they trusted me to understand what they were saying.

Obviously, the fact that I have a rural background colours the way I perceive various things, especially topics related to rural life. It was my goal to remain cognizant of this throughout the study, especially when it came to assuming I understood what participants meant in conversation with me and eventually analyzing the data generated by the study. Central to my efforts to overcome the potential for faulty assumptions was asking follow-up questions to ensure I was grasping meanings correctly, considering alternate meanings when rereading the transcripts or my notes, and completing a round of member-checking at the conclusion of the study.

After joining each group, I asked permission to record our conversation. Roughly half of the groups objected to this; in those cases, I took detailed notes. In each case, I began by asking participants what their biggest political concerns were—a question that was so broad and open-ended that participants were free to take the conversation in any number of ways. There were places in the ensuing conversation where I would ask a follow-up question to ensure clarity or a more direct question to slightly guide the conversation back to politics (it was not uncommon for the conversation to drift in all sorts of directions). But above all, my job was to listen. In the vast majority of groups, participants quickly grew comfortable and the conversations flowed openly—these people clearly had things they wanted to say. In fact, one of the clearest themes to emerge

in this work was the degree to which many rural citizens feel overlooked and ignored in general. Participants often expressed their gratitude that "someone who mattered" actually wanted to hear what they had to say.

At the conclusion of these chats, which lasted anywhere from 45 minutes to over three hours, I made brief field notes summarizing some of the patterns that stuck out in the conversation before eventually reading through the transcript or the notes I had taken, hand-coding them into specific topics, and entering quotes into a master data display spreadsheet (Cramer 2016, 42; Miles and Huberman 1994; Verdinelli and Scagnoli 2013). This document included basic demographic information for each group and separated the comments made by participants into a series of topic categories. These categories included ideological preference, rural identity and rural-specific challenges, concerns over local economy, western alienation, environmental concerns, attitudes toward immigrants and Indigenous peoples, and attitudes towards Donald Trump, among others. This method of data reduction and organization allowed for a thorough and quick comparison of the comments made about a particular topic between various groups and also provided a clear visual cue as to the topics that each group were most eager to speak to. Studying the evolving data display as the project progressed allowed for the identification of clear patterns with respect to attitudinal positions across groups and, more importantly, of ways in which various topics were linked together for participants across groups. As certain patterns became apparent, both in terms of what issues mattered most and how participants were making sense of these issues, I added certain questions or probes to my informal protocol in order to test whether or not the pattern persisted across other groups. After entering the data from my last "coffee chat," I again studied the data display and identified the themes that were most consistently present. Finally, I engaged in a round of member-checking wherein I revisited four randomly-selected groups and asked them directly about the central themes I had noticed and the ways in which these issues seemed to be connected for participants. Although some groups had not directly spoken to one or all of the central themes in their initial conversation with me, all four groups enthusiastically agreed with my findings and often elaborated on these themes in additional detail.

While I did encounter small pockets of ideological diversity among participants, it is fair to say that the vast majority of citizens I spoke with leaned strongly conservative in their ideology and party preference. Given that rural Alberta has endorsed conservative-leaning candidates with 67%, 65%, 87%, and 72% of the vote in the 2008, 2012, 2015, and 2019 provincial elections, this was not at all surprising.[1] Nor was it a surprise to encounter a fair bit of discontent given how the Alberta economy has struggled since 2014. What was perhaps more unexpected was both the breadth and depth of political anger in rural Alberta—a strong sense of discontentment that branches out from multiple grievances with many distinct implications.

Ideological discontent surfaced often in the conversations I participated in, directed largely at the policies of the Alberta New Democrat Party, who had been recently defeated at the time of this study, and the federal Liberal government led by Justin Trudeau. But over the course of the conversations, it became apparent that there was much more going on for these individuals than a general unhappiness with the ideological persuasion of certain governments. Rather, three distinct types of alienation—western, political, and rural—emerged as important factors in how they were viewing various political issues, each of which related much more strongly to a particular social identity held by participants than a basic ideological preference or even the particularities of their own personal situation. Indeed, the vast majority of participants across age and gender categories, including those most outspoken in their political anger, were either gainfully employed or comfortably retired. In other words, the various alienations identified in these conversations were rarely the product of personal struggles. Rather, they were related to participants' feelings that *the groups* to which they felt strongly connected were being treated unfairly. It was only after partaking in several coffee chats that I was able to see both the extent of participants' discontent and the particular ways in which many citizens in rural Alberta have come to understand seemingly different political issues as tightly connected.

IDENTITY AND ALIENATION IN RURAL ALBERTA

Upon completing her study of rural Wisconsin, Cramer (2016, 5–6) defined rural consciousness as "an identity as a rural person that includes much more than an attachment to place. It includes a sense that decision makers routinely ignore rural places and fail to give rural communities their fair share of resources, as well as a sense that rural folks are fundamentally different from urbanites in terms of lifestyles, values and work ethic."

Wuthnow (2018), whose research team completed over 1,000 in-depth interviews with citizens from across rural America, largely concurs. He argues that that rural communities are best understood as moral communities "in which people feel an obligation to one another and to uphold the local ways of being that govern their exceptions about ordinary life…and doing the right thing" (4). Central to these "ways of being" is a deeply-rooted identity in one's particular town, an intense pride in being "practical, productive, and down-to-earth," and an unspoken assumption that their moral order is predicated on "whiteness" (4). However, there is also a pervasive sense of rage given that rural citizens often share a sense that their moral community is "under siege" in general and being "left behind" in particular (6–11). Hochschild's (2016) study of Louisiana, while not exclusively rural focused, similarly identified shared cultural values and an emerging sense that "ordinary people" literally feel like "strangers in their own land" as key to understanding the political resentment that motivated such strong support for the anti-establishment Tea Party movement.

These descriptions of the rural United States strongly resemble the sense of identity and alienation that became apparent in the conversations I took part in across rural Alberta. Indeed, a deep-seated sense of "rural identity," a sense that rural citizens were fundamentally different in certain ways from urban Canadians, was apparent in almost every conversation. This was not a surprise. I and others have previously mused about the existence of a particular "rural" or "agrarian" identity in Canada and the associated political implications for urban-rural relations (Banack 2021; Epp 2008; Sandwell 2016). Beyond a basic sense of pride in rural life, the land some tend, the community spirit they feel, or the types of work many rural people engage in, a loosely defined but shared moral

"code" emerged over the course of this study that proved to be important to how rural citizens understood themselves in relation to nonrural citizens. This code also proved important to how rural Albertans interpreted various political issues.

The code often bordered on a brand of libertarianism, but with a unique collective streak. I heard several references to qualities such as common sense, hard work, self-reliance, being "down-to-earth," treating people equally and with dignity, and being good neighbours. I also heard participants identify themselves as very much being "ordinary people." Surely, much of this code is standard conservative fare, but there was also a clear sense that this outlook was a key component of the moral fibre of the rural, as opposed to urban, community to which they belonged:

Group 16

Me: Do you ever think about moving?

Speaker 1 *(female over 45)*: I'm not moving to Edmonton, thank you very much!

Speaker 2 *(male over 45)*: I understand that city people probably look down on our way of life, that they could never imagine living here. Well, I could never imagine living there. And I tried. I was in Calgary for five years. Great job, but I could never feel at home there. It's just different in the city. The way people go about things. They don't seem to want to work hard. I have six grandchildren. I love them all equally, but I'd only hire two of them, the two that stayed here. They are the only two who truly know how to work.

Group 12

Speaker 1 *(male over 45)*: We here in rural Alberta, in small towns, we just want to be left alone by government. We know how to solve problems; we know how to work together to solve issues we have in the community. We do not need the government getting involved, telling us how to do it.

Speaker 2 *(male over 45)*: It's simple—rural Albertans believe each and every individual should be able to pull your own weight. We are self-reliant. If a guy is down on his luck, fine, we will

help him. No problem. But we work hard and are not open to people looking for handouts. We feel shame if we end up on welfare or employment insurance. There are too many people in this country who don't feel that shame.

Speaker 3 (male over 45): Too many provinces too!

Speaker 2 (male over 45): Right. They are okay with waiting for the next handout and complaining even louder if they don't get it.

Group 21

Speaker 1 (male over 45): There has been a shift in demographics in this area. You're getting an urban type of attitude coming into the rural area. Urban people moving onto acreages and stuff, commuting to Edmonton. And we're seeing our small community halls and such kind of fall apart because the people that have been doing it, the rural people, have been doing it for 25 years, right? And the urban-type people, they are not into community things so they don't want to help out.

Attached to this sense of identity was a clear sense of layered alienation that traversed three distinct issues. The first and most obvious source of political anger in rural Alberta is that which is currently an Alberta-wide phenomenon. As a multitude of recent polls have confirmed (Andrew-Gee 2019; Angus Reid Institute 2019), a strong sense of "western alienation," or perhaps a more specific "Alberta alienation," has reemerged and is influencing how citizens make sense of politics throughout the province. In nearly every single conversation, the notion that Alberta was being treated unfairly by both the federal government and certain provinces was the first issue participants brought up. They often elaborated on this issue at great length, and in many cases described Alberta as being "under attack." Indeed, it is difficult to exaggerate how passionately held these views are among rural Albertans.

Second, the vast majority of rural Albertans that I shared coffee with, including many of the less frequent left-leaning citizens, also felt an acute sense of structural, political alienation. The notions that

"politicians do not listen to the people," that "politicians are only after your vote," that "the political game is rigged and we only see half of what's going on," and that party discipline means "the local politician is essentially useless" were rampant in these conversations. As one individual put it, "it just gets you so angry, it just turns you right off. The lack of common sense, the lies, the games. And the parties sour everything. I want to follow it, but I just have to turn it off."

Third, the type of political anger each of Cramer (2016), Wuthnow (2018), and Hochschild (2016) documented in the rural United States related to the seeming lack of respect rural communities receive was an unmistakable ingredient in how many rural Albertans were making sense of their political world. Closely attached to study participants' attempts to articulate what "being rural" meant were denunciations of city-dwellers and "their" governments overlooking rural areas, looking down upon rural citizens, and often taking advantage of them. There were several references throughout the conversations to specific cutbacks to services and program funding that hurt rural towns. Rural crime, and the government's seeming indifference to it, was another area of common concern.

Whatever the issue, participants largely shared the view that, given the relatively small size of rural populations, the government is not truly interested in helping rural communities. In addition, a sense that their "way of life" was under attack was widespread, be it due to a serious policy issue like the introduction of a carbon tax ("I have absolutely no other option. I simply have to pay more. I can't take the bus. I can't afford an electric car. And I couldn't plug it in anywhere if I could. How is this anything but an extra tax on rural people?") or the seemly mundane (the growing popularity of vegan burgers, which threatens the cattle industry, for instance). Yet the sense that urbanites "do not understand" rural citizens was the link that tied these issues together and generated a widely shared source of latent anger that often emerged in these conversations, especially when paired with the real-world concerns these citizens felt governments were ignoring. Note how three different groups responded to the question "Do you think that people who live in larger cities understand rural areas? Rural citizens?":

Group 19

Speaker 1 (male under 45): There seems to be a disconnect when it comes to how this country was built and the continuing importance of rural areas for this country. We are feeding you! And we are doing a good job of it. Our produce is safe and healthy and we work hard to make sure it's done. We do not make much money doing that work, yet the cities completely turn their noses up at us. We are just a bunch of ignorant hillbillies and whatever ideas we might have, whatever problems or issues we might raise, well the politicians don't need to really listen.

Group 17

Speaker 1 (female over 45): Oh, they don't know we exist. I'm surprised you could find us, coming from the big university. Did you know we existed before you found us on the highway driving by?

Group 13

Speaker 1 (male over 45): Absolutely not! We might as well be from different planets. And the government workers, the politicians, the professors from Edmonton? They are the worst of all. They are on their high horse about all this shit. They simply don't understand what it is really like out here.

Speaker 2 (male over 45): Ah, most of those professors see us as rednecks who can barely get our pants on by ourselves. I don't have a college degree, so I'm an idiot. I know that's what they are thinking. I worked from nothing to a senior management position in a successful oil company. But I'll always be a redneck in their eyes.

Speaker 3 (female over 45): Oh, yes, they think we are rednecks. Were you at that meeting where Notley was supposed to come but at the last minute she sent some others from Edmonton instead? They looked at us like we were fools. They weren't listening to anything we said…It is nice that

you came out here. Nice that someone wants to listen. Do you think anyone will listen to what you write?

THE IMPLICATIONS OF LAYERED ALIENATION: UNDERSTANDING RACIAL PREJUDICE IN RURAL ALBERTA

The above was but a tiny snippet of the political anger and the different senses of alienation that were shared with me by a several groups across rural Alberta. Although it was expressed in slightly different ways, the notions that Alberta as a whole is being taken advantage of by the rest of the country, that politicians simply do not listen to "ordinary people" like themselves, and that rural communities and rural citizens in particular are often misunderstood, looked down upon, or overlooked entirely by urban dwellers and "their" governments were strongly held. Given the broad scholarly consensus on the connection across pockets of the Western world between increasing economic inequality and political alienation on the one hand and right-wing populism on the other (Mudde 2007; Norris and Inglehart 2018; Brown 2019), it should come as no surprise that, in the conversations observed over the course of this study, the strong majority of participants expressed both misgivings about the reliability of traditional media sources as well as strong admiration for anti-establishment politicians, especially former American president Donald Trump.

A more overtly troubling link that emerged in these conversations was that between a rampant sense of rural communities being mistreated and overlooked in a variety of ways and the "advantages" and "benefits" seemingly bestowed by "government" on newcomers to Canada and Indigenous peoples. Indeed, the level of anger that participants expressed around such issues was somewhat startling. I definitely encountered examples of blatant prejudice expressed against certain cultural groups, the recitation of hurtful stereotypes with respect to the "intentions" of Muslims or the "work ethic" of Indigenous peoples, and a certain ignorance when it came to a whole realm of related topics. Frankly, I was expecting elements of this. But more common was the sense that for many rural Albertans, including several who expressed knowledgeable, nuanced, and even sympathetic views towards cultural minorities, newcomers, and Indigenous peoples, there exists a clear

connection between their own sense of alienation, their own sense of being overlooked and judged by others, and a sense of anger at state and societal efforts to address *instead* the concerns of cultural, racial, and religious minorities and Indigenous peoples. What emerged here was a strong sense that central aspects of the broader moral code present in rural Alberta, especially as it relates to "hard work and self-reliance" and "equal treatment," are routinely violated by various levels of government when it comes to such issues. Echoing the precise sentiments of the Tea Party supporters in Louisiana interviewed by Hochschild (2016, 135–40), many rural Albertans feel that, given the layered alienation they experience, they, rather than various minority groups, are the true losers in contemporary politics. Consider the following exchanges:

Group 17

Speaker 1 *(male over 45)*: There is no celebration of the working man. The guy who spends his life heading to work at 6 a.m. every day for 40 years or 50 years. That's what we all did... [Today] it's all these special interests that get their handouts for this and for that. And government gives it to them. There's no money to fix the roads around here, but these refugees crossing the borders with their nice suitcases and cell phones? These immigrants you see sitting around the mall in the middle of the day, no need for a job? And Christ, these Natives? Don't get me started. The government will put its back out to help them. Jesus, the billions and billions. But people like us? Our little town? Ha! I guess we are lucky to have the loonie for this coffee.

Group 8

Speaker 1 *(male over 45)*: You see them [recent immigrants] walking around town. You know the government is paying them. They don't have jobs, but they are living better than I am. I'm struggling to survive. I've been laid off for nearly a year. I'm looking for work but there is none around here. I don't blame them for that. I know it's the oil field, the lack of a pipeline. Fucking Trudeau. And the fucking crime in

the rural areas now. The government isn't doing anything
to stop that. But the government always finds a way to help
them.

Speaker 2 (male over 45): Oh, they are too busy showering the
Natives or the refugees with cash or flying around the world
and staying in suites on the taxpayer's dime to worry about
rural crime or jobs in Alberta. They don't care about us.

Speaker 1 (male over 45): Right. Why aren't the politicians sitting
here with us like you are, asking us about how we see things?
They come around at election time and that's it.

Speaker 2 (male over 45): And if we do tell them that things are
not fair, well then it's, "You don't understand your white
privilege!" Jesus Christ. Do we look privileged? But we are
just a bunch of racist hicks out here, right?

Although citizens routinely shared opinions about various cultures that spoke to an obvious lack of familiarity with their practices and beliefs, not to mention the very real struggles both newcomers and Indigenous peoples face, it was also true that many of the views expressed in these conversations, especially as they pertained to Indigenous peoples, were rooted in the real-life experiences of rural citizens. Many of the social ills that plague Indigenous communities in Canada and that academics frequently lament in statistical form are often encountered head-on by rural citizens in their daily lives and do much to shape their perceptions. Although somewhat jarring to hear, these experiences, in conjunction with their own grievances, were frequently alluded to as a way to justify their anger at state support for Indigenous peoples:

Group 9

Speaker 1 (male under 45): I went to school with many, many
Natives. In elementary, it was almost 50/50, whites and
Natives. Then every year, more and more drop out. So
many Natives from my school would get tens of thousands
of dollars from the Band and their oil reserves when they
turned a certain age and they immediately quit school

and pissed it away. I didn't get that. My parents had barely enough to get by on but they helped where they could. Their parents are drunk, they don't help. By the time I graduated, there was one Native in my class. All the others dropped out. That's on the system. Pouring money onto the reserve just makes it worse.

Speaker 2 (male under 45): I understand now, I think we all understand now, better than we did before, that some bad things happened in the past. I know what [Speaker 1] has just described is related to this history. I'm fine with trying to make amends. But how long do we need to go on apologizing? How many more billions do we need to pour into these issues without seeing anything get better? The issues never go away. The reserves are shit holes. We see the houses trashed and broken when we drive through. We know about the crime, the drugs. We see the Natives wandering the streets, not working. The water's not safe to drink. Even after all the money poured in. Why can't they pull themselves up? Why don't they have that drive?

Speaker 3 (male under 45): Because they are coddled. They don't have to work like we do. It's a culture built on demanding handouts and getting them from government. Welfare breeds welfare.

Speaker 1 (male under 45): And it never ends. It's all about wanting more. And as soon as a group wants more than what is equal, I am going to have a problem with that.

Group 17

Speaker 1 (male over 45): They won't work, but they are looking for millions here and billions there. And the government is giving it to them.

Speaker 2 (male over 45): Yeah, this local reserve has tried all sorts of things to get guys working. They've open manufacturing plants on the reserve, then it was a forestry company, then they were making hay, then more manufacturing of some kind. And every one of those operations have closed

up because they can't get anyone to show up for work. Why would they work when the government will just pay them anyway? And the government just shells out more money for the next big plant or shop or whatever that they want to build for jobs for these people. Give me a break.

Speaker 1 (male over 45): Do you think Trudeau is running this way with cash to get any white people working in rural Alberta? To set up these make-work projects for the thousands laid off from the patch? Hell no.

IMPLICATIONS FOR BUILDING INCLUSIVE RURAL COMMUNITIES

No doubt, many of the comments quoted above point to a lack of understanding with respect to the ramifications of the Canadian State's historical treatment of Indigenous peoples, or how the immigration and refugee systems in this country actually operate, or the specifics of "government handouts" for newcomers or Indigenous peoples. They similarly ignore the efforts that both federal and provincial governments have made over the years to address issues related to rural infrastructure and job creation.

Employing an ethnographic approach in an effort to better understand political opinion formation across rural Alberta allowed me to better see, beyond a certain level of ignorance around "who gets what," the way in which distinct grievances are often layered together in the minds of these citizens. I began to understand how these grievances are connected to individuals' own identities as rural Albertans, and are particularly strongly linked to the various forms of alienation they experience—the different ways in which they feel misunderstood, mistreated, and overlooked. These connections animate their thinking on issues related to newcomers and Indigenous peoples. In other words, while these views do reflect a certain ignorance that many will find distasteful, there is also a certain logic at work in their formulation. There are winners and there are losers in the minds of these rural Albertans, and it is becoming increasingly clear that they are understanding themselves as occupants of the latter category.

On one level, there is little new in claiming that a connection exists between a sense of alienation, a sense of "losing," and growing support

for anti-establishment politics and resentment toward minority groups. What is novel, I suggest, is how ethnography can demonstrate, in ways that surveys may miss, the detailed manner in which citizens are making connections between issues in the formation of specific political opinions. This is especially so in terms of unveiling the specific ways in which citizens directly connect these issues in their minds when discussing political issues among themselves.

Practically speaking, this ethnographic unveiling can be of significant help for policy-makers and community educators who are tasked with addressing issues of racial prejudice in rural communities and building more inclusive communities. Survey data on attitudes toward racialized minorities or Indigenous people in rural areas can, to be sure, help us determine whether more "education" or "intercultural dialogue" is required. But ethnography can complement survey work by highlighting the importance of designing such interventions in a way that takes into account the specific manner in which rural citizens are processing these issues. In other words, any attempt to address racial prejudice in rural Alberta will, I expect, encounter a fair bit of resistance from citizens unless the deep-seated layers of alienation felt in these areas is acknowledged within such efforts. The manner by which citizens have come to hold these views are often a product of a particular type of personal experience that cannot be just waved aside or immediately ridiculed as ignorant and bigoted. There is a logic at play in the minds of these citizens and any efforts to improve cultural relations in rural communities must take this logic into account in their program design. They must acknowledge with empathy the anger and fear that so often sits at the heart of these attitudes. Only then will the opportunity arise for authentic learning, bridge-building, and reconciliation across cultural divides in rural communities. Only then can one hope to move in the direction of "deep equality."

AUTHOR'S NOTE

This chapter is an abridged and revised version of the following article, printed with permission: Clark Banack, "Ethnography and Political Opinion: Identity, Alienation and Anti-establishmentarianism in Rural Alberta," *Canadian Journal of Political Science* 54, no. 1 (2021): 1–22.

NOTE

1. Although this is not a perfect representation of the "rural vote" in Alberta, these calculations demonstrate the percentage of vote share captured by both the Progressive Conservative and Wild Rose parties in the 2008, 2012, and 2015 provincial elections and the United Conservative Party's vote share in the 2019 provincial election in ridings outside of Edmonton, Calgary, Red Deer, and Lethbridge.

REFERENCES

Andrew-Gee, Eric. 2019. "Is the West Fed Up with Canada?" *Globe and Mail*, March 22, 2019. https://www.theglobeandmail.com/canada/article-is-the-west-fed-up-with-canada-what-a-new-survey-shows-about-the/.

Angus Reid Institute. 2019. "Decades after Reform's Rise, Voters Open to a New Western Canada Party." *Angus Reid Institute*, February 5, 2019. http://angusreid.org/western-canada-separatism/.

Auyero, Javier. 2006. "Introductory Note to Politics under the Microscope: Special Issue on Political Ethnography 1." In "Politics under the Microscope", edited by Javier Auyero, special issue, *Qualitative Sociology* 29: 257–59. https://doi.org/10.1007/s11133-006-9028-7.

Banack, Clark. 2021. "Rural Identity in an Urban Canada: Minority Rights for Agrarian Communities?" *American Review of Canadian Studies* 51 (4): 628–48.

Bauman, Zygmunt. 1992. *Hermeneutics and Social Science: Approaches to Understanding*. Hampshire, UK: Gregg Revivals.

Bayard de Volo, Lorraine, and Edward Schatz. 2004. "From the Inside Out: Ethnographic Methods in Political Research." *PS: Political Science and Politics* 37 (2): 267–71.

Benzecry, Claudio E., and Gianpaolo Baicchi. 2017. "What Is Political about Political Ethnography? On the Context of Discovery and the Normalization of an Emergent Subfield." *Theory and Society* 46 (3): 229–47.

Boswell, John, Jack Corbett, Kate Dommett, Will Jennings, Matthew Flinders, R.A.W. Rhodes, and Matthew Wood. 2019. "State of the Field: What Can Political Ethnography Tell Us about Anti-politics and Democratic Disaffection." *European Journal of Political Research* 58 (1): 56–71.

Brown, Wendy. 2019. *In the Ruins of Neoliberalism*. New York: Columbia University Press.

Cramer-Walsh, Katherine. 2009. "Scholars as Citizens: Studying Political Opinion through Ethnography." *Political Ethnography*, edited by E. Schatz, 165–82. Chicago: University of Chicago Press.

Cramer-Walsh, Katherine. 2012. "Putting Inequality in Its Place: Rural Consciousness and the Power of Perspective." *American Political Science Review* 106 (37): 517–32.

Cramer, Katherine. 2016. *The Politics of Resentment*. Chicago: University of Chicago Press.

Epp, Roger. 2008. *We Are All Treaty People: Prairie Essays*. Edmonton: University of Alberta Press.

Geertz, Clifford. 2003. "Interview with Clifford Geertz." By Neni Panourgiá and Pavlos Kavourasin. *Qualitative Methods* 1 (2): 27.

Hochschild, Arlie Russell. 2016. *Strangers in Their Own Land: Anger and Mourning on the American Right*. New York: New Press.

Kumar, Satendra. 2014. "The Promise of Ethnography for the Study of Politics." *Studies in Indian Politics* 2 (2): 237–42.

Miles, Matthew, and A. Michael Huberman. 1994. *Qualitative Data Analysis*. 2nd ed. Thousand Oaks, CA: Sage Publications.

Mudde, Casse. 2007. *Populist Radical Right Parties in Europe*. Cambridge: Cambridge University Press.

Norris, Pippa, and Ronald Inglehart. 2018. *Cultural Backlash: Trump, Brexit and The Rise of Authoritarian Populism*. Cambridge: Cambridge University Press.

Sandwell, Ruth W. 2016. *Canada's Rural Majority, 1870–1940: Households, Environments, Economies*. Toronto: University of Toronto Press.

Schatz, Edward. 2009. "Ethnographic Immersion and the Study of Politics." *Political Ethnography*, edited by Edward Schatz, 1–22. Chicago: University of Chicago Press.

Thomas, Paul. 2007. "Moving On from 'Anti-Racism'? Understanding of 'Community Cohesion' held by Youth Workers." *Journal of Social Policy* 36 (3): 435–55.

Verdinelli, Susana, and Norma I. Scagnoli. 2013. "Display Data in Qualitative Research." *International Journal of Qualitative Methods* 12 (1): 359–81.

Vrij, Aldert, Lucy Akehurst, and Beverley Smith. 2003. "Reducing Ethnic Prejudice: An Evaluation of Seven Recommended Principles for Incorporation in Public Initiatives." *Journal of Community and Applied Social Psychology* 13: 284–99.

Vrij, Aldert, Emil Van Schie, and Julie Cherryman. 1996. "Reducing Ethnic Prejudice Through Public Communication Programs: A Social-Psychological Perspective." *The Journal of Psychology* 130 (4): 413–20.

Wacquant, Loïc. 2003. "Ethnografeast: A Progress Report on the Practice and Promise of Ethnography." *Ethnography* 4 (1): 5–14.

Wedeen, Lisa. 2009. "Ethnography as Interpretive Enterprise." *Political Ethnography*, edited by Edward Schatz, 75–93. Chicago: University of Chicago Press.

Wuthnow, Robert. 2018. *The Left Behind: Decline and Rage in Rural America*. Princeton: Princeton University Press.

Yanow, Dvora. 2006. "Neither Rigorous nor Objective?" In *Interpretation and Method: Empirical Research Methods in the Interpretive Turn*, edited by Dvora Yanow and Peregrine Schwartz-Shea, 97–119. New York: M.E. Sharpe.

5

DRIVING INTO NOWHERE

Refugee Resettlement and Integration in Rural Canada

Stacey Haugen

THE PHRASE "DRIVING INTO NOWHERE" can describe the experiences of refugee newcomers arriving in rural Canada for the first time. While speaking with Syrian refugees across the country, I heard stories of newcomers surprised by the immense space, frigid cold, and absolute quiet of rural places. Unfamiliar with Canadian geography and given little information about their destination, refugees were often unsure of their new communities. One Syrian man confided that upon arriving in Toronto, he was told that he would not be staying in the city but would be travelling north. Although he was assured that his family would be resettled in a rural community in southern Ontario, he was convinced that they were headed for Alaska. Another refugee family attempted to search the name of their destination in Google before they arrived. Unfortunately, the rural place they were headed to is so small that Google could not accurately locate it for them. Instead, the search engine suggested the community they were looking for was an urban centre in southern Ontario. With this information in hand, the family was more than a little surprised when they arrived in a small prairie town in the middle of February.

These stories capture only a fraction of the surprise and uncertainty that characterize refugee resettlement and integration in rural

areas. In this chapter, I explore the unknowns of rural resettlement. As an important counterpoint to Banack (this volume), who documents degrees of hesitancy expressed by some rural citizens toward supporting newcomers to Canada, I document how rural places across the country are, in fact, welcoming increasing numbers of refugees into their communities. This remains largely understudied and absent from conversations concerning national immigration. From my research, I have found that resettlement can offer benefits both to smaller communities and to refugees. Communities can benefit from the new skill sets and cultures that refugees bring with them, and refugees can benefit from the housing affordability, social networks, employment opportunities, and space found in rural areas. The rural residents and refugees I spoke with recognize and enjoy the benefits that smaller communities can offer all residents, including the ability to, as one of my interviewees put it, "let the kids run free, have a garden, and have lots of space."[1]

However, there are also many challenges present in rural communities. In the absence of government-funded services and other supports, the role of integrating newcomers falls largely to the individuals who live in rural places. Thus, community attitudes, religious biases, and individual assumptions matter a great deal. Through considerations of hospitality, gratitude, and expectation, I trace the ways in which rural residents are welcoming newcomers into their communities and question the assumptions and expectations present throughout this process. I conclude by considering how communities can work to ensure rural places are integrating and including newcomers as "good neighbours"—that is, in ways that resemble deep equality (Beaman 2017; see also Banack and Pohler, introduction to this volume)—rather than simply tolerating their presence until they move elsewhere.

BACKGROUND

In Canada, while government-assisted refugees are almost exclusively resettled to urban centres that receive federal funding, privately sponsored refugees can be resettled anywhere a private sponsorship group has formed (Government of Canada 2018). Canada's system of private sponsorship is unique in that it allows Canadians to raise funds to bring refugees into their community, regardless of the community's population

size or distance from an urban centre. Sponsors take on the resettlement and integration needs of the refugees; in particular, they are responsible for supporting the newcomers financially and socially during their first year in Canada. Established by the Immigration Act of 1976, private sponsorship has been used to accept large numbers of refugees into Canada. During the Indo-Chinese crisis in the 1970s, Canadians in communities across the country sponsored 34,000 refugees (Labman 2016, 69).

More recently, private sponsorship was used to bring thousands of Syrian refugees to Canada. Since the fall of 2015, more than 58,000 Syrian refugees have been resettled in more than 350 Canadian communities, including small and rural centres (Government of Canada 2022; Government of Canada 2021a). Rural Canadians have been involved in refugee resettlement and integration largely through private sponsorship, and while governments and academia have largely ignored resettlement in rural places (Yoshida and Ramos 2013), the Canadian media has highlighted the experiences of some rural sponsors and refugees (Moulton 2015; McDonald 2016; Presse 2016; Taylor-Vaisey and Shendruk 2016).

When refugees are resettled into rural areas, they experience the challenges that are inherent to life in rural Canada. Small and rural places struggle with a lack of services and adequate infrastructure, diminishing and ageing populations, youth out-migration, and environmental degradation (Moazzami 2015; Gadsby and Samson 2016). Newcomers, including the individuals I spoke with, often face additional barriers including a lack of access to multilingual service providers, ethnic food items, and advanced language training (RDI 2016; FCM 2011). A lack of public transportation in rural areas is one of the biggest challenges newcomers face. A rural service provider I spoke with contended that the "biggest challenge initially [for refugees to access services] was transportation."

Further, in the absence of services and government supports, rural places rely on social connections and community networks to accomplish essential tasks and achieve goals; these include, among other things, integrating newcomers (Besser and Miller 2015, 174; Flora and Flora 2013). Community relationships and sponsor connections are essential to the integration of refugees and the provision of essential services such as language classes, housing, transportation, and employment. Despite the challenges, rural residents organize informal

English language lessons, volunteers drive refugees into the nearest urban centre for appointments, local grocers order in halal meats and pita bread, and sponsors reach out to the community for donations and support. One sponsor I spoke with commented, "We had so many donations that we had to turn stuff away."

From starting English language schools in church basements to creating newcomer welcome centres, rural communities are finding creative ways to welcome newcomers into their communities and to help them find a sense of belonging (Haugen 2019; McMorrow and Caufield 2016). The community members and sponsors I spoke with were eager to share their stories of rural welcome and excitement around hosting newcomers. One sponsor commented that "there was a lot of community excitement about actually doing something to help the situation in Syria…The support from the community never waned." Another community member stated that "the general community sense is very positive—people get involved and want to meet them."

While there is a lack of data and research comparing urban and rural resettlement, my research clearly shows that there is something distinct to rural places and their resettlement efforts. For example, when speaking about the differences between urban and rural places, a rural resident I spoke with stated that "we are more cohesive as a community because we are intimately involved in each other's lives because of geography." Expanding on the geographical size of smaller places, another community member commented on the realities of living in a small community where everyone knows everyone, stating, "A tight knit community is a blessing and a curse—it takes a while to break into the community." While this was a common sentiment among rural residents, those I spoke with often indicated that once newcomers were included and embraced by the community, they experienced the benefits of these close social networks. An English-language service provider explained how they played a role in helping newcomers integrate into the community, saying, "We want our volunteers to spend time with our students [the newcomers]…We want volunteers to take them for coffee, take them shopping…and help them in the garden. That way, too, you get volunteers that are more committed because they are part of their life." My research also demonstrates that, despite the challenges, rural residents make real efforts to band together

and support newcomers. For example, one sponsor commented that "whatever they [the newcomers] need, we'll do our best."

In the rural context, when resettlement services are largely provided through informal community organizing, rural sponsors, volunteers, and community networks play a significant role in the integration process. Community attitudes, assumptions, and expectations become particularly important. Before refugees arrive, rural sponsors make assumptions about broader community attitudes and intolerance towards newcomers. After refugees arrive, community expectations of how a refugee should look and act impact relationships between community members and newcomers. Expectations of gratitude on the parts of sponsors and community members affect integration processes as both communities and newcomers offer hospitality and navigate new relationships. Private sponsors, as the first point of contact with the refugees they are sponsoring, are the link between the community and the newcomers; they are, in effect, gatekeepers to the community. Because sponsors play such a key role in the success of rural resettlement, their expectations and assumptions of refugees and the sponsorship process are particularly important.

My goal here is to explore the broader community attitudes and religious biases that I encountered in my research in rural communities, specifically considering how community and sponsor expectations of how a refugee should look, act, and express gratitude influenced processes of integration. Through understandings of hospitality and the guest-host relationship, I offer insight into what it takes for a community as a whole and for individuals to recognize, meet, and move past their assumptions to accept, welcome, and include newcomers.

METHODS

In the spring of 2017, I travelled across Canada to explore how rural communities were welcoming and integrating Syrian refugee newcomers. With funding from the International Development Research Centre, I visited four rural regions across the country where Syrian refugees had been resettled in 2016. In addition to phone calls, emails, and preliminary visits, I spent approximately one week in each place conducting semi-structured interviews and attending informal social events and local

activities. I chose the communities because they are located in different provinces and have varying population sizes, geographies, and economies. Two of the communities were chosen based on my own personal connections to and prior knowledge of resettled refugees in those regions. The other two communities were asked to participate because of their location and the way in which the refugees living there had come to be sponsored in the community. While five of the six Syrian families I spoke with were resettled through the private refugee sponsorship program—the primary way in which refugees settle in rural Canada—one family arrived in Canada through government-assistance, then came to live in their rural community with support from a private sponsorship group.

I have assigned a letter to each community I visited, in the order in which I visited them:

- Community A is in southwestern Ontario. It has a population of 8,000 and is approximately 150 kilometres from the nearest metropolitan centre. One Syrian family was resettled into this community.
- Community B is a rural region in Nova Scotia where a coalition of individuals from two neighbouring communities had come together to sponsor three refugee families. Two of the Syrian families were resettled into a community of 3,000 people about 20 kilometres from the nearest urban centre. The other Syrian family was resettled in a neighbouring community of about 500 people that is 50 kilometres from the nearest metropolitan centre.
- Community C is in southern Alberta and has a population of 800 people. It is about 100 kilometres from the nearest urban centre. One intergenerational Syrian family was sponsored by members of this community.
- Community D is in central Saskatchewan. With a population of 6,000 people, this community is about 110 kilometres from the nearest metropolitan centre. One Syrian family lives here.

In total, I spoke formally with over 45 private refugee sponsors, community members, and service providers, and six Syrian refugee

families. I recorded a large portion of the interviews and also relied heavily on my interview notes, particularly for unrecorded interviews. When analyzing the data, I looked for key themes and findings across the interviews. While the private sponsors were my initial contacts in each community, I made further connections after I arrived through community service providers, other volunteers, and the refugees themselves, in an effort to speak with and hear from as many individuals as possible within the community.

Attending community events such as farmers' markets, church picnics, and refugee family gatherings, I spoke informally with many, many more individuals than I formally interviewed and had the opportunity in some places to speak with other immigrants and refugees in the region. It is important to note that I had an Arabic translator present for only one interview; all other interviews were conducted in English. While the refugees I spoke with had at least a working knowledge of English, this was a limiting factor of the project. The study was also limited by the fact that some refugees were hesitant to share critical reflections of their resettlement experience, since they still depended heavily on their sponsors in many aspects of their lives.

UNDERSTANDING HOSPITALITY AND THE HOST-GUEST RELATIONSHIP

When a private sponsorship group welcomes a refugee family, a relationship of hospitality is created between those who are displaced or exiled—the guests—and those who feel at home in their country and community—the host. While understandings of hospitality can differ between cultures, Avril Bell (2010, 240) found in her study of immigration that "in all cases hospitality encompasses a complex and power-laden set of relations between people and place. The act of welcome invokes a spatialized relationship between the host who is 'at home' and the guest/newcomer who arrives from elsewhere." As long as newcomers are seen as guests, they are understood as outsiders who have come "from away" and do not belong to the community. A power imbalance is created between the sponsors and those who are new to the community, culture, and, often, language. Thus, the host may find it difficult to establish an equal and reciprocal relationship with the guest, who is always at a disadvantage in the host's world.

Understandings of hospitality inform expectations of gratitude within this uneven relationship. In her consideration of feminist understandings of hospitality, Ileana Szymanski (2010, 123) argues that the guest–host relationship is often "coupled with the idea that exiles are guests that are handed something out and, consequently, they are expected to behave as polite guests; namely, to take what is given to them, be grateful, and leave promptly." The host is understood as having agency while the guest is entirely passive, thus leaving the guest at a great disadvantage. In the context of refugee resettlement, the refugee is constructed as the othered, passive, thankful guest in contrast to the citizen who is an active agent (Moulin 2012, 55). In this context, inclusion and belonging become conditional. The refugee is accepted as a guest and is expected to act as such (Bell 2010, 252).

Varying understandings of hospitality and assumptions and expectations of the other, the newcomer, can help describe the relationships between refugees and private sponsors in rural Canada. In the context of private refugee sponsorship, sponsors are at home in their communities: they have resources, knowledge, skills, and networks to rely on. Refugees are disadvantaged as they often lack the language skills to communicate, networks of family and friends to lean on, and knowledge of Canadian systems and norms. In her study of newcomers in a small community in New Brunswick, Stacey Wilson-Forsberg (2012, 114) found that because native residents are at home in their community, they have more control over intergroup relationships. The attitudes of residents towards newcomers thus play a key role in the outcomes of acculturation processes.

Further entrenching this power dynamic is the fact that private sponsors provide refugees with financial support for their first year in Canada and are the primary network that the refugees have to rely on in rural places. Seen as the guest, refugees are considered to be passive participants in the resettlement process—the ones receiving hospitality and in need of help. Receiving communities tend to regard immigrants as a population that needs to be helped by the local community and that has its needs met by government or community service providers (Wilson-Forsberg 2012, 67). In Canada, these conceptions of hospitality are constructed within international migration patterns and national

immigration policy. As an industrialized country, Canada benefits from migration by receiving highly trained professionals from other parts of the world. In this context, Wilson-Forsberg (2012, 149) argues that the "social worth of immigrants is largely evaluated on their ability to augment the country's productivity so that those already in the country can benefit from immigration. Accordingly, immigrants at the very least cannot be burdens to those already in the country." This results in a "needs-based analysis" of immigration in which Canadian citizens reach out to immigrants to help them adjust to a Canadian way of life. Within this narrative, Canadian citizens are constructed as the "White acceptors" at the centre of the nation who have the ability to "exercise tolerance" and "grant such inclusion" to "the other" (Bell 2010, 249).

These host-guest relationship dynamics were evident in the rural communities that I visited. Private sponsors were particularly aware of what they considered to be the broader community's assumptions of and biases toward refugee newcomers. All of the groups I spoke with assumed that their largely white, Christian communities held prejudicial, unwelcoming, or intolerant attitudes towards newcomers. Sponsorship groups largely understood their communities as being "more white and less tolerant" (O'Connell 2010, 537). Thus, before the refugees arrived, every group took steps to mitigate these attitudes, inform their communities about the newcomers, and get the community involved in the process through volunteer activities. Sponsorship groups held community meetings and fundraisers, made presentations to town council, and asked for donations and community volunteers. These activities encouraged the community to work together and those involved became invested in the success of the sponsorship.

While the efforts of the sponsorship groups largely resulted in positive reactions and increased involvement from the community, there were a few negative comments made by community members either over social media or in person to private sponsors. However, sponsors indicated that the communities were overwhelmingly supportive of their efforts. Overall, the groups were surprised that their communities were welcoming and everyone was excited to receive the newcomers when they arrived. One sponsor commented that "the community as a whole has been very accepting. Everybody wanted to be involved." Another

community member stated that the community was intentional about visiting the refugee family, stating that "there wasn't really a day they [the newcomers] didn't have people at their place." A refugee newcomer commented that "everybody in the community wants to help." Yet another rural resident stated that the "wider community as a whole is very accepting."

COMMUNITY EXPECTATIONS AND BIASES

While the sponsors worked hard to ensure that the community welcomed the newcomers, these efforts did not necessarily address the religious bias that existed in some form in each community. There was a common sentiment from some sponsors and community members that a Christian refugee family would "fit" into their community better than a Muslim family. In one community, in particular, the sentiment of wanting a Christian refugee family was a divisive point between two local churches that had partnered to undertake the sponsorship. One church was adamant that a Muslim family would not fit into the small community, while the other was not partial to a Christian or Muslim family. A Christian leader in the community played a strong role in advocating for and ensuring a Christian refugee family was sponsored. When I spoke with this particular individual, they commented that they had "pushed" the congregation to sponsor a refugee family that the community "had the most in common with," meaning a Christian family. They stated that they "thought settlement would go better that way, and maybe they [the newcomers] would stay in the community longer." A sponsor in the community made comments to the same effect, stating that they "wanted to sponsor a Christian family for their ease of integration in a very Christian community."

Churches are one of the main social institutions in rural places. While they did not play a prominent role in every sponsorship case in this study, they did play a role in most, and a significant role at that. In each community, at least a few sponsorship members were affiliated with Christian community churches. Church spaces were often used to hold events and meetings, and Christian churches, as well as local Muslim associations or mosques if present in the community, participated in fundraising and volunteering activities.

The particular ways in which community churches were involved in private sponsorship differed by community. In one community, a Christian church welcomed a Muslim refugee family to use their space for catering activities. In another community, a local pastor was part of a secular sponsorship group supporting a Muslim family. Local churches hold diverse attitudes regarding newcomers and while individuals in one church may be adamant that only a Christian family will "fit" into their community, individuals in another may welcome and support a Muslim family. Religious biases can also exist outside of the church and it is not possible to categorize every religious institution as either welcoming or unwelcoming to outsiders or other religious beliefs. Churches, as both social and religious institutions in rural places, can play a diverse and important role in fostering welcoming attitudes within their communities.

While private sponsors as a whole were prepared to encounter and address prejudicial or unwelcoming attitudes within their communities, they were largely unprepared to deal with expectations and assumptions of how a refugee should look, act, and express gratitude. There was an overall expectation across the participating communities that refugees should be poverty stricken, have little money, and lack agency. Once the refugees arrived in Canada, many community members and sponsors expressed concern that the newcomers were not the poorest of the poor. Private sponsors articulated that the refugees they sponsored were not "the most in need." For one sponsor, the fact that the family they sponsored had an apartment, access to international relief funds, and some form of employment and housing in Lebanon meant that "this was not a family that was actually most in need."

The expectation was that a "true" refugee family would come to Canada from a refugee camp with little to no money or resources. Another sponsorship group indicated that many volunteers expected the refugee family to look and behave "more in need" than they did. There was tension among members of another group about finding a family in the direst of situations, implying that some refugee situations were not dire enough. These feelings existed even though the refugees had qualified for resettlement under the UNHCR's standards, were legally admitted into Canada, and were granted permanent residency (Government of Canada 2019a; Government of Canada 2019b).

Mass media images and media representations of refugee resettlement influence the public's understandings of refugee newcomers. Wilson-Forsberg (2012, 67) suggests that cultural stereotypes and media images inform understandings of refugees and immigrants, and specifically contribute to expectations that they are in need of help in all aspects of their lives and that they are incapable of making any decision for themselves. Tyyska et al. (2018, 162) further contend that media outlets in Canada "continue to depict refugees along an inaccurate and misleading continuum between being needy and lacking agency, and as a possible threat." While it is unclear how each sponsor or community member constructed their understanding of what it means to be a refugee, my findings indicate that media images of the Syrian crisis played a large role in understandings of the war and the community's desire to sponsor. When asked why they decided to become private sponsors, everyone I spoke with mentioned the photo of Alan Kurdi as a catalyst for their decision.[2] One sponsor stated that "the images of the little boy on the beach started coming through the media and I know I was really moved and just appalled that that could happen to people and I think other people in this community were the same way." Thus, private sponsors and community members were forming images and assumptions of how the refugees would look and act before they even considered getting involved in private sponsorship.

The results of these expectations were two-fold. When refugees did not live up to expectations, and volunteers were not willing to change their understanding of who a refugee should be, expectations caused a rift between sponsors and community members and refugees. When refugees are understood as extremely poor, disadvantaged, and coming from refugee camps, the Canadian public assumes that they should be grateful for everything they are given, including the "gift" of being in Canada. The unsaid assumption is that refuge is not a human right but something that is awarded to a lucky few. Thus, newcomers must prove that they are worthy of accepting this gift through expressions of gratitude and hard work.

In one community in this study, some sponsor group members were unwilling to change their expectations and assumptions. These individuals clashed with other sponsors, community members, and the refugee

family over several issues, including employment opportunities. One sponsor from this group explained the situation stating, "Early on, our group was really hopeful that they [the refugee family] would be able to be supporting themselves by the end of the year...I don't know if our group would have taken a refugee family if we felt like at the end it was going to be a situation where they were having to live on unemployment insurance. I think that we really had hopes that they would come and we would be able to help them integrate well and they would be functioning in society like all of us are." For these sponsors, belonging and acceptance were tied to the contribution that the newcomers could make to their community.

Another sponsor from the same group recognized that unmet expectations had contributed to disagreements with the refugee family, stating, "We just thought that we were bringing a [refugee] family that was in need, that has seen the worst in life, they lost their house, they live in a camp, they don't have money, so, as a human being, for me, I thought that coming into a different country and basically having a house, having furniture, having clothing...I would expect them to say 'thank you'... What we saw from this family was 'give us more', 'this is not enough'—and that's where a lot of our frustrations came from." In these instances, the sponsors' desire for gratitude was inflated and requests from the refugees were seen as extravagant or over the top.

However, in other instances, sponsors were able to acknowledge, modify, and move past their expectations to accept the refugees and work with them based on their humanity. For example, one sponsor indicated that "no matter what, they are better off in their situation here than they would have been in Lebanon." Another indicated that "I've changed my expectations." One sponsor was very aware of unrealistic expectations, saying, "If you have expectations of any kind, you are only going to guess wrong and set yourself up for disaster at the worst and, at the least, disappointment." It is, however, important to recognize the context in which expectations are created. The last quote was provided by a sponsor who was involved in the intentional sponsorship of a Christian refugee family who had been identified for resettlement by a Christian organization. Thus, while this participant recognized the fallibility of expectations, they also already knew what to expect regarding the refugee family's religious beliefs and some of their cultural practices.

Sponsors who were mindful of the impacts of false assumptions expressed frustration with other sponsors or community members who wanted refugees to conform to both their expectations and, at the same time, act "exactly like Canadians." One sponsor expanded on the challenges associated with the expectations of their community, saying:

> People expect refugees that are extremely down trodden, extremely poor…and want to help those people who are in the worst situations, but then the reality when they arrive, if they are in very bad shape and need a lot then they are very demanding, they need a lot, they need a lot of help, medical issues, dental issues, driving, so it's this very fine line that refugee families have to walk. They can't be too demanding because then people will be frustrated with them, but they can't be too self-sufficient because then people will be like…maybe they didn't need our help after all…They have to thread that needle just right to meet the expectations of the community.

In most instances, sponsors recognized that they had agreed to provide services and supports to the refugees when they undertook the sponsorship, regardless of their assumptions or expectations of gratitude.

WHERE DO WE GO FROM HERE?

While many rural residents and sponsors are actively working to create welcoming communities for newcomers, integration and inclusion involves more than acts of hospitality or attitudes of tolerance. Newcomers must be encouraged to find their own identity and sense of belonging within the community—one that is not based solely on what the newcomer can do for or add to the community. Wilson-Forsberg (2012, 138) argues that "with any luck, this needs-based perspective will evolve into a more progressive community model, which recognizes the newcomers as full citizens, accords them respect, and welcomes them as valued and equal partners in the progressive development of the communities." While welcoming and hospitality can begin the process of inclusion, a more equal relationship must be developed.

Marguerite La Caze (2013, 133), in her writing on hospitality and refugee resettlement, contends that "hospitality accounts for our initial response to asylum seekers and refugees, but does not articulate the terms of a continuing interaction, where people may stay for many years and eventually become citizens in the new community." The integration process cannot be unidirectional. Private sponsors and host communities must enter into the process as participants, not just facilitators. While power imbalances are inherent to any system of resettlement, inequalities can be addressed if those involved work towards more reciprocal acts of hospitality in ways that align more concretely with the idea of becoming "good neighbours," as discussed by both Henderson and Epp in this volume. A theologian and ethics scholar, Thomas Ogletree (1985, 4), states that "the equality of host and stranger finally shows itself in reciprocal acts of hospitality that reflect reversals in the relational order. My readiness to welcome the other into my world must be balanced by my readiness to enter the world of the other." Within a relational understanding of hospitality and integration, tolerance is not enough. Only when a community is able to garner mutual respect for the refugees they are sponsoring can the barriers of paternalistic attitudes, false assumptions, and judgment be shifted. One sponsor recognized this, stating, "It's all about relationship, relationship, relationship, and it's not about teaching and telling."

In rural communities where informal relations are vital to integration, inclusion, and service provision, welcoming refugees as active agents and as equal community members is crucial. Addressing false and harmful assumptions and expectations is important for dispelling myths of immigrant and refugee populations among Canadian sponsors and community members, ensuring that newcomers can retain their own identity while also feeling a sense of belonging within their new community. Rural communities in particular do not often have formal resources or government services to lean on and must recognize the impacts that the opinions and attitudes of community members and volunteers have on newcomers.

Placing all of the responsibility on the newcomer to change their behaviours and assimilate into the community not only harms the newcomer, but also prevents growth and positive change from taking

place within the broader community. A community's ability to adapt and change is crucial for the survival of rural and smaller places where depopulation and out-migration are very real challenges (Bollman, this volume; Pohler et al., this volume). Rural communities need newcomers to address diminishing populations and services. Rural communities that bring in newcomers through private sponsorship or other means need to make themselves aware of the biases, assumptions, and expectations present in their communities and of the work that will be needed to fully accept newcomers as equal members of the community. This is important both for immigrants and refugees who will be entering the communities in the future, and for those already present.

In this context, where do rural communities begin to address community and individual expectations and assumptions? In many cases, the individuals I spoke with said that more information and clarity surrounding the resettlement process would have helped sponsorship groups and refugees manage and address many unmet expectations. For example, the refugees I spoke with also had expectations and assumptions of the resettlement and sponsorship process. Prior to their arrival in Canada, refugees had little or no understanding of the communities or areas in which they would be resettled. After they arrived in Canada, they communicated with other refugees and shared their experiences. The expectations that arose from exchanged information between refugees frustrated some sponsors. Prior to the arrival of the refugees, it would have been useful if sponsors understood that often, refugees receive little background information regarding their resettlement, do not know what to expect, and thus lean on the experiences of other refugees and immigrants to fill in the blanks.

Many refugees were also confused about what the sponsorship group was responsible for and who exactly they were. In retrospect, groups said that it would have been very helpful for everyone involved if the sponsors had explained, at the very beginning and in detail, the role of the sponsorship group in the process—in particular, that they were private citizens and not government officials—at the very beginning. Of course, prior experience with sponsorship or resettlement can also be helpful. While individual sponsors or community members may have been involved in refugee sponsorship before in some capacity, all of the groups I spoke with

were new to the sponsorship process. Moreover, the refugee families they sponsored were the only refugees who had been resettled in each community that year.

Two of the groups in this study went on to sponsor another refugee family. Both of these groups mentioned to me some of the changes they were making based on their previous experience. For example, one group said that they were being very intentional about involving community members with a wide range of perspectives, skills, and professions in the second sponsorship in an effort to create a broader network for the refugees to access and to provide a diverse set of viewpoints and opinions to the group. As one sponsor put it regarding this decision, one must "use the resources of the people that you have." Doing so strengthens attempts to cultivate equal relationships, address community assumptions and expectations, and address misunderstandings when they arise from the start of the sponsorship. While formal programs and community networks can develop specific skills, building a mutual relationship based on acceptance and understanding are crucial for refugees to find a sense of belonging, which is different from tolerance or inclusion. Wilson-Forsberg (2012, 159) expands on this, stating that "formal programs play a critical role in the adaptation and integration of immigrant adolescents in the receiving community, but it is informal relations that really count when one is searching for a sense of belonging and that feeling of being at home. What is required are the forms of social organization that make these informal relations flourish."

The assumptions and expectations of both private sponsors and other community members in rural Canadian communities impacted the resettlement of refugees in these places. How sponsors responded when their assumptions or expectations were challenged by the refugee newcomers speaks to the guest-host relationship and the power embedded within this process. Some sponsors were able to critically reflect on their own opinions and beliefs in ways that ultimately allowed them to accept the refugees as they are, on the basis of their humanity, and build mutual relationships with them as neighbours (see also Henderson, this volume; Epp, this volume).

Other sponsors' expectations of what refugees should look like and how they should express gratitude led to conflict and tension with the

refugee families they were sponsoring. While these tensions did lead to some issues and points of conflict between the sponsors and refugees I spoke with, and in one case the dissolution of a sponsorship group, these frictions did not necessarily result in the refugee families leaving the communities. In one case in which the refugees' relationship with the private sponsors became strained, other community members stepped in to help support the refugees. This refugee family ultimately decided to settle permanently in the small community because they liked the smaller centre, they had made friends and created a support network, and they were able to buy a home. This finding speaks to the agency of refugees, the integral role of community supports, and the complex nature of resettlement and integration. There is nothing simple about these processes or a refugee's decision to stay.

Some issues and tensions were also tied to rural sponsors not knowing what to expect when they started the private sponsorship project—something I heard from many of them. This common comment speaks to both a lack of supports given to private sponsors in general and a lack of specific knowledge regarding rural resettlement and integration. Because they are absent from much of the scholarship and government narrative on immigration and resettlement, rural places often feel as though no one sees or recognizes the work that they are doing to improve their communities and address barriers and challenges. This dearth of information also contributes to rural places often being unaware of the work being done in other smaller communities to welcome and integrate newcomers. Further considering how expectations influence the sponsor and refugee relationship can help explain why some sponsorship groups break down and others go on to sponsor more refugees, as well as how rural communities can better address commonly held assumptions in order to more intentionally build welcoming and inclusive attitudes among residents.

More broadly, understanding how the Canadian government portrays refugees and how Canadians expect refugees to look and act is vital to understanding the interactions between Canadian residents and refugees and the processes of integrating and welcoming newcomers into Canadian society. Understanding how the expectations and assumptions of rural sponsors and community members influence their interactions

with refugees is particularly important as both federal and provincial governments look to direct immigrants and refugees to rural communities in an attempt to revitalize these places (Government of Canada 2021b). In the global context, as the number of refugees continues to rise, considering rural resettlement as a durable solution to displacement is one way to address Canada's resettlement responsibilities. If newcomers are to be welcomed and accepted into rural places as equal members of the community—as new neighbours instead of only guests—we must recognize the work that rural residents and sponsors are already doing, but we must also find ways to go beyond simply promoting tolerance. We must, that is, begin addressing the assumptions, expectations, and biases among Canadians that can limit inclusion, prevent belonging, and threaten deep equality.

NOTES

1. Uncited quotations in this chapter come from transcripts of interviews I conducted with rural residents and refugees in the four study communities (see Methods section, this chapter) in May and June 2017.
2. The photo in question was taken by Turkish photojournalist Nilüfer Demir in September 2015. For more information on the impact of the Alan Kurdi photo in Canada, see Kurdi (2018).

REFERENCES

Beaman, Lori. 2017. *Deep Equality in an Era of Religious Diversity*. Oxford: Oxford University Press.

Bell, Avril. 2010. "Being 'At Home' in the Nation: Hospitality and Sovereignty in Talk about Immigration." *Ethnicities* 10 (2): 236–56.

Besser, Terry, and Nancy Miller. 2015. "Latino/a Immigration, Social Capital, and Business Civic Engagement in Rural Prairie Towns." In *Social Capital at the Community Level: An Applied Interdisciplinary Perspective*, edited by Steven C. Deller and John M. Halstead, 174–89. New York: Routledge.

FCM (Federation of Canadian Municipalities). 2011. *Starting on Solid Ground: The Municipal Role in Immigrant Settlement*. Ottawa: Federation of Canadian Municipalities. http://boards.amssa.org/research/members/viewPost/post_id:10258.

Flora, Cornelia Butler, and Jan L. Flora. 2013. *Rural Communities: Legacy and Change*. Boulder, CO: Westview Press.

Gadsby, Leona, and Ron Samson; Essential Skills Ontario. 2016. *Strengthening Rural Canada: Why Place Matters in Rural Communities*. Report prepared for Strengthening Rural Canada Initiative. Vancouver: Decoda Literacy Solutions; Ottawa: Essential Skills Ontario. http://www.decoda.ca/wp-content/uploads/Strengthening-Rural-Canada_Final.pdf.

Government of Canada. 2018. "Syrian Refugees Family Composition—Ad Hoc IRCC (Specialized Datasets)." Last updated October 10, 2018. https://open.canada.ca/data/en/dataset/ca243c40-a6d3-4a46-a578-b4fad4369df0.

Government of Canada. 2019a. "How Canada's Refugee System Works." Last updated November 27, 2019. https://www.canada.ca/en/immigration-refugees-citizenship/services/refugees/canada-role.html.

Government of Canada. 2019b. "Understand Permanent Resident Status." Last updated November 11, 2019. https://www.canada.ca/en/immigration-refugees-citizenship/services/new-immigrants/pr-card/understand-pr-status.html.

Government of Canada. 2021a. "#WelcomeRefugees: Key Figures." Government of Canada. Last updated January 11, 2021. http://www.cic.gc.ca/english/refugees/welcome/milestones.asp.

Government of Canada. 2021b. "Rural and Northern Immigration Pilot: About the Pilot." Last updated March 2, 2021. https://www.canada.ca/en/immigration-refugees-citizenship/services/immigrate-canada/rural-northern-immigration-pilot.html.

Government of Canada. 2022. "Find Help to Adjust Refugees." Last update February 28, 2022. https://www.canada.ca/en/immigration-refugees-citizenship/services/refugees/help-within-canada/government-assisted-refugee-program/providers.html.

Haugen, Stacey. 2019. "'We Feel Like We're Home': The Resettlement and Integration of Syrian Refugees in Smaller and Rural Canadian Communities." *Refuge: Canada's Journal on Refugees* 35 (2): 53–63.

Kurdi, Tima. 2018. "Boy on the Beach: How Alan Kurdi's Family Are Turning Their Grief into a Fight to Help Refugees." Interview with Laura Lynch, *The Current*, CBC, April 17, 2018. https://www.cbc.ca/radio/thecurrent/the-current-for-april-17-2018-1.4622103/april-17-2018-full-episode-transcript-1.4623819.

La Caze, Marguerite. 2013. *Wonder & Generosity: Their Role in Ethics and Politics*. Albany: SUNY Press.

Labman, Shauna. 2016. "Private Sponsorship: Complementary or Conflicting Interests?" *Refuge: Canada's Journal on Refugees* 32 (2): 67–80.

McDonald, Joanne. 2016. "Syrian Family Finds a Home with St. Helen Parish." *Niagra This Week*, May 6, 2016. http://www.niagarathisweek.com/news-story/6531244-syrian-family-finds-a-home-with-st-helen-parish/.

McMorrow, Joseph, and Catherine Caufield. 2016. "Canada's Small Towns Can Make Refugees Feel at Home." *Edmonton Journal*, April 7, 2016. https://edmontonjournal.com/opinion/columnists/joe-mcmorrow-and-catherine-caufield-canadas-small-towns-can-make-refugees-feel-at-home.

Moazzami, Bakhtiar. 2015. *Strengthening Rural Canada: Fewer & Older: Population and Demographic Challenges Across Rural Canada: A Pan-Canadian Report*. Prepared for Strengthening Rural Canada Initiative. Vancouver: Decoda Literacy Solutions; Ottawa: Essential Skills Ontario; Regina: Saskatchewan Literacy Network; St. John's: Literacy Newfoundland and Labrador; Québec: RESDAC.

Moulin, Carolina. 2012. "Ungrateful Subjects? Refugee Protests and the Logic of Gratitude." In *Citizenship, Migrant Activism and the Politics of Movement*, edited by Peter Nyers and Kim Rygiel, 54–72. New York: Routledge.

Moulton, Carlyn. 2015. "Canada's Small Communities Can Be Ideal for Syrian Refugees, Says Rural Sponsor." Interview with Carol Off, *As It Happens*, CBC, December 2, 2015. http://www.cbc.ca/radio/asithappens/as-it-happens-tuesday-edition-1.3345339/canada-s-small-communities-can-be-ideal-for-syrian-refugees-says-rural-sponsor-1.3347410.

O'Connell, Anne. 2010. "An Exploration of Redneck Whiteness in Multicultural Canada." *Social Politics: International Studies in Gender, State & Society* 17 (4): 536–63.

Ogletree, Thomas. 1985. *Hospitality to the Stranger: Dimensions of Moral Understanding*. Philadelphia: Fortress Press.

Presse, Michelle. 2016. "Nightime Walks and Other Pleasures: Syrian Refugees Learn to Love Smalltown Canada." *Globe and Mail*, May 10, 2016. http://www.theglobeandmail.com/news/national/nightime-walks-and-other-pleasures-syrian-refugees-learn-to-love-smalltown-canada/article29956968/.

RDI (Rural Development Institute). 2016. *Community Report: Immigration in 5 Rural Manitoba Communities With a Focus on Refugees: Case Studies*. Brandon, MB: Brandon University. https://www.brandonu.ca/rdi/files/2016/09/Immigration-in-5-Rural-Manitoba-Communities-with-a-Focus-on-Refugees-Case-Studies-August-2016.pdf.

Szymanski, Ileana. 2010. "Feminism, Hospitality, and Women in Exile." In *Feminism and Hospitality: Gender in the Host/Guest Relationship*, edited by Maurice Hamington, 125–62. Toronto: Rowman & Littlefield Publishers, Inc.

Taylor-Vaisey, Nick, and Amanda Shendruk. 2016. "True North Refugees: Where 25,000 Syrians Have Settled in Canada," *Macleans*. March 2, 2016. http://www.macleans.ca/news/canada/true-north-refugees-where-25000-syrians-have-settled-in-canada.

Tyyska, Vappu, Jenna Blower, Samantha Deboer, Shunya Kawai, and Ashley Walcott. 2018. "Canadian Media Coverage of the Syrian Refugee Crisis: Representation, Response, and Resettlement." Geopolitics, History and International Relations 10 (1): 148–66.

Wilson-Forsberg, Stacey. 2012. *Getting Used to the Quiet: Immigrant Adolescents' Journey to Belonging in New Brunswick, Canada*. Montréal: McGill-Queen's University Press.

Yoshida, Yoko, and Howard Ramos. 2013. "Destination Rural Canada: An Overview of Recent Immigrants to Rural Small Towns." In Social Transformation in Rural Canada, edited by John Parkins and Maureen Reed, 67–90. Vancouver: UBC Press.

III

PRACTICAL TOOLS FOR BUILDING INCLUSIVE RURAL COMMUNITIES

A NOISY SILENCE

Challenges for Rural Teacher Education

Michael Corbett, Jennifer Tinkham, and Claudine Bonner

ACROSS CANADA, teacher education has instituted sociologically informed equity and inclusion courses as core features of the preparation of professional teachers. This chapter explores key tensions identified by the authors to query and analyze the particular challenges of current programming relating to race and racialization in the context of rural communities. In this writing, we explore the tensions between rural community sensibilities, the intersection of popular local settler histories and critical historical narratives, and the difficulty of finding a voice that many university-age, rural youth exhibit in challenging conversations about race, racialization and equity.

Our point of entry into this conversation about rural teaching is the persistent challenges we have faced working with undergraduates, most of whom are learning to be professional teachers, as they enact what Tuck and Yang (2012) call "moves to innocence." We find that rural undergraduates often tend to imagine their communities and their lives as largely disconnected from the issues of racialization, which they imagine to be either the misguided bigotry of marginal individuals who operate outside the mainstream of polite community opinion in their home places and/or things that happen in distant times (i.e., the historical past) and places (e.g., in the United States or in large cities) from which they are removed.

Discussions of the structural nature of racism and social inequality are subsequently framed in a psychological register that blames aberrant individuals, ignoring the need for both taking personal responsibility and understanding how racism is systemic.

Complicating common psychologized understandings of racism requires an engagement in a different kind of conversation—one that requires both "breaking the silence" on racism and developing insights into how ordinary social institutions such as schools and workplaces unintentionally reproduce that silence, often through practices considered to represent progressive whiteness (Han and Laughter 2019; Matias 2016). We conclude by cautioning against blaming rural preservice teachers for what they do not know, and recommending increased attention to the social sciences and humanities in teacher education.

METHOD

Educators often sit together over a meal. The conversation often turns at some point to classroom practice. While for many this is simply "shop talk," it is also a way of working through our teaching practices, problems we encounter, and our frustrations and challenges with colleagues who are understanding yet constructively critical. The process of seeking to improve our practice is, at its heart, self-study research (Lassonde, Galman, and Kosnik 2009; Mitchell, O'Reilly-Scanlon, and Weber 2005). This method seeks to "understand the relationship between the knower and the known" and to "understand what is the form and nature of reality" (Kuzmik and Bloom 2008, 207). According to Brown (2004, 520), "self-study is uniquely suited to contribute to an understanding of race and social class issues in education." In coming together to think critically about issues of equity and social justice and what they mean to us as educators, we created a space of critical collaborative inquiry geared toward improving our own understandings of our practice and our thinking about teaching and learning in a rurally located Canadian university.

We—Michael, Jennifer, and Claudine—work at a small, primarily undergraduate university in eastern Canada, where we are responsible for teaching sociologically informed material to undergraduates who come from predominantly white rural and small-town places. Demographically, Nova Scotia is, by one Statistics Canada definition,

approximately 40% rural (Statistics Canada 2022). This, however, tells us little about the nature of rural social space, which, as Reid and colleagues (2010) argue, combines people, place, and production. The mythology of Nova Scotia as a rural, anti-modern space apart has a long and resonant history, dating back at least a century and promoted by cultural intellectuals and conservative political forces alike (McKay 1994; McKay and Bates 2010). This mythos contains a subregional typology of European descent that defines the rural areas of the province as exclusive, Anglo-European spaces in which the erasure of diversity and racism are deeply engrained cultural tropes.[1] Today, this mythos takes both the mundane shape of the resentment embedded in rural coffee shop conversations, such as those documented by Cramer (2016) and Banack (this volume), and the racialized violence illustrated by confrontations, fishing gear destruction, and the late-2020 burning of a lobster plant in southwest Nova Scotia in the wake of the opening of an Indigenous fishery.

Michael and Jennifer work with preservice teachers, while Claudine teaches postsecondary students in the Department of Sociology. What brought us together is a common "stone in the shoe" (Neilsen 1994): the "noisy silence," as we have coined it, that arises in our classes when issues of race are taken up. We sometimes deal with preservice teachers who reject sociological analysis as a set of excuses and diversions, and who occasionally accuse us of racism for mentioning race at all. But we feel it more deeply in our students' silences—particularly, their reticence to engage in discussions of economic, gender, and racial inequality beyond gestural expressions of pity or regret that "this kind of thing still happens" out there somewhere.

We feel and experience what has been called the "right shift" in our teaching context. Thus, our dialogue began with the political context; with the ways we did or did not see the extreme views of the alt-right manifested in the language and actions of preservice teachers in our classrooms. As we talked, we acknowledged continuing concerns related to the ability of the formal education system to address the changing factors of race, gender, age, language, and culture within the constraints of the modern bureaucratic schooling structures as we know them (Howard 2016; Ryan 1999). Take, as one glaring example, the ways in which schools are failing Black youth. The reality is that the processes

of education continue to provide unequal opportunities and create negative outcomes, especially for racialized and Indigenous students and students from low socioeconomic family backgrounds (Butler 2019; Dei and Karumanchery 1999). Why and how this is happening, and what should be done to address it, are issues of ongoing debate (Dei et al. 1997; Solomon 1992; Dei 2008).

Canadian provincial governments have made attempts to address some of these issues by developing more inclusive curricula, addressing teacher training issues, promoting culturally responsive pedagogies, and putting forward policy initiatives geared toward meeting social justice concerns. Yet at the same time, Stephen Harper's ignominious words about "committing sociology" return to us as our students steer away from social analysis and toward comfortably applying dispositional, attitudinal, meritocratic analysis to explain school success and failure.[2] Applying a self-study methodology to our own practices provides insight into how we might reflectively adjust our own approaches to better understand the dynamics of race in the particular rural context in which we work. We fully understand that our account is incomplete and ultimately subjective, but we hope it is a story that will raise useful questions about noisy silences. We also recognize the complexity surrounding issues of race in rural contexts, including the default assumption that rural people hold less inclusive social and political views (Banack and Pohler, introduction to this volume). This type of discourse has consequences for our rural students who are navigating complex, intersectional identity questions, some of which frame their families and communities in deficit terms, and many of which they are encountering for the first time. It is vital that rural preservice teachers engage in conversations about race, equity, and inclusion, both in their education and ultimately in their own classrooms, with their own students. As we suggest below, however, navigating these questions requires many rural students to not only learn a whole new system of etiquette and propriety, but a new vocabulary. From a learning perspective, we believe that it is crucial to create spaces in which rural students can understand themselves in academic discourses not as inherently less accepting than their urban peers, but as human beings capable of learning, changing, and being accountable to their social responsibilities.

Our self-study method in this chapter involves moving between and among three paths of inquiry: analysis of relevant literature, research engagements with colleagues and students, and three-way dialogues with one another. We use these paths as methodological tools to explore our beliefs and experiences in the classroom. Our methods in this chapter are inspired by an insightful piece by Joanne Tomkins (2002), who used a self-study methodology to probe her own learning and unlearning. Tomkins's work unsettles foundational assumptions about place, power, history, and identity by exploring how rural Nova Scotia came to be the kind of place it is today.[3] Tomkins interrogated her own perceptions as well as those of her students with the goal of better understanding how settler privilege infuses the way her predominantly rural, white, Nova Scotian students understood not just race, but also education and teaching. We are attempting something similar here.

RURAL TEACHER EDUCATION: IGNORANCE AS INNOCENCE

It is now widely accepted that teacher education needs to engage lived experience of racial and ethnic identities, but research shows that it does not. As a result, many teachers enter professional practice without diversity experience. According to Peck (2010, 576), "the development of ethnic identity is both a personal and social process, which occurs through inter- and intra-group boundary formation." Peck (2011, 308) also argued that ethnic identity "may change depending on the social, political, and/or cultural context in which one finds oneself." We, too, argue that there can be no unified ethnic identity among diverse groups because all aspects of identity are situation dependent. Contemporary literature has also established that students' ethnic backgrounds can influence their learning (Abu-Laban and Stasiulus 2000; Barton and Levstik 2004; Barton and McCully 2004; Epstein 1998, 2000; Hall 2003; Peck 2010, 2011).

Santoro (2009) notes that when preservice teachers lack knowledge about their students' cultures and identities, they struggle to engage them and find it difficult to design lessons that are accessible and relevant to diverse backgrounds. This negatively impacts their abilities to integrate relevant and accessible teachings and materials. Knowing what and how to teach in diverse classrooms depends on teachers' understandings of

their students' learning needs and of blind spots in the curriculum they were taught to use. It also depends on whether teachers are self-reflective as to how their own knowledge, biases, and privileges influence their teaching practices (Corbett 2010; Egbo 2011; Kanu 2005; Ragoonaden, Sivia, and Baxan 2015; Santoro 2009). According to Egbo (2011), critical self-reflection and examination can enable teachers to understand the different variables that affect how students learn and succeed both in and out of the classroom.

Tinkham, Martineau, and Bonner discovered preservice teacher resistance to incorporating Indigenous perspectives into the curriculum.[4] They categorize this resistance into three themes: (1) "not my culture"; (2) "difficult history"; and (3) "colonial ideological ascription." The first theme focuses on concerns about appropriation and resistance to making mistakes. It highlights the teacher's own perceived lack of knowledge. The second theme is focused on the teacher's personal reactions to content or experiences. These can include but are not limited to disbelief, shame, guilt, and anger. Within this theme, there is often an identified fear of recreating trauma. The third theme is focused on the teacher seeking to resist critical examinations of colonization and desiring to maintain the status quo. In this study, the first and second themes were common, albeit weakly articulated, among preservice teachers. The third theme was expressed by only one participant. In all cases, these themes categorized instances in which preservice teachers avoided issues of race rather than theorizing and engaging them.

Teaching Indigeneity

One Nova Scotia study conducted by Jennifer Tinkham looks at the degree to which rural preservice teachers felt prepared to infuse Indigenous education into their classrooms.[5] A rural preservice teacher interviewed by Tinkham believes that "it will be challenging to teach from an Indigenous perspective considering I am not Indigenous myself... Regardless how much we read and research, as a non-Indigenous citizen, student and educator, I feel I will never truly understand what it means to be Indigenous." She worries that her intent will be called into question, but she is mostly concerned with teaching in a way that does not harm her students and/or their families:

As a teacher, I do not want to ever say anything or start a discussion about anything that may spark a negative memory or story any of my students may have heard or been told. I think it is very important as a teacher to realize that some of our students' parents or grandparents may have attended residential schools and may not want to have them discussed in our classrooms.

Another of Tinkham's interviewees gestures to his rural heritage as he highlights his hesitancy around tackling Indigenous issues in the classroom. This research participant believes he is powerless to make any change, commenting: "I used to think that I wasn't a part of the colonial oppression of Aboriginal Persons in Canada but lately it seems that Canadians of all backgrounds are being told that they have failed Aboriginal People." He continues:

I cannot properly teach Aboriginal perspectives because I am not Aboriginal. Having someone teach about someone else's history takes away from the positive impact it can have on the students learning experience...Students in a rural school growing up not being around Aboriginal students and communities might find it hard to relate to the Aboriginal perspectives being taught in class. This was certainly my experience; it wasn't until I got to grade ten that I was exposed to self-identifying [Mi'kmaw] students.

A third preservice teacher in Tinkham's study identifies a modified "not in my backyard" notion, which seems to suggest that if there is no diversity in the immediate surroundings, there isn't much point in teaching about it. He then employs a strategy that we call an "innocence of ignorance." According to this logic, because he does not have deep experiential knowledge of Indigenous issues and can claim no experience with racism, he can be excused from having to deal with the subject matter as a teacher. This preservice teacher goes on to acknowledge problems and express sympathy while simultaneously absolving himself of responsibility as an ordinary, allegedly powerless bystander:

> If I look at myself honestly, I can say that while I am very sympathetic to the issues of Aboriginal people, especially what students face with the current education structure, I haven't really done much other than to say I think the current model is not working. This is not so different from what the vast majority of Canadians do today...There is only one group that has the power to enact the changes needed, that's the federal government.

While he does express sympathy for the educational experiences of Indigenous students, that sympathy is caught up in an unresponsive politics of incapacity. Battiste (2004, 10) refers to this as cognitive imperialism: "a form of cognitive manipulation used to disclaim other knowledge bases and values." She argues that "Eurocentric humanity has proved to be not about being a universal human and whole, healed and empowered, but is still located in social constructions of superiority and dominance" (10). For Battiste, cognitive imperialism is an exclusionary vehicle for denying existence, culture, and identity, which ultimately "maintains legitimacy of only one language, one culture, and one frame of reference" (10). She emphasizes that "curriculum does not address poverty, nor oppression amongst the Aboriginal people that has resulted from colonialism. The images and stories told in the public system portray the government, settlers, and their policies that nearly eradicated the Aboriginal culture, language and way of life in a manner that paints the colonists in a positive light" (6; see also Battiste 1998).

Battiste points to the need to critically examine how Indigenous people and groups are being portrayed in curriculum and what messages are being delivered through the subject matter. A key feature of the innocence of ignorance is the sense that conversations about race are sensitive, difficult, and potentially solvable by some powerful others. This is a failure to take responsibility nested in an equally ineffective and ultimately conservative retreat into guilt, innocence, or, indeed, both.

Indigeneity in/and Rural Nova Scotia
From the rural Nova Scotian university within the ancestral and unceded territory of Mi'kma'ki, Tomkins (2002) offered a carefully constructed critical analysis of her practice as a teacher educator working to help

students understand how their own privilege inflects the way they imagine their work. Tomkins brings together the problems of educating teachers in rural Atlantic Canada and the way that a genuine commitment to Indigenous education, equity, and inclusion can be understood more broadly. This work situates Atlantic Canadian teacher education in a larger discussion about the complex intersection of rurality and Indigeneity that has received attention in the academic literatures on teacher education, place-conscious education, environmental education, place and space in education, and Indigenous education.

In terms of Indigenous education in teacher education, reconciliation has two aspects. The first is to educate Indigenous students about who they are and why this matters; the second is to educate Canadians about Indigenous histories and experiences (Truth and Reconciliation Commission 2015). Tinkham (2013) calls this "cultural responsibility" and contends that teacher education programs focus not on teaching Indigenous culture but rather on teaching Canadian students how to work with Indigenous students and content. Teacher education should focus on helping preservice teachers facilitate this learning in their own classrooms, helping them set their practice within a decolonizing framework. In other words, reconciliation is not Indigenous work, but Canadian work (Palmer and Popcock 2020).

Following Tomkins's (2002) analysis and drawing on critical Indigenous education scholarship, others have argued that teacher education reinforces settler identities rather than disrupting them, pointing, at least gesturally, to rurality (Aitkin and Radford 2018; Schick 2014; Tinkham 2017; Tupper 2011). Our analysis above of the comments made by the third preservice teacher in Tinkham's Nova Scotia study point to one element of how race is understood and framed by many rural preservice teachers.[6] In that preservice teacher's words, we find a sensibility that resonates with Sarah Neal's (2012) concept of the "rurally included": a process that naturalizes conceptions of who does belong in rural places—specifically, multigenerational white families—and who does not. The idea is that everyone is ostensibly welcome in many rural places so long as they are "known," or part of the "rurally included." This level of analysis of exclusive forms of "rural inclusion" is not well developed in the rural education literature beyond Tomkins's

productive start all the way back in 2002 and a handful of later echoes in a series of articles and responses in the *Journal of Research in Rural Education* (Corbett 2009; Faircloth 2009; Greenwood 2009).

OUR DIALOGUE:
A NOISY SILENCE IN RURAL TEACHER EDUCATION

Trying to make sense of our own practice in the classroom, we came together to discuss some of the challenges and frustrations we have encountered in the rural university classroom. We have shared experiences of watching our classrooms go very quiet when equity subjects are raised and how, when the silence is broken, it is typically by a student from an urban centre. We considered, in particular, how to interpret these silences when they occurred in conversations about race.

Silence, Discomfort, and Etiquette

If rural (white) silence is a common experience in discussions of race, what meanings might we apply to it? Robin DiAngelo (2012) has, in her work, unpacked a number of ways in which white silence exists in racial discussions. Silence, she says, can be productive when it is used to allow the Other to speak or to have an honest discussion. Silence can, however, also be a tool of whiteness when it is not being used to challenge the systemic structures of racism. Here, Claudine wonders how much this is an issue of rurality in particular, and how much it is an issue of the broader Canadian struggles around identity and nation-building in general. Is this form of silence a response to the general discomfort many Canadians feel when the concept of race arises in open dialogue? Is it also an all-too-common hubris as we smugly watch racial animosity fester in the United States, secure in the unsupported belief that "this doesn't happen here"? Dei, Calliste, and Aguiar (2000, 16) highlight that, in everyday Canadian discourse, race is the "category that often gets lost... in part because of the discomfort of speaking about race and racism." We retreat into coded discourses and the use of euphemisms to replace difficult language. In particular contexts, we even retreat into silence. Both of these tactics have the effect of turning race into something that we do not raise in polite conversation, effectively rendering it both distant and invisible.[7]

In our research, race is seen to exist outside immediate place and time for many rural students in Canada. In a sense, the race discussion has been papered over by notions of the happy community, of close-knit sociability, and of an imagined world where there are no racial tensions, largely because race is thought to be absent. Other topics of social concern also promote discomfort. For instance, questions of gender and social class are often experienced as vaguely uncomfortable, but also vaguely relatable. When it comes to race, however, many rural preservice teachers wonder how it relates to them at all. They tend to see themselves, and the genteel consensus in their communities, as separate from the whole issue. The only people who talk about race are outside that consensus. They are the overt bigots, constructed as rogue others, who represent exceptions to the rule of imagined rural politeness, decency, and solidarity.

The university classroom is not exempt from the silent regime of politeness and civility that abounds in rural Nova Scotian mythology. Through our conversations with one another, we have explored experiencing a construction of politeness amongst rural postsecondary students in which speaking of race is considered unsavoury and unbecoming. It is possible that for these rural postsecondary students, the tone of the school is thought to be somehow "above" such conversation. Questions of race then enter the realm of the null curriculum—abject topics that are best left unsaid for fear of causing offense, or that are properly left to families and private discussion (e.g., sex education particularly as it relates to gender). In many rural school communities and for many teachers, any discussion of race is beyond the pale of careful, respectful speech. Conversations constructed as "appropriate" take the form of appeals to colour-blindness, low-stakes expressions of solidarity, or "good whiteness" that demand little or nothing of those who express them (Saul and Burkholder 2020).

It is important to note, however, that even while rural preservice teachers may *conceive* of race as a concept that is absent from or foreign to rural communities, they certainly do not *feel* it to be absent. In fact, the discomfort that rural preservice teachers express around topics of race illustrates the powerful presence it has for them. As Banack and Pohler (introduction to this volume) note, the default assumption of rural ignorance, exclusivity, and racism confounds what might otherwise be read as a high degree of sensitivity to the complexity of race in rural

communities, even if this sensitivity reinforces established sociocultural hierarchies.

Finding Words

Connected to the issue of conceiving of race as something alien to rural communities is an issue of vocabulary. We have found that the language required to discuss questions of race is unavailable or alien to many rural postsecondary students. Some appear to feel guilty about not knowing what they consider to be the "politically correct" or culturally sensitive language, or even the factually correct information required to discuss sensitive topics. They might see this lack of knowledge or what Han and Laughter (2019) call racial literacy as a marker of their ignorance and point of shame or, alternatively, as a feature of their valued rural cultural and social capital. Like some of Tinkham's Nova Scotian interviewees, rural preservice teachers often lack (or, because they have never focused on it before, think they lack) experiential knowledge of race and racism.

For our current study, one of our colleagues, whose name has been withheld to protect her confidentiality, spoke to us of her sense of how these silences among rural preservice teachers reflect what is perceived as an embarrassing ignorance and another marker of their rural alterity in the academy:

> What's compelling me these days is how many things people have to think about so that they get the language right. I watch them struggling under the weight of that. They don't want to do it wrong, but they feel like they're completely unable to speak because they don't have the language or the latest term. In some ways, the weight of that makes them bitter and then there is this fight against it because they can't find their place in it. They can't find their place in diversity if they're white and they come from just enough money to send them to university. They feel really left out in the conversation and I think that's one of the hard places these days. They just feel tongue-tied and they don't want to be left out of the conversation.

These preservice teachers often find the discussion of race and racialization alien and even shocking because, in their schooling and communities, information about historic injustices, residential schools, and race violence was never discussed, or only discussed as a problem in the United States and/or the isolated action of warped psychologies. When race, more broadly speaking, entered the curriculum, it was boxed in some corner of a long-past history or a distant geography (i.e., the Middle East or South Africa) rather than presented as an issue of contemporary Canadian politics—and by extension, as an element of what they would need to know to be effective teachers in Canada. When confronted with uncomfortable histories and sociologies, things obviously do not become simpler or easier. The words of Tinkham's third Nova Scotian preservice teacher, quoted above, illustrate the problems of recognition and acceptance of historical injustice and of what teachers are supposed to do about and with it all once they know. For some, the answer is to do nothing. Since these are structural problems, many preservice teachers feel powerless to effect change. The problems are simply too big, and rationalizations follow easily. Preservice teachers respond in a number of ways when confronted with the argument that change can only occur through community. Common responses that we have heard include: "Well, I don't really agree with those radical groups," or, "I'm not very political," or, "I just want to teach." We have, however, also encountered the converse: "I'm so frustrated by the people I work with who don't care. I can't do this work alone." Performative expectations can also be a barrier: "I have all these outcomes to meet; I have no time for this." Others express a personal distaste for politics and activism: "I got into this to work with kids, not to change the world."

Still others simply reject the problem, arguing that the playing field has been equalled, if not tilted in favour of racialized groups and minorities. For some of these preservice teachers, a common strategy is to turn the argument about race back on those who point out the structural dimensions of racism. By psychologizing the issue, it becomes possible to go beyond the notion that race-talk is about marginal bigots and rude or unsavoury folks, to the notion that such talk blames "innocent" white people for things they had nothing to do with, creating a climate of misinformation, fear, and loathing. Thus, the real racists are those who

identify race as important and use it as a mechanism for blaming others for their own problems, creating unfair advantages for undeserving people, or even promoting the hateful agendas of social justice ideologues.

TEACHING COMPLEXITY IN TESTING TIMES

Schools continue to be about competition, which highlights the importance of curriculum and assessment. All curriculum involves the selection of material and emphasis. Perhaps more importantly, high-stakes assessments and what they are imagined to contain drive teachers' selection of content and test-ready pedagogical techniques. "Will it be on the test?" is now not just a question that teachers control and that students must anticipate; it is also a question that teachers themselves have to consider in the context of published standardized test results. Seldom are the relationships among place, race, colonialism, capitalism, rurality, and curriculum considered (Chambers 2008; Corbett 2020b).

This is not lost on rural preservice teachers, who have absorbed the rural-deficit discourse common in media accounts of rurality and who see their most important task as "closing the gap" between the country and the city. Allegedly neutral content that is easily testable seems to provide a shelter from complexity and judgment, offering clear targets for knowledge transmission. Conversations about equity and inclusion go beyond transmission, making uncomfortable epistemological demands on preservice teachers to both understand and accept structural social analysis. There is no recipe for this kind of work. It is much easier to get a "fun" activity for students in your classroom or a test that assesses some cognitive ability or mastery of "neutral" content. Encountering the complexity of theory, social analysis, and alternative histories that challenge the "comfortable lies" (Loewen 2007) that North American students of western European descent learn in school is one part of it. Another part is finding oneself in the story (or in multiple stories); this is what a university education ought to do.

Our original research questions brought us to think about the difference we might be making. Jennifer thinks we are planting a crop of ideas in each student. When the "garden" moves on, we can't be sure how it all turns out. But we get glimmers here and there. For instance, Jennifer saw a resistant young teacher's practice change once he actually began

teaching. Claudine spoke to how students relate in their assessments of her courses that they encountered new ideas and concepts and that this new stuff was "good for me to learn." Is there an expansion of moral/ethical consciousness happening here? There might be. We do not track this very well, and perhaps we should.

We will have to see what impact things like mandatory culturally responsive training and the Indigenization initiative at our rural university will make as time unfolds. Both the universities and the schools are now in a period of transition that may at least challenge the grand narratives of progress and academic knowledge production that these institutions tell themselves about themselves. It is also becoming increasingly clear that rural areas are not separate worlds set apart from urban diversity. Demographic change in rural Canada is nothing new (Bollman, this volume), and pandemic-related migration (i.e., flight from larger to smaller cities, towns, and rural locales), rural labour shortages, temporary worker programs, pro-immigration policy, real estate markets, and other social pressures have changed the formerly alarmist conversation about population decline in Nova Scotia to emerging questions of diversity and growth.

At the tertiary level in Nova Scotia, with its nine small universities that have mostly evolved out of exclusive religious institutions, and its community colleges that have long reproduced gender, social class, and racialized occupational structures, there is an *institutional* silence that needs a deep unpacking. While this work is in its early stages, as Saul and Burkholder (2020) argue, universities have become oases of fine words and the noble sentiments that express a strategic but effectively disengaged institutional and personal ethical positioning they call "good whiteness." There is no question in our minds that our university, with its majority rural Nova Scotian student intake, is a very silent place indeed. We address this as well in our conversations with each other. There are few public discussions of sensitive topics or difficult histories that are initiated by students themselves. Rather, there is what appears more as a rural university patrician aloofness from the messiness of complex street politics—a mildly activist politeness bathed in an intellectualized vocabulary our students feel they are expected to learn. And perhaps they, too, see through its façade.

BREAKING THE NOISY SILENCE

Thus, we are left with questions. Are the rural students actually this silent, or does the system encourage and reward their silence? St. Denis (2007, 1086) pointed out that "the argument that addressing racism and doing anti-racist education is too negative and that we need to focus on the positive often results in tinkering with the status quo." St. Denis insisted that schools begin conducting an interrogation of race and racism and commit themselves to the principles of anti-racist education. She also cautioned in the context of Indigeneity that, if this work is not done carefully, "instead of doing anti-racist education that explores why and how race matters, educators can end up doing cross-cultural awareness training that often has the effect of encouraging the belief that the cultural difference of the Aboriginal 'Other' is the problem. Offering cultural awareness workshops can also provide another opportunity for non-Aboriginals to resent and resist Aboriginal people" (1086).

We do think that it is time to talk about race, and about why and how it matters. We need to have these conversations in more than cursory ways, and extend them into discussions of other spaces, such as policing. Change is needed not just in teacher education but within the Nova Scotia curriculum. We believe that understanding racism is also key to understanding history. Participating in a dialogue about race can help students begin to see why some stories have been privileged over others, and why some historical and present-day events took place or are currently taking place. It can help everyone begin to point out racist practices, beliefs, attitudes, microaggressions, and systemic inequalities. It can problematize rural, down-home, East Coast politeness. Learning new things and unlearning old habits must be at the centre of this curriculum, which, we think, should include a cold-eyed analysis of the politics of property, the distribution of resources, and the multiple forms of vulnerability that the recent COVID-19 pandemic has uncovered.

We see a number of implications emerging from this analysis. First, it is our view that rural teacher education requires strong foundational work that explicitly and directly challenges the allegedly "close-knit" mythology of rurality. At the very least, idyllic rural fabrications, including how we think about "neighbourliness" (Banack and Pohler,

introduction to this volume), need to be challenged with a clear historical analysis of settler-colonial history. Courses in Indigenous education, critical race theory, culturally responsive pedagogy, whiteness studies, and the history, geography, and sociology of education can provide important foundational backgrounds for preservice teachers. We believe such courses will support a more complete understanding among preservice teachers of educational equity and the need for active promotion of inclusive education. Our research illustrates that the way many rural communities understand cultural, racial, and ethnic differences (as well related differences of gender, sexuality, and language) tends to be rooted in a sensibility that assumes a white, cisgender, able-bodied, European-descended, anglophone subject as well as the exceptionality of rural places as normative pillars of the larger society or even as the "natural" homeland of the allegedly real, *pur laine*, born-and-bred people of the region and the nation.

Secondly, our research has revealed that for many rural preservice teachers, racialization, Indigenous issues, and culturally responsive pedagogy are still understood to be issues exclusive to urban spaces, or to the supposed homogeneity of minority-language neighbourhoods and communities of colour. This view tends to reinforce the idea that rural places are relatively homogenous cocoons that are not significantly connected to other places. There tends to be for these preservice teachers great interest in place-based education and pedagogies that focus on the local (Corbett 2020b). While we do believe, following Dewey and the pragmatist tradition, that all learning begins from experience, it is also important that local experience be expanded through engagements that enrich conceptions of time and space.

Rural youth and those who teach them require, we argue, a stronger grounding in the social sciences and humanities. These areas of study serve as foundations for more complex understandings of the modern world. Ironically, in many small, rural secondary schools with restricted timetables and limited options, social studies and humanities courses are often scheduled against university-preparatory science and math offerings. As a result, many academically motivated rural students, including many who eventually become teachers, feel that they must choose university-preparatory courses, particularly

advanced math and science streams that allow students to keep their "options open" (which is code for choosing the university option). It is also important to note that in Nova Scotia, teachers are no longer required to report on social studies outcomes at the elementary level. Additionally, preservice teacher education programs serving predominantly rural teacher education candidates should also consider enhanced foundational sociocultural content in their programs. Here, we challenge the more instrumental, subject-area-focused teacher training that is preoccupied with method and realist knowledge "outcomes" to engage with the messiness of complex intellectual and social problems, relational ethics, and critical inquiry (Perry 2013).

Finally, rather than blaming rural preservice teachers for their lack of knowledge of the language and concepts relating to discussion of contemporary equity and inclusion, it is our view that this issue be addressed in a way similar to how educators try to address, for instance, differences in cultural capital or in broadband access. We suggest here that diversity talk is itself a complex set of discursive practices that are not evenly distributed across social class and regional spaces. Supporting rural students as they enter into difficult conversations and break the noisy silence about topics considered inappropriate in their home places can be approached sensitively and supportively. They need to be addressed in ways that work explicitly against alienating the sensibilities of rural preservice teachers, yet that do not release them from the responsibility of educating themselves and their students about enacting the thoroughgoing changes recommended by the Truth and Reconciliation Commission and the generation of scholarship that has sought to make schools more diverse places that provide opportunity for all. This is perhaps best characterized as what Han and Laughter (2019) call "racial literacy." Literacy, in this context, is not a mechanical skill that one learns once and for all through a mastery of some set of basics, but a lifelong practice of learning, change, and development. In the end we have realized that we ourselves need to explore more effective and inclusive ways to engage these difficult conversations with our rural students, and to help break the noisy silence.

NOTES

1. The work of novelist and travel writer W.R. Bird is significant here. Bird chaired Nova Scotia's Historical Sites and Monuments Advisory Council from 1938 to 1966 and was one of a group of cultural intellectuals who designed a tourism strategy that Ian McKay (1994) has dubbed "tartanism." This strategy constructed the province as a quintessentially Anglo-European space in which each of its regions contained what Bird (1950) called racial "types" (Irish, Scottish, British, French, German). Bird's 1950s travel books are guides for the Ontario or New England motor tourists who were suddenly able, along newly paved roads, to escape the hurly-burly of modernity for the mythic, simple past of fisherfolk and crafts people. Bird frames race as something closer to what we would today understand as culture, but at the same time assumes whiteness to be dominant and normal. Nova Scotia's tourism strategy retains significant elements of tartanism. Further, as Ursula Kelly (2013) argues using the case of Newfoundland, the trope of a therapeutic, uncomplicated space outside modernity remains central to Atlantic Canadian mythos.

2. This was a statement made by Harper at a 2013 news conference following the Boston Marathon bombing and in relation to other similar terrorist incidents. His comments—meant to be a critique of the position taken by then Leader of the Opposition Justin Trudeau—dismissed the idea that diverse social factors play a role in criminal behaviour, instead insisting that individual responsibility is all that matters in crime and punishment. According to this view, swift, targeted punishment, not an analysis of who is being punished and why, is all that is required in such situations (Brym and Ramos, 2013). To think beyond the individual was for Harper a kind of sin which mirrors Margaret Thatcher's similar notion that society is a fiction.

3. More recently, scholars have argued that Indigenous education is not only crucial to promoting justice and positive social change on Turtle Island, but also highlights how it must go further and support "the repatriation of Indigenous land and life" (Tuck and Yang, 2012, 1; see also Alfred 2009; Madden 2015). Until very recently, the field of rural education in Canada has had little significant interaction with issues of Indigeneity and race (Corbett 2020a; Corbett and Gereluk 2020).

4. Jennifer Tinkham, Christine Martineau, and Claudine Bonner, "Learning to Teach; Teaching to Unlearn: Teacher Education and Indigenous Content," (unpublished manuscript, September 2019).

5. Jennifer Tinkham, "Beyond a 'Cultural Prop': Pre-Service Teacher Perceptions of the Challenges and Opportunities of Mandatory Indigenous Education Courses," (unpublished manuscript, January 2020).
6. Tinkham, "Beyond a 'Cultural Prop'."
7. In *Playing in the Dark: Whiteness and the Literary Imagination*, Toni Morrison (1992, 9–10) suggested that "the habit of ignoring race is understood to be a graceful, even generous, liberal gesture. To notice is to recognize an already discredited difference. To enforce its invisibility through silence is to allow the black body a shadowless participation in the dominant cultural body. According to this logic, every well-bred instinct argues *against noticing* and forecloses adult discourse" (emphasis in original).

REFERENCES

Abu-Laban, Yasmeen, and Daiva Stasiulis. 2000. "Constructing 'Ethnic Canadians': The Implications for Public Policy and Inclusive Citizenship: Reply to Rhoda Hoaward-Hassman." *Canadian Public Policy—Analyse de Politiques* 26 (4): 477–87.

Aitken, Avril, and Linda Radford. 2018. "Learning to Teach for Reconciliation in Canada: Potential, Resistance and Stumbling Forward." *Teaching and Teacher Education* 75: 40–48. https://doi.org/10.1016/j.tate.2018.05.014.

Alfred, Taiaiake. 2009. *Peace, Power, Righteousness: An Indigenous Manifesto*. Oxford: Oxford University Press.

Barton, Keith C. & Linda S. Levstik. 2004. *Teaching History for the Common Good*. New York: Routledge.

Barton, Keith C., and Alan W. McCully. 2004. "History, Identity, and the School Curriculum in Northern Ireland: An Empirical Study of Secondary Students' Ideas and Perspectives." *Journal of Curriculum Studies* 36 (6): 1–32.

Battiste, Marie. 1998. "Enabling the Autumn Seed: Toward a Decolonized Approach to Aboriginal Knowledge, Language, and Education." *Canadian Journal of Native Education* 22 (1): 16–27.

Battiste, Marie. 2004. "Animating Sites of Postcolonial Education: Indigenous Knowledge and the Humanities." Paper presented at the annual meetings of the Canadian Society for Studies in Education, Winnipeg, MB, May 29, 2004.

Bird, Will R. 1950. *This Is Nova Scotia*. Toronto: Ryerson Press.

Brown, Enora. 2004. "The Significance of Race and Social Class for Self-Study and the Professional Knowledge Base of Teacher Education." In *International Handbook of Self-Study of Teaching and Teacher Education Practices*, edited by J. John Loughran, Mary Lynn Hamilton, Vicki Kubler LaBoskey, and Tom Russell, 517–74. Dordrecht: Kluwer.

Brym, R. J., & Ramos, H. 2013. "Actually, Now's the Perfect Time to 'Commit Sociology'." IPolitics, April 26, 2013. https://www.ipolitics.ca/news/actually-nows-the-perfect-time-to-commit-sociology.

Butler, Alana. 2019. "Socioeconomic Inequality and Student Outcomes in Canadian Schools." In *Socioeconomic Inequality and Student Outcomes: Cross-National Trends, Policies, and Practices*, edited by Louise Volante, Sylke V. Schnepf, John Jerrim, and Don A. Klinger, 169–87. Singapore: Springer.

Chambers, Cynthia. 2008. "Where Are We? Finding Common Ground in a Curriculum of Place." *Journal of the Canadian Association for Curriculum Studies* 6 (2): 113–28.

Corbett, Michael. 2009. "Assimilation, Resistance, Rapprochement, and Loss: Response to Woodrum, Faircloth, Greenwood, and Kelly." *Journal of Research in Rural Education* 24 (12): 1–7. https://jrre.psu.edu/sites/default/files/2019-08/24-12.pdf.

Corbett, Michael. 2010. "Backing the Right Horse: Teacher Education, Sociocultural Analysis and Literacy in Rural Education." *Teaching and Teacher Education* 26 (1): 82–86.

Corbett, Michael. 2020a. "Relocating Curriculum and Reimagining Place Under Settler-Capitalism." In *Curriculum Challenges and Opportunities in a Changing World: Transnational Perspectives in Curriculum Inquiry*, edited by Bill Green, Philip Roberts and Marie Brennan, 167–83. London: Palgrave Macmillan.

Corbett, Michael. 2020b. "Place-Based Education: A Critical Appraisal from a Rural Perspective." In *Rural Teacher Education: Connecting Land and People*, edited by Michael Corbett and Dianne Gereluk, 279–98. Singapore: Springer.

Corbett, Michael, and Dianne Gereluk, eds. 2020. *Rural Teacher Education: Connecting Land and People*. Springer.

Cramer, Katherine, 2016. *The Politics of Resentment: Rural Consciousness in Wisconsin and the Rise of Scott Walker*. University of Chicago Press.

Dei, George. 2008. "Schooling as Community: Race, Schooling and the Education of African Youth." *Journal of Black Studies* 38 (3): 346–66.

Dei, George, Agnes Calliste, and Margarida Aguiar, eds. 2000. *Power, Knowledge and Anti-racism Education: A Critical Reader*. Halifax: Fernwood Publishing.

Dei, George, and Leeno Karumanchery. 1999. "School Reforms in Ontario: The Marketization of Education and the Resulting Silence on Equity." *The Alberta Journal of Educational Research* 25 (2): 111–31.

Dei, George, Josephine Mazzuca, Elizabeth McIssac, and Jasmin Zine. 1997. *Reconstructing 'Drop-out': A Critical Ethnography of the Dynamics of Black Students' Disengagement from School*. Toronto: University of Toronto Press.

DiAngelo, Robin. 2012. "Nothing to Add: A Challenge to White Silence in Racial Discussions." *Understanding and Dismantling Privilege—The Official Journal of the White Privilege Conference* 2 (1): 2–17.

Egbo, Benedicta. 2011. "What Should Preservice Teachers Know about Race and Diversity? Exploring a Critical Knowledge-Base for Teaching in 21st Century Canadian Classrooms." *Journal of Contemporary Issues in Education* 6 (2): 23–37.

Epstein, Terrie. 1998. "Deconstructing Differences in African-American and European-American Adolescents' Perspectives of U.S. History." *Curriculum Inquiry* 28 (4): 397–423.

Epstein, Terrie. 2000. "Adolescents' Perspectives on Racial Diversity in U.S. History: Case Studies from an Urban Classroom." *American Educational Research* 37 (1): 185–214.

Faircloth, Susan C. 2009. "Re-Visioning the Future of Education for Native Youth in Rural Schools and Communities." *Journal of Research in Rural Education* 24 (9): 1–4.

Greenwood, David A. 2009. "Place, Survivance, and White Remembrance: A Decolonizing Challenge to Rural Education in Mobile Modernity." *Journal of Research in Rural Education* 24 (10): 1–6.

Hall, Stuart. 2003. "New Ethnicities." In *Identities: Race, Class, Gender, and Nationality*, edited by Linda M. Alcoff and Eduardo Mendieta, 90–95. Oxford: Blackwell.

Han, Keonghee Tao, and Judson Laughter, eds. 2019. *Critical Race Theory in Teacher Education: Informing Classroom Culture and Practice*. New York: Teachers College Press.

Howard, Gary R. 2016. *We Can't Teach What We Don't Know: White Teachers, Multiracial Schools*. Teachers College Press.

Kanu, Yatta. 2005. "Teachers' Perceptions of the Integration of Aboriginal Perspectives into the High School Curriculum." *Alberta Journal of Educational Research* 51 (1): 50–68.

Kelly, Ursula. 2013. "Find Yourself in Newfoundland and Labrador: Reading Rurality as Reparation." In *Rethinking Rural Literacies: Transactional Perspectives*, edited by Bill Green and Michael Corbett, 53–74. London: Palgrave Macmillan.

Kuzmik, Jeffrey J., and Leslie R. Bloom. 2008. "'Split at the Roots': Epistemological and Ontological Challenges/Tensions/Possibilities and the Methodology of Self-Study Research." In *The Seventh Internation Conference on Self-Study of Teacher Education Practices: Pathways to Change in Teacher Education: Dialogue, Diversity and Self-Study*, edited by Melissa L. Heston, Deborah L. Tidwell, Katheryn K. East, and Linda M. Fitzgerald, 207–12. Cedar Falls, IA: University of Northern Iowa.

Lassonde, Cynthia A., Sally Galman, and Clare M. Kosnik, eds. 2009. *Self-Study Research Methodologies for Teacher Educators*. Rotterdam: Sense Publishers.

Loewen, James W. 2007. *Lies My Teacher Told Me: Everything Your American History Textbook Got Wrong*. Rev. ed. New York: Touchstone.

Madden, Brooke. 2015. "Pedagogical Pathways for Indigenous Education With/In Teacher Education." *Teaching and Teacher Education* 51: 1–15.

Matias, Cheryl E. 2016. *Feeling White: Whiteness, Emotionality, and Education*. Rotterdam: Brill Sense.

McKay, Ian. 1994. *The Quest of the Folk: Antimodernism and Cultural Selection in Twentieth-Century Nova Scotia*. Montréal: McGill-Queen's University Press.

McKay, Ian, and Robin Bates. 2010. *In the Province of History: The Making of the Public Past in Twentieth-Century Nova Scotia*. Montréal: McGill-Queen's University Press.

Mitchell, Claudia, Kathleen O'Reilly-Scanlon, and Sandra Weber, eds. 2005. *Just Who Do We Think We Are? Methodologies for Autobiography and Self-Study in Education*. New York: Routledge.

Morrison, Toni. 1992. *Playing in the Dark: Whiteness and the Literary Imagination*. New York: Vintage Books.

Neal, Sarah. 2012. *Rural Identities: Ethnicity and Community in the Contemporary English Countryside*. Farnham: Ashgate.

Neilsen, Lorri. 1994. *A Stone in My Shoe, Teaching Literacy in Times of Change*. Winnipeg: Peguis.

Palmer, Jane, and Celmara Pocock. 2020. "Aboriginal Colonial History and the (Un)Happy Object of Reconciliation." *Cultural Studies* 34 (1): 49–69. https://doi.org/10.1080/09502386.2019.1602153.

Peck, Carla. 2010. "'It's Not Like [I'm] Chinese Canadian. I Am In Between': Ethnicity and Students' Conceptions of Historical Significance." *Theory and Research in Social Education* 38 (4): 574–617.

Peck, Carla. 2011. "Ethnicity and Students' Historical Understandings." In *New Possibilities for the Past: Shaping History Education in Canada,* edited by Penney Clark, 305–24. Vancouver: UBC Press.

Perry, George. 2013. *The Grand Regulator: The Miseducation of Nova Scotia's Teachers, 1838–1997*. Montréal: McGill-Queen's University Press.

Ragoonaden, Karen, Awneet Sivia, and Victorina Baxan. 2015. "Teaching for Diversity in Teacher Education: Transformative Frameworks." *Canadian Journal for the Scholarship of Teaching and Learning* 6 (3): 1–18.

Reid, Jo Ann, Bill Green, Maxine Cooper, Wendy Hastings, Graeme Lock, and Simone White. 2010. "Regenerating Rural Social Space? Teacher Education for Rural-Regional Sustainability." *Australian Journal of Education* 54 (3): 262–76.

Ryan, James. 1999. *Race and Ethnicity in Multi-ethnic Schools: A Critical Case Study*. Clevedon, UK: Multilingual Matters.

Santoro, Ninetta. 2009. "Teaching in Culturally Diverse Contexts: What Knowledge about 'Self' and 'Others' Do Teachers Need?" *Journal of Education for Teaching* 35 (1): 33–45.

Saul, Roger, and Casey Burkholder. 2020. "Intellectualizing Whiteness as a Response to Campus Racism: Some Concerns." *Ethnic and Racial Studies* 43 (9): 1636–53.

Schick, Carol. 2014. "White Resentment in Settler Society." *Race Ethnicity and Education* 17 (1): 88–102. https://doi.org/10.1080/13613324.2012.733688.

Solomon, R. Patrick. 1992. *Black Resistance in High School: Forging a Separatist Culture*. New York: SUNY Press.

St. Denis, Verna. 2007. "Aboriginal Education and Anti-racist Education: Building Alliances Across Cultural and Racial Identity." *Canadian Journal of Education* 30 (4): 1068–92.

Statistics Canada. 2022. "Population Growth in Canada's Rural Areas, 2016 to 2021." Accessed March 1, 2022. https://www12.statcan.gc.ca/census-recensement/2021/as-sa/98-200-x/2021002/98-200-x2021002-eng.cfm.

Tinkham, Jennifer. 2013. "That's Not My History! Examining the Role of Personal Counter-Narratives in Decolonizing Canadian History for Mi'kmaw Students." PhD diss., University of Alberta. ERA. https://doi.org/10.7939/R3ND7J.

Tinkham, Jennifer. 2017. "That's Not My History! Reflections from Mi'kmaw Students on the Role of Their Teachers in Decolonizing Social Studies Education in Nova Scotia." In *Visioning a Mi'kmaw Humanities: Indigenizing the Academy*, edited by Marie Battiste, 228–52. Sydney: Cape Breton University Press.

Tomkins, Joanne. 2002. "Learning to See What They Can't: Decolonizing Perspectives on Indigenous Education in The Racial Context of Rural Nova Scotia." *McGill Journal of Education / Revue Des Sciences de l'éducation de McGill* 37 (3): 405–22.

Truth and Reconciliation Commission of Canada. *The Final Report of the Truth and Reconciliation Commission of Canada*. 6 vols. Montréal: McGill-Queens University Press, 2015.

Tuck, Eve, and K. Wayne Yang. 2012. "Decolonization Is Not a Metaphor." *Decolonization: Indigeneity, Education & Society* 1 (1): 1–40.

Tupper, Jennifer. 2011 "Disrupting Ignorance and Settler Identities: The Challenges of Preparing Beginning Teachers for Treaty Education." In "[Indigenous Education] in Education," edited by Rainey Gaywish, Linda Goulet, Joanne Pelletier, and Larry Steeves, special issue, *In Education* 17 (3): https://doi.org/10.37119/ojs2011.v17i3.

PROMOTING UNDERSTANDING AND EQUITY IN RURAL CANADA

The Role of Community Education

Michelle Lam

The one year, me and my cousin were at grandpa's house with my dad [on Halloween]...And this kid came to the door dressed up all in black. My grandpa opens the door and says, "Oh, look, a little n----r." And my dad, me, and my cousin is like, [gasps]. And, like, we're old enough to know that he shouldn't be saying that. My dad just kind of looks at him and he's like, "He doesn't know any better. He's never been taught anything different."...No one's ever taught him any different.
—RURAL MANITOBA RESIDENT, quoted in Lam
(2021, 120; emphasis added).

RURAL AREAS ACROSS CANADA face many challenges related to the out-migration of youth as well as aging populations, as outlined in detail in Bollman's chapter in this volume. Meanwhile, citizens in many larger urban centres face skyrocketing housing costs and deteriorating infrastructure. The solution often touted to address each of these challenges is to direct a segment of incoming immigrants away from large urban centres and toward rural areas instead (Esses and Carter 2019). Rural areas are frequently encouraged to tout their much lower costs of living, the availability of jobs, and the various social advantages of "small-town

living" in order to woo newcomers to come and stay (Valade 2019). Government initiatives like the Atlantic Immigration Pilot Program (Keung 2017) or the Rural and Northern Immigration Pilot (IRCC 2019) aim to work with rural centres in this process, assisting newcomers in settling outside of large urban centres.

However, as newcomers are encouraged to move to rural areas, and these areas become more diverse, there remains a corresponding need to increase the supports and initiatives designed to educate rural citizens about this increasing cultural, linguistic, and religious diversity. As Banack and Pohler (introduction to this volume) note, attitudes toward immigration tend to be less favourable in rural areas. As Haugen (this volume) further makes clear, even those eager to support refugees settling in rural communities sometimes hold problematic assumptions about newcomers that can impede community inclusion and integration. Furthermore, newcomers may unknowingly step into a powder keg of long-standing rural disillusionment and perceived government abandonment that can increase tensions between racial and cultural groups (Azano 2015; Epp 2008; Epp and Whitson 2001). Indeed, as Banack (this volume) demonstrates, there seems to be a link in rural areas between a sense of growing economic instability and political alienation and more negative attitudes towards newcomers. These concerning trends in rural areas lend themselves to deepening resentment, racism, and disillusionment. As Robertson (2005, 411) notes, the barriers to employment for newcomers are a "bitter reality and shattered dreams create fertile soil for social hostility." This social hostility, in turn, can lead newcomers to leave the rural communities where they intended to settle, opting instead for larger urban centres (Esses and Carter 2019). This creates a vicious cycle in which small communities work to recruit newcomers and facilitate early stages of settlement services—efforts that are costly, time-consuming, and often volunteer-driven—only to be forced to begin recruitment and settlement again as newcomers leave for the large city. This outcome is surely some distance from the goal of deep equality (Banack and Pohler, introduction to this volume).

To overcome this cycle, rural communities must plan for the long term, focusing on factors that promote newcomer retention in rural areas, especially practical initiatives to create an equitable and inclusive

environment. This chapter focuses on community education's role in facilitating and creating this type of environment and the importance of "two-way" education for both newcomers and rural residents. Two-way education serves not only to integrate newcomers into the rural community but also to expose nonnewcomer residents to newcomers' challenges with the aim of fostering understanding and, ultimately, empathy.

After exploring in more detail what this type of two-way education may look like in rural communities, this chapter closes with a discussion of a study I conducted in 2021, which centred around assessing the effectiveness of a board game I created as part of a two-way-street approach. As the story of the grandpa that began this chapter illustrates, education that fosters inclusivity is necessary not only for newcomers but also for community members more broadly.

WHAT IS INTEGRATION?

In a book about inclusivity in rural areas, it is important to ask: Who is being included into whose systems? This same critique is levelled at the terminology of integration. While the term *integration* is still commonly used by settlement practitioners and policy-makers, and the Government of Canada (2011) defines integration as a "two-way street" in which both the newcomer and the host society adapt and benefit, *integration* is not a neutral term. We still need to ask: Who is being integrated into whose systems? Moreover, as Haugen (this volume) asks, to what degree are they, in fact, integrated? Are newcomers simply viewed as guests, or do they become neighbours, with mutual expectations of reciprocity? These questions raise issues of power, colonialism, "white-saviourism," and race, and call into question the impacts of "good intentions" (Gorski 2008). Many of these themes are explored in detail throughout this book.

In the early days of Canadian immigration, newcomers were expected to assimilate and adopt Canadian traits. Ethnic communities—that is, non-white, non-European communities—were considered a barrier to assimilation (Shan 2015). The ideology of assimilation shifted to integration after the Second World War, as mass movements of people from Europe settled in Canada. This integration ideology, characterized by "mutual obligations" rather than unidirectional assimilation, remains today (Shan 2015, 21). However, despite these inclusive definitions of

integration that emphasize a reciprocal process, immigrants are still compared to and expected to match native-born Canadians in economic performance and cultural standards. They are expected to eventually "resemble Canadians in terms of behaviour and psychology profiles" (Hébert 2013, 4). In the words of Shan (2015, 22), "how to integrate this ideal [integration] into practice remains a challenge." While equitable two-way-street definitions of integration abound in pedagogical theory, conformity and cultural imperialism remain in pedagogical practice, with settlement workers and teachers often taking a prescriptive approach to teaching "Canadian" culture (Hébert 2016; Shan 2015). One example of this can be seen in the work of Ali (2012), who explored the efforts of Canadian teachers to "help" immigrant parents learn Canadian ways of parenting. These teachers did not, however, make an effort to recognize the different and equally valuable methods of parenting among immigrant families, which could have been sources of mutual learning.

There are significant social benefits for immigrants who have assimilated and diminished their visibility. Despite Canada's ideologies of multiculturalism, inclusion, and equitability, newcomers still experience benefits for changing their linguistic, social, and economic behaviour (Li 2002). The current emphasis on "soft skills" and "clear communication" can be critiqued as socially acceptable ways of discriminating against newcomers (Hébert 2016; Reitz, Curtis, and Elrick 2014; Lam 2021). Faced with this discrimination, newcomers make decisions about adopting "standard" accents and behaving, dressing, managing conflict, and leading in ways that are deemed understandable and acceptable to the nonnewcomer (white) majority (Lam 2021).

As Canadian society becomes increasingly diverse, many Canadians feel that shared values are necessary (Hébert and Wilkinson 2011; Jedwab 2016). Yet there is a fine line between the discourse about "absorptive capacity" of various cities and communities, which is taken to mean availability of jobs, housing, schools, health, and social services (Esses et al. 2010; Government of Canada 2011), and discussions of "social cohesion," which, as Hébert (2013, 5) notes may be understood as a euphemism for more overt "racist considerations of non-white immigrants as being 'too many'" (see also Jedwab 2016, 14). In Wong and Guo's (2018, 5) words,

"Contemporary racism in Canada is formulated and invoked as a defence of Canadian and western values and is profoundly a form of cultural fundamentalism that is racist in nature." I argue with Li (2003, 330) that integration should mean giving newcomers the "right of contestation, the legitimacy of dissent, and the entitlement to be different." In other words, integration involves evening out the power imbalances that currently define it in practice. Only then can it truly become a two-way street.

TWO-WAY-STREET EDUCATION

To live up to this idealized definition, integration must include the creation of a society that can acknowledge past and ongoing injustices; discuss deeper issues related to values, beliefs, and practices; share personal stories; and negotiate ways to work together in pursuit of common goals (Ali 2012). In other words, two-way-street integration requires true two-way-street education.

Education for Newcomers

One direction of the two-way-street model involves providing education and supports for newcomers. Newcomers often list better education opportunities for themselves and their children as motivational factors for immigration. In many cases, parents are willing to endure jobs for which they are overqualified to provide a better future for their children.

Language education is an area of need for newcomers. Language ability plays a significant role in the selection criteria for immigrant intake and is a crucial determinant of integration after arrival in Canada (Kilbride and Ali 2010). Language is also a critical factor in labour market success (Wilkinson and Garcea 2017). If newcomers do not have the opportunity to gain French or English proficiency, they will need to find employment in positions that do not require that proficiency, even if they have very high levels of education in other areas (Kilbride and Ali 2010).

Newcomers, particularly women, experience multiple barriers to achieving this language proficiency. These include high costs of housing, difficulty with credentialing, needing two incomes, lack of information about programs, and lack of available and affordable child care. These barriers result in further challenges, including those related to

mental health, loss of social networks, exclusion, isolation, and domestic violence (Kilbride and Ali 2010). In rural areas, barriers can be amplified. Providing quality language education in rural areas can be difficult because of sparse funding, difficulty recruiting qualified professionals, accessibility of interpreters, and lack of childcare (Sawatzky 2018). However, innovative educators and community members have built on rural strengths, such as a deeply connected community base and strong volunteer engagement, and have harnessed technology to address gaps (Lam 2019). For example, in 2015, the town of Altona, Manitoba, sponsored enough refugees to increase its population by 1%. There were so many children among these refugees that an entire class had to be added to the local school. The town organized English conversation practice groups in the basement of a local church and held classes in the local mall (Anderssen 2017). They used Google Translate to aid communication and organized a bevy of volunteer drivers to provide transportation to and from Winnipeg, an hour and a half away. Altona is an excellent example of a rural community that responded to their particular context's challenges by building on their strengths. However, questions remain about the long-term viability of these volunteer-driven solutions. As newcomers in rural areas have higher mobility than both the Canadian population and newcomers in larger cities (Hellstrom 2018)—that is, they more frequently move away from their initial place of settlement—rural areas are welcoming new newcomers in a seemingly never-ending cycle of early, demanding stages of settlement. That rural areas rely on volunteer community members, without training or support, to provide the bulk of settlement and integration work at this stage on an ongoing basis for the foreseeable future is problematic.

Educational programs that target youth integration tend to focus on the initial settlement period only, without providing longer-term support. This is perhaps because children and youth are often assumed to be resilient, adaptive, and quick learners. It is assumed, in other words, that after the first year or two in Canada, newcomer children and youth will be fully integrated and won't need such supports.

This is not the case. In fact, educational and labour outcomes are poorer for refugee and newcomer youth with lower French or English language skills, those incorrectly placed in classes, and those with

significant gaps in their education (Wilkinson et al. 2012). Even after becoming conversationally adept in a new language, as newcomer students advance through their school career, they are chasing a constantly moving target of academic language aptitude. Language learning supports need to support academic language acquisition, which takes longer to master (Cummins 2011). Supports are needed even for the second generation, who may become disillusioned with the myth of "Canadian multiculturalism" as they encounter systemic barriers and racism in the larger society (Ali 2008). Newcomer and second-generation students also face challenges of credentialization, lack of support systems, trauma, and adaptation (Wilkinson et al. 2012). The resiliency of youth alone is not enough to overcome these barriers and challenges. Newcomer students require longer-term support (Hébert 2016).

It is crucial to remember, however, that although this programming is essential, it is only one direction of an equitable, two-way education model. The other direction—that of developing education for nonnewcomer Canadians—is also needed and has often been left out of education and immigration discussions.

Education for Nonnewcomers

As human migration increasingly becomes a polarizing and politicized topic, and as xenophobic and anti-immigrant sentiment rise around the world (Banack and Pohler, introduction to this volume), education becomes a powerful and necessary force in enhancing understanding of difference, implementing equity, and combatting racism. This type of education should be implemented at the broad community scale, including volunteers, teachers, refugee sponsors, and community members.

This education is needed in several key areas. First, it is needed in the employment space for employers who are hiring newcomers. Racism and ethnic discrimination, although no longer overtly part of Canada's immigration strategy, are still felt through institutional and systemic discrimination, cultural and ideological discourse, individual microaggressions, and hate crimes (Wong and Guo 2018). Increasing Islamophobia and anti-Asian discourse, changes to provincial health care coverage that limit access to international students, and a dramatic rise in racial profiling against Black peoples are all examples of the prevalence of racism

in Canada (Wong and Guo 2018). In my own work, I have also found that Canadians generally view immigrants as cheap labour, and rural areas are no exception in this regard. As one study participant told me:

> I was talking to a guy, and he's, you know, he delivers stuff. I just casually asked, "Hey, you know, how are you doing" or whatever. And he said, "Not good." And we chatted about it, and he said his boss had called him in and said—and he was getting paid well for what he does. Like I mean, he's been doing his job for a long time. And he says, "Um, you're too expensive. We're going to have to work on cutting your hours or something like that because we're, you know, *I can hire six immigrants for the cost of you*. (quoted in Lam 2021, 191; emphasis added)

Employers need to be aware of the exclusion facing newcomers after arrival, which includes raising awareness of racism, barriers, and the dehumanizing discourses of being seen as only valuable for labour market contributions.

Second, education is needed for educators. The majority of teachers are white, middle-class women who have limited experience working cross-culturally and whose ideas about cultural norms and what is normal in areas of child development, teaching, and professional expertise are based mainly on their own cultural communities (Ali 2012; Howard 2016). Many immigrant children enter these classrooms feeling immense pressure to succeed, as their families often see success in Western education as the pathway to broader success in life (Ali 2012). In rural areas, educators may be unfamiliar with these, and other realities of their newcomer students' lives. It is necessary to provide educational pathways for educators to learn about these realities. Corbett (2010, 83) describes this as anthropological learning:

> To know how to teach is to know a great deal about where you are teaching and the conditions experienced by people in that place. This involves an immersion in the culture of the place, its history, the way power is exercised there, how resources are distributed, the racial, gender and class dynamics that shape

social life, the way school has been experienced historically in the community by different kinds of families, and things of this order.

While this type of knowledge is needed across the board, the vast disconnect between the lived realities, experiences, and expectations of newcomer parents and nonnewcomer teachers (who are primarily white in rural areas) sets this need in bold relief (Ali 2012).

To demonstrate this type of learning, Ali (2012) interviewed teachers and immigrant parents. When she asked immigrant parents about positive experiences with teachers, they responded with instances in which teachers had asked to learn more about cultural practices, accommodated religious needs, showed appreciation, and informed parents about their children's successes. However, most immigrant parents interviewed believed that teachers were prejudiced, did not communicate well, and did not value the input of parents in the school other than for fundraising. The positive experiences mentioned were mainly individual teachers' efforts and not the results of broader institutional systems or organizational policies. School systems and educational policies, procedures, and pedagogy designed for relatively homogenous populations have not yet been adapted to meet diverse populations' needs and strengths (Ali 2012; Hamm 2014).

Finally, it is also necessary to provide education for community members at large. Recall the grandpa who uttered racist slurs without realizing they were offensive because he had "never been taught any different." Two-way education in this regard requires that community members have access to education about newcomers and newcomer experiences.

After working as a teacher of English as an additional language in a rural area, I recognized the need for education to further cultural awareness and sensitivity. While many volunteers, educators, administrators, and community supporters are well intentioned, they are human, and humans are all raised within a particular culture at a specific time. This limited outlook can result in hurtful impacts despite good intentions. I also recognized that mandating a class or professional development exercise for employers, educators, and community members that focused on diversity,

equity, and inclusion could be met with resistance from people who do not see themselves as needing such content or learning. As one of my participants aptly stated, "Why would grandpa need to go to that class anyway? Grandpa's living just fine" (quoted in Lam 2021, 214). I wanted to create an educational tool that would address these issues—something that would appeal to employers, educators, and community members and at the same time give them access to the type of anthropological learning described earlier by Corbett (2010). A discussion of this tool, and the study I conducted around it, make up the remainder of this chapter.

REFUGEE JOURNEYS

As has been discussed, educating rural employers, educators, and community members is a necessary aspect of two-way integration of newcomers into rural communities. It does, however, come with challenges. For instance, as one study participant said, "education can only go so far as the person being educated is willing to receive" (quoted in, Lam 2021, 163). In light of this challenge, I wanted to create an engaging, practical, portable tool that would explore the topic of integration, be able to foster deep discussion, and bring relevant research on newcomers and integration into an accessible and nonthreatening educational environment. The *Refugee Journeys Board Game* (Lam 2017) is the result of this desire.

Board Game Approach and Development

I began making *Refugee Journeys* by collecting newcomer experiences from scholarly articles, news, and media. I also included my own experiences and those shared with me by my students over the years. I used these experiences to populate spaces on the game board and to create "experience cards," which function as discussion prompts during the game (see Figure 7.1). To play the game, players move around the board, much like in the game *Snakes and Ladders*: players may move backwards or forwards, progressing towards a goal (see Figure 7.2).

Early uses of the game showed that some players progressed by moving forward and backward without engaging in an in-depth discussion about the topics on the experience cards. After consulting with board game designer Rob Gosselin of Birdlight Games, I added "identity cards" to the game, which

FIGURE 7.1

FIGURE 7.2

FIGURE 7.3

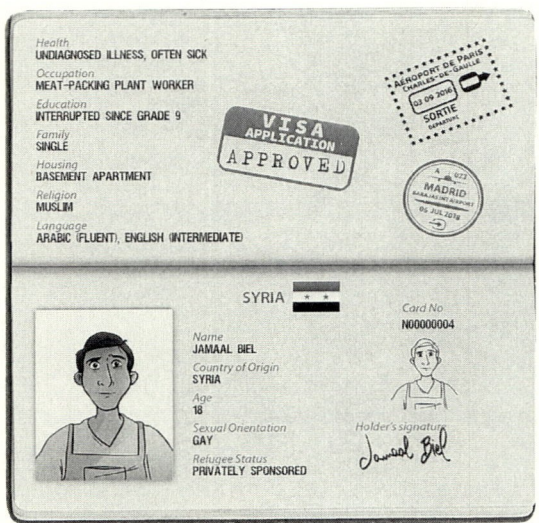

describe many aspects of individual and social identity that can impact integration (Figure 7.3). To avoid stereotypes, the cards were randomly generated from lists of individual and social identity traits that can impact integration, such as religion, country of origin, language, gender, and sexuality. The identity cards are a way for players to conceptualize intersectionality's theoretical lens, positing that there are multiple and intersecting layers of socially determined identity factors that can compound experiences of marginalization. These intersecting identities form points of discussion in the game and also impact the "paths of integration" that players may follow on the game board. For example, in one session, a player landed on a space that said, "Are you male? Move ahead 2." After consulting her identity card, she realized she was unable to progress because she was not male, which led to an in-depth discussion about gender barriers.

These game design elements highlight systemic discrimination and the ways in which different events impact various identities. Building on critical race theory (Crenshaw 1989), which does not question whether racism exists but instead seeks to understand its impacts, this game opens spaces for discussions of race, bias, and systemic discrimination, including the ways various social identities can impact these experiences.

Learning Objectives

Fostering empathy is an essential goal of this game. As Esses and colleagues (2008, 25) have written, "Campaigns that elicit admiration and respect for group members, perhaps by demonstrating the hardships that they have successfully overcome, may prevent negative attitudes and behaviour." Another goal of the game is to understand how relevant policies affect newcomers. After each experience card is played, players have a discussion guided by questions on the board. For example, after a player draws an experience card that says, "You are a 65-year old grandma. You are attending an English class, but the topic is always about how to find a job. Move back two spaces," the group has a discussion about this situation from the perspective of their identity card or their personal experience. The game also includes a deck of question cards to prompt discussion. This deck includes one card that asks about players personal experiences, which allows for deep engagement.

One of the challenges in creating educational tools for equity, diversity, and inclusion is that they often rely on marginalized groups or individuals to educate the majority. This is a form of free labour, and I wanted to avoid this in my game. As one second-generation newcomer participant shared with me:

> People on the end of being educated get touchy and wounded, and maybe they get defensive. They minimize and sometimes gaslight, and that stinks…I never actually articulated it that way, why these conversations were, why I dreaded having these conversations or why I tried to run away because the emotional cost is very real, you know? (quoted in Lam 2021, 163)

At the same time, I still wanted to provide an opportunity to share experiences from minority perspectives, *if they so chose*. To navigate this tension, I designed each question card to include several options for discussion, and framed discussion topics as suggestions. Players can then choose the items they wish to discuss, meaning that sharing personal experiences is entirely optional.

The discussion is the richest place of learning in the game. For example, after drawing the experience card about the grandmother

learning English, one participant might share a story about their own grandmother, another might express frustration over the educational pathways available to newcomers when their needs are not reflected in the topics of the class, while another participant might sympathize with the teacher, pointing out that all classes have diverse requirements and perhaps the majority of the students wanted to learn about employment. A discussion sparked by this card would be influenced by the personal backgrounds, experiences, opinions, and perceptions of the players. The discussion space in the game is thus a profoundly educational space, as players imagine, explore, and learn from one another.

The design of the game highlights many other aspects of integration, such as the cyclical path of integration, or how players may sometimes feel like they take one step forward and two steps back. It involves immobilizing culture shock (miss a turn) and identity changes (draw a new identity card). Because the game's end goal is simply labelled "finish," the design also leads to discussions about where, exactly, the process of integration actually ends. When I facilitate game play sessions (which I continue to do), I always ask groups how they would know they had "finished" the integration journey. Even among newcomer players, there are significant differences in how they view the destination of integration. For some, having "arrived" means they are financially independent or employed in a job that matches their skills and qualifications. Others mention the ability to sponsor family members. Still others describe goals related to language ability, social connections, or more affective dimensions like belonging. This illustrates the complex nature of terms such as *settlement* and *integration*. In every group, these differences only emphasize the need to provide spaces for discussion, recognition of diversity, and inclusive learning. *Refugee Journeys* offers one such space (Figure 7.4).

Outcomes

After collecting feedback from players, I found they commonly expressed the outcomes of their gameplay experience. I have written in more detail about the process of creating the game and the complexities of understanding its effectiveness elsewhere (Lam 2018b, 2020, 2021), so my summary in this chapter will be brief. Participants reported that

FIGURE 7.4

they had learned new information, felt an emotional impact, enjoyed the engaged conversation, formed new, critical perspectives, and increased empathy. Participants used words like *highly engaged* and *thought-provoking* to describe the experience. One participant wrote, "This opened my eyes as to how many challenges and little things that a refugee could experience and how big an impact could be" (quoted in Lam 2020, 151).

In my experience running workshops, focus groups, research projects, classes, and community events around the topic of rural immigration and integration, participants are quick to acknowledge the reality of discrimination and racism in their communities, yet they often point out that this racism is unintended. This serves as a conversational detour since it moves the conversation from the discomfort that arises after racism is acknowledged to a more comfortable place—namely "good intentions" (Gorski 2019; Lam 2021). As one of my participants said about his father-in-law,

> He's the kindest, most gentlest man around. But he can say very racist things...But it's also interesting, you know, he wouldn't again see himself as racist. I don't think he—well, I mean we judge a generation that we have little understanding of. (study participant, 2021)

Regardless of intent, the results of these racist interactions are felt in painful ways by racialized communities, as illustrated by another participant, this time a racialized teacher living in a rural prairie city:

> Why didn't I say anything back then? Because you know, you talk about having relational clout? You know, the relational currency to speak into these things? I just felt like I wasn't able to say anything, and even if I did say anything, I don't know if I would've been taken seriously or heard. Part of it too was resignation, you know? This is just the way it is for immigrants and newcomers to Canada. (quoted in Lam 2018a, 42)

These well-intended but ultimately ignorant interactions are not going to be solved by merely playing a board game. But a board game can open the door to questions and it can create the space for conversations and sharing, which can increase understanding and empathy.

Integration in Canadian contexts is often compared to a two-way street, where both the host society and the newcomer adapt and benefit (Government of Canada 2011). To actually achieve the goal of true, two-way-street integration, settlement and integration initiatives must follow a similar two-way framework in which educational programming serves not only to integrate newcomers, but also to educate nonnewcomer community members to respect and value the diverse perspectives, backgrounds, and experiences of newcomers arriving in their communities. Through the development and use of practical tools, rural community education has a vital role to play in establishing an ethos that respects and values diverse community members' rich backgrounds and experiences.

In rural communities where resources dedicated to integration may be sparse, tools like the *Refugee Journeys Board Game* can provide a platform for education to happen on both sides of the two-way street. It

allows for the sharing of perspectives, experiences, and knowledge. It inspires imagination and empathy by encouraging participants to think about ways that different identities may experience settlement and integration. Learning happens from the research-based experiences built into the game and the discussion that ensues after each experience is shared. It is immensely practical and also appropriate for rural citizens who are already motivated by the ideas of inclusion and neighbourliness, but who are perhaps not yet versed in the very real challenges newcomers and refugees face in the process of integration. This tool, and the discussions it leads to, could also help rural students overcome the "noisy silences" highlighted by Corbett, Tinkham, and Bonner (this volume). While it will not single-handedly achieve deep equity in rural communities, it just might be something that grandpa will try.

REFERENCES

Ali, Mehrunnisa Ahmad. 2008. "Second-Generation Youth's Belief in the Myth of Canadian Multiculturalism." *Canadian Ethnic Studies* 40 (2): 89–107. https://doi.org/10.1353/ces.2010.0017.

Ali, Mehrunnisa Ahmad. 2012. "The Shadow of Colonialism on Relations between Immigrant Parents and Their Children's Teachers." *Alberta Journal of Educational Research* 58 (2): 198–215.

Anderssen, Erin. 2017. "Welcome to the Country: Refugees Are Helping a Prairie Town Grow." *Globe and Mail*, November 12, 2017. https://www.theglobeandmail.com/news/national/welcome-to-the-country/article30820904/.

Azano, Amy P. 2015. "Addressing the Rural Context in Literacies Research." *Journal of Adolescent and Adult Literacy* 59 (3), 267–69. https://doi.org/10.1002/jaal.480.

Corbett, Michael. 2010. "Backing the Right Horse: Teacher Education, Sociocultural Analysis and Literacy in Rural Education." *Teaching and Teacher Education* 26 (1): 82–86. https://doi.org/10.1016/j.tate.2009.08.001.

Crenshaw, Kimberlé. 1989. "Demarginalizing the Intersection of Race and Sex: A Black Feminist Critique of Antidiscrimination Doctrine, Feminist Theory, and Antiracist Politics." *University of Chicago Legal Forum* 1: 31.

Cummins, Jim. 2011. "Literacy Engagement: Fueling Academic Growth for English Learners." *The Reading Teacher* 65 (2): 142–46. https://doi.org/10.1002/TRTR.01022.

Epp, Roger. 2008. *We Are All Treaty People: Prairie Essays*. Edmonton: University of Alberta Press.

Epp, Roger, and David Whitson. 2001. *Writing Off the Rural West: Globalization, Governments and the Transformation of Rural Communities*. Edmonton: University of Alberta Press.

Esses, Victoria M., and Charlie Carter. 2019. *Beyond the Big City: How Small Communities Across Canada Can Attract and Retain Newcomers*. Toronto: Public Policy Forum.

Esses, Victoria M., Leah K. Hamilton, Caroline Bennett-AbuAyyash, and Meyer Burstein. 2010. *Characteristics of a Welcoming Community*. Ottawa: Citizenship and Immigration Canada.

Esses, Victoria M., Scott Veenvliet, Gordon Hodson, and Ljiljana Mihic. 2008. "Justice, Morality, and the Dehumanization of Refugees." *Social Justice Research* 21 (1): 4–25. https://doi.org/10.1007/s11211-007-0058-4.

Gorski, Paul. 2019. "Avoiding Racial Equity Detours." *Educational Leadership: Journal of the Department of Supervision and Curriculum Development* 76 (7): 56–61.

Government of Canada. 2011. "Evaluation of the Welcoming Communities Initiative." Last updated September 15, 2011. http://www.cic.gc.ca/english/resources/evaluation/wci/section1.asp.

Hamm, Lyle. 2014. "The Culturally Responsive Classroom: A Proactive Approach to Diversity in the Classroom." *Education Canada*, 20 September 2014. https://www.edcan.ca/articles/the-culturally-responsive-classroom/.

Hébert, Yvonne. 2013. "Cosmopolitanism and Canadian Multicultural Policy: Intersection, Relevance and Critique." *Encounters on Education* 14: 3–19. https://doi.org/10/.15572/ENCO2013.01.

Hébert, Yvonne. 2016. "Youth in Plural Cities, Multiculturalism and Citizenship: Policy Challenges and Opportunities." *Foro de Educación* 20: 199–230.

Hébert, Yvonne, and Lori Wilkinson. 2011. "Meeting the Challenges of the New Century: Creating Common Values as Fundamental to Citizenship." In "55th Annual Conference of the Comparative and International Education Society (CIES)," edited by Ratna Ghosh, special issue of *Canadian Issues / Thèmes canadiens* 2011 (Spring): 28–34.

Hellstrom, Mikael. 2018. *Refugees Discuss Their Settlement Experience in New Brunswick*. Research brief for Migration in Remote and Rural Areas. https://www.uwinnipeg.ca/ceri-network/docs/hellstrom-mirra-research-brief.pdf.

Howard, Gary R. 2016. *We Can't Teach What We Don't Know*. 3rd ed. New York: Teachers College Press.

IRCC (Immigration, Refugees and Citizenship Canada). 2019. *Rural and Northern Immigration Pilot: About the Process*. Ottawa: Government of Canada. https://www.canada.ca/en/immigration-refugees-citizenship/services/immigrate-canada/rural-northern-immigration-pilot-about.html.

Jedwab, Jack. 2016. "Pick a Number: The Value of Annual Consultations on Immigration Levels." *Canadian Diversity* 13 (1): 11–17.

Keung, Nicholas. 2017. "Immigration Pilot Program Aims to Draw Newcomers to Atlantic Canada." *Star*, November 25, 2017. https://www.thestar.com/news/immigration/2017/11/25/immigration-pilot-program-aims-to-draw-newcomers-to-atlantic-canada.html.

Kilbride, Kenise M., and Mehrunnisa Ahmad Ali. 2010. "Striving for Voice: Language Acquisition and Canadian Immigrant Women." *Current Issues in Language Planning* 11 (2): 173–89. https://doi.org/10.1080/14664208.2010.505075.

Lam, Michelle. 2017. *Refugee Journeys: Identity, Intersectionality, and Integration*. Board game. Self-published, Birdlight Games.

Lam, Michelle. 2018a. "'I Put Myself in My Parents' Shoes:' Dignity and Dehumanization in EAL Classrooms." *Canadian Journal for New Scholars in Education / Revue Canadienne Des Jeunes Chercheures et Chercheurs En Éducation* 9 (2). http://journalhosting.ucalgary.ca/index.php/cjnse/article/view/43276.

Lam, Michelle. 2018b. "'We Can't Paint Them with One Brush': Creating Opportunities for Learning about Refugee Integration." *Refuge: Canada's Journal on Refugees* 34 (2): 103–12.

Lam, Michelle. 2019. "Language Education for Newcomers in Rural Canada: Needs, Opportunities, and Innovations." *Journal of Rural and Community Development* 14 (1): 37–47. https://journals.brandonu.ca/jrcd/article/view/1596.

Lam, Michelle. 2020. "Understanding the Effectiveness of an Anti-racist Educational Intervention." *Journal of Higher Education Theory and Practice* 20 (13): 147–153.

Lam, Michelle. 2021. "Friendly Manitoba? A Brandon Case Study on Welcoming Newcomers Outside the Big City." PhD diss., University of Manitoba. https://hdl.handle.net/1993/35327.

Li, Peter. 2002. *Destination Canada: Immigration Debates and Issues*. Oxford: Oxford University Press.

Li, Peter. 2003. "Deconstructing Canada's Discourse of Immigrant Integration." *Journal of International Migration and Integration / Revue de l'integration et de la migration internationale* 4 (3): 315–33. https://doi.org/10.1007/s12134-003-1024-0.

Reitz, Jeffrey G., Josh Curtis, and Jennifer Elrick. 2014. "Immigrant Skill Utilization: Trends and Policy Issues." *Journal of International Migration and Integration* 15 (1): 1–26. https://doi.org/10.1007/s12134-012-0265-1.

Robertson, Heather Jane. 2005. "Lost in Translation." *Phi Delta Kappan* 86 (5): 410–11. https://doi.org/10.1177/003172170508600516.

Sawatzky, Laurie. 2018. "Perspectives on Refugee Settlement and Integration Across Canada." Paper presented at the Metropolis Conference, Calgary, AB, March 23, 2018.

Shan, Hongxia. 2015. "Settlement Services in the Training and Education of Immigrants: Toward a Participatory Mode of Governance." *New Directions for Adult and Continuing Education* 146 (Summer): 19–28. https://doi.org/10.1002/ace.20128.

Valade, Marc. 2019. "From Immigrant-Friendly to Immigrant-Competent: Improving the Immigrant 'Dating Game' of Smaller Communities." *Migration in Remote and Rural Areas*. Winnipeg: University of Winnipeg and Community Engaged Research on Immigration Network.

Wilkinson, Lori, and Joseph Garcea. 2017. *The Economic Integration of Refugees in Canada: A Mixed Record?* Washington, DC: Migration Policy Institute. https://www.migrationpolicy.org/research/economic-integration-refugees-canada-mixed-record.

Wilkinson, Lori, Miu Chung Yan, A. Ka Tat Tsang, Rick Sin, and Sean Lauer. 2012. "The School-to-Work Transitions of Newcomer Youth in Canada." *Canadian Ethnic Studies; Calgary* 44 (3): 29–44.

Wong, Loyd, and Shibao Guo. 2018. "Canadian Ethnic Studies in the Changing Context of Immigration: Looking Back, Looking Forward." *Canadian Ethnic Studies Journal* 50 (1): 1–9.

CONTEXTUAL BIBLE STUDY

An Effective Practice to Promote Inclusivity in Rural Communities and Faith Groups

Coleen Lynch

RURAL CHRISTIANS have often been stereotyped and stigmatized as intolerant. Reimer (this volume) does much to systematically address, and in many ways falsify, this stereotype, at least with respect to "evangelical" Christians in Canada. However, it is undeniably true that some Christians, rural and urban, Protestant and Catholic, have interpreted Christian scriptures (the Bible of the Old and New Testament) in ways that support, if not actually promote, intolerance. It does not have to be this way. Indeed, rural churches of all denominations possess the potential to play incredibly important roles in transforming the attitudes of congregations across Canada on issues related to cultural and religious inclusion. It is clear that religious adherence and attendance has seen an overall decline across Canada, including rural Canada. However, church service attendance levels do generally remain higher outside of major urban centres (Clark 2003, 4). For many rural communities across the country, the church or churches remain key institutional pillars. Given the foundational role churches often play in rural communities, it is necessary to acknowledge the spiritual underpinnings of such communities and recognize that they present an important avenue for action and change as we strive for deep equality across rural Canada (Banack and Pohler, introduction to this volume).

Rural churches have an enormous and very real potential to create and support inclusivity in their communities. This chapter illustrates one way in which churches can realize this potential: through the effective use of a form of spiritual capital to address intolerance in rural communities. More specifically, I will introduce Contextual Bible Study (CBS) as a transformative tool of spiritual capital—a values-based initiative that holds the potential to bring about change in the attitudes and actions of Christian participants on issues related to inclusion and neighbourliness. In fact, CBS interactions often lead to creative and effective actions for the positive transformation of real-life issues in rural communities.

The chapter begins with discussions of the notion of spiritual capital and the concept of CBS. I then describe a CBS I facilitated at a denominational women's meeting held in rural Alberta in September 2018. This event included a group discussion of two broad themes: the plight of immigrants and refugees in Canada on one hand, and that of Indigenous peoples on the other. The Biblical story of the flight into Egypt and the story of Our Lady of Guadalupe from the Christian tradition provided the material for reflection and interaction connecting to the themes. In this CBS, a positive and pronounced change was observed among participants with respect to their attitudes towards these often-marginalized groups—an outcome that demonstrates that, under certain guidance, rural people can mutually engage their deeply held spiritual values and beliefs to bring about needed transformation in addressing important local issues.

Before I begin, however, a brief caveat related to the uniqueness of this chapter. Although I reference various academic work throughout, including a small academic case study I presided over, much of this chapter is based upon my own personal experiences. With nearly 50 years of rural ministry experience in Canada and in Peru, I have learned the significance of scripture and Christian tradition for rural populations. Facilitating CBSs in Canada and using a similar method in Base Christian Communities in Peru, I witnessed the empowering effect of reflection on scripture and Christian tradition in open dialogue with others. This simple process can transform deeply entrenched attitudes and help participants engage in definitive actions that address often difficult and challenging issues for local rural communities. Although I hope many academics will find the following discussion interesting, the audience

I am mostly aiming at with this chapter are Christians who call rural Canada home, and especially rural Canadian church leaders who possess the opportunity to use CBS as a tool to address issues of cultural and religious intolerance in their communities.

WHAT IS SPIRITUAL CAPITAL?

Spiritual capital is a form of social capital. *Social capital* is a term frequently used to convey levels of interpersonal trust; shared norms, values and identity; and willingness to act co-operatively or with reciprocity that exist within any given community. It is generally understood to be the product of communal interaction of various sorts. It is often argued that higher levels of interaction in a society lead to higher levels of social capital in any given community, leading to a variety of positive outcomes for the community as a whole as well as individuals within that community. As Flora, Flora, and Gesteyer (2016) have argued, the measure of social capital is a key factor in understanding how relationships operate in a society as assets for both individuals and groups.

As a form of social capital, spiritual capital results from our interactions with those processes that form our values, give meaning to our existence, and determine our approach to life (Baker and Skinner 2006). The notion of spiritual capital is premised especially on the idea that religions and religious communities can represent a key component of a community's overall social capital. This is due to the well-known effects that spiritual and religious practices, beliefs, networks, and institutions can have on an individual's approach to interacting with fellow citizens and participating civically to improve communal life. Indeed, American sociologist Robert Putnam—perhaps the best-known proponent of using social capital as an indicator of community health—sees churches as a significant resource for communities in this regard. Putnam (2000, 66) notes that "faith communities...are arguably the single most important repository of social capital in America." I would argue that the same point can be made for rural communities across Canada. It is true that religious adherence and attendance has declined across both urban and rural Canada. But it is also true that, for a sizable segment of the population, especially those in rural centres, the church remains a key spiritual and civic institution from which much social capital can accrue.

Spiritual capital is often used as an umbrella term that includes religious capital and religious human capital. Although religious capital and spiritual capital are sometimes used interchangeably (Adjibolosoo 2013; Baker and Miles-Watson 2006; Friedli 2001; Guest 2007; Iannaccone 2003; Hammerli 2011; Woodberry 2003), for my purposes, religious capital is directly related to the practice of religion while spiritual capital is a broader idea that extends beyond specific membership in a religious organization. Spiritual and religious capital operate in conjunction with each other. Spiritual capital creates the atmosphere and motivation for actions that result in religious capital. Religious capital relates to religious traditions and their practices, both individual (Iannaccone 1990) and collective (Baker and Miles-Watson 2006; Baker and Skinner 2006; Baker and Smith 2011). For Christians, personal and community prayer, pastoral visits, worship, Christian education, and Bible study are all examples of religious capital that accrue spiritual capital within individuals and community members. *Religious human capital* is a related though less frequently used term, which describes a mixture of both personal skills and experience accrued within the family and the religious group. To accrue this form of capital, one must participate in the celebration of rituals, the acquisition of faith knowledge, and congregational fellowship (Iannoccone 1990, 299). As a result, churches are depositories of both religious (human) capital and individual and collective spiritual capital that can be tapped on occasion to influence the broader well-being of the local community.

Importantly, spiritual capital is something that can empower individuals not only to alter the way they interact with their most familiar fellow citizens, but also to experience transformation with respect to how they see and understand those largely unfamiliar to them. Speaking specifically to the issue of cultural or religious tolerance, clearly one's background—their "home" culture—is a fundamental component of understanding the views any given individual holds. If one grew up in an environment devaluing other cultures or being suspicious and negative towards certain groups of people, then we are not likely to easily change the views of this individual unless they encounter a compelling experience, a new knowledge, or a transformed relationship that can alter their worldview. If religious viewpoints have substantially formed one's way of seeing and understanding the world—as is this case in the Christian communities across rural

Canada with whom I work—then examining the origin of those religious beliefs, principles, and outlooks on life becomes critical to one's interactions with others. For religious individuals, an openness to a change in worldview equals an openness to consider different ways of understanding God or different expressions of values. Such openness can lead to important changes in individuals and communities with respect to understanding and welcoming those from different cultural or religious backgrounds.

CBS AS A TOOL FOR CHANGE

CBS provides an important example of a tool that can unlock this potential for positive change. It is a form of dialogue and interpretation that empowers ordinary Christians to engage the Bible and each other in helpful ways. Nadar (2009, 387) defines CBS broadly as "an interactive study of particular texts in the bible, which brings the perspectives of both the context of the reader and the context of the bible into dialogue, for the purpose of transformation." Similar to the liberation theology movement in Latin America in the 1970s, CBS was coined in the 1980s in South Africa as a "form of liberation hermeneutics" (West 2014, 2). It was devised as a practical tool to engage the expertise and insights of ordinary Bible readers and academic Biblical scholars in a group or community quest to address a communal problem by encouraging individual transformations. The CBS method is also closely connected to the "See, Judge, Act" approach (West 2014). In this approach, the "See" phase highlights the need to analyze the local or community context, the "Judge" phase involves examining a Biblical text that speaks to this local context, and the "Act" phase consists in carrying out a course of action that was illuminated by the reflection and sharing that took place within the group setting (West and Ujama Centre Staff 2007). The critical components are always the real-life local context of a situation and the subsequent action plan for transformation to address the presenting issue that emerges out of this communal reflection (Nadar 2009).

CBS, which incorporates this "See, Judge, Act" approach, is an effective tool for changing attitudes because it is not simply a content course taught to those who are curious about a particular issue. Rather, it is an interactive exercise designed to empower community members to take action on an issue they are already invested in by facilitating

participatory study of the issue and relevant Biblical texts (West and Ujama Centre staff 2007; Nadar 2009). Nadar (2009, 390–99) illustrates this by outlining the five Cs of CBS: community (interactive); context (context of the reader); criticality (context of the bible); conscientization (critical dialogue and raising awareness); and change (transformation).

Overall, CBS promotes an "embodied theology" (West and Ujama Centre Staff 2007, 62). It is grounded in the deep belief that God speaks into our life: "The Bible itself shows that God speaks specifically to specific people in specific life situations" (17). More importantly for our purposes, CBS is spiritual capital in action. The knowledge, wisdom, and openness that accrue in believers as a result of worship, prayer, and Christian study invite the believer into a rich environment of ongoing learning towards positive transformation of the self and the world, guided by an evolving worldview. CBS is one way of actively participating in this learning—in other words, it is the embodiment of spiritual capital.

One way for facilitators to use CBS as a tool for this type of personal and communal transformation is by engaging a community or congregation about local concerns through social media, café chats, focus groups, town meetings, or casual conversation at church, cultural events, or just on the street. The facilitator then invites participants to attend a meeting at which they will collaboratively categorize and prioritize the issues raised in their initial conversations. After a consensus is reached regarding what issues need to be addressed first, the facilitator invites participants to return to a follow-up meeting, where they will engage in a CBS. Participants do not require knowledge of the Bible, only a willingness to address the issue named and a commitment to engage in CBS as a guide for dialogue and action planning. The facilitator, who must have sufficient Biblical knowledge and group facilitation skills, then examines scripture to find passages relevant to the issue, which the group will read and discuss at the follow-up meeting.

The follow-up meeting uses a CBS process. The facilitator presents the Biblical text or texts that relate to the issue that the group marked as a priority at their first meeting. The facilitator may give some brief historical or literary context for the passage. The group then examines the Biblical personalities present in the passage—their character traits, motivations, probable worries and concerns, emotions expressed and

withheld, and choices and strategies used to address issues. Continued dialogue results in connecting the Biblical text with the issue being addressed by the group. At the end of the meeting, the facilitator asks how the group wants to address their issue. The group brainstorms both individual and collective actions, then consensually decides on a plan of action. The entire meeting lasts an hour and a half to two hours. The facilitator concludes by suggesting a later meeting to evaluate the outcomes of the action plan.

CBS AND THE ISSUE OF RELIGIOUS AND CULTURAL INCLUSIVITY IN RURAL COMMUNITIES: A BRIEF CASE STUDY

In September 2018, I used CBS as a vehicle for attitudinal change on the issue of religious and cultural inclusivity in a regional denomination meeting. Forty-seven Anglican women (25 from rural areas, 22 from urban) gathered for their annual Yellowhead-Edmonton West Regional Anglican Church Women meeting. The women represented 10 rural parishes and seven urban parishes. The planning committee invited me to preach at the opening church service and to be the guest speaker at the meeting. I chose to use this opportunity to engage this community in a CBS process, and to evaluate the effectiveness of the CBS approach with regard to issues of inclusivity.

Basic surveys were administered to the participants both before and after the CBS. The "before" survey asked participants what resources they used to form their views about immigrants and refugees: family, school, work, internet/television/newspaper, personal experience, or experiences of people you know. The same question was then asked with respect to Indigenous people. Overall, participants responded that they used the following resources to form their views on refugees, immigrants, and Indigenous people: family (21%); school (6%); work (13%); internet/television/newspaper (64%); personal experience (49%); and experiences of people you know (38%). In general, rural and urban respondents formed their views from similar sources; however, urban respondents relied more on internet/television/newspaper as a resource while rural respondents relied more on the experiences of people they knew.

The "before" survey also used a five-point Likert scale to rate participant dissatisfaction or satisfaction with Canada's treatment of immigrants and refugees, with a brief explanation of their choice. Similar questions were then asked for Canada's treatment of Indigenous people. Twenty percent of rural respondents and 27% of urban respondents were dissatisfied with Canada's treatment of refugees and immigrants. Twenty-four percent of rural responses and 55% of urban respondents were dissatisfied with Canada's treatment of Indigenous people. Participants were then asked to describe how their local community was involved with immigrant and refugee issues and Indigenous issues. The diversity of responses ranged from a firm "I have no idea!" to stating that their parishes were sponsoring a refugee family. There were few initiatives involving Indigenous people, though some respondents, possibly from the same parish, had participated in the blanket exercise—an exercise designed to help non-Indigenous people try to understand historical land issues from the perspective of Indigenous people.

After this first survey was completed, I facilitated a CBS on the issue of inclusivity using the Christian story of the flight into Egypt (Matt 2:13–18). This is a well-known passage for Christians that tells the story of the plight of Joseph and Mary and their newborn baby Jesus, who some were already calling the "King of the Jews." Interpreting him as a serious threat to his rule, King Herod sought to murder the child, going so far as to order the execution of all male children under the age of two in the vicinity of Bethlehem. In the story, an angel appears to Joseph in a dream and instructs him to take Mary and Jesus to Egypt to maintain their safety from Herod's wrath.

After the presentation of the Biblical text, I facilitated a conversation focused on how Mary, Joseph, and newborn Jesus might have experienced the journey to Egypt, the arrival in a foreign land, and the challenges of settling into a new culture with no job and no family ties. Participants named issues of language barriers, no work tools, no friends or relatives, unfamiliar culture and food, travel with a newborn, and the reason that compelled them to go in the first place: the safety of their child. Very quickly, participants connected the experience of the Holy Family trying to protect their child with the motivation of contemporary immigrants and refugees looking for a better life for their family

in spite of all the struggles and challenges they must face on their migration journey.

I then moved on to present a second story—the story of Our Lady of Guadalupe—to examine issues relating to Indigenous people. This story is not from scripture but has a long history in the Christian tradition. According to the traditional account, in sixteenth-century Mexico, Mary, the virgin mother of Jesus, appeared to a poor Indigenous peasant named Juan Diego. She had brown skin and spoke Juan Diego's native language. Mary requested that a shrine be built to honour her. Hearing the story, the local Bishop initially did not believe Juan Diego and demanded a "sign" before moving forward with the construction. In response, Mary left an embedded portrait of herself on the inside of Diego's cloak. In 1895, Pope Leo XIII approved this image for veneration. It is thus a widely known story in Catholic circles, as well as among Protestants who have travelled in, or know people from, Spanish-speaking countries. The relevance of this still-popular image is significant because it highlights both an Indigenous witness to a Marian apparition and an Indigenous rendering of the Blessed Virgin Mary herself.

In the discussion that followed my presentation of this story, participants identified issues that Juan Diego faced: prejudice, poverty, power (the Bishop), invalidation of personal experience, and scorn of Indigenous culture and language. The participants reluctantly admitted that local Indigenous people on reserves and in the city probably experienced similar issues. Several participants expressed annoyance because they felt bombarded by the continuing focus on the negative stories about Christians, which had become more prominent since the Truth and Reconciliation Commission meeting held in Edmonton in May of 2014. Others expressed a desire to just move on from the residential school issue and talk about something else. Some participants also noted that they were tired of what they perceived as Indigenous people receiving monetary assistance without doing anything to help themselves out of situations of addiction and criminal activity.

After these discussions, I administered a second survey that asked participants to rate, using a five-point Likert scale, how helpful the study of the Bible story was in informing their views on refugees and immigrants and how helpful the study of the Christian traditional story

was in informing their views on Indigenous people. Participants wrote a brief explanation for each of their responses. Eighty percent of rural participants and 68% of urban participants found the Bible story very helpful or extremely helpful in informing their views on refugees and immigrants. With respect to their views on Indigenous people, 56% of rural participants and 59% of urban participants found the example from Christian tradition very helpful or extremely helpful in forming their views.

The final questions on the "after" survey asked what action, if any, the participant would personally take towards refugee and immigrant issues and Indigenous issues. Eighty percent of rural participants replied that they would take personal actions towards helping or welcoming refugees and immigrants, and 52% of rural participants were prepared to take personal actions towards helping or welcoming Indigenous peoples.

UNDERSTANDING THE OUTCOMES

Of course, these are the results of but one small case study. Although I am unable to make any substantive claims with respect to the impact this type of CBS can have on changing the attitudes of different groups of Christians across rural Canada, the results of my surveys in this case show that people can change their minds on sensitive topics when they reflect on their viewpoints, often inadequately formed, through shared dialogue with others on relevant scripture passages and appropriate examples from the Christian tradition. It is worth reiterating, however, that all study participants were women. It has long been assumed that gender plays an important role in the formation of racist or anti-immigrant views, with women in particular tending towards more positive or open viewpoints (see, e.g., Johnson and Marini 1998). Although more recent research has cast some doubt on this long-held assumption (Hughes and Tuch 2003; Ponce 2017), the fact that all study participants were women does place an additional limitation on our hopes to extrapolate broad conclusions about the effectiveness of CBS as a tool for overcoming cultural and religious intolerance in rural Christian communities. Many more studies of this sort are needed to academically verify the effectiveness with which this type of CBS can affect attitudinal change in practicing Christians across rural Canada

on issues related to immigrants, refugees, and Indigenous people. But my strong hunch, after having worked in rural ministry for over 40 years, is that there is something very promising in this method.

Interestingly in this case study, although one could note positive progress in terms of participants' attitudes towards both groups, participants seemed more positively inclined towards immigrants and refugees than Indigenous people. There is a whole host of potential reasons why this may be the case, some of which are related to the CBS approach itself. For instance, Biblical stories like the flight to Egypt may hold more weight for practising Christians in rural Canada than stories from Christian tradition such as Our Lady of Guadalupe. Other reasons are related to participants' own personal histories. The practical realities of the lived context of study participants may affect their responses. For instance, historical interactions or deeply engrained societal-level stereotypes may contribute to rural participants' views about one group (Indigenous people) being more hardened than their views about another (immigrants and refugees). Again, more research is needed to better understand this outcome.

That said, I maintain that communal study, through the lens of scripture, of specific issues affecting rural communities has the potential to change long-held attitudes and actions of rural Christian communities. Specifically, it has the potential to move people towards a greater openness and willingness to explore actions that could help address real-life rural issues and concerns around tolerance and inclusion. The power of CBS is in its simplicity. It is designed to be an effective, practical vehicle for engaging any participant to reflect openly on ordinary life issues. Through study and dialogue, individuals and groups can transform destructive thoughts and strategize actions for positive outcomes through the application of Christian scripture to contemporary issues. It is also worth noting that, despite my personal experience using CBS from a Christian perspective, CBS could be developed by any faith tradition by using its authoritative resources in writing, ritual, and other traditions. Furthermore, secular spiritual capital may also be used to motivate a focused study among nonreligious or nonspiritual participants using the resources of literature, history, and philosophy. I have aimed this chapter specifically at rural Christian communities,

but CBS is a tool that can be applied much more widely than I have documented here.

Of course, CBS is not a panacea that will alter all negative views toward otherness among Christian believers. It is clear from the particularly limited sample examined that tolerance with respect to Indigenous people in particular is a relevant and ongoing concern for rural communities. Building more positive relationships between adjacent reserves and rural towns and villages will require an intentional effort from both parties. Anecdotally, cultural events in both rural communities and on reserves certainly help to bring diverse groups together in a friendly environment. This form of social capital is critical because forming key relationships of mutual trust, especially among leaders, promotes mutual advocacy for further contacts and improved relationships. This same principle provides a model for new immigrants and refugees to share cultural values through conversations engendered in events that often start with a showcase of ethnic treasures of food and dress. Relationships often begin and continue over shared meals and fellowship. These intentional actions tend to break down past bias and prejudice. Often, they result in participants realizing that people are people all over the world and that, perhaps surprisingly, they share similar values.

What if one person changes their views and takes action to be factually informed about people and cultures unfamiliar to them? What if one person commits to building a relationship with someone from another way of life? What if churches, religious groups, and people with values of inclusion and caring for all humankind made an effort to listen to one another and learn from difference? What if we all began to welcome the stranger—the person whose culture, language, or even values are different from our own—like the Good Samaritan at the heart of Roger Epp's analysis in this volume? What if we sought to find solutions together to confront the damage of intolerance? What if we all boldly began to accept one another and to hear out our neighbours' stories of pain and prejudice—their challenges and suffering, hopes and dreams? We can be more inclusive, we can be better neighbours, whether in rural communities or anywhere else. In the rural context, churches can play an important role in encouraging greater tolerance and, ideally, compassion, inclusiveness, and deep equality. We will only be able to achieve this when we decide to allow difference

to be a catalyst for changing negative attitudes and embracing acceptance of others as a way to transform ourselves and our world.

There is now a growing interest in Intercultural Bible Study, which has groups from different nations and social classes examine the same issue and Bible text and share their insights (de Witt and Dyk 2015; Prior 2015; Schipani 2015; Segovia 2015; Van Zyl 2015; West 2014). For the issue of tolerance in rural communities, Intercultural Bible Study using a CBS method could potentially succeed in changing negative attitudes towards difference. By joining diverse groups in dialogue through technology—FaceTime, Zoom, email—study groups from across the world can gain access to different viewpoints and actions that can be mutually inspiring and life-transforming for those involved. Indeed, to foster even greater inclusion and rural community solidarity among neighbours of different religious backgrounds, interfaith CBS may be an approach that could be explored. For an ecumenical Bible study to move towards actions, we need to hear and honour all voices.

"We are transformed when we acknowledge we need each other, the academic and the 'ordinary reader', when we experience how intercultural conversations shock and liberate, disturb and challenge, prod and sensitize, refute and confirm, question and transform, interfere and create anew" (Prior 2015, 94). Difference is not our enemy. Whatever methods we use to facilitate greater awareness and openness with one another in rural areas promises the hope of greater tolerance. CBS is one such viable option for rural churches to lead the way of transformation towards the goal of building more inclusive rural communities.

REFERENCES

Adjibdosoo, Senyo. 2013. *Spiritual Capital: Its Meaning and Essence*. Bloomington: West Bow Press.

Baker, Chris, and Jonathan Miles-Watson. 2006. "Faith and Traditional Capitals: Defining the Public Scope of Spiritual and Religious Capital—A Literature Review." *Implicit Religion* 13 (1): 17–69.

Baker, Chris, and Hannah Skinner. 2006. *Faith in Action: The Dynamic Connection Between Spiritual Capital and Religious Capital*. Final report of the William Temple Foundation research project (2002–2005) Regenerating Communities: A Theological and Strategic Critique. Chester, UK: William Temple Foundation.

Baker, Chris, and Greg Smith. 2011. "Spiritual, Religious and Social Capital: Exploring Their Dimensions and Their Relationship with Faith-Based Motivation and Participation in UK Civil Society." Paper presented at the BSA Sociology of Religion Group Conference, Edinburgh, UK, April 2011.

Clark, Warren. 2003. "Pockets of Belief: Religious Attendance Patterns in Canada." *Canadian Social Trends* 68 (Spring): 2–5.

de Witt, Hans, and Janet Dyk, eds. 2015. *Bible and Transformation: The Promise of Intercultural Bible Reading*. Atlanta: SBL Press.

Flora, Cornela Butler, Jan L. Flora, and Stephen P. Gasteyer. 2016. *Rural Communities: Legacy and Change*. 5th ed. Boulder, CO: Westview Press.

Friedli, Lynne. 2001. "Social and Spiritual Capital: Building 'Emotional Resilience' in Communities and Individuals." *Political Theology* 2 (2): 55–64.

Guest, Mathew. 2007. "In Search of Spiritual Capital: The Spiritual as a Cultural Resource." In *A Sociology of Spirituality*, edited by Peter C. Jupp, 181–200. Oxfordshire: Taylor and Francis.

Hammerli, Maria. 2011. "Religion and Spirituality between Capital and Gift." *Religion and Theology* 18: 195–210

Hughes, Michael, and Steven A. Tuch. 2003. "Gender Differences in Whites' Racial Attitudes: Are Women's Attitudes Really More Favorable?" *Social Psychology Quarterly* 66 (4): 384–401.

Iannaccone, Laurence R. 1990. "Religious Practice: A Human Capital Approach." *Journal for the Scientific Study of Religion* 29 (3): 297–314.

Iannaccone, Laurence R. 2003. "Spiritual Capital: An Introduction and Literature Review." Paper presented at the Spiritual Capital Planning Meeting, Cambridge, MA, October 2003.

Johnson, Monica Kirkpatrick, and Margaret Mooney Marini. 1998. "Bridging the Racial Divide in the United States: The Effect of Gender." *Social Psychology Quarterly* 61 (3): 247–58.

Nadar, Sarojini. 2009. "Beyond the 'Ordinary Reader' and the 'Invisible Intellectual': Shifting Contextual Bible Study from Liberation Discourse to Liberation Pedagogy." *OTE* 22 (2): 384–403.

Ponce, Aaron. 2017. "Gender and Anti-Immigrant Attitudes in Europe." *Socius* 3: 1–17.

Prior, John M. 2015. "The Ethics of Transformative Reading: The Text, the Other and Oneself." In de Witt and Dyk, *Bible and Transformation*, 75–97.

Putnam, Robert. 2000. *Bowling Alone: The Collapse and Revival of American Community*. London: Simon and Schuster.

Schipani, Daniel. 2015. "Transformation in Intercultural Bible Reading: A View from Practical Theology." In de Witt and Dyk, *Bible and Transformation*, 99–116.

Segovia, Fernando. 2015. "Intercultural Bible Reading as Transformation for Liberation: Intercultural Hermeneutics and Bible Studies." In de Witt and Dyk, *Bible and Transformation*, 19–51.

Van Zyl, Danie. 2015. "Toward Transformation: Factors in Transformative Reading." In de Witt and Dyk, *Bible and Transformation*, 117–29.

West, Gerald. 2014. "Locating 'Contextual Bible Study' within Biblical Liberation Hermeneutics and Intercultural Biblical Hermeneutics." *HTS Theological Studies* 70 (11): 1–16.

West, Gerald, and Ujamaa Centre Staff. 2007. *Doing Contextual Bible Study: A Resource Manual*. South Africa: The Ujamaa Centre for Biblical and Theological Community Development and Research.

Woodberry, Robert. 2003. "Researching Spiritual Capital: Promises and Pitfalls." Paper presented at the Spiritual Capital Planning Meeting, Cambridge, MA, October 2003.

IV

A RURAL APPROACH TO ANTI-RACISM AND SETTLER–INDIGENOUS RELATIONS

Co-operation and Neighbourliness

9

CO-OPERATIVE DEVELOPMENT POSSIBILITIES IN RURAL SETTLER AND INDIGENOUS COMMUNITIES

Lessons from the Co-operative Innovation Project and Co-operatives First

Dionne Pohler, Jen Budney, Murray Fulton, Darcy Overland, Aasa Marshall, Trista Pewapisconias, and Kyle White

TAKING SERIOUSLY THE GOAL OF BUILDING more inclusive rural communities also requires taking seriously the challenges facing people in these communities. Both rural and remote settler and Indigenous communities in western Canada are experiencing the negative effects of a growing development "gap" between the rural peripheries and urban centres, although the challenges they face are not identical.[1] Indigenous communities, which have been marginalized and oppressed since the very early days of colonization, continue to deal with the havoc inflicted on their communities by colonial policies, such as the attempted destruction of their social capacity through the residential school system and the severe constraints placed on Indigenous economic autonomy by the Indian Act.[2] By contrast, settlers residing in agrarian-based rural communities and once-vibrant regional manufacturing centres are experiencing more recent losses of primary industries and employers due to globalization, the competitive pressure for economies of scale in agricultural production, and the fossil fuel industry downturn. All of these factors have resulted in increasing exclusion of rural settlers from the labour market as family farms give way to corporate agriculture, businesses shut down, and skills

become obsolete. In both rural settler and Indigenous communities, we witness an under-investment in basic services such as health care, childcare, gas, and groceries, low or diminishing rates of volunteerism, a steady rise in addictions and mental health crises, and out-migration of those who are young and ambitious. These are all indicators of a prolonged or growing lack of community self-reliance.

The resultant (and for the most part, justified) perception of scarcity has not helped to alleviate, and indeed further contributes to, high levels of distrust between settler and Indigenous communities. While this distrust is widespread across Canada, it is incredibly pronounced in the rural west (see Joseph 2018; Banack, this volume), where the two groups often live in close geographic proximity but remain socially isolated from one another due to deeply embedded institutional and political barriers (e.g., the provincial municipality and federal reserve systems). Notwithstanding the fact that many of these settler and Indigenous communities have similar needs, people living in these places are subject to institutionally imposed segregation that limits their ability to work together and build trust within and across their communities. This segregation also impacts the increasing numbers of immigrants beginning to settle in rural municipalities, who are experiencing higher levels of social isolation and exclusion than new immigrants in urban centres (Patel et al. 2019). While some of these experiences may be the result of racism or bigotry, they are also inextricably linked to structural impairments and development challenges facing rural communities—for instance, depopulation (as outlined by Bollman, this volume) and the lack of community-based services.

The primary purpose of this chapter is to highlight the importance of addressing socioeconomic needs in rural settler and Indigenous communities in western Canada, and to explore whether co-operative development might be one feasible strategy for addressing community needs in an inclusive way. Co-operatives, or co-ops, are unique approaches to community development that can build social cohesion. That being said, they also require a certain degree of existing social cohesion and community capacity to form in the first place—two factors that may be in short supply in rural communities facing particularly high needs. We outline the challenges of co-op development in

rural settler and Indigenous communities and the conditions under which co-operative development is most likely to occur. Our insights are drawn from the data and findings of the Co-operative Innovation Project (CIP), a two-year, community- and action-based research project we undertook from 2014 to 2016 in rural settler and Indigenous communities in western Canada. In this chapter, we explore and extend several of the questions we asked in our research project: (1) What are the needs in rural and remote settler and Indigenous communities in western Canada? (2) Is the co-operative model (still) relevant and feasible in these communities for inclusive economic and social development? And (3) if it is, what is needed to encourage community members to develop inclusive and sustainable co-operatives to address their needs?

The key findings of the CIP project that we report in this chapter suggest that those rural settler and Indigenous communities that would receive the greatest benefit from the development of co-ops—those with the greatest needs—are also those facing the biggest hurdles in creating and sustaining inclusive development through co-ops. We suggest that inclusive development goals in rural settler and Indigenous communities are unlikely to be met through co-operatives unless efforts are made to establish a supportive co-operative development environment. This may require the creation of resources focused on encouraging and supporting co-operative development in rural communities. In particular, we see a need for resources supporting co-operation between and across rural settler and Indigenous communities to address their shared needs. We conclude our chapter by describing one such resource, Co-operatives First, a nonprofit organization that was established following the CIP to address the development challenges in rural western Canadian settler and Indigenous communities. Co-operatives First encourages and supports co-operative work at a local level to address communities' identified needs. We highlight several examples of new co-ops that have formed in rural communities with assistance from Co-operatives First. We note that, as a development tool, co-ops have unique potential to inclusively address local needs by breaking down barriers between rural settler and Indigenous communities. In particular, they can bring rural settlers and Indigenous peoples together to work on meaningful grassroots projects with a common goal: overcoming long-standing divisions within and

across these communities and ultimately creating the potential for settlers and Indigenous peoples living in close proximity to each other in the rural west to become deeply equal neighbours (Banack and Pohler, introduction to this volume; see also Henderson, this volume; Epp, this volume).

BACKGROUND ON COMMUNITY DEVELOPMENT AND CO-OPERATIVES

Development scholars have long viewed self-reliance as "not merely a necessity but a matter of survival" (Galtung et al. 1980). The UNHCR describes self-reliance as "the social and economic ability of an individual, a household or a community to meet essential needs (including protection, food, water, shelter, personal safety, health and education) in a sustainable manner and with dignity. Self-reliance, as a programme approach, refers to developing and strengthening livelihoods of persons of concern, and reducing their vulnerability and long-term reliance on humanitarian/external assistance" (International Labour Organization 2005, 1).

Building community self-reliance is an important component of building inclusive and sustainable societies insofar as self-reliance means that communities are able to develop resilience by actively building and engaging the capacity of their members to thrive in environments characterized by change, uncertainty, unpredictability, and surprise (Magis 2010). Resilient systems are inherently diverse and redundant, with built-in overlap and reserve resources to ensure that they can continue to function in the face of shocks and in times of need (Mazur 2013). Inclusive, local-level participation and control over decision-making are essential to governance in resilient communities; mere assets alone do not build resiliency.

Unfortunately, the importance of self-reliance and resiliency in building inclusive and sustainable communities has not always been well understood by government. For generations, Canada's federal government kept Indigenous communities dependent on meager government handouts. In 1990, the National Indigenous Economic Development Board (NIEDB) was established to assist the federal government in developing and implementing policies and programs that responded to the needs and circumstances of Indigenous people. According to its "Our Work" page on its website, the federally appointed NIEDB now works to "bring visibility

to the economic disparity between Indigenous communities and other Canadian communities, and to support Indigenous people in increasing participation in the economy." Yet despite nearly 30 years of programming, the NIEDB's (2019) Indigenous Economic Progress Report concluded that while the overall economic outcomes for Indigenous peoples are improving, this is only to varying and sometimes very small degrees.

Similarly, since 1987, the federal Department of Western Economic Diversification has been mandated to expand industry and generate increased economic and social stability in Canada's western provinces, with a combined role of coordinating and communicating all federal programs and activities that could contribute to economic development and diversification in the region, as well as representing the interests of western Canada in the development of national policies and programs. This department, like other regional development agencies in Canada, has faced criticism. Many programs lack transparency or are perceived as pork-barreling, and the results of 30-plus years of investment are mostly "either impossible to assess, or simply disappointing" (Kaplan 2018). In general, the top-down approach to socioeconomic development has not effectively enabled rural settler or Indigenous communities to pursue the kind of inclusive and sustainable development that would allow them to become self-reliant and resilient.

There are, of course, alternatives to top-down development models—alternatives that hold the promise of greater inclusivity, community participation, and self-determination. Social enterprises have been shown to be an effective way for communities to improve their own financial, social, and environmental well-being (Loney 2018). These are businesses whose primary reasons for being include the attainment of inclusive social and economic objectives that are determined by the communities themselves. In recent years, social enterprises and social innovation have garnered increasing attention. For instance, in 2018 the Government of Canada announced the creation of a Social Finance Fund—$755 million over ten years—to support innovative solutions on a broad range of social challenges and to attract private investment to the social finance sector (Employment and Social Development Canada 2018). Social enterprises are expected to be significant recipients of these funds. Concurrently, there is growing awareness that Indigenous

sovereignty—the ability of Indigenous communities to make their own decisions about what development approaches to take, or what Corntassel (2008) calls "sustainable self-determination"—is essential to successful and inclusive social and economic development on reserves.[3]

The co-operative organization—where the members are both the owners and the primary users of the organization's services—is a particularly versatile form of social enterprise. It is also a form of organization that is compatible with Indigenous sovereignty, based as it is on the values of self-help, self-responsibility, democracy, equality, equity, and solidarity. Co-ops, in fact, have a long history in the rural west. Where conventional development models failed in this region's past, co-ops were often able to fill the void. The most successful of these early co-ops have, over the long term, become fixtures of western Canadian landscape. They include, among others, Co-op grocery stores and gas stations, UFA (United Farmers of Alberta) cardlocks and farm and ranch supply stores, natural gas suppliers, and the many credit unions with branches in small towns that banks do not service. And while the historical co-operative movement is implicated in the strategies of colonization, assimilation of Indigenous labour, and consolidation of settler control over land and resources in the Canadian west (Sengupta 2015), scholars have noted the similarities between traditional modes of Indigenous self-governance and co-operative governance (Hammond-Ketilson 2004; Findlay 2006; Thompson and Emmanuel 2012). Co-operative values and principles are compatible with the aims of "quadruple bottom line organizations" (Scrimgeour and Iremonger 2004), which aim to meet Indigenous communities' unique combinations of economic, social, environmental, and cultural goals.

Co-ops typically operate with a lower cost of capital and provide local community members with opportunities for employment, education, and training, as they are often the last remaining organizations in depopulating or declining rural areas (Royer 2018; Mavenga and Olfert 2012). Importantly, community members have greater control of co-operative enterprises through their local ownership and the members' participation in governance. Local control is essential because it allows the community to balance multiple locally defined goals such as inclusive service provision, employment opportunities, and financial sustainability, rather than being subject to the whims of outside investors.

TABLE 9.1 Estimates of co-operative incorporations in rural settler and Indigenous communities in western Canada, 2000 to 2015

Year	Manitoba			Saskatchewan			Alberta			British Columbia			Total
	Settler	Indigenous	Subtotal	Settler	Indigenous	Subtotal	Settler	Indigenous	Subtotal	Settler	Indigenous	Subtotal	
2000	3	0	3	1	0	1	1	0	1	1	0	1	6
2001	5	0	5	3	0	3	3	0	3	3	0	3	14
2002	1	0	1	9	0	9	6	0	6	1	0	1	17
2003	7	0	7	1	0	1	0	0	0	4	0	4	12
2004	1	0	1	2	0	2	3	0	3	4	0	4	10
2005	4	0	4	4	0	4	1	0	1	2	0	2	11
2006	7	0	7	3	0	3	0	0	0	6	0	6	16
2007	4	0	4	6	0	6	1	0	1	1	0	1	12
2008	5	0	5	1	0	1	2	0	2	2	0	2	10
2009	5	1	6	2	0	2	2	0	2	2	0	2	12
2010	3	0	3	2	0	2	3	0	3	2	0	2	10
2011	2	0	2	4	0	4	2	0	2	5	0	5	13
2012	2	0	2	7	0	7	3	0	3	6	2	8	20
2013	-	-	-	4	0	4	1	0	1	7	0	7	12
2014	-	-	-	5	0	5	2	0	2	1	0	1	8
2015	-	-	-	3	0	3	-	-	-	-	-	-	3
Total	49	1	50	57	0	57	30	0	30	47	2	49	186

Source: CIP (2016).

Note: Some Indigenous-community co-ops are incorporated or registered in larger urban centres. Data for these co-ops may be missing.

Co-ops build social capital among members and strongly contribute to community self-reliance and resilience. Yet despite the potential advantages of co-ops, they are not always successful (Fairbairn, Fulton, and Pohler 2015; Fulton and Larson 2009). What's more, they have not been forming at the same rate in rural communities as they once did (Duguid and Karaphillis 2015), and Indigenous co-ops have been declining in number steadily for the past 50 years (Hammond-Ketilson and MacPherson 2001; Canadian Co-operative Association 2012). As Table 9.1 shows, between 30 and 57 co-operatives were formed in each of the four western provinces (British Columbia, Alberta, Saskatchewan, and Manitoba) over a 16-year period. This translates into roughly three co-ops per year per province. It was this realization that new co-op development has been declining that served as the initial motivation for the CIP.

MOTIVATION FOR THE CO-OPERATIVE INNOVATION PROJECT

Over the past few decades, many Western industrialized societies have been experiencing troubling socioeconomic changes, including labour market restructuring due to global outsourcing and automation (Acemoglu 2006; Acemoglu and Restrepo 2019), rising income inequality (Green, Riddell, and St.-Hillaire 2016), and significant political realignments characterized by growing partisanship. In some cases, they have also seen dramatic weakening of the authority of the established political classes and parties and alarming increases in health disparities within populations due to factors including addiction and lack of access to health resources (Case and Deaton 2020). The troubles are not evenly dispersed, but largely geographical and/or racialized (Kodras 1997). In Canada, rural settler communities have experienced these changes as more recent upheavals, while for most rural Indigenous communities the effects are part of a long continuum under colonial rule.

Both rural settler and rural Indigenous communities are experiencing intensified social and economic pressure due to changing demographic patterns, urbanization, and shifting government priorities and programs (Bollman, this volume). Remote, resource-based communities have seen sharp declines in population growth (Winkler et al. 2007). Many prairie settler communities have experienced population losses due to the increasing concentration and size of family farming operations, while others have experienced growth along with cultural changes as new immigrants arrive to work in an increasingly industrialized agricultural sector (Kandel and Brown 2006). The industrialization and incorporation of agricultural businesses have been encouraged by the growth of new technologies (for example, genetically modified crops), trade regimes (such as the World Trade Organization), marketing systems (including the elimination of marketing boards such as the Canadian Wheat Board), and "chickenization" (wherein very large corporations control all stages of agricultural production in contract-based factory farming systems). The result is an agricultural sector that is virtually unrecognizable from what it was 30 years ago.

Likewise, many Indigenous communities are experiencing large demographic shifts. Some are experiencing rapid population growth

due to high birth rates while others face declining growth rates, with continued out-migration from reserves to cities (Barrera 2017). Significant—sometimes abject—poverty due to lack of employment opportunities, poor paying jobs, substance abuse, deteriorating housing, and inadequate education have thrown some communities into states of permanent crisis (United Nations 2015). Others (though many fewer) have witnessed influxes of financial resources from Treaty Land Entitlement payments (Government of Canada 2015), successful operations of urban reserves (Poholka 2016), or other business ventures. At the same time, Indigenous political structures are facing new challenges and opportunities due to factors such as the push for Indigenous self-government and the federal duty to consult.

Historically, socioeconomic upheavals like these have been catalysts for individuals to form co-ops and other social economy organizations to collectively address economic or social need. We can find examples from the Industrial Revolution, European settlement of the Great Plains of North America, and the Great Depression (MacPherson 1979). There are many different kinds of co-ops, including worker co-ops, consumer co-ops, producer co-ops, and multi-stakeholder co-ops. Co-ops can be either nonprofit or for-profit enterprises. As Schneiberg and colleagues (2008, 637) note, the flexible structure of co-operatives has historically been used by groups of individuals to mobilize "against bureaucracies, markets, and corporations to promote community, economic self-sufficiency, local ownership, regional development, and workplace democracy." However, despite today's socioeconomic challenges (which could also be described as crises), co-ops are not forming in any great number in rural Indigenous or settler communities in Canada (Table 9.1). The lack of co-operative development in the face of major challenges within these communities is particularly interesting given the long and relatively successful history of co-operatives in rural settler communities across the prairie provinces (MacPherson 1979), the general congruity of co-operative principles and Indigenous values (Hammond-Ketilson 2004; Findlay 2006; Thompson and Emmanuel 2012), and the existence of some large, successful settler and Indigenous co-operatives operating in rural and remote regions of Canada (notably, Federated Co-operatives Limited and Artic Co-operatives Limited).

The primary motivation of the Co-operative Innovation Project (CIP) was to investigate why co-operative development appears to be stagnating in these communities and what might be done about it. The project sought to explore whether co-ops are a viable development model for these communities and, in particular, whether an inclusive approach to development through co-ops is feasible and sustainable. The ultimate goal of the project was to develop insights about the viability of the co-operative model in different rural settler and Indigenous communities, along with recommendations about how to support co-operation within and across these communities to address their identified needs.

METHOD

To date, the CIP is the largest project to simultaneously explore the needs and development experiences of both settler and Indigenous communities in rural western Canada. A brief overview of the methodology employed in the CIP is provided in this section. More detailed information on the research design, methods, and instruments used (as well as other results not reported here) can be found in the project's final report (CIP 2016). The CIP was funded by Federated Co-operatives Limited, a wholesaling, manufacturing, logistics, and distribution co-op collectively owned by more than 160 independent local consumer co-operative associations across British Columbia, Alberta, Saskatchewan, and Manitoba. The research was undertaken by a team of university academics, students, and staff at the University of Saskatchewan, much of it in collaboration with various partner organizations (e.g., Federated Co-operatives Limited, the Plunkett Foundation, and the International Centre for Northern Governance and Development, among others) as well as, most importantly, rural and remote settler and Indigenous communities and their leaders and members.

The CIP employed mixed methods, including:

- A randomized telephone survey of 2,025 settler and Indigenous community members in rural western Canada
- A web-based survey of 359 community administrators across the four western Canadian provinces

- Interviews with seven co-operative developers (i.e., staff and consultants usually employed by co-operative associations to help groups and communities form co-ops)

Desktop research of government economic development policies and the business development landscape coupled with literature reviews and interviews with co-operative developers helped us understand the broader institutional and organizational supports for co-operative development in western Canada, particularly as they compare to more conventional approaches to community economic and business development. The surveys of rural settler and Indigenous community members and community administrators were primarily used to identify quantitative patterns of similarity and difference across a broader random sample of rural communities and individuals in terms of perceived needs, social cohesion, business capacity, and knowledge of the co-operative model.

Additionally, from December 2014 to June 2015, community engagement meetings were held across the four western Canadian provinces, inviting people in and around 13 Indigenous and 50 settler communities to attend one of 26 meetings. Communities were initially selected based on a stratified random sampling procedure, and researchers contacted leaders, administrators, band council members, and Elders in the selected communities to describe the objectives of the project and to determine if their community was interested in participating. Each community that participated was provided a report based on the research that was tailored to their own community, including a summary of the discussions that occurred at the meeting.

The community meetings involved in-depth explorations of the lived experiences of community members, including the needs they perceived within their community, as well as the attitudes of community members toward their own and others' communities. The meetings were also used to explore solutions to the challenges highlighted by community members, including the possibility that co-operatives and collectively owned community enterprises could address some of their needs. Through these combined methods, the CIP reached 37% (649 out of 1,731) of rural settler and Indigenous communities in western Canada.

RESULTS

An interdisciplinary literature review of research in rural development economics, rural sociology, Indigenous studies, co-operative development, governance, history, and the social economy more generally initially highlighted three elements that were necessary conditions for the development of co-operatives: (1) the presence of a well-defined community need; (2) community business capacity (business know-how and experience); and (3) community social capacity (group trust, cohesion, and shared goals).

At the beginning of the project, our primary interest was to explore whether the lack of recent co-operative development was the result of community-specific factors (e.g., needs, capacities). As the project progressed, however, it became clear that the presence of certain community-specific factors were necessary but insufficient conditions for co-operative formation. Structural and institutional factors, including broader knowledge of the co-operative model, a supportive co-operative development environment, and ample social capital were also necessary for co-ops to develop and thrive in rural communities. These findings spoke to the notion of resilient systems as being inherently diverse and redundant. They also indicated that co-operative development may be best approached as part of an iterative process of inclusive development in which social capital contributes to the building of economic capital, which in turns helps to produce more social capital, and so forth.

Community-Specific Factors

To successfully address their needs through co-ops, communities require three necessary but insufficient components: (1) a need that is not being met; (2) business capacity; and (3) social capacity or cohesion. We found that each of these components exists to a greater or lesser degree in different communities.

Community Needs

Community needs were explored with community members during the 26 community meetings held across western Canada. There were key differences across settler and Indigenous communities in the needs identified, but also many similarities. Table 9.2 shows the top community needs in each type of community as determined by the frequency with

TABLE 9.2 Top 12 needs in Indigenous and settler communities in western Canada

Indigenous communities' needs	Settler communities' needs
Health care	Health care
Support services	Housing
Community barriers	Industry/business development
Seniors' services	Volunteerism
Accessing services	Transportation
Transportation	Seniors' services
Housing	Infrastructure
Industry/business development	Recreation facilities/programming
Recreation facilities/programming	Support services
Infrastructure	Community barriers
Education	Youth engagement and services
Addictions services	Shopping

which they appeared in the community meeting notes, a proxy for the amount of time that was devoted to discussing the need by the community members.

Health care was the top need identified in both settler and Indigenous communities. As one community member expressed, highlighting a widely shared perception that Canada's universal health care is not easily accessible to rural community members, "Health care—what health care? You have to decide when you will be sick." Access to mental health and addictions services were among the top health care–related needs identified by Indigenous community members. Lack of volunteers and services for youth were key challenges in settler communities. Indigenous communities identified a higher need for support services (e.g., support for the homeless, newcomers, families, women, and children). While housing was identified as among the top needs in all communities, settler communities more frequently identified housing as a need than Indigenous communities, in particular the shortage of low-income and good-quality rental housing. Most communities identified specialized housing for seniors as an area of concern, and seniors' services were also more generally discussed in several of the community meetings: "Seniors need extra help—no services or taxis here mean they either rely on the support of their family or move out."

One interesting challenge that was discussed in both settler and Indigenous communities was the presence of barriers to working within and across communities, though this concern was raised more often in the Indigenous community meetings. As one participant noted, "There is lots of politics and lots of competitiveness within and amongst these [surrounding] communities."

Community Business Capacity and Social Cohesion

The telephone and web surveys provided information from a larger random sample of respondents across provinces and communities that allowed us to explore relationships between community needs, business and social capacity, and quality of life. The surveys asked respondents to rate the level of different needs in their communities, and these surveys identified higher average levels of need in Indigenous communities when compared to settler communities. We also asked survey respondents to answer a series of perceptual questions about their communities' characteristics (e.g., the levels of general business skills, technology and labour, community volunteerism, occurrence of property crime, trust). Based on these perceptual questions, we developed measures for our two key theoretical constructs: business capacity and social cohesion. The social cohesion measure was further separated into two constructs, which we labelled "sense of safety and security" and "willingness to work together."

The most interesting relationships among these variables are summarized in Figure 9.1. There is a clear negative correlation between community needs and business capacity, and between needs and social capacity. In other words, needs increase as business and social capacity decrease (and vice versa). This is suggestive of the vicious cycle that we referred to earlier: needs increase as human capital leaves rural communities in search of employment opportunities and better access to services, which produces greater insecurity and reduced social cohesion, which leads in turn to perceptions of increased needs.

The implication of these results is that those communities with the greatest need will have the least ability to create and sustain co-ops that can address their challenges, as human capital and social cohesion are required for co-operative development. Furthermore, the ability of a community to address its own needs deteriorates over time as needs

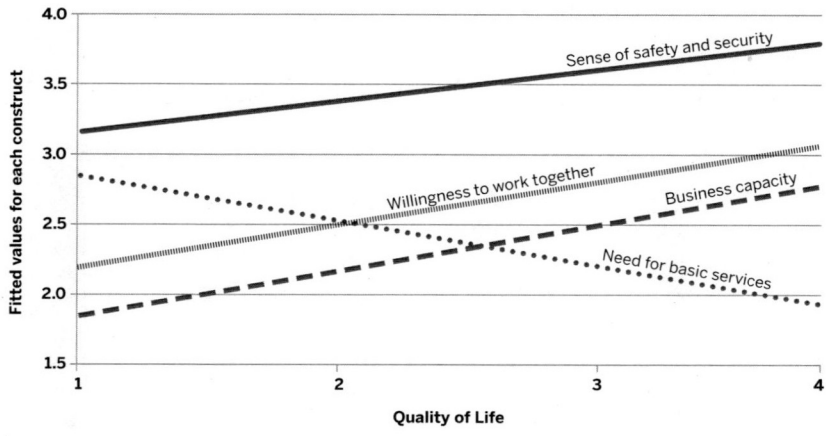

FIGURE 9.1 Relationships between community need, capacity, and quality of life

Source : CIP telephone survey of rural community members, 2015.

Note : A rating of 1 is low. A rating of 4 is high.

grow and capacity continues to diminish. As might be expected, there is also a strong positive correlation between community capacities and respondents' perceived quality of life in their community, and a negative correlation between community needs and quality of life.

Other Factors Required for Co-operative Development in Rural Communities

Knowledge of Co-ops

The telephone and web surveys both asked: "Do you know what a co-operative is?" As outlined in Figure 9.2, 23% of settlers and 41% of Indigenous respondents to the telephone survey indicated that they had no knowledge of co-ops.

The town and band administrators who responded to the web survey had much greater knowledge of co-ops. Approximately 91% of those who responded to the web survey were aware of co-ops, and we found similar levels of knowledge between administrative leaders in both settler and Indigenous communities. However, successful co-ops are member-driven organizations, and for this reason community administrators are not

FIGURE 9.2 Percentage of respondents answering "no" to the question, "Do you know what a co-operative is?"

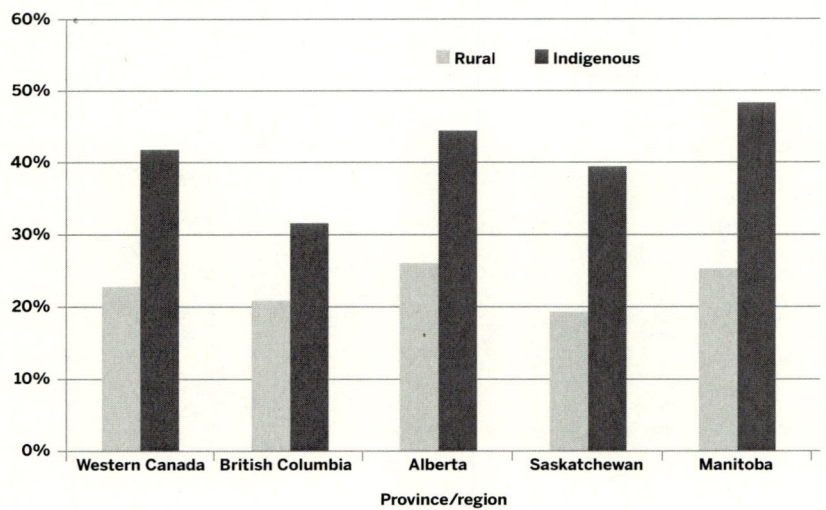

Source: CIP telephone survey of rural community members, 2015.

usually the primary leaders of community co-operative development initiatives. Additional evidence of the general lack of knowledge of the co-operative model was present in the community meetings. When community members were asked to identify ways that they thought the top needs of their communities could be addressed or how a service they were lacking could be provided, almost no one identified a co-operative enterprise as an option to address these needs. The primary solutions identified by community members were government, nongovernmental organizations, independent entrepreneurs, corporations, and volunteer associations.

At the community meetings, it also became apparent that even when people were somewhat aware of the co-operative model, knowledge was restricted to specific organizational examples such as the local co-operative grocery store, gas station, or credit union. While many people in these communities were members of co-ops themselves, they often could not state the particular advantages and disadvantages of the co-operative ownership, governance, and business model relative to

other forms of business development. Few could imagine ways to expand from the primary examples of retail and credit union co-ops to develop new co-ops to address contemporary challenges.

When exposed to examples of co-ops that had formed in other communities similar to their own, however, community members became highly engaged in exploring possible innovative, collective approaches as solutions to the challenges and needs that had been raised earlier in the discussion. For instance, in one community, after the facilitators highlighted some examples of worker co-ops, two young women began an animated discussion about the possibility of starting a worker-owned taxi co-op to provide community members with transportation to medical appointments in the nearest town with medical services without having to rely on taxis from the city. This opened up the possibility of addressing two community needs: creating a transportation service for senior residents of the community and creating employment opportunities for the community's younger residents.

Co-operative Development and Co-operative Catalysts

Co-ops are most likely to form and thrive in situations where community members themselves take a leadership role in adapting conventional development strategies to address community needs. They are less likely to thrive when leadership and development strategies are imposed on a community from an external party. Local people understand the primary issues in their communities and are often seen as more legitimate within their communities than outsiders, meaning that the ideas they introduce are more likely to be accepted by the community. Local ownership and control are also important for the success of collective endeavours, as locals are much better able to establish and enforce the norms and rules necessary to guide collective behaviour (Ostrom 2000).

However, co-operative development still requires someone (or preferably a group of people) to take a much more active role in furthering the co-operative development process within their community. We refer to these people as "co-operative catalysts." Based on our interviews with co-operative developers and the literature review on co-operative development, the CIP researchers identified some unique characteristics, skills, and competencies possessed by effective co-operative catalysts

that help them to both build support within the community and leverage necessary resources outside the community to undertake development projects (see also Overland 2017).

Co-op catalysts must be passionate about development opportunities that meet the needs *in their community, for their community*. Rural settler and Indigenous communities have seen numerous proposals for development initiatives from governments come and go. Co-op catalysts must be willing to undertake substantial effort, often foregoing personal recognition or compensation, particularly in the short-term, to sustain inclusive community engagement in the co-operative development project over the long term. Co-op catalysts require a great deal of perseverance. Developing co-operatives can take longer than creating other types of organizations as the more inclusive and democratic nature of their ownership and governance structures slows decision-making and adds other transaction costs in the way of time.

Effective co-operative catalysts have the ability to manage interpersonal and group conflict. The creation of a co-op to address a community need has a great deal of disruption potential, especially in cases where the development may impact existing formal or informal political structures and power bases. For instance, the co-op may be perceived to compete with services being offered by an established individual or business, or community members may begin to turn to co-op leaders rather than elected officials or town and band administrators to help them solve their problems. While co-op leaders generally place community development objectives above politics, they must be aware of the political dynamics that exist within and between communities to be able to understand who in the community holds levers of influence and how these formal and informal "gatekeepers" may enable or hinder the formation and work of the co-op. Political and conflict resolution skills enable them to gain consensus among key community players, including both advocates and potential gatekeepers, for the development project.

Effective co-operative catalysts may even figure out how to transcend traditional community barriers altogether to build a more inclusive model. For instance, Shellie Gleave, the entrepreneurial "co-op champion" of the Eco Cooperative Community Services Centre in British Columbia, went outside the borders of her own village to bring together people from Fraser

Lake, Nadleh Whut'en First Nation, and Stellat'en First Nation by creating a regional hub for community services such as education and market access for local food production. In Gleave's words, "what makes sense for when you bring communities together is co-operation...to be able to think of us instead of just being a community, we're a regional community...That makes sense to us, because we're providing opportunity for everybody" (quoted in Marshall 2017).

However, inclusive co-operative development is time-consuming, and rural communities with the greatest development needs often cannot afford to devote the time required. Moreover, if development efforts are unsuccessful, it can lead to erosion of trust and community support for future co-operative development initiatives. Effective co-operative catalysts and community leaders need to be aware of various models that could be used to solve the needs in the community, but they must also possess the acumen to be able to understand why a co-op may (or, just as importantly, may not) work in their community, particularly if other development models have failed.

Co-operative catalysts can be formal leaders in the community but they can also be informal leaders—people who are not in positions of authority, but who are trusted because of their deep connections to the community and its members. These connections enable catalysts to understand both the community's problems and its dynamics. As a result, they are effective at framing the problems and potential solutions in a way that allows different community members to see the connection. In short, although they may be operating in communities with low levels of social capital, co-operative catalysts themselves must possess not only leadership qualities but also relatively high levels of social capital in their community.

Broader Structural and Institutional Environment

Our results highlight that even when communities have a well-defined need, adequate levels of business capacity and social cohesion, knowledge of the co-operative model, and the presence of co-operative catalysts, successful co-operative development still requires a broader enabling environment that is supportive of collective or group entrepreneurship. A review of the business development ecosystem in Canada uncovers much

less explicit support for and knowledge of co-operative development as compared to that for individual entrepreneurship and corporate business development. The CIP project determined that co-operatives would be unlikely to be developed unless a development initiative was to be introduced that focused on inspiring people in rural communities to consider a co-operative solution to meet their needs. Such an initiative would help communities explore whether the co-operative approach is the right one for their specific needs. It would also develop supports to help communities create new co-operative organizations and provide ongoing support for co-ops' sustainable growth and development so they can thrive.

In response to the conclusion reached by the CIP research team about the need for a broader enabling and supportive environment for co-operative development, Federated Co-operatives Limited decided to fund the creation of Co-operatives First, a co-operative business development organization dedicated to helping rural settler and Indigenous communities address their own needs through co-operative enterprises. Co-operatives First was incorporated as a nonprofit co-operative development organization in 2016 and receives $1 million per year from Federated Co-operatives Limited for its operation. The current board of directors is drawn from business, co-operative, and Indigenous communities throughout western Canada. In 2016, the founding board members (one of whom is an author on this paper) hired an executive director, Audra Krueger. The organization has since grown to six employees under Krueger's leadership.

Co-operatives First has been an institutional innovation in the business development environment in western Canada focused on inclusive, community-based approaches to development through co-ops. In the next section, we review the challenges and successes of the first few years of Co-operatives First's operations.

CO-OPERATIVES FIRST

Three of the authors of this chapter work for Co-operatives First, and the data and information we provide in this section is largely based on their experiences. Co-operatives First had some very early successes in encouraging and supporting co-operative development and has also experienced substantial growth since its creation in 2016. Based on information

provided by the nonprofit on October 1, 2020, Co-operatives First had taken on 100 projects since it first began operations, resulting in 44 new co-operative incorporations to date. Most of its support has been provided to new start-ups, though staff also provide support for existing co-ops. Their main website receives an average of 170 visits per day, including about 90 visits per day to the resource page.

Supporting Community Knowledge of Co-ops

Despite these early successes, Co-operatives First faces some significant challenges in its goals to increase understanding of the co-operative business model in rural communities and help community groups and leaders grow their economies and improve their communities through sustainable co-operative development efforts. One of the major challenges, which is consistent with the findings of the CIP project, is that general knowledge of the co-op model is quite low (and in some cases people associate it exclusively with a gas station or grocery store). Where people have had some interaction with co-ops, that experience has not been uniformly positive. Thus, part of the work of Co-operatives First involves changing people's perception about the possibilities available for community-based economic development through the co-operative model. Part of this process has involved a major learning curve in transitioning from a community- and action-based academic research project to a nonprofit co-operative development organization. Co-operatives First staff had to learn how to explain the co-operative model to people through the use of examples and stories that would resonate with rural settler and Indigenous community members. Standard technical presentations that define a co-op and go through the steps of how to form one were not as effective.

The development of nontechnical and easily navigable online resources was a critical early success. Co-operatives First created an online resource (Co-op Creator)[4] inspired by a desire to make it as easy as possible for people to access the necessary information to start a co-op. Prior to the creation of Co-op Creator, online information about co-operative development was patchy, highly technical, and somewhat intimidating for those who were not as familiar with the co-operative business model or co-operative development. Co-operatives First also

started a podcast called *The Common Share*, which covers different issues in business, community, and co-operative development, often through the use of real stories and examples.

Community members have approached Co-operatives First for assistance in developing co-ops in a diverse range of services and industries. The organizations that have formed with assistance from Co-operatives First range from daycare co-ops to rural broadband co-ops, and models that go beyond consumer co-ops to include producer co-ops (Indigenous artisans, farmers, etc.), worker consulting co-ops, investor co-ops, and marketing co-ops. Finding or developing the expertise to help communities build a business plan across such a diverse range of industries and co-operative models can be a challenge, and the staff at Co-operatives First are continuously cultivating relationships with a wide network of people that they can call upon to provide technical assistance (e.g., business plan writers) and tailor business advice to communities.

Another challenge Co-operatives First has faced as it builds this support network for communities is finding consultants that have knowledge of the co-operative model. While the CIP limited its interviews to developers who were well aware of the co-operative model, staff at Co-operatives First have had to work closely with business consultants and economic development officers to educate them about the structural and governance differences between co-ops and other types of organizations. It is not always clear whether a community is in greater need of technical business support or training on how to undertake a co-operative model of development.

Co-operatives First has sought to address this issue by building a workshop—Creating Connections—to educate economic development professionals about the co-operative model. The workshop has been delivered to just under 300 people. To build wider public awareness of the co-operative governance model, the organization has also partnered with the University of Saskatchewan to create and deliver an introductory course on co-ops—Co-ops 101—and an open, online co-operative governance course that has been delivered to over 2,000 people.

Addressing Structural Barriers to Co-operative Development

While the lack of knowledge of the co-operative model among community members and those involved in economic development is a major barrier to co-operative development, it is not the only one. As we noted earlier, several structural, institutional, political, and community barriers also continue to hinder the development and success of co-ops.

First, as was identified in the CIP project and as is consistent with the on-the-ground experiences of Co-operatives First staff members, co-operative development has political economy implications that must be considered. Co-operative development places decision-making power in the hands of specific people in a community. These individuals are not necessarily connected to the broader political and economic environment within a region or a country, and so they may be unaware of, or unable to access, all the resources they need. Furthermore, community and co-operative development efforts may clash with established community power dynamics and/or result in distributing community benefits in ways that may or may not be inclusive of those who face the greatest need. Gatekeepers—those with formal or informal power in the community and beyond—can help or hinder co-operative development, often depending on whether they stand to gain or lose. Gatekeepers include policy-makers, regulatory agencies, local business elites, and/or local community and political leaders. Consideration of their role, as well as the potential for community member advocacy for and against the development of a co-op, is crucial to understanding the feasibility of a co-op's establishment and, ultimately, its sustainability. As outsiders to the community, co-operative developers at Co-operatives First typically try to avoid political controversy within and beyond the communities they work with by focusing on co-ops as practical tools to help groups of individuals solve problems within their community. However, it is often necessary for co-operative catalysts to work through long-standing community issues and barriers that could hinder co-operative development efforts. For influential gatekeepers who feel they will lose something if a co-op forms, trying to identify ways to connect these gatekeepers' individual interests with collective community interests is important.

Second, one of the key roles of Co-operatives First is encouraging rural people to push back against the dominant policy and academic

narratives that rural communities are "dying" and "not viable" and focus instead on solutions to identified needs. Community members must understand that they have the permission and power to make changes for themselves and to experiment with different models and solutions to their needs. They don't need to wait on help from outside (which often never comes). Still, to this end, having people within the community with the technical know-how to run a nonprofit or business is helpful. For instance, the not-for-profit Heart Linked Community Services Co-operative, which provides programming for at-risk youth in northern Saskatchewan communities, was started by a group of co-operative catalysts, one of whom who has a background in accounting and law (Co-operatives First 2020a). Where people with these skills are not available, or even where they are, Co-operatives First can connect the community to people with the technical skills required to help get the co-op off the ground. Importantly, community members must be able to adapt government and funding program criteria to undertake community development initiatives that fit the local context. For instance, policy-makers should encourage a community's positive deviations from government requirements to access program or development funding if the purpose is to find inclusive and sustainable economic development solutions to challenges that support the needs of local community members.

Insights from Co-operatives First
Communities require space and permission from government to experiment. Based on the results of CIP and the experiences of Co-operatives First, we propose that co-operatives are less likely to be successful in achieving sustainable and inclusive economic and social development if the creation of these organizations and/or the benchmarks of their success are imposed from outside the communities as a matter of "good" government policy. Inclusive development must be seen as an iterative process that fosters resiliency in communities by building both social and economic capital in tandem. In our research and experience, rural setter and Indigenous community members want three things: (1) an atmosphere where governments at all levels support local innovation (instead of creating barriers); (2) flexible financial support that can be

targeted to suit local community needs; and (3) direction, not dictation, on what might be possible. These results mean that policy and development goals and benchmarks should ideally be developed by the communities themselves, possibly with some outside assistance in navigating the more technical aspects of the economic and co-op development process. If broader policy and development goals must be set by outside parties like governments, they are more likely to be met when these objectives are aligned with solutions to locally identified community needs.

In keeping with the idea of inclusive development as an iterative process of the co-development of social and economic capital, the early stages of co-operative development will likely take place within individual rural settler and Indigenous communities. However, as these communities become more resilient, we should see increasing possibilities for inclusive co-operative development and partnerships, providing opportunities for rural people to work together not only within, but also across communities.

Indeed, we already see a few examples of co-ops serving as bridges between Indigenous and settler communities. One example is the Eco Cooperative Community Services Centre in British Columbia, mentioned earlier, which brings together people from Fraser Lake, Nadleh Whut'en First Nation, and Stellat'en First Nation. Another is the Nehiyawaskiy Indigenous Peoples Art Co-op, which enables talented Cree, Dene, and Métis artists in Lac La Biche, Alberta, to sell their goods to a wider market through partnerships with the Lac La Biche Canadian Native Friendship Centre, Métis Crossing, and the University of Alberta gift store (Co-operatives First 2020b). Yet another example is the Indigenous Technical Services Co-operative (formerly the Saskatchewan First Nations Technical Services Co-operative), which, according to its website, brings together member First Nation communities to "ensure Saskatchewan First Nations speak with one voice protecting their collective interests by providing high quality, standardized and efficient technical services through coordinated service delivery" on reserve in areas such as housing development, water treatment, and engineering (White 2016). As knowledge of the co-operative model grows in rural Indigenous and settler communities, and as education towards reconciliation continues throughout school systems and other institutions, we might expect

more bridging co-ops to develop that could facilitate common projects across these communities. While co-ops do require some initial social cohesion to develop, the process of co-operative development can also build alliances and strengthen social connections by bringing rural Indigenous and settler neighbours together to work toward meeting their shared needs and goals.

INCLUSIVE CO-OPERATIVE DEVELOPMENT AMONG RURAL NEIGHBOURS

Rural settler and Indigenous communities in western Canada face a range of challenges in developing resilient and socially inclusive economies. Historically, members of these communities worked together to develop formal or informal co-operative enterprises to meet their needs (though mostly within individual settler and Indigenous communities, rather than across these communities). Since many community needs can only be addressed collectively, development models that allow for the coordination of local collective action—for instance through co-ops—are particularly important. Co-operative development also has the potential to break down barriers and bring people together within and across rural settler and Indigenous communities to address shared needs.

However, the number of new co-operative formations in western Canada has stagnated. This is problematic, as co-ops have unique advantages over other types of organizations for sustainable and inclusive development in rural settler and Indigenous communities. In co-operatives, the members are both the owners and the primary users of the organization's services and are more likely than other types of organizations to provide opportunities for meaningful control and ongoing inclusive participation by local community stakeholders. If the barriers to co-operative development we identified can be overcome, we propose that co-ops hold great potential not only as a community development model, but also for improving relations within and between members of different communities. In particular, we see great potential for the co-operative model to connect rural settlers and Indigenous people who often face similar needs and live in close proximity to each other, yet must overcome institutionally imposed segregation that limits their ability to work together, build trust, and repair relations

with each other and across their communities. Co-operative work is not simply learning how to tolerate each other; it is the real work of learning how to become good neighbours.

In the CIP, we found a strong correlation between very high needs and very low business capacity and social cohesion. This finding suggests that communities with the greatest needs will have the least ability to bring people together to create and sustain co-ops that can inclusively meet these needs. In these communities, there will continue to be a role for governments to play in addressing basic individual needs through more directed social policies. However, policy-makers should understand that these interventions, unless they are carefully carried out, are unlikely to build community capacity, resiliency, or inclusivity in either the short or long term, and indeed may serve to further reduce the ability of a community to address its own challenges. Inclusive development, even in the communities of highest need, should be viewed as an iterative process in which government intervention should be aimed towards projects and programs that will lead to eventual community self-reliance.

The challenges the CIP identified with co-operative development in western Canada have important implications for whether co-ops are feasible and sustainable in specific communities, and whether they are a viable, inclusive economic and social development strategy in rural Canada more broadly. These challenges include a mix of community-based factors, as well as the supporting structural and institutional environment around co-operative development. More specifically, if co-ops are to play a role in achieving inclusive development goals, the current lack of co-operative knowledge in rural communities in western Canada and the broader lack of institutional support for economic development through co-operative models suggests a need for more active interventions to encourage new co-operative formations.

The responsibility for driving these interventions will likely fall to local municipal governments, existing co-ops, and other local organizations, community groups, and leaders. Indeed, the CIP led to the formation of Co-operatives First, which has been solely funded to date by Federated Co-operatives Limited, an organization deeply embedded in and committed to rural western Canadian communities. Without

an investment by local organizations, it is unlikely that co-ops can be an effective policy tool to address rural community needs, particularly because these interventions may be too costly for communities to undertake on their own, and they may not have all the resources they need within their own communities. However, these collective enterprises are also less likely to be effective and sustainable—or, most importantly, inclusive—if they are accountable to development criteria created by outside stakeholders, agencies, and other levels of government (e.g., federal). Local stakeholder and community dedication to co-operative development is more likely to ensure the sustainability of any co-ops that are formed. That said, it is possible for federal governments to provide funding for co-operative development, as long as this funding is not explicitly tied to the achievement of a narrow set of objectives that do not align with current community needs, as identified by the community members themselves.

In this chapter we have highlighted the socioeconomic needs in rural settler and Indigenous communities in western Canada and how co-operative development is one feasible strategy for inclusively addressing these community needs. Co-ops are a unique approach to community development that can help build more inclusive and equal communities. Yet they require social cohesion and community capacity to form—factors that may be in short supply in rural communities facing high needs and strained relationships, especially between settler and Indigenous communities. Repairing relations between rural settler and Indigenous neighbours will thus require taking seriously the challenges facing people in their communities and exploring alongside them the possibility for developing co-operative, inclusive solutions to their challenges.

NOTES

1. In Canada, the term *settler* refers to individuals who are not Indigenous. While the data drawn upon in this paper is collected from both rural and northern (more remote) settler and Indigenous communities, to simplify the writing, we primarily use the term *rural* throughout. Rural communities are broadly defined in this paper as the territory lying outside an urban area, and formally designated in Statistics Canada categorizations as census subdivisions located outside of census metropolitan area or census agglomerations. A census metropolitan area is an area with a population of at least 100,000, of which more than 50,000 live in the core. A census agglomeration has a core population of at least 10,000. At the time of this research, there were 1,731 rural settler and rural Indigenous communities in western Canada.
2. See Truth and Reconciliation Commission of Canada (2015) for a full report on the history of the residential school system and its consequences for Indigenous wellbeing.
3. For more on Indigenous sovereignty and sustainable self-determination, see the work of the Harvard Project: https://hpaied.org.
4. To access the tool, go to https://coopcreator.ca/.

REFERENCES

Acemoglu, Daron. 2006. "Globalization and Inequality." *Brown Journal of World Affairs* 13: 19–28.

Acemoglu, Daron, and Pascual Restrepo. 2019. "Automation and New Tasks: How Technology Displaces and Reinstates Labor." *Journal of Economic Perspectives* 33 (2): 3–30.

Barrera, Jorge. 2017. "Indigenous Population Growing Rapidly, Languages Surging: Census." *CBC News*, October 25, 2017. https://www.cbc.ca/news/indigenous/indigenous-census-rapid-growth-1.4370727.

Canadian Co-operative Association. 2012. *Co-operatives in Aboriginal Communities in Canada*. Ottawa: Canadian Co-operative Association.

Case, Anne, and Angus Deaton. 2020. *Deaths of Despair and the Future of Capitalism*. Princeton: Princeton University Press.

CIP (Co-operative Innovation Project). 2016. *Final Report*. https://coopinnovation.wordpress.com/final-report/.

Co-operatives First. 2020a. *June Newsletter*. Saskatoon: Co-operatives First. https://mailchi.mp/5c5eaaa8e116/june-20-newsletter-7790865?e=236bfc670b.

Co-operatives First. 2020b. *July Newsletter*. Saskatoon: Co-operatives First. https://mailchi.mp/4c604f35cd9c/july-20-newsletter-7850541.

Corntassel, Jeff. 2008. "Toward Sustainable Self-Determination: Rethinking the Contemporary Indigenous-Rights Discourse." *Alternatives: Global, Local, Political* 33 (1): 105–32.

Duguid, Fiona, and George Karaphillis. 2015. *Economic Impact of the Co-operative Sector in Canada*. Ottawa: Co-operatives and Mutuals Canada.

Employment and Social Development Canada. 2018. *Backgrounder: The Social Finance Fund*. Ottawa: Government of Canada. https://www.canada.ca/en/employment-social-development/news/2018/11/backgrounder-the-social-finance-fund.html.

Fairbairn, Brett, Murray Fulton, and Dionne Pohler. 2015. *Governance as a Determinant of Success and Failure: What Other Co-ops Can Learn from Co-op Atlantic*. Saskatoon: Centre for the Study of Co-operatives.

Findlay, Isobel. 2006. "Putting Co-operative Principles into Practice: Lessons Learned from Canada's North." ICA *Review of International Co-operation* 99 (1): 44–52.

Fulton, Murray, and Kathy Larson. 2009. "Overconfidence and Hubris: The Demise of Agricultural Co-operatives in Western Canada." *Journal of Rural Cooperation* 37 (2):166–200.

Galtung, Johan, Peter O'Brien, and Roy Preiswerk, eds. 1980. *Self-Reliance: A Strategy for Development*. London: Bogle-L'Ouverture.

Government of Canada. 2015. "Success Stories: Agreements and Land Claims." Last updated April 20, 2015. https://www.rcaanc-cirnac.gc.ca/eng/1306932724555/1539953769195.

Green, David A., Craig Riddell, and France St.-Hillaire, eds. 2016. *Income Inequality: The Canadian Story*. Montréal: Institute for Research on Public Policy.

Hammond-Ketilson, Lou. 2004. "Aboriginal Co-operatives in Canada." *Review of International Cooperation* 97 (1): 38–47.

Hammond-Ketilson, Lou, and Ian MacPherson. 2001. *A Report on Aboriginal Co-operatives in Canada: Current Situation and Potential for Growth*. Saskatoon: Centre for the Study of Co-operatives.

International Labor Organization. 2005. *Handbook for Self-Reliance*. Geneva: United Nations High Commissioner for Refugees.

Joseph, Kevin. 2018. "Racist Farmers and Thieving Indians." *Prince Alberta Daily Herald*, February 12, 2018. https://paherald.sk.ca/2018/02/12/racist-farmers-thieving-indians/.

Kandel, William A., and David L. Brown, eds. 2006. *Population Change and Rural Society*. Vol. 16 of *The Springer Series on Demographic Methods and Population Analysis*, edited by Kenneth C. Land. Netherlands: Springer.

Kaplan, Mischa. 2018. "Canada Needs to Rethink Its Approach to Economic Development." *Macleans*, March 15, 2018.

Kodras, Janet. 1997. "The Changing Map of American Poverty in an Era of Economic Restructuring and Political Realignment." *Economic Geography* 73 (1): 67–93.

Loney, Shaun. 2018. *The Beautiful Bailout: How a Social Innovation Scale-up Will Solve Government's Priciest Problems*. Self-published, Friesens.

MacPherson, Ian. 1979. *Each For All: A History of the Co-operative Movement in English Canada, 1900–1945*. Toronto: Macmillan of Canada.

Magis, Kristen. 2010. "Community Resilience: An Indicator of Social Sustainability." *Society and Natural Resources* 23 (5): 401–16. https://doi.org/10.1080/08941920903305674.

Marshall, Aasa. 2017. "Every Co-op Needs a Co-op Champion." *Co-operatives First Blog*, December 22, 2017. https://cooperativesfirst.com/blog/2017/12/22/every-co-op-needs-a-co-op-champion/.

Mavenga, Fortunate, and M. Rose Olfert. 2012. "The Role of Credit Unions in Rural Communities in Canada." *Journal of Rural Cooperation* 40 (1): 1–28.

Mazur, Laurie. 2013. "Cultivating Resilience in a Dangerous World." In *The State of the World 2013: Is Sustainability Still Possible?*, edited by Linda Starke, 353–63. Washington, DC: Island Press.

NIEDB (National Indigenous Economic Development Board). 2019. *The Indigenous Economic Progress Development Report*. Available from http://www.naedb-cndea.com/.

Ostrom, Elinor. 2000. "Collective Action and the Evolution of Social Norms." *Journal of Economic Perspectives* 14 (3): 137–58.

Overland, Darcy. 2017. "Cooperative Leadership: Social and Spatial Regeneration in Rural Western Canada." In *Social Regeneration and Local Development: Cooperation, Social Economy and Public Participation*, edited by Silvia Sacchetti, Asimina Christoforou, and Michele Mosca, 117–32. New York: Routledge.

Patel, Asiya, Jennifer Dean, Sarah Edge, Kathi Wilson, and Effat Ghassemi. 2019. "Double Burden of Rural Migration in Canada? Considering the Social Determinants of Health Related to Immigrant Settlement Outside the Cosmopolis." *International Journal of Environmental Research and Public Health* 16 (5): 678. https://doi.org/10.3390/ijerph16050678.

Poholka, Holli. 2016. "First Nation Successes: Developing Urban Reserves in Canada." Master's thesis, Queen's University. QSpace. http://hdl.handle.net/1974/14951.

Royer, Jeffrey S. 2018. "Measuring the Cost of Capital in Co-operative Businesses." *Agribusiness* 35 (2): 249–64.

Schneiberg, Marc, Marissa King, and Thomas Smith. 2008. "Social Movements and Organizational Form: Cooperative Alternatives to Corporations in the American Insurance, Dairy, and Grain Industries." *American Sociological Review* 73 (4): 635–67.

Scrimgeour, Frank, and Catherine Iremonger. 2004. "Maori Sustainable Economic Development in New Zealand: Indigenous Practices for the Quadruple Bottom Line." Working paper, Waikato Management School, University of Waikato, Hamilton, New Zealand.

Sengupta, Ushnish. 2015. "Indigenous Co-operatives in Canada: The Complex Relationship Between Cooperatives, Community Economic Development, Colonization, and Culture." *Journal of Entrepreneurial and Organizational Diversity* 4 (1): 121–52.

Thompson, Matthew, and Joy Emmanuel. 2012. *Assembling Understandings: Perspectives of the Canadian Social Economy Research Partnerships, 2005–2011.* Victoria: University of Victoria.

Truth and Reconciliation Commission of Canada. 2015. *The Final Report of the Truth and Reconciliation Commission of Canada.* 6 vols. Montréal: McGill-Queens University Press.

UNHCR (United Nations Human Rights Committee). 2015. *International Covenant on Civil and Political Rights: Concluding Observations on the Sixth Periodic Report of Canada* (catalogue no. CCPR/C/CAN/CO/6).

White, Kyle. 2016. "Indigenous Co-op Development." *Co-operatives First* Blog, October 29, 2016. https://cooperativesfirst.com/blog/2016/10/29/indigenous-coop-development/.

Winkler, Richelle, Donald R. Field, A.E. Luloff, Richard S. Krannich, and Tracy Williams. 2007. "Social Landscapes of the Inter-Mountain West: A Comparison of 'Old West' and 'New West' Communities." *Rural Sociology* 72 (3): 478–501.

10

INCLUSION ON WHOSE GROUNDS?

Against Liberal Essentialisms and toward Radical Neighbourliness in Rural Anti-racism

Phil Henderson

IN JULY OF 2019, Owen Sound, Ontario, experienced a rash of white supremacist vandalism. Racist stickers were affixed throughout public spaces in this small town in the predominantly rural federal riding of Bruce-Grey-Owen Sound. Lightposts, mailboxes, handrails, street signs, and park benches were remade into messaging boards for hatred, unified under white identitarianism (Finlay-Stewart 2019). Furthering this atmosphere of hate, on July 11 and 12, 2019, the Owen Sound Muslim Association—a place of communal worship—was also vandalized. Eggs, tomato sauce, and condiments were smeared onto the windows, walls, and roof. A chain restaurant operated by members of the Muslim community was similarly defaced.

At a regularly scheduled city council meeting on July 15, Mayor Ian Boddy denounced these events, labelling them as hate crimes, and comparing them to a series of arsons that rocked the city in 2015. Echoing sentiments also expressed by Muslim Association spokesperson Waleed Aslam, Boddy argued that these actions were unreflective of Owen Sound (Langlois 2019). Boddy instead praised the roughly 70 people who attended a solidarity vigil at the Muslim Association on July 13, held in hopes of deterring a third night of vandalism. Whether because of their presence or some as-yet-unknown reason, no further vandalism

249

occurred. In his statement at the close of the council meeting, Mayor Boddy urged the public to report any incidences or further vandalism to the police so that investigations could be conducted (Owen Sound City Council 2019, 2:23:00–2:30:00). On July 16, a 22-year-old white male was charged in relation to the vandalizing of both the Muslim Association and the restaurant. It is unknown whether this individual is connected to the racist stickers, some of which have appeared since his arrest (Owen Sound Police Service 2019; Langlois 2019). What is certain, however, is that an emboldened white identitarianism exists in Owen Sound—a small town 190 km northwest of Toronto with a population of around 22,000, defined largely by its relationship to the surrounding rural counties of Bruce and Grey.[1] As a consequence, local racialized communities are experiencing an increased sense of visibility and vulnerability as their safety and place within this community is threatened.

This chapter reflects on the politics of hate in rural communities. Contrary to much of the scholarly literature, I attempt to position my reflection in ways that are committed to thinking with rural people rather than merely about them. To this end, I begin this chapter by reviewing the literature on politically mobilized hatred in rural communities against the backdrop of the racist vandalism in Owen Sound. I show that, while there are strengths, the literature largely depoliticizes and reifies hatred. In the next section I consider the ways in which scholars and public officials, in their responses to the politics of hate, fall back again and again on the language of tolerance and inclusion. Tracing the liberal conceptual containers and institutional frameworks that are reinforced by both scholarly and official examples of this discourse, I argue that tolerance and inclusion are relatively thin bases for thinking about real communities and practices of solidarity. Moreover, I show how reliance on notions of tolerance makes presumed cultural differences seem immutable, thereby entrenching dominant and exploitative social relations. I then consider the relationship of neighbouring and the imperative of neighbourliness as concepts of solidarity that function as community responses to acts of hate amongst rural people, ultimately concluding that neighbourliness, on its own, has also failed to be a sufficient theory of anti-racist praxis in Owen Sound. I close the chapter by speculating about

a different kind of neighbourliness—radical neighbourliness—and what this might look like in rural communities.

A COTTAGE INDUSTRY ABOUT COTTAGE COUNTRY

The vandalism described in this chapter's introduction is an attempt to (re)cast the public space of Owen Sound as at once the property of whiteness and overtly hostile towards racialized residents (Moreton-Robinson 2015). Since the city was established in 1857, the area has undergone a rapid demographic transition. Through the dispossession and displacement of the Anishinaabek and the (at times legal, at times merely de facto) exclusion of other racialized communities, the population of Owen Sound today has been demographically constructed as 96% white (Statistics Canada 2017c). Given this history, the 2019 vandalism remains in the realm of more mundane acts of hatred. Indeed, by the standard of local historical incidences of hatred, the escalation and organization behind these hate crimes appears relatively nascent. As in most of North America, extreme acts of racist and colonial violence are never far from the surface of living memory. In mid-1995, which is remembered as "the Summer of Hate," the Owen Sound area was gripped by anti-Indigenous violence, culminating in boat burnings and the stabbings of four Indigenous youths (Chippewas of Nawash 2005; Koenig 2005; Wallace 2013). In 2015, the Member of Parliament for the riding, Larry Miller, made overtly white-nationalist declarations, asserting that people wearing niqabs ought to "stay the hell where [they] came from" (quoted in Hannay 2015). Even given this history, it is difficult to miss the ways in which the actions of July 2019 reflect a general rise in hate crimes (Habib 2019). Not only do they portend a growing appetite for white identitarianism—given that Owen Sounders' process of identity formation is often in direct opposition to urban centres like Toronto—they also exemplify the rural inflection that many observers have identified in this wave of hatred.

A veritable cottage industry of literature on the alleged atavism and revanchism of rural communities has sprung up, largely in the wake of the 2016 US presidential election. In some cases, this literature is a timely update to older works, such as Catherine McNicol Stock's

(2017) revisitation of her 1996 classic *Rural Radicals*. Following the Oklahoma City bombings, Stock investigates the "politics of hatred" directed against the American government and a supposed conspiracy of nondominant groups to whom the state had capitulated, against the interests of "average" (read: propertied, white, straight, cisgendered, able-bodied, anglophone, and male) Americans (2). What Stock found were manifestations of deep legacies of "rural radicalism" that she suggests precede and in fact birth the United States itself (3–10).

Locating this politics of hatred in its specifically rural manifestations, Stock seems well placed to comment on the Trump era and its seemingly dichotomous rural-urban divides. In her preface to the 2017 edition of *Rural Radicals*, Stock observes that the politics of hatred is more extreme in its rhetoric and actions, and in its relationship to the political mainstream. Simply put, overt displays of hatred are both more likely to be publicly denounced now than in 1996, even as the perpetrators are more emboldened (Stock 2017, x). Stock further observes that, as so much of contemporary political discourse migrates online, the primary grievances expressed in today's politics of hatred are often "disaggregated from the experience of rural America," even as they are more "easily reinforced and normalized in isolated areas" (xi).

The strength of Stock's work is evinced in its resonance with the situation in Owen Sound. Whereas the racist violence of the Summer of Hate was embedded in the local grievances that white settlers concocted against the fishing rights of two First Nations, the vandalizing of the Muslim Association and the stickering campaign appear more deterritorialized in both their origins and orientation. The events of 2015 and 2019 are both despicable acts of hatred, yet the more recent actions manifest the disaggregated qualities of the contemporary politics of hatred to which Stock points. That this disaggregated yet resurgent white identitarianism is fomenting seems well founded; the question of why, however, is the subject of much discussion.

Whereas Stock takes a primarily descriptive approach to this question in *Rural Radicals*, others position themselves as diagnosticians of the problem. A primary example of this is Robert Wuthnow's (2018) *The Left Behind*, which seeks to explain why a radicalizing of the rural-urban dichotomy emerged as one of the "clearest conclusions"

of the 2016 American election (2). Throughout his analysis of the "rural outrage" that he alleges propelled Trump to the White House (12), Wuthnow makes several astute observations, chief amongst these being that inasmuch as general appraisals of the election have noted the roiling sense of rage in the rural United States, they do so in ways that individualize grievances. Wuthnow argues that this tends to be "all about private resentments and personal attitudes" and that what follows "has nothing to do with the communities in which rural Americans live" (160). Disentangled from the racist and reactionary rhetoric and actions in which it typically presents itself, the fact that this rural outrage is communal rather than individual opens a conversation about material power imbalances, exploitation, and domination as experienced by, within, and across rural communities. It is a mistake to dismiss this communal sense of grievance out of hand, even as the reactionary scapegoating that accompanies it must be rejected. The deleterious effects that rural communities experience at the hands of both increasingly rapacious capitalism and an (at best) indifferent state are deserving of serious consideration. They also go some way to explaining the causes of rural outrage and understanding how a politics of hatred displaces class antagonisms. Structural and materialist analyses are also enormously helpful in visioning pathways towards a grassroots intersectional solidarity (Grossman 2017; Taylor 2017; Haider 2018). Unfortunately, in his analysis, Wuthnow (2018, 2) eschews structural and materialist analyses, arguing that the rural-urban divide is primarily cultural.

Wuthnow treats the phenomenon of reactionary rural politics as a cultural antagonism. He writes that residents of rural communities fear that "the nation and the culture have moved on" from the normative commitments that define rural cultures, even as rural people remain nostalgically committed to a belief "that the heart of America still beats in small communities" (6). Wuthnow posits that atavism and revanchism manifest in a culture under siege. The idea that reactionary politics are part of rural culture is echoed throughout this literature. It is also a staple of left-liberal and even radical political analyses. From Thomas Frank's (2004) *What's the Matter with Kansas*—which posits that cultural antagonisms are mobilized to placate the very real material and class

interests of rural communities—through to Marx and Engels's ([1848] 2005) comments on the "idiocy of rural life," there exists plenty of scholarly tropes for Wuthnow and others to implicitly rely upon in buttressing their assessment that "rural culture" lends itself to a politics of hatred.

In effect, moving research on reactionary politics in rural communities away from structural and materialist analyses and towards an interrogation of cultural difference as such enables essentialist and depoliticized reading of these movements (Ashwood 2018). Absurd leaps in analysis are glossed over with relative ease if an act of hatred is correlated to rurality. Stock's (2017) reliance upon these tropes is exemplary. She implies that Timothy McVeigh's rural background is the primary factor in understanding his attack on the Federal Building in Oklahoma City, rather than the fact that his army training physically and psychologically conditioned him to do violence in the service of America's imperial war against the people of Kuwait and Iraq (Ashwood 2018, 739).

Participating in online discussions about the 2019 vandalizing of the Muslim Association and the racist stickering, I noticed parallel logics. Several members of a local anti-racist group expressed that racism of this sort is inevitable in a rural community like Owen Sound and that no one should be surprised by it. Troublingly, most of these interlocutors were rural people themselves, or else ex-urbanites now living in the Owen Sound area. These discussions relied heavily upon tropes about rural communities having distinctly intolerant cultures—assertions that fly in the face of my own experience of participating in anti-racist work in both rural *and* urban communities.

In some ways, the burgeoning literature on reactionary rural politics both relies upon and reinforces a core problem in rural anti-racist movements: self-erasure. Anti-racist work in rural communities (and its evidence of the internally contested character of those communities) is invisibilized and the work made more difficult by the nearly hegemonic appraisal of an essential rural backwardness. Very little space seems to exist for rural people to at once acknowledge that politically mobilized hatred exists within our communities, but also to recognize that this problem spans the rural-urban divide, to discuss its structural and institutional manifestations, and to highlight that common cause could be made within and between communities typically pitted (or pitting

themselves) against one another. Instead, the massive success of tracts like J.D. Vance's (2016) *Hillbilly Elegy* suggests a public hungry for self-reporting informants who position themselves within the supposedly inveterately xenophobic culture of rural communities, while also maintaining a degree of plausible distance in order to convincingly denounce said culture. This confessional approach to combatting hatred seems unlikely to fundamentally challenge the conditions in which these hatreds were produced.

At its best, the move to read the reactionary politics of Timothy McVeigh, Appalachian hillbillies, or vandalism in Owen Sound as manifestations of rural culture interrogates how these are not idiosyncratic events, but rather part of a daily lived reality within a society suffused with deference to hierarchy, whiteness, hypermasculinity, and capital. Unfortunately, as evidenced by this growing literature, the move towards culture as the analytic has more often fallen into essentialism. This is evidenced by recurring descriptions of an explicitly and spatially distanced rural culture that is singular and separable from the culture writ large. This is perhaps best exemplified by Arlie Russell Hochschild's (2016) *Strangers in their Own Land*. Hochschild attempts to get at the "deep story" of these cultures—what she calls the "feels-as-if story" (135). Her method thus "removes judgement. It removes fact" when appraising these stories (135). Because Hochschild identifies the reactionary anger of her rural interlocutors as a cultural object, it becomes immovable and unquestionable. Such an approach is, to be frank, patronizing. It erases struggles against reactionary politics that occur within rural communities; it reifies the urban observer as the proper knowledge-producing and necessarily tolerant subject; and it trivializes the real—though never unproblematic—capacity of rural people to produce meaningful knowledge about, and accounts of, our communities.

While I am suspicious of the normative commitments underpinning this literature, I appreciate that it creates a toehold on which to build a conversation. Although this literature presents rurality by constructing and spatializing cultural difference in order to denounce a rural other, I do not reject the move to think through the politics of hatred from a place of specificity. As the Combahee River Collective—a

group of radical Black queer socialist feminists—made clear in their 1977 statement of organizing principles, individuals and communities approach political struggles in ways that are informed and framed by their lived experiences (Taylor 2017). Understanding how the specificities of a person's or community's identity are constructed through relatively persistent, yet fully mutable, power relations is a cornerstone of rigorous and impactful political analysis. Thus, insofar as it becomes a starting place for an intersectional critique of structural and material relations of power, rurality offers as much as an analytic. Examples of this approach include Zoltán Grossman's (2017) *Unlikely Alliances*, which details the perhaps surprising depths of solidarity built between Indigenous peoples and agriculturalist settlers when a shared environment comes under threat. Similarly, *Left Elsewhere* (Catte 2019) offers compelling insights into the resonant legacies and promising possibilities of liberatory politics emerging from struggles in rural communities. However, for this approach to be impactful, it must also shed some of the conceptual baggage that many scholars have been carrying—normative commitments that should at the very least be noted, if not abandoned. One way I think scholars can go about shedding this baggage is to engage more closely with their rural interlocutors as producers, not merely recipients, of rich and complex political theories and anti-oppressive frameworks.

IS TOLERATION ANOTHER WORD FOR URBANE BIGOTRY?

The literature on reactionary rural politics reproduces several problematic tropes, not the least of which is how it continually (re)spatializes the politics of hatred. Politically mobilized hatred is made to appear sporadic or irregular, even if it might be asserted as common in a given place or time. Approached in this way, the politics of hatred is always described as some kind of break: that's how *they* thought *then*, that's how *they* act *there*, this hateful *event* is the *exception*, not the rule; it isn't reflective of *us*. These common refrains construct idealized accounts of the social relations of a given community, nation, or state. Acts of hatred are spatialized to a peripheral outside. Whether that outside is temporal, geographical, cultural, or otherwise is often a matter of historically contingent convenience.

Responses from public figures to the racist vandalism in Owen Sound exemplify this attempt to (re)spatialize hatred. Mayor Boddy and Waleed Aslam, the Muslim Association spokesperson, crucially refused to essentialize Owen Sound and the surrounding rural area as being inherently racist. The rhetoric of their refusals, however, further displaces the politics of hatred into an underdetermined space that is somehow somewhere outside of the community itself. Boddy's sentiment that these acts do not represent Owen Sound and Aslam's assertion that the vandalism is not "an indicator of what's Owen Sound and what's Grey County" (quoted in Langlois 2019) are not only hard to square with the fact that an elected representative of the riding has been a prominent promulgator of anti-Muslim sentiments, but also that the Canadian state has a long history of hatred against Muslims (Razack 2008; Dhamoon and Abu-Laban 2009).

In comments to *The Hub*, all five candidates in the Bruce-Grey-Owen Sound riding during the 2019 federal election denounced the vandalism in ways that position the acts of hatred outside of the community, and outside of Canada more generally. In some cases, the (re)spatialization of hatred was done without subtext, such as when the Conservative Party candidate stated that "racism and hate *have no place* in Canada" (quoted in Ruff 2019; emphasis added). Other candidates relied on metaphor to achieve the same ends. Both the People's Party and New Democrat candidates evoked images of disease when denouncing the problem of racism (Townsend 2019; Stephen 2019), implying the supposedly alien nature of racism to the otherwise healthy body politic. Echoing the Liberal candidate, the People's Party candidate also asserted that hatred is rooted in ignorance, thereby constructing the perpetrators as being outside of an enlightened community of tolerance (Townsend 2019; Den Tandt 2019).

While such sentiments can be viewed generously as normative appeals to how our social relations ought to be structured, they nevertheless work to obscure actually existing conditions. Discursively spatializing hatred outside the community encourages us to ignore its ongoing role in the genocidal dispossession of land from Indigenous peoples (Wolfe 2006; Coulthard 2014; Estes 2019) and in the construction of exploitable pools of labour of differentially racialized communities (Abu-Laban and Gabriel 2002; Kuokkanen 2009; Karuka 2019). Moreover, political hatred

is clearly manifest in the use of policing and incarceration to construct and contain undesired groups (Camp and Heatherton 2016; Stark 2016; Maynard 2017; Crosby and Monaghan 2018); in the heightened exploitation of the (reproductive) labour of persons typically read as women or femme (Brodie 1994; Federici 2004); and in a bloody foreign policy of empire (Webber and Gordon 2016; Shipley 2017). These, and myriad other forms of exploitation and domination, are structurally necessary to the relatively smooth reproduction of dominant social relations, but are erased if hatred is treated as merely episodic. In short, the interlocking forms of exploitation, dispossession, domination, and violence that Ktunaxa scholar Joyce Green (2001, 715–16) calls "Project Canada" go fully unnamed, even as the reproduction of these forms of domination relies on an organized politics of hatred. While it may be the case that that politics typically takes the form of indifference (Povinelli 2011; McCallum and Perry 2018), when structures of domination are challenged, those who benefit or perceive themselves as benefitting from the status quo often defend it rancorously (Faludi 1991; Hirschman 1991; Dudas 2008; Anderson 2016; Mackey 2016; Haiven 2020).

Representing the politics of hatred as somehow something other than, or spatializing it outside of, the dominant social, political, legal, and economic order has many consequences. What I am particularly interested in here are the ways in which the politics of hatred—understood as aberrant and cultural rather than structural and material—merely leads to calls for greater toleration and inclusion, which are apparently conceptualized as the only remedies necessary to combat hate.

Tolerance defines what public figures called for in response to the vandalism in Owen Sound. Mayor Boddy told council that while he is not naïve to the fact that there are "still people out there that don't understand the differences between us," he nevertheless expressed how "frustrating" these hate crimes are in light of the efforts to "eliminate hatred and eliminate the differences between us" (Owen Sound City Council 2019, 2:23:00–2:30:00). In short, he is concerned that the project of maintaining the public sphere by requiring the minimization and toleration of our supposedly fixed differences remains incomplete.

Coming from across the partisan spectrum, these responses from public officials evidence Wendy Brown's (2006, 3) observation that, in

contemporary liberal democracy, "tolerance knows no political party." Uncritically accepting Brown's assertion that toleration is hegemonic would be irresponsible at the best of times, but this is especially so given that the political right in North America is, at time of writing, enthralled in the so-called Ahmari-French debates over whether the values and institutions of liberalism can serve the political goals of the conservative movement (Ahmari 2019; French 2019). Nevertheless, given the consistency with which all local candidates denounced these hate crimes, appealing explicitly to principles of toleration, Brown's observation maintains its validity. Indeed, the rhetoric of toleration remains strong enough in this context that even candidates whose party leaders have spoken at rallies alongside prominent white nationalists like Faith Goldy felt compelled to issue denunciations (Khandaker 2019).

In many ways it is encouraging that, regardless of their position on the partisan spectrum and of the grassroots alliances upon which their parties depend, all candidates at least offered lip-service to the principles of toleration. Such unanimity marks toleration as a core principle of the governing consensus. However, the constellation of power relations on which that governing consensus rests must be interrogated. It is precisely because of the ways in which "tolerance talk" obscures questions of power that toleration becomes what Brown (2006, 4) calls a language of governmentality: toleration is a discourse that fences political conduct within (and in order to reproduce) relations of power as they already exist. Put more clearly, toleration discourses obscure the reality of institutionalized white supremacism behind images of Canadians as benign and magnanimous tolerators faced with supposedly inevitable intercultural conflict with the infiltrative, yet still tolerated, Other. If toleration is our principle response to the politics of hatred, we rest contented on false "conceits that right attitudes produce justice," rather than grappling with how actually to reorder relationships of power (Brown 2006, 18).

Brown (2006, 178) explains the ways in which toleration discourses serve as an "incorporative practice" that, in the case of the hate crimes in Owen Sound, "promises to keep the peace" by bringing the Muslim Association more fully within the wider community. This obscures historically contingent questions of structural and material power relations in order to construct "group conflict as rooted in ontologically

natural hostility toward [and between] essentialized religious, ethnic, or cultural difference" (15). Crucially, this is achieved primarily by requiring that the tolerated group divest themselves of any particularities or peculiarities that might hinder them from fitting comfortably within dominant social relations. Brown thus summarizes that "the aim of learning tolerance is not to arrive at equality or solidarity with others but, rather, to learn how to put up with others by weakening one's own connections to community and claims of identity" (184). Considered in this light, Boddy's appeal for toleration of the "differences between us" is, in effect, a refusal to build conditions of meaningful social equality that are premised not on the absence of overt conflict but on the presence of real solidarity. Toleration discourses, as evidenced above, displace political analyses by creating a "binary of the ignorant and parochial hater and the [tolerant] cosmopolitan sophisticate" to whom the former inevitably accedes (Brown 2006, 184).

GOOD NEIGHBOURS DON'T NEED FENCES, RADICAL NEIGHBOURS TEAR THEM DOWN

Interestingly paralleling the shifting politics of hatred, this turn towards discourses of toleration and inclusion similarly disaggregates and deterritorializes our responses to hatred. Tolerance talk is not necessarily inauthentic in Owen Sound, nor in rural communities more generally, yet the frames of toleration and inclusivity feel quite far from the lingua franca in which the greater portion of the community responds to acts of hatred. My supposition is that there exists within all communities a number of vernaculars used to talk about and against hatred, even if those particular valances are not always immediately apparent. Moreover, I suspect that, as a result of their more common circulation, these other discourses also mobilize thicker notions of community than does "tolerance talk." This seems to be the case—though, as I show, not unproblematically—for one of the primary anti-hate discourses in Owen Sound: neighbourliness.

Those who live in, work with, or research rural communities likely recognize neighbours and neighbourliness as matters of core concern (see, e.g., Epp, this volume). For rural people, our neighbours and the degree to which they embody neighbourly behaviour are matters of

frequent conversation (Buckley 1983; Crow, Allan, and Summers 2002; Dunkelman 2014). As is the case with much intellectual work by those without institutional accreditation, scholars commonly miss the ways in which neighbourliness is at once a practice and a political theory (Painter 2012, 516). In the wake of the vandalizing of the Muslim Association, those supporting the solidarity vigil noted that "our neighbours, our friends" were experiencing acts of hatred, and that this obligated the formation of "a protective circle of neighbours" to ensure their safety (Boltman 2019). The neighbour functions as a relational subject position that creates both ethical and political responsibilities for care, concern, and solidarity; moreover, neighbourliness is a lingua franca or common-sense politics of anti-hate.

Indeed, this is only the most recent manifestation of a longer history of praxis and theorizing about neighbourliness in Owen Sound. In the midst of the waves of anti-Indigenous violence that defined the Summer of Hate, the Neighbours of Nawash was formed by a grassroots group of predominantly white settlers to combat the rampant politics of hatred in their community. The Neighbours organized anti-hate education sessions and fundraising through their existing networks within the settler community (Wallace 2013, 86–89). Marilyn Struthers, a member of the Neighbours, notes that the group named itself advisedly. While many misattribute the name as the "Friends of Nawash," Struthers (2010, 371) highlights that "being a neighbour carries a different politics of relationship…There are certain traditional obligations to being a 'neighbour.' Helpfulness, hot casseroles when there is a death…and money in a public bank account if there is a survival threatening event…[like] a boat burning." Animated by obligations emerging from the ethicopolitical relationship of being neighbours to the Chippewas of Nawash, it is possible to see a grounded anti-racist framework travelling under the label of "neighbourliness." This community's political theory of anti-racism is remarkable for the ways in which it enables (though may not always achieve) an eschewal of the often abstract and depersonalizing language that accompanies tolerance talk while simultaneously refusing to ground obligation or commonality in the framework of citizenship—which, try as it might to offer a universal vision of belonging, continues to reify an imperial state-building project.

As with all political relationships, however, even something as seemingly mundane as a neighbour cannot be presumed. It needs interrogating. A plainer way of putting this is simply to ask: If neighbourliness is a praxis, then who is my neighbour? The very question invokes an entire tradition of thought. The obligations owed to our neighbours have long preoccupied Christian practitioners and scholars with debates largely hinging on whether the parable of the Good Samaritan implicated a particularist or a universalist understanding of the neighbour (Winch 1987; Lerner 2002; Lynch, this volume; Epp, this volume). In other words, is the neighbour that Christ invokes another member of a shared ethnos or imagined community, or is the neighbour the Other, an outsider. Joe Painter (2012, 523) suggests that this dichotomy is unhelpful, as both the particularist and the universalist understanding of the neighbour are faulty: the former is too exclusionary and prone to "limiting neighbour-love only to the in-group," while the latter is so expansive as to amount to a "utopian extension of the social contract."

Against both these readings, Painter offers what I call a materialist understanding of the neighbour, insofar as he focuses on the real conditions of neighbouring. Tracing the etymology of the word, Painter suggests that "neighbour initially connoted no particular social relationship beyond dwelling nearby, and not necessarily very nearby" (523). Quoting Philip Abrams, Painter argues that the relationship of a neighbour is "neither universal nor specific; it is framed by propinquity and…little else" (523). Far from denuding our understanding of the neighbour, its reduction to a relationship of nearness "opens the concept of the neighbour…to ambiguity, difference, and agonism" (524). Through this understanding, the neighbour is neither required to share in a common particular ethnos or community, nor are they necessarily a radical Other forced to divest themselves of those distinctions in order to appeal to a shared universal humanity. In the propinquitous neighbour, difference not only remains, but remains unessentialized.

Given the degree to which the Neighbours of Nawash were enmeshed with local faith groups—several Neighbours were faith leaders—one might expect that their understanding of the neighbour was shaped by the (universalist) Christian tradition. However, Struthers' account bares far more resemblance to Painter's materialist understanding of the

neighbour. She writes that a "neighbour is 'someone who lives in proximity'...defined simply and explicitly by proximity" (Struthers 2010, 371).

While neighbourliness has clearly functioned endogenously within Owen Sound as a powerful anti-racist praxis, it has not been without severe limitations. As Struthers notes, the Neighbours failed to ask a crucial question: "What do neighbours do about the *structural inequities* that produce localized conflict?" (374; emphasis added). They failed also to articulate their interventions within and against "the broader arena of systemic racism [and imperialism]" (374). As Struthers implies, the Neighbours remained committed to seeing those who perpetrated violence as having equal claim to the obligations of neighbourliness as those who withstood the onslaught—in this case, the Chippewas of Nawash. Others have made similar criticism (Wallace 2013, 102). Because of this perspective, the Neighbours were unwilling to uphold their responsibilities to Nawash in ways that their white settler neighbours might deem "too radical" (Wallace 2013, 102). As one Neighbour put it, their primary "interest was in it not blowing up" (Wallace 2013, 88). Though this indicates an aversion to further violence, it belies a desire to return to normalcy and to preserve a status quo (Struthers 2010, 368, 371; Wallace 2013, 106). In this flattened vision of the politics of neighbourliness, we are never called upon to take up truly difficult positions when doing so might itself be deemed unneighbourly for having inconvenient or even marginally deleterious effects on another neighbour.

A radical praxis of neighbourliness must question the very conditions of possibility through which the relationship of neighbouring is (re)produced. It asks, How do I stand with my neighbours when they are harmed by other neighbours? Where are the neighbours who have been removed or barred entry due to displacement and gentrification? Whom among my neighbours has been kept from public life due to cisheteropatriarchy? What becomes of neighbours forced into transience by exclusionary state-based citizenship and labour regimes? What of those who suffer violence at the hands of racist policing and carceral systems? Are my neighbours able to weather the storm of climate change? Finally, but maybe foremost within settler-colonial contexts like Canada, a radical approach to neighbourliness begins by asking: How can I be a good neighbour when the very ground on which I make my home is being

expropriated from the Indigenous peoples who have governed and cared for it since time immemorial? How can I be both neighbour and *guest*?

These questions are all endemic to the language and ethos of a materialist understanding of neighbourliness. They root neighbourliness—that unavoidable relation of propinquity—not in colonial regimes of proprietorship but in place-based relationships of proximal solidarity. Questions like these and the radical neighbourliness on which they speculate help to bypass fetishisms of power—even as they attend to power's structural and material consequence—foregrounding the very real responsibilities that we have to our neighbours.

NEIGHBOURING ON SOMETHING DIFFERENT

While imperfect and incomplete, this discussion about neighbourliness as an anti-racist praxis and political theory endogenous to Owen Sound refutes much of the literature with which this chapter opened. Whereas this literature (re)locates the politics of hatred to rural communities, a grounded appraisal reveals neither simply revanchist roughnecks nor peaceable pastoralists. Instead, there are real, complicated, and internally contested communities struggling over how they understand themselves and what they want to become.

The vandal, the protective circle of neighbours, and the Muslim Association *all* stake claims of belonging to Owen Sound. It is this contestation over the meaning of the community itself that should interest us. Importantly, our interest should resist the desire to proclaim which of these positions has the "authentic" understanding of the community as an abstract thing, as this flattens out contradictions and reifies an idealized community that never was. Nevertheless, we can never hesitate to align ourselves with, uplift, and learn from those struggling for liberatory understandings of their communities and towards abolition of actually existing relations of exploitation and domination.

Loka Ashwood (2018, 714) says, "We need a better vocabulary to capture rural politics." This begins by striving to think with rather than merely about rural communities—to understand rural people as producers not merely of commodities or services, but also of political theories and practices. So much of scholarship and popular discussion focuses on the interventions that outside actors deemed necessary to build

inclusive or tolerant rural communities. Few consider that sustainable resolutions to these conflicts are likely to be immanent to the communities themselves. Furthermore, there has been a refusal throughout much of the literature to interrogate the very concepts of inclusivity and toleration. Though these frameworks are dominantly presumed to be palliatives for the politics of hatred, they reify and depoliticize the structural and material inequities that are foundational to liberal democratic state-building projects and capitalist social relations. But truly striving to be good neighbours—that is, radical neighbours—could become the basis upon which rural people build a liberatory struggle.

NOTE

1. Statistics Canada (2017c) reports a population decline of 1.4% in Owen Sound from 2011 to 2016, which deepens trends already established during the previous census period. According to the 2016 Census of Population, Owen Sound has a population density of roughly 1,000 people per kilometre. The counties adjacent to Owen Sound, Bruce, and Grey, have populations of 68,000 and 94,000 respectively. Bruce county's population density is 16 people per kilometre, and Grey county's is 20 people per kilometre (Statistics Canada 2017a, 2017b).

REFERENCES

Abu-Laban, Yasmeen, and Christina Gabriel. 2002. *Selling Diversity: Immigration, Multiculturalism, Employment Equity, and Globalization.* Peterborough: Broadview Press.

Ahmari, Sohrab. 2019. "Against David French-ism." *First Things*, May 29, 2019. https://www.firstthings.com/web-exclusives/2019/05/against-david-french-ism.

Anderson, Carol. 2016. *White Rage: The Unspoken Truth of Our Racial Divide.* New York: Bloomsbury Publishing.

Ashwood, Loka. 2018. "Rural Conservatism or Anarchism? The Pro-state, Stateless, and Anti-state Positions." *Rural Sociology* 83 (4): 717–48.

Boltman, Aly. 2019. "I Won't Be Complacent." *The Hub*, July 14, 2019. https://owensoundhub.org/opinion/7667-i-won-t-be-complacent.html.

Brodie, Janine. 1994. "Politics on the Boundaries: Restructuring and the Canadian Women's Movement." 8th Annual Robarts Lecture, York University, Toronto, ON, March 1, 1994.

Brown, Wendy. 2006. *Regulating Aversion: Tolerance in the Age of Identity and Empire*. Princeton: Princeton University Press.

Buckley, Anthony. 1983. "Neighbourliness: Myth and History." *Oral History* 11 (1): 44–51.

Camp, Jordan T., and Christina Heatherton. 2016. *Policing the Planet: Why the Policing Crisis Led to Black Lives Matter*. London: Verso.

Catte, Elizabeth, ed. 2019. *Left Elsewhere: Finding the Future in Radical Rural America*. Cambridge, MA: MIT Press.

Chippewas of Nawash. 2005. *Under Siege: How the People of the Chippewas of Nawash Unceded First Nation Asserted Their Rights and Claims and Dealt with the Backlash*. Neyaashiinigmiing: Ipperwash Inquiry.

Coulthard, Glen Sean. 2014. *Red Skin, White Masks: Rejecting the Colonial Politics of Recognition*. Minneapolis: University of Minneapolis Press.

Crosby, Andrew, and Jeffery Monaghan. 2018. *Policing Indigenous Movements: Dissent and the Security State*. Halifax: Fernwood Publishing.

Crow, Graham, Graham Allan, and Marcia Summers. 2002. "Neither Busybodies nor Nobodies: Managing Proximity and Distance in Neighbourly Relations." *Sociology* 36 (1): 127–45.

Den Tandt, Michael. 2019. "We Are Better than This." *The Hub*, July 9, 2019. https://owensoundhub.org/letters/7636-we-are-better-than-this.html.

Dhamoon, Rita, and Yasmeen Abu-Laban. 2009. "Dangerous (Internal) Foreigners and Nation-Building: The Case of Canada." *International Political Science Review* 30 (2): 163–83.

Dudas, Jeffery R. 2008. *The Cultivation of Resentment: Treaty Rights and the New Right*. Redwood City, CA: Stanford University Press.

Dunkelman, Marc J. 2014. *The Vanishing Neighbor: The Transformation of American Community*. New York: W.W. Norton & Co.

Estes, Nick. 2019. *Our History Is the Future: Standing Rock versus the Dakota Access Pipeline and the Long Tradition of Indigenous Resistance*. London: Verso.

Faludi, Susan. 1991. *Backlash: The Undeclared War Against American Women*. New York: Crown Publishing Group.

Federici, Silvia. 2004. *Caliban and the Witch: Women, the Body and Primitive Accumulation*. Brooklyn: Autonomedia.

Finlay-Stewart, Anne. 2019. "Calling Out Racism and Hate." *The Hub*, July 9, 2019. https://owensoundhub.org/opinion/7635-calling-out-racism-and-hate.html.

Frank, Thomas. 2004. *What's the Matter with Kansas: How Conservatives Won the Heart of America*. New York: Henry Holt & Co.

French, David. 2019. "What Sohrab Ahmari Gets Wrong." *National Review*, May 30, 2019. https://www.nationalreview.com/2019/05/david-french-response-sohrab-ahmari/.

Green, Joyce. 2001. "Canaries in the Mines of Citizenship: Indian Women in Canada." *Canadian Journal of Political Science* 34 (4): 715–38.

Grossman, Zoltán. 2017. *Unlikely Alliances: Native Nations and White Communities Join to Defend Rural Lands*. Seattle: University of Washington Press.

Habib, Jacky. 2019. "Far-Right Extremist Groups and Hate Crime Rates Are Growing in Canada." *The Passionate Eye*, CBC, July 13, 2019. https://www.cbc.ca/passionateeye/m_features/right-wing-extremist-groups-and-hate-crimes-are-growing-in-canada.

Haider, Asad. 2018. *Mistaken Identity: Race and Class in the Age of Trump*. London: Verso.

Haiven, Max. 2020. *Revenge Capitalism: The Ghosts of Empire, the Demons of Capital, and the Settling of Unpayable Debts*. London: Pluto Press.

Hannay, Chris. 2015. "Remarks on Women Wearing Niqabs Were 'Inappropriate', Tory MP Says." *Globe and Mail*, March 17, 2015. https://www.theglobeandmail.com/news/politics/remarks-on-women-wearing-niqabs-were-inappropriate-tory-mp-says/article23496326/.

Hirschman, Albert O. 1991. *The Rhetoric of Reaction: Perversity, Futility, Jeopardy*. Cambridge: Harvard University Press.

Hochschild, Arlie Russell. 2016. *Strangers in Their Own Land: Anger and Mourning on the American Right*. New York: New Press.

Karuka, Manu. 2019. *Empire's Tracks: Indigenous Nations, Chinese Workers, and the Transcontinental Railroad*. Oakland: University of California Press.

Khandaker, Tamara. 2019. "Andrew Scheer Criticized for Support of United We Roll Convoy." *Vice*, February 20, 2019. https://www.vice.com/en/article/a3bjb4/andrew-scheer-criticized-for-support-of-united-we-roll-convoy.

Koenig, Edwin C. 2005. *Cultures and Ecologies: A Native Fishing Conflict on the Saugeen-Bruce Peninsula*. Toronto: University of Toronto Press.

Kuokkanen, Rauna. 2009. "Indigenous Women in Traditional Economies: The Case of Sámi Reindeer Herding." *Signs: Journal of Women in Culture and Society* 34 (3): 499–504.

Langlois, Denis. 2019. "Mosque in Owen Sound Vandalized; Members Feeling Unsafe." *Sun Times*, July 12, 2019. https://owensoundsuntimes.com/news/local-news/mosque-in-owen-sound-vandalized-members-feeling-unsafe.

Lerner, Berel Dov. 2002. "Samaritans, Jews and Philosophers." *Expository Times* 113 (5): 152–56.

Mackey, Eva. 2016. *Unsettled Expectations: Uncertainty, Land and Settler Decolonization*. Halifax: Fernwood Publishing.

Marx, Karl, and Frederick Engels. (1848) 2005. *The Communist Manifesto*. Reprint, Chicago: Haymarket Books.

Maynard, Robyn. 2017. *Policing Black Lives: State Violence in Canada from Slavery to Present*. Halifax: Fernwood Publishing.

McCallum, Mary Jane Logan, and Adele Perry. 2018. *Structures of Indifference: An Indigenous Life and Death in a Canadian City*. Winnipeg, University of Manitoba Press.

Moreton-Robinson, Aileen. 2015. *The White Possessive: Property, Power, and Indigenous Sovereignty*. Minneapolis: University of Minnesota Press.

Owen Sound City Council. 2019. "July 15 2019 Council Meeting." Owen Sound. Uploaded July 17, 2019. YouTube video, 2:30:09. https://www.youtube.com/watch?v=aM118uERcb4.

Owen Sound Police Service. 2019. "Male in Custody for Mischief to Religious Property." *The Hub*, July 16, 2019. https://owensoundhub.org/police/7676-male-in-custody-for-mischief-to-religious-property.html.

Painter, Joe. 2012. "The Politics of the Neighbour." *Society and Space* 30 (3): 515–33. https://doi.org/10.1068/d21110.

Povinelli, Elizabeth. 2011. *Economies of Abandonment: Social Belonging and Endurance in Late Liberalism*. Charlotte, NC: Duke University Press.

Razack, Sherene H. 2008. *Casting Out: The Eviction of Muslims from Western Law and Politics*. Toronto: University of Toronto Press.

Ruff, Alex. 2019. "No Place in Canada." *The Hub*, July 10, 2019. https://owensoundhub.org/letters/7650-no-place-in-canada-1.html.

Shipley, Tyler A. 2017. *Ottawa and Empire: Canada and the Military Coup in Honduras*. Toronto: Between the Lines.

Stark, Heidi Kiiwetinepinesiik. 2016. "Criminal Empire: The Making of the Savage in a Lawless Land." *Theory & Event* 19 (4): article no. 633282. https://www.muse.jhu.edu/article/633282.

Statistics Canada. 2017a. "Bruce, CTY [Census division], Ontario and Ontario [Province]." Data table in *Census Profile, 2016 Census* (catalogue no. 98-316-X2016001). https://www12.statcan.gc.ca/census-recensement/2016/dp-pd/prof/index.cfm?Lang=E.

Statistics Canada. 2017b. "Grey, CTY [Census division], Ontario and Ontario [Province]." Data table in *Census Profile, 2016 Census* (catalogue no. 98-316-X2016001). https://www12.statcan.gc.ca/census-recensement/2016/dp-pd/prof/index.cfm?Lang=E.

Statistics Canada. 2017c. "Owen Sound [Population centre], Ontario and Ontario [Province]." Data table in *Census Profile, 2016 Census* (catalogue no. 98-316-X2016001). https://www12.statcan.gc.ca/census-recensement/2016/dp-pd/prof/index.cfm?Lang=E.

Stephen, Chris. 2019. "Anti-immigrant Sentiments Are Fueling Intolerance." *The Hub*, July 10, 2019. https://owensoundhub.org/letters/7649-anti-immigrant-and-anti-refugee-sentiments-are-fueling-intolerance.html.

Stock, Catherine McNicol. (1996) 2017. *Rural Radicals: Righteous Rage in the American Grain*. Rev. ed. Ithica: Cornell University Press.

Struthers, Marilyn. 2010. "Reflections on the Politics of Neighbourliness in Aboriginal/White Alliance-Building from the Fishing Wars of 1995." In *Alliances: Re/Envisioning Indigenous-non-Indigenous Relationships*, edited by Lynne Davis, 368–75. Toronto: University of Toronto Press.

Taylor, Yeeanga-Yamahtta. 2017. *How We Get Free: Black Feminism and the Combahee River Collective*. Chicago: Haymarket Book.

Townsend, Bill. 2019. "We Need to Study, Discuss and Understand." *The Hub*, July 10, 2019. https://owensoundhub.org/letters/7637-we-need-to-study-discuss-and-understand.html.

Vance, J.D. 2016. *Hillbilly Elegy: A Memoir of a Family and Culture in Crisis*. New York: HarperCollins.

Wallace, Rick. 2013. *Merging Fires: Grassroots Peacebuilding Between Indigenous and Non-Indigenous Peoples*. Halifax: Fernwood Publishing.

Webber, Jeffery R., and Todd Gordon. 2016. *Blood of Extraction: Canadian Imperialism in Latin America*. Halifax: Fernwood Publishing.

Winch, Peter. 1987. "Who Is My Neighbour?" In *Trying to Make Sense*, by Peter Winch, 154–66. Oxford: Blackwell.

Wolfe, Patrick. 2006. "Settler Colonialism and the Elimination of the Native." *Journal of Genocide Research* 8 (4): 387–409.

Wuthnow, Robert. 2018. *The Left Behind: Decline and Rage in Rural America*. Princeton: Princeton University Press.

11

THE WORK OF NEIGHBOURS

A Rural Ethos for Reconciliation

Roger Epp

We have left our rural relations out of the work toward reconciliation.
—MAX FINEDAY, Plains Cree,
  "I Do Not Want to Fight About This Anymore"

The choice here in Canada is one that must be made among friends and neighbours. We must face the underlying tensions. We must understand them and resolve them. Neither side believes that the other is going anywhere. This is home...We share space in a common land.
—FRED KELLY, Anishinaabe Elder, quoted in Aaron Mills,
  "What Is a Treaty?"

ACROSS MUCH OF THE RURAL WEST, Indigenous and non-Indigenous peoples live in adjacent communities, or in the same community, though the relationships between them often have been marked by tensions, fears, and side-by-side solitudes. This is scarcely a bold observation; for many people, it is simply lived reality. While the Truth and Reconciliation Commission affirmed in its final report that the work of building "a new way of living together" belonged to all Canadians, a follow-up national

survey suggested that people on the prairies—especially the rural prairies—are strikingly less willing to acknowledge racism, systemic barriers, the need to settle outstanding land claims, or the residential school legacy. Moreover, they are more likely to attribute to Indigenous peoples "a sense of entitlement when it comes to support from government" (Environics Institute for Survey Research 2016, 6; see also Banack, this volume). Not surprisingly, the Winnipeg-based Frontier Centre for Public Policy, a self-described think tank, chose to target small-market radio stations in Saskatchewan in 2018 with an ad challenging the residential school "myth" (MacPherson 2018). In the controversy that followed, the Centre was accused of "deliberately sowing deceit and division" (FineDay 2018)—presumably, though, on fertile ground. By that point, the Truth and Reconciliation Commission's 94 Calls to Action had been overwhelmed by the sharply polarized reaction to the shooting death of a young Indigenous man, Colten Boushie, on a Saskatchewan farm, and the farmer's acquittal on all charges in a Battleford courtroom. This series of events also exposed the lack of connective tissue across the reserve and nonreserve communities strung along Saskatchewan's Highway 4 (Friesen 2016; Hubbard 2019; Johnson 2019).[1] The Saskatchewan Association of Rural Municipalities (SARM 2017), which had been notably silent on the Truth and Reconciliation Commission and the subject of reconciliation at its annual conventions, passed a resolution demanding that the federal government "expand the rights and justification for an individual to defend or protect himself, herself, and persons under their care and their property"—in short, stand-your-ground legislation. Two years later, SARM achieved a partial victory in tougher provincial anti-trespass legislation.

This chapter begins from three premises. The first is that while it is relatively easy to summon a countryside of unresolved tensions and unacknowledged racism, it is dangerous—and false—to conclude that no other narrative is possible in the rural West. The second is that the most difficult, most urgent, and most meaningful work of reconciliation, of making a new way of living together, is necessarily local in character (Epp 2008). It is too important to be left by proxy to a national government and the wedge politics of national elections. The third is that the language of diversity and inclusion is insufficient to the task. Not only does such

language misrepresent the status of Indigenous peoples as minorities in a multicultural mosaic or as individual rights-bearers seeking to take their place in a liberal society of equals; in rural places, it is just as likely to be regarded as a matter of imposition by outsiders (Wuthnow 2018, 10–11).

To that end, I want to explore the case for an alternative ethical and political subject: that of the neighbour. My hunch is that this language has a much closer cultural fit with a rural sense of obligation and practice, but also that it has an intellectual range, a critical edge, and perhaps—I want to be cautious here—a complex compatibility with reemergent traditions of Indigenous legal thinking and what they say about the everyday enactment of treaty relations. All this is to explore. Any language, any ethos, of course, presents its own openings and limitations. I want to be clear at the outset that my interest here is neither in restating comfortable home-truths nor in minimizing the settler-colonial history of how land became property across the Canadian West. Instead, it is to unsettle and reframe what has been a difficult conversation in rural places around the ethical subject of the neighbour. The term is inherently relational and reciprocal. Neighbours live in geographic proximity. Their histories are entangled, like it or not. They cannot always avoid one another. Unlike "citizens," "refugees," and "Indians," neighbours are not defined in law by the state; their positive obligations to each other do not depend on the courts. To be a neighbour is to act like one. The language of the neighbour, meanwhile, operates on more than one level. It can describe elements of an everyday code of conduct ("neighbourliness"); it has a well-established place in the common-law tradition; and it surely draws some of its theoretical strength from a powerful story, inherited from the Christian tradition, that responds to a question asked in search of justification: Who is my neighbour? In other words, Who is deserving of my respect and care? What are the limits of that circle? The outcome of the story is to disrupt the settled prejudices of those who hear it, to redraw the circle.

NEIGHBOURLINESS AS AN ORDINARY VIRTUE
In his book *The Ordinary Virtues*, Michael Ignatieff (2017, 24) concludes that the twentieth-century project to establish human rights as the principled core of a shared set of universal values and solidarities has succeeded only among an "influential but thinly spread stratum"—that

is, among "people paid to think abstractly or campaign for a living." What he finds instead, whether in the crowded favelas, the multicultural cities, or the fragile postconflict, postapartheid, and postdisaster zones of a superficially globalized world, are people who live by "ordinary virtues." By that he means "skills in moral conduct and discernment," acquired through experience, which are "not abstract and theoretical, but intensely practical, contextual, and local" (27–28). Those virtues typically begin with generosity and welcome. They hinge on trust and reciprocity, not logical consistency. They make no claim on humanity as a whole; they focus on the "human beings we know" (209). They operate as an unwritten code, a shared moral order, one that "works to live and let live as an organizing assumption in dealings with others, but retreats to loyalty toward one's own when threatened" (29). Ordinary virtues sometimes draw sharp lines between insiders and outsiders. At their best, though, Ignatieff writes, they not only keep ordinary vices in check. They also help people resist the peddlers of "global clichés" about inevitable clashes of civilizations or religions, the kind that can turn "neighbors into enemies"; they do so by "creating the space"—local space—"to do real politics together" (135).

Whether Ignatieff succeeds as an anthropologist of comparative ethical codes is not my concern. His global itinerary includes no intentional rural stops. Nonetheless I want to claim the idea of ordinary virtue as resonant with the ethos of the neighbour: not abstract, but practical, contextual, and local. In this sense, it echoes some prominent and otherwise very different recent scholarly treatments of the rural. James Scott (2012, 37–38), for example, treats the community as the basic "unit of moral obligation," by which he means "a pattern of finely grained mutual reciprocities which govern social relations and which are enforced by the sanctions of local approval or censure." The critical distinction here is between insiders and outsiders. In his book *The Left Behind: Decline and Rage in Rural America*, Robert Wuthnow (2018) also begins with face-to-face communities, which, for all their acknowledged limits and fault lines, are experienced by those who live in them as places of identity, loyalty, and especially "moral obligation." That sense of obligation is lived out in relation to one's family, to one's neighbours, and to community projects, institutions, and organizations. As

Wuthnow writes, "these are not the ideals of a utopian order that are seldom put into practice. They are the implicit constraints of ordinary life to which people adhere enough of the time to function as community norms" (15). They serve to include as well as exclude: "Residents can live there and be so independent that they rarely speak to anyone else. But if they do live that way, they are treated as outsiders" (14). Beyond that, the community norms of neighbourliness are not readily catalogued; they may vary from location to location, and they may be highly elastic depending on circumstances. In Wuthnow's account, they connect to everyday practices such as simply acknowledging others on the street, attending community events (he does not get so detailed as setting up the tables, bringing a pie, or making sure the sound system works), working hard, keeping up one's property (but not showing off), and being ready to volunteer one's skills and tools when called on to help others. That might mean singing at funerals or clearing snow after a blizzard or delivering a meal to a family preoccupied with a medical situation. Expectations and roles can be individual as well as gendered. But in rural communities, people know what it means for them to be neighbourly. As Barney (2004, 29) observes, "members of a community defined by a mutual moral obligation usually know what to do, or what not to do, without having to be told. Habituation to obligation, rather than its declaration, is the mark of a community whose bond is moral." Their obligations extend well beyond the minimal-interference legal standard of the "good neighbour" who keeps fences maintained, animals inside them, weeds and noises down, and storm water or spring melt well channelled when it crosses a property line—who is, in short, not a nuisance.

Social relations among neighbours have been characterized in terms of exchange or reciprocity—not altruism—that extend over time and that include elements of trust, sociability, help, and respect of others' privacy (Abrams 1986, 30). They do not require sameness or intimacy. In fact, they are marked by the paradox of physical proximity and yet a measured emotional distance. The neighbour is distinct from a friend or family member, though those identities may overlap. To be a neighbour is to act like one. It is to respond appropriately, to take time, to keep an eye out, to be reliable. It is to exercise tact and forbearance—another way in which neighbourliness involves a different, long-range register of time. It is, in

other words, to learn through practice a set of ordinary virtues, which are *not* an automatic response on the part of rural people either to their relative proximity or to their presumed interdependencies. Proximity or adjacency, like familiarity, can as easily breed contempt and potential conflict. Practices of neighbourliness, moreover, can be corroded or forgotten or never really developed in the first place.

In Wuthnow's (2018, 11) account, community norms can also exclude people who cannot meet expectations—for reasons of poverty, for example—just as they can hide racism and misogyny "in the patterns of life that nearly all-white communities have come to accept." But they also serve to mediate real difference and manage conflict in places where people live with each other for a lifetime. Because of the higher value they assign to direct experience and to personal connections—the "human beings we know"—over against abstract principle, they work to soften the rhetorically energetic rural support that is often enlisted for political positions that would hold the line against LGBTQ+ rights, say, or refugee resettlement. Neighbourliness offers a way to make one's place in the community—not just to be "tolerated"—because it represents the more relevant moral test. It does not need to erase difference; if anything, difference may be its realization. For that matter, *neighbourliness* is neither a "progressive" word nor a "conservative" word; it moderates a polarized politics of friends and enemies, which vulnerable rural communities can least afford. As a consequence, the person routinely at the microphone for local events might well be the one whose ballot-box politics are known to be out of step with the majority, but whose demonstrated skill in public, continued willingness to accept the role, and track-record as a reliable neighbour make it unthinkable for people to question what, to an outsider, might seem an ironic situation.

Like Henderson (this volume), I am wary of presenting what might seem an idealized account of this kind of ordinary virtue in rural contexts—or, equally, a naïve account of how neighbourliness might in reality serve as ideological cover and compensation for the neoliberal retreat of the state from so much of the countryside. Or how it might assume and therefore reinforce a regime of land as private property.[2] Those imagined charges might signify a difference in metropolitan and

rural sensibilities.³ In the concluding essay of *Writing Off the Rural West*, a book that critically explored the restructuring and abandonment of rural places to global market forces, the scholar-farmer Nettie Wiebe (2001) strikes a very different note. Rural people, she writes, who are "rooted in place" and who "not only remember but continue to live in relationships of trust, cooperation, and *neighbourliness* are models for the possibility of such human community" (2001, 330; emphasis added). They are more than the individualized subjects of neoliberalism, which means they can also imagine and act on alternative projects. From this angle, the word *neighbour* is not somehow outside of politics. If anything, it is the precondition of politics. Where it represents practices of trust and reciprocity, it mitigates what the political theorist Hannah Arendt (1958, 52–53) once called the loss of a "common world...that gathers us together and yet prevents our falling over each other" (see also Talisse 2019). It might even affirm that in an age when intense polarization, anger, and blame-seeking are the defining features of a top-down, hollowed-out public realm, there is no way for people to decide to do something new together in the countryside unless they are neighbours first.

WHO IS MY NEIGHBOUR?

To this point, my purpose has been to sketch out an account of the neighbour and neighbourliness that, first, is recognizable to a rural context and, second, represents a coherent, substantial example of ordinary virtues at work—an account with a political capacity that is still to be realized. But this account is also problematic or incomplete in terms of the larger interest in building a new way of living together, Indigenous and settler, in the rural West. In a sense, its enduring cultural strength in rural communities that have weathered one or two generations of political-economic restructuring may also be its limitation, for the ethos of neighbourliness can easily be reserved for a shrinking, hardening circle of trust and reciprocity, while a more hostile or fearful attitude prevails in relation to those who are regarded as outsiders.

As a next step, then, I turn to what is commonly known as the story of the Good Samaritan. While the story has a particular point of origin in the Christian Gospels, where it echoes and queries an older, two-fold injunction in the Hebrew scriptures to love God and love one's neighbour

as oneself, it is also part of a wider cultural inheritance that is reflected, for example, in the adoption of "Good Samaritan laws" to describe the duty to assist in an emergency. As such, the story of the Samaritan is easily reduced to an edifying story of a good deed done. But such a reduction strips it of much of its depth and critical potential. The title is, in fact, a problematic imposition on the biblical text. Read in the context of the interpretation I develop, "Good Samaritan" sounds suspiciously like "Good Indian"—that is, someone who is better than most of his kind. In that way, it serves to reinforce what is at stake. In the Book of Luke (10:25-37), the story is presented as Jesus's indirect response to a challenge from a learned man who first asks what he must do to inherit eternal life. The question may have been a trap or a bit of late-night sophistry. When the learned man is prompted for the commandments to love God and neighbour, then told simply to do so, he shifts into a limit-seeking approach: "Who is my neighbour?" In other words, Who is not? Who is beyond the circle of obligation? Significantly, the story turns on the figure of the neighbour rather than that of the stranger, for whom protocols of hospitality would have applied. But it also accepts the ambiguity of the neighbour—the one who is near.[4] What can that mean?

The story concerns a man who sets out on a journey on a dangerous stretch of road, who is beaten, robbed, and left for dead beside the road, and who is eventually helped to safety and bed-rest, not by the respectable members of his own society—who hurry past—but by a generous outsider, a Samaritan. Presumably, the first listeners to this story, and Christian insiders ever since, have identified with the traveller. He is one of "us." But the story is meant to undercut civilizational hierarchies and insider-outsider distinctions. In locating the problem of obligation on the edge of the circle, the story reaches scandalously across a bitter we-they divide of peoples living side by side. Who is the neighbour? Not the one you expect, not the one who is like you, and not necessarily the one you have been taught to respect. The neighbour is the one who acts like a neighbour, and who takes no small risk in doing so. As one commentator has suggested, had the victim known who had come to rescue him, he might have refused the assistance, or been too afraid to accept it (Mescher 2020; Gaster 1962). But think also of the risk the Samaritan took in stopping to help—how someone coming on the scene while he was tending to

the victim might have interpreted it. Then tell that story in a contemporary setting on Highway 4 between Biggar and Battleford in west-central Saskatchewan. Replace Samaritan with Cree. Who is the neighbour? Who takes the initiative? Who takes the time? Who shows compassion and courage? And who stands in need of help?

The parable of the neighbour has attracted plenty of interpreters over two millennia—theologians, of course, but also recent generations of social and political theorists (e.g., Žižek, Santer, and Reinhard 2013; Fierke 2014; Painter 2012). It might still be the sermon text on occasional Sunday mornings in the many small churches across the rural West, some of them, indeed, on reserves and in predominantly Métis communities. While it is commonly read as a lesson that turns a particular ethic (the love of one's own people) into a universal one (the love of humanity), this reading is insufficient or misleading. The story gives a very specific identity—Samaritan—to its principal character. (Prompted by Jesus to identify who is the neighbour, the learned man cannot bring himself to say the word *Samaritan*, only "the one who showed mercy.") Likewise, the setting is not generic. It is the hilly border region between Jerusalem and Jericho, where side-by-side relations are tense, where presumably there is no history of small, routine reciprocities and not enough connecting tissue. But the story is still about the neighbour, the one who is near. It does not vacate the local for the universal. It does not imagine an abstract world of infinite neighbourly obligations—a world of reciprocity and trust without limit, a contradiction in terms. Finally, it does not require that the Samaritan cease to be a Samaritan. No doubt he goes home. Though he returns the next day to settle up with the innkeeper, he does not seize the moment to ask to assimilate, to "move up," leveraging his generosity for admission into a "better" society. The story doesn't undermine itself in that way. It does not matter whether "deep down, we are all the same," or whether the Samaritan is "becoming more like us." When he acts as a neighbour in so fraught a space, he does not erase the circle of reciprocal obligation; he redraws and unsettles it.

THE NEIGHBOURS WERE ALREADY THERE

In March 2019, Kristian Ayoungman, a young man from Siksika First Nation in Treaty 7 territory in southern Alberta, was shot dead after an

altercation in the nearby town of Strathmore (Walker 2019). Well known locally as a Junior B hockey player, he had just played in an alumni game. After an altercation later that evening, he and his friends were headed back to the reserve on a rural highway with another vehicle in chase. Ayoungman, a passenger in his friend's truck, was struck by a bullet fired at long range. Two local men—brothers—were charged with first-degree murder. This case, however, was not the Boushie case. For one thing, it involved no defence of a farm "castle"; for another, it has received far less public attention. But it had the potential to trigger similar local and regional tensions around the death of another young Indigenous man in what seemed initially to be a racially motivated crime.[5] The young man's mother, Melodie Ayoungman, was blunt in a televised interview about the racism that led to the shooting. But she and Siksika community leaders also said that they were concerned about the possibility that young people would seek retribution in Strathmore. Siksika First Nation councillor Buck Breaker worried that violence would escalate so that "the jail cells would have been full and the morgue would have been full and the courthouse would have been full" (quoted in Walker 2019). Melodie Ayoungman told a journalist that she drew on the Blackfoot teachings learned from her grandparents to choose a different path. Among other things, she organized a candlelight vigil for which people travelled from Siksika to Strathmore. There, they were met by local people, including the mayor, Pat Fule, a long-time resident. The vigil led to regular meetings between Siksika and Strathmore leadership, apparently a new practice although the communities are not far apart.

    For the purposes of this chapter, though, the mayor's response to the vigil is of particular interest. In a letter to the local paper, he wrote: "Until we can admit that racism is here—and due to the recent murder, our *neighbours* now worry about coming to Strathmore—we can't improve" (quoted in Walker 2019; emphasis added). While the unvarnished references to racism may have displeased some of the town's residents, his choice of the word *neighbour* is an intriguing one in light of the preceding analysis. Note that the mayor is not somehow exercising his authority, on behalf of an enlightened community, to recognize and confer a new status on people who live on the reserve. Instead, the neighbours were already there. What remained was simply to see them as such, to understand their

apprehension, and then through that encounter to see himself as a neighbour, too—one who needed, for a start, to acknowledge those he meets in town, not look the other way, and who needed to accept an invitation when it was offered.

ENACTING TREATY RELATIONS OF MUTUALITY

If my readings of rural practices of mutuality and the parable of the neighbour have any claim in the countryside, they suggest that rural people have the resources they need, first, to reframe relationships with their Indigenous neighbours; second, to understand themselves as treaty people and to enact treaty relationships; and third, to step outside the powerful settler mythology that has worked for several generations to dull any lingering uneasiness about their historic presence on the land.[6] This is, I appreciate, a tall order. But I am emboldened by stories across the rural West that point to new ways of living together. These stories owe less to academic critiques of colonialism or the United Nations Declaration on the Rights of Indigenous Peoples than to cultures of neighbourliness and the gift of proximity. Some examples:

- In the Cariboo region of central British Columbia, a retired rancher and sawmill owner donated a half-section of land and accompanying water rights back to the Esk'etemc First Nation, which never believed it had surrendered them. Chief Charlene Belleau of Esk'etemc First Nation says the man has employed many First Nations members over the years, and she agreed with an interviewer's suggestion that he is a "good neighbour" (Belleau 2017; see also Lamb-Yorski 2017).[7]
- In central Alberta, a farmer invited Elders to conduct reburial ceremonies for the nineteenth-century remains of an adolescent Cree girl, likely pushed up by a badger, beaded clothing still partially intact, in a corner of his field where he has made provision for ongoing visitors (Reith and Stewart 2016).
- In Saskatchewan, settler descendants in a farming district have worked with members of the Young Chippewayan First Nation, whose allocated reserve on the same triangle of land was made available to homesteaders in the 1890s, to build relationships

around ceremony, food, a sacred hill-site, friendship, and an ongoing campaign for recognition of an outstanding land claim. Their first joint declaration more than a decade ago asserted: "We are all treaty people" (Leitch 2016; Epp 2012).

- In the adjacent communities of St. Paul, Alberta, and Saddle Lake First Nation, whose members once engaged in a year-long, multi-million-dollar boycott of St. Paul businesses, a racist incident at a local theatre led local people to form a joint reconciliation committee and hold community meetings, a walk, and a rally that filled the hockey arena (Morin 2018). In a film that emerged from this work, *Treaty Talk* (Leitch 2018), one self-described settler ally who has learned enough Cree to introduce herself at length, talks about a failure to share land—for deer, berries, or ceremony—and asks: "What is our responsibility to treaty?"

- In west-central Saskatchewan, Cree Elders were invited in the summer of 2019 to conduct a pipe ceremony and share lunch with community members at a ranch that was to be bisected by a municipal road, the scheduled construction of which came as a surprise since preparatory work had just unearthed a richness of 10,000-year-old artifacts. First Nations leaders had not been consulted about the discoveries or the road, except by local farmers. The next step was a formal agreement to work together to stop the road. Rancher Mitzi Gilroy said: "I think they want to make a heritage site of some kind here, and we're on board" (quoted in Warick 2019; see also Short 2019).

- In southern Manitoba, where a Dakota two-spirit woman Geraldine McManus has kept a prayer camp at the site where Enbridge's replacement Line 3 will cross into the United States, local people—a handful at least, for the pipeline is a big employer—have kept an eye out when she has been away and helped host a Thanksgiving feast in fall 2018 for people from across the region, including the nearest reserve (Martin 2019).[8] When she needed a burning barrel, a teacher who had brought ceremonial tobacco promised to ask a farmer.

- In central Alberta, on Samson Cree First Nation, along a bend in the Battle River, an Elder revived the practice of the water ceremony, once outlawed, in co-operation with the regional watershed alliance over a four-year cycle. The event included a pipe ceremony, blessing, and feast. The hosts had "invited their neighbours from across Battle River Country"(wearecree.com). People came.

Taken together, these examples present a rural West at odds with the conventional picture. They are consistent with a study based on focus-group interviews in Toronto and two communities in northern British Columbia. This study suggested that participants in the BC focus groups leaned much more towards a sense of local, personal—not delegated—responsibility for reconciliation (de Costa and Clark 2016). While the impact of these examples might be modest, it should not be underestimated. Each of them raises the question: If something like this can happen in one rural locality, why not others? Each reflects something of the work of neighbours. It is relational, respectful, and reciprocal. It sometimes starts with a crisis or problem. It builds trust. It involves openness to ceremony, to the exchange of food and knowledge, and to the lived experience of Indigenous participants. Not least, it involves a small but significant shift away from simple, zero-sum definitions of land as property—as exclusive domain—and toward forms of shared use based on responsibilities that arise from the land and its history. For the most part, this work happens without federal or provincial governments anywhere near. It does not lead with lofty pronouncements. It is practical, local, and contextual. It comes close to what I want to describe as enacting treaty relationships.

In this context, the work being done to rearticulate Indigenous legal traditions ought to be read by rural people of good will as an invitation essentially to think about what they are doing. While this work is diverse, its general purpose is to establish an alternative to what is conventionally understood to be the basis for Indigenous reengagement with Canada. More specifically, it aims to shift the focus away from the priority of advancing Indigenous interests in the Canadian court system, tacitly

accepting its constitutional authority and its mode of reasoning in hopes of favourable decisions, to that of reclaiming and developing traditions that guided decision-making, dispute resolution, and intersocietal relations for generations prior to colonization. Typically, those traditions are story-based and land-based (e.g., Napoleon and Friedland, 2016). They begin with an affirmation of relatedness; their objective is closer to harmony than to justice, understood in more abstract or win-lose terms. Indeed, John Borrows (2010, 199), a leading Indigenous scholar in this shift, has commented that Canadian constitutional law frustrates "the more fundamental work to be done to harmonize Indigenous peoples' relationships *with their neighbours*" (emphasis added). In Borrow's work, the neighbour is commonly invoked even when he is describing conflict, say, over land or fisheries. The language localizes, deescalates, and reconstitutes. The tone is hospitable, though the political implications of taking Indigenous law seriously would be far-reaching.

Among the Plains Cree, the governing concept is *wahkohtowin*. Wildcat (2018, 14) defines *wahkohtowin* as referring simultaneously to a worldview of interrelatedness; to law, or "the obligations and responsibilities people have to maintain good relationships"; and to good conduct. As Harold Cardinal and Walter Hildebrandt (2000, 14–15) write on the basis of extensive interviews with Elders: "The teachings and ceremonies are the means given to First Nations to restore peace and harmony in times of personal and community conflict. These teachings also serve as the foundation upon which new relationships are to be created." Thus, the principle of *wahkohtowin* is foundational for the treaties, understood as an "enduring and lasting relationship between the First Nations, the Crown, and her subjects. These relationships were, in part, to consist of mutual ongoing caring and sharing arrangements between the treaty parties, which included a sharing of duties and responsibilities for land" (15).

I have no authority to offer further commentary on Cree teachings or understandings of Treaty 6. My purpose here is simply to suggest possible bridges of recognition and understanding for those who start from rural practices of neighbourliness. The same holds for what Aaron Mills (2017, 231) calls an Anishinaabe constitutionalism, which understands that interdependence is foundational, that "each of us needs the

gifts we don't have in order to be free," and that freedom is, in fact, experienced through the "needs and demands of others"—not by autonomous individuals. This "carefully developed orientation towards the other" is consistent with the priority of harmony (233). It requires the cultivation of self-control and "personal practices of mutual aid which we may call living in right relation" (236). Mutual aid, in turn, is the basis for treaty, a "framework for right relationships" (225)—not just rights—and a stark alternative to the "bald exercise of power," fear, and unspoken assumptions about settler supremacy (220). Mills acknowledges that the idea of a treaty-based constitutionalism "risks unwinding the world I know and all that I have in it" (220). Nonetheless, he argues, it represents an invitation to be partners—"different and together" (209)—in shared space, one by which "settler lives can be accounted for and legitimized" (238).

THE WORK OF NEIGHBOUR

The figure of the neighbour is, if anything, less likely to be encountered in Western political and social theory than the Cree principle of *wahkohtowin* is likely to appear in a contemporary law-school curriculum. That's not about to change. The neighbour in the strong rural sense I have explored may seem an anachronism in highly urbanized settings where relationships are chosen on the basis of commonalities, not defined by proximity, where needs are met by strangers in specialist occupations, and where mobility over a lifetime is assumed. That said, my interest in this chapter is in rural places where people—Indigenous and non-Indigenous—must routinely decide how they will live together, since they do not have the option of reconciliation from a safe distance. In such places, where people confront the everyday challenges of distance, access to public services, health care, schools, economic opportunity, food security, and environmental balance in a resource-based countryside—here the ordinary virtues of the neighbour have not lost their relevance. They may represent the best hope for reframing treaty as something other than a one-time land transaction that cleared the West for settlement generations ago. They can help redraw the circle of reciprocity, different and together, one encounter at a time. For there will be no new way of living together in the diverse regions of the rural West if it is not through the work of neighbours.

AUTHOR NOTE

I am indebted to Laticia Chapman for her research assistance and for our ongoing conversations about the subject of the neighbour, especially her insights with respect to time and forbearance; to Darin Barney, Will Braun, Dwayne Donald, Philip Henderson, and Patricia Makokis for their thoughtful comments on an earlier draft; and to Tanya Fontaine Porozni, Mick Friesen, and Shannon McPhail for encouraging conversations from different rural contexts.

NOTES

1. Harold Johnson, Cree author, lawyer, and former Crown prosecutor, who died in 2022, recounted that on the long drive through sparsely populated country in western Saskatchewan, his wife asked him to make a roadside stop, but adamantly not at a farmyard. Johnson (2019, 4) wrote, "I realized that this tough woman, who lives with me on a trapline, who regularly walks trails alone in the dark knowing there are wolves out there, whom I have never seen to be afraid of anything, was now afraid of farmers. And if we believe Gerald Stanley [the farmer accused in the Boushie case], the farmers were afraid of her."

2. This is a complex point, whose complexity only increases as rural property ownership is concentrated, often in the hands of outside speculators who push prices beyond the reach of local people and land-based livelihoods. This may be where neighbourliness as idea and practice shows itself as a limited, ordinary virtue. By itself, it cannot ground a full-scale critique of property, not even when a pattern of land transactions undermines neighbourliness; nor can it unravel the settler-colonial history of North America. Nonetheless, I would argue that the idea contains fragments of an ancient, Aristotelian sense of property in land as being important, not as wealth or as an acquisition, but as the basis of one's standing in the community, one's generosity, and one's responsibilities. In this sense, neighbourliness tempers property as exclusive domain. It might once have elicited the donation of land for a school or a cemetery; it might still mean the decision to adopt ecological practices in farming, for example, or to sell within the community rather than to the highest potential bidder in a global market. That emphasis on property as responsibility is consistent with the kinds of initiatives described later in this chapter and, using the term *titleholders* rather than *landowners*—a vocabulary I've begun to hear—to describe

prairie farmers and ranchers. I am grateful to Philip Henderson for pushing me on this point and for the critical distinction he brings to his treatment of the neighbour in Chapter 10 of this volume.

3. One of those differences involves the word *community*: "It is now typically used to describe self-chosen clusters of people who, in a world of strangers, share some essential characteristic, for example, profession, ethnicity, sexual preference, or, behind gates, wealth. In rural contexts, however, it continues to mean something quite opposite: living unavoidably with, and having to rely upon, people who are not like you, and doing so possibly over a lifetime" (Epp 2008, 48).

4. The *Oxford English Dictionary* (3rd ed.) traces the word *neighbour* to Germanic and Old English sources; in one possible etymology, it suggests that the word descends from *nēahgebūr*, a combination of *nēah* (nigh, near) and *gebūr* (inhabitant, peasant, farmer). The same spatial sense of the neighbour as near-dweller is ascribed to the Greek word used in the Gospel of Luke: πλησίος (plesios) (Beck 1962, 534–35; Young 1982, 691).

5. More than a year later, when the first of two brothers charged in the shooting entered a guilty plea to a charge of manslaughter and his lawyer asked the court for a Gladue report before sentencing, it emerged publicly that the accused were also Indigenous, though evidently not from Siksika. That fact does not diminish either the emotions generated in the aftermath of the shooting or the responses described here. The second brother was found guilty of manslaughter later in 2021.

6. The settler mythology as I have described it says: (1) there was no one here when we came; (2) this country gave us freedom—land—and we made something of it through our own hard work and sacrifice: and (3) as members of a higher civilization, we are natural successors on the land (Epp 2017).

7. In a CBC interview, Chief Charlene Belleau (2017) was asked if the donor, Kenneth Linde, was a good neighbour: "Yes…our communities are small. Whenever he needed to come down and visit, you know our doors were open. Whenever we needed to see him we could always be able to visit. So… like any rural area, people are close. Everybody knows each other. When you need support for one another, we're always there for each other."

8. In April 2020, the wigwam built at the site was burned to the ground in what police called an arson and potentially a hate crime. No charges have been laid. McManus (2020) told an interviewer that while "racism is well and alive in Gretna…I just really try to let that go and focus on the good people that came out there. The ones that made me feel good to be a human being and doing what I'm doing."

REFERENCES

Abrams, Philip. 1986. *Neighbours*, edited by Martin Bulmer. Cambridge: Cambridge University Press.

Arendt, Hannah. 1958. *The Human Condition*. Chicago: University of Chicago Press.

Barney, Darin. 2004. "Communication versus Obligation: The Moral Status of Virtual Community." In *Globalization, Technology, and Philosophy*, edited by David Tabachnick and Toivo Koivukoski, 21–41. Albany: SUNY Press.

Beck, H.F. 1962. "Neighbor." In *Interpreter's Dictionary of the Bible*, Vol. 4, edited by George Arthur Buttrick. Nashville: Abingdon Press.

Belleau, Charlene. 2017. Interview by Carol Off. *As It Happens*, CBC, May 12, 2017. https://www.cbc.ca/radio/asithappens/as-it-happens-friday-edition-1.4112585/may-12-2017-episode-transcript-1.4116036#segment3.

Borrows, John. 2010. *Canada's Indigenous Constitution*. Toronto: University of Toronto Press.

Cardinal, Harold, and Walter Hildebrandt. 2000. *Treaty Elders of Saskatchewan: Our Dream Is That Our Peoples Will One Day Be Clearly Recognized as Nations*. Calgary: University of Calgary Press.

de Costa, Ravi, and Tom Clark. 2016. "On the Responsibility to Engage: Non-Indigenous Peoples in Settler States." *Settler Colonial Studies* 6 (3): 191–208.

Environics Institute for Survey Research. 2016. *Canadian Public Opinion on Aboriginal Peoples: Final Report*.

Epp, Roger. 2008. *We Are All Treaty People: Prairie Essays*. Edmonton: University of Alberta Press.

Epp, Roger. 2012. "'There Was No One Here When We Came': Overcoming the Settler Problem." *Conrad Grebel Review* 30 (2): 115–26.

Epp, Roger. 2017. "Rural Prairie West: Last Frontier for Reconciliation?" *Prairie Messenger*, January 11, 2017.

Fierke, Karin M. 2014. "Who Is My Neighbour? Memories of the Holocaust/Al Nakba and a Global Ethic of Care." *European Journal of International Relations* 20 (3): 787–809.

FineDay, Max. 2018. "'I Do Not Want to Fight About This Anymore': Residential School Denial Is Poisonous." *CBC News Opinion*, September 30, 2018. https://www.cbc.ca/news/canada/saskatoon/opinion-orange-shirt-day-radio-ad-residential-schools-1.4843779.

Friesen, Joe. 2016. "The Night Colten Boushie Died: What Family and Police Files Say About His Last Day, and What Came After." *Globe and Mail*, October 20, 2016. https://www.theglobeandmail.com/news/national/colten-boushie/article32451940/.

Gaster, T.H. 1962. "Samaritans." In *Interpreter's Dictionary of the Bible*, Vol. 4, edited by George Arthur Buttrick. Nashville: Abingdon Press.

Hubbard, Tasha, dir. 2019. *nîpawistamâsowin: We Will Stand Up*. Ottawa: National Film Board. https://www.nfb.ca/film/nipawistamasowin-we-will-stand-up/.

Ignatieff, Michael. 2017. *The Ordinary Virtues: Moral Order in a Divided World*. Cambridge, MA: Harvard University Press.

Johnson, Harold. 2019. *Peace and Good Order: The Case for Indigenous Justice in Canada*. Toronto: McClelland and Stewart.

Lamb-Yorski, Monica. 2017. "Rancher Gifts Land to Esk'etemc During Title and Rights Ceremony." *BC Local News*, May 10, 2017. https://www.bclocalnews.com/news/rancher-gifts-land-to-esketemc-during-title-and-rights-ceremony.

Leitch, Brad, dir. 2016. *Reserve 107*. Vancouver: Rebel Sky Media. https://www.reserve107thefilm.com.

Leitch, Brad, dir. 2018. *Treaty Talk: Sharing the River of Life*. Vancouver: Rebel Sky Media. https://www.treatytalk.com.

MacPherson, Alex. 2018. "'Repeating It Causes Damage Over and Over and Over Again': Frontier Centre Radio Ad Describes Residential School Harm as a 'Myth,'" *Saskatoon Star-Phoenix*, September 24, 2018. https://thestarphoenix.com/news/local-news/frontier-centre-radio-ad-describes-residential-school-harm-as-a-myth/.

Martin, Melissa. 2019. "Guided by Spirits, Undaunted by Threats." *Winnipeg Free Press*, June 21, 2019. https://www.winnipegfreepress.com/local/right-place-right-time-guided-by-spirits-undaunted-by-threats-511633712.html.

McManus, Geraldine. 2020. "Spirit of The Buffalo: An Interview With Geraldine McManus From The Frontlines Of Resistance To The Enbridge Line 3 Pipeline." By Yahya Apánii. *Branch Out*, May 8, 2020. https://branchoutnow.org/spirit-of-the-buffalo/ (May 8, 2021).

Mescher, Marcus. 2020. *The Ethics of Encounter: Christian Neighbor Love as a Practice of Solidarity*. Maryknoll, NY: Orbis Books.

Mills, Aaron [Waabishki Ma'iingan]. 2017. "What Is a Treaty? On Contract and Mutual Aid." In *The Right Relationship: Reimagining the Implementation of Historic Treaties*, edited by John Borrows and Michael Coyle, 208–47. Toronto: University of Toronto Press.

Morin, Brandi. 2018. "'We're So Used to Not Saying Anything': Standing Up Against Racism in St. Paul, Alta." *The Discourse*, February 3, 2018. https://thediscourse.ca/urban-nation/used-not-saying-anything-standing-racism-st-paul-alta.

Napoleon, Val, and Hadley Friedland. 2016. "An Inside Job: Engaging with Indigenous Legal Tradition through Stories." *McGill Law Journal* 61 (4): 725–54.

Painter, Joe. 2012. "The Politics of the Neighbour." *Environment and Planning D: Society and Space* 30 (3): 515–33.

Reith, Terry, and Briar Stewart. 2016. "Ancient Grave in Alberta Farmer's Field Unearths Historical Mystery." *CBC News*, January 4, 2016. https://www.cbc.ca/news/canada/edmonton/ancient-burial-site-viking-alberta-1.3368518.

SARM (Saskatchewan Association of Rural Municipalities). 2017. "Rural Crime." Resolution 34-17A. https://sarm.ca/advocacy/resolutions/resolution-full?id=1024.

Scott, James. C. 2012. *Decoding Subaltern Politics: Ideology, Disguise, and Resistance in Agrarian Politics*. London: Routledge.

Short, Amanda. 2019. "FSIN and Farmers Sign Agreement to Protect Land Where Artifacts Found." *Saskatoon Star-Phoenix*, June 11, 2019. https://thestarphoenix.com/news/local-news/fsin-and-farmers-sign-agreement-to-protect-land-where-artifacts-found/.

Talisse, Robert. 2019. *Overdoing Democracy: Why We Must Put Politics in Its Place*. New York: Oxford University Press.

Walker, Connie. 2019. "Shooting Death of Young Indigenous Man Forces Rural Community to Confront Racism." *CBC News*, November 6. 2019. https://www.cbc.ca/news/indigenous/kristian-ayoungman-shooting-strathmore-alberta-1.4866823.

Warick, Jason. 2019. "Saskatchewan First Nations Want Road Project Stopped after Rare Artifact Discovery." *CBC News*, June 5, 2019. https://www.cbc.ca/news/canada/saskatoon/saskatchewan-indigenous-artifacts-1.5162189.

Wiebe, Nettie. 2001. "Rewriting the Rural West." In *Writing Off the Rural West*, edited by Roger Epp and Dave Whitson, 325–30. Edmonton: University of Alberta Press.

Wildcat, Matthew. 2018. "Wahkohtowin in Action." *Constitutional Forum* 27 (1): 13–24.

Wuthnow, Robert. 2018. *The Left Behind: Decline and Rage in Rural America*. Princeton: Princeton University Press.

Young, Robert. 1982. *Young's Analytical Concordance to the Bible*. Nashville: Thomas Nelson.

Žižek, Slavoj, Eric L. Santner, and Kenneth Reinhard. 2013. *The Neighbor: Three Inquiries in Political Theology*. Chicago: University of Chicago Press.

CONCLUSION

Clark Banack and Dionne Pohler

WE INTRODUCED THIS VOLUME by posing several questions about cultural, racial, and religious inclusiveness in rural Canada—a topic that, to date, has not received much scholarly attention. To what degree does cultural, racial, and/or religious intolerance exist in rural Canadian communities? What does such intolerance look like in rural Canada and how do such attitudes manifest? How should such attitudes be addressed in the context of the realities of rural life? What examples exist of organizations and individuals working to counter such attitudes and build more inclusive rural communities? How can institutions like schools, churches, co-ops, and community groups, so fundamental to everyday life in rural communities, play a central role in this work? And more generally, what do more inclusive rural communities look like? While we have not provided definitive answers, the volume's contributing authors have explored each of these questions in ways that provide much-needed starting points for future academic and practical work in this area.

Taken together, the chapters in this volume provide distinct ways of considering the racial, cultural, and religious diversity that exists in rural Canada (a place more diverse than many realize); the attitudes that exist towards racial, cultural, and religious minorities and Indigenous peoples in rural Canada (attitudes that are often more complex than

most realize); and a multitude of approaches to think about the issue of inclusivity in rural areas, not to mention a number of practical tools that can be used to work toward building inclusive rural communities where each person feels like they belong. Throughout the volume, we have sought to make a rural-specific contribution to the topic of anti-racism, with a particular emphasis on "everyday anti-racism" wherein individuals and communities in rural Canada work to welcome, accept, and treat equally all individuals and groups, irrespective of race, culture, or religion. To describe our normative project, we adopted the language of neighbourliness and deep equality—lived virtues, ideas, and processes "enacted and owned by so-called ordinary people in everyday life" (Beaman 2017, 13). The overarching goal of such a project is to move beyond mere "tolerance" of the other, and toward a genuine embrace of equality, acceptance of meaningful difference, and, above all, desire to be in community together, much like good neighbours. Each of the chapters contributes, in its own way, to our understanding of rural Canadian communities and of the paths that must be taken to move closer to deep equality and the type of neighbourliness described in Epp's chapter in this volume. We hope that this has resonated with readers of the volume, and most especially with those who are undertaking the daily work of building more inclusive communities together with their rural neighbours.

There were several risks associated with developing an edited volume like this. First, it would have been easy to begin from the premise that rural Canada is "White and Christian," an assumption that erases the cultural, racial, and religious diversity that already exists in rural Canada. We hope that Bollman's and Hirsch and Borri-Anadon's chapters, which began this book, have challenged that premise by highlighting the "invisibilization" of diversity in rural areas, particularly when comparing rural communities to urban centres. We believe it is especially important to understand that while Indigenous peoples have always lived throughout Turtle Island, their presence today is especially visible in rural Canada, where they make up a growing proportion of the population.

A second noteworthy risk in a project such as this is to overemphasize either the welcoming and "friendly" nature of rural communities or, alternatively, the intolerance and bigotry of rural peoples. It would,

in other words, be easy to perpetuate well-worn myths about rural communities and peoples, and just as easy to create new, but equally misrepresentative, ones. The chapters in this volume, whether drawing upon quantitative or qualitative methodological approaches, avoid simple explanations for their findings, digging deeper into the literature, data, community contexts, and language to facilitate understanding and empathy without ignoring the very real challenges of building inclusion in rural communities. For instance, in Chapter 5, Haugen simultaneously highlights the problematic assumptions rural people can make about refugees (often due to a lack of knowledge about what to expect); the myriad ways rural people and organizations work to help newcomers build a home in the community; and the self-reflection rural people engage in through their interactions and relationships not only with their newcomer neighbours, but also with each other. Haugen's approach to exploring the multiple overlapping dimensions that shape interactions between longer-term rural residents and newcomers to rural communities avoids what Henderson critiques in Chapter 10 as "essentializing" rural peoples, communities, or cultures. And importantly, the lack of knowledge rural residents in Haugen's research had about newcomers highlights why a two-way community education approach like the one outlined by Lam in Chapter 7 can be so effective, especially when coupled with practical tools like Lam's board game or the Contextual Bible Study described by Lynch in Chapter 8.

There are also some limitations in this volume that present important opportunities for future research in this area. First, we focus almost solely on issues of race, culture, and religion, rather than on other equally significant forms of diversity related to, for example, gender, sexual orientation, or disability. The scope of our work simply did not allow us the room to pursue these other dimensions of diversity, nor the unique challenges of inclusion they present in rural communities, in the depth they deserve. Although Reimer noted in Chapter 3 that gender norms and ideas about sexual diversity in evangelical Christian communities may prove to be bigger barriers to deep equality in rural communities than either race or culture, we leave the broader research questions that such issues raise to future scholars who are keen to expand considerations around inclusion in rural Canada.

Second, aside from many of Henderson's critical insights in Chapter 10, we have not dedicated much space to the ways in which structural and systemic racism in Canada impact Indigenous and racialized residents in rural communities. Nor have we considered in much depth the way in which White settlers in rural Canada respond to claims that Canada suffers from a deep and systemic racism that infects its institutions in a variety of ways. Such claims, without being unpacked in ways that rural citizens can truly understand, may, we suspect, have the effect of hardening attitudes towards anti-racism work in general, although this has not been clearly verified. We noted in the introduction to this volume that we believe the most promising initial path towards building inclusive communities in much of rural Canada are grassroots approaches that work with individuals and groups through local and trusted institutions such as rural schools, churches, co-operatives, and other community-embedded organizations. However, it remains true that questions related to the systemic racism that permeates institutions at the national, provincial, and even local levels in Canada, and especially the way this impacts Indigenous and racialized residents in rural communities, require much additional research going forward.

Third, we only briefly explore the structural and political barriers facing rural communities and residents, and the possible ways to overcome these barriers, as they undertake the difficult work of building more inclusive communities. For instance, as Pohler and colleagues note in Chapter 9, settler and Indigenous communities and peoples in rural Canada have many similar needs and live in close proximity to each other, but they have been subject to historical and ongoing institutionally imposed segregation that limits their ability to work together and build trust within and across their communities. While it is difficult to think about how community-level initiatives can overcome these barriers, these authors outline how the development of co-operatives may provide opportunities for rural neighbours to work together to solve problems and build trust. As Epp so beautifully notes in the last paragraph of Chapter 11, we cannot forget the critical importance of relationships between people living in proximity to each other; in rural areas, "the ordinary virtues of the neighbour have not lost their relevance. They may represent the best hope...They can help redraw the circle of reciprocity,

different and together, one encounter at a time. For there will be no new way of living together...if it is not the work of neighbours."

Finally, while our volume contributors are not exclusively White settlers, the voices and experiences of Indigenous people and racial/religious minority settlers living in rural Canada are not the primary focus of this volume, nor are they the target audience. That most contributors to this volume cannot claim to have lived experience with the discriminatory attitudes we seek to overcome is certainly a point worth acknowledging and is, for some we are sure, a very real drawback of the volume. It would be ideal if future work in this direction explicitly incorporated more diverse perspectives, including from Indigenous and racialized settler residents who have experienced racism in rural Canada firsthand, and particularly from those working on anti-racism approaches and practices in rural communities. Indeed, the deep listening approach that Banack, in Chapter 4, used among coffee groups in rural Alberta could also be an effective methodology to explore the perspectives of more diverse groups on these issues.

Having acknowledged these limitations, however, it is important to recognize that Indigenous and racialized peoples should not be the only ones responsible for undertaking anti-racism work. Rather than trying to "speak for others," the contributors of this volume were, by and large, asked to think about how they might engage with rural settlers from their home communities on topics related to racism and inclusivity. It is also worth reiterating that this volume was premised on the idea that pursuing something akin to Beaman's deep equality requires, as a first step, meeting rural Canadians "where they are" when it comes to the topic of everyday anti-racism. Based on our experiences with rural communities and peoples, we are convinced that this requires cautious first steps led by those whom rural citizens would be likely to trust and to whom they are willing to listen. We hope that our work will encourage rural settlers to engage in their own self-reflection and basic education related to everyday anti-racism so more substantive work in the form of intercultural, interfaith, and interracial dialogue involving Indigenous peoples, racialized settler residents, and their White settler neighbours will find more fertile ground. Nevertheless, this contention and our preferred approach requires further testing, and we encourage other scholars, from

all manner of backgrounds and lived experiences, to consider doing more work in this area.

Despite these limitations and corresponding areas for future research, we remain convinced that this volume does make several very important contributions. First and foremost, this book cuts a novel path through academic terrain that has been, for the most part, untilled, both by scholars of rural studies in Canada and by those interested in the prevalence and development of appropriate responses to racism in Canadian society. That the contributing authors of this volume come from very different academic disciplines and communities and employ different ontological and epistemological perspectives has ensured a rich mixture of observations and prescriptions for moving the conversations on racism, both academic and practical, forward in rural Canada. Of course, this rich mixture also posed a unique challenge for us, as editors. It quickly became clear that combining all of these perspectives into a single volume with a common approach and thematic framework would prove difficult. Although we did push authors to think through how notions of inclusion, neighbourliness, and deep equality fit into their arguments, we acknowledge that not all authors came to see these terms in identical ways. Rather than struggle to impose a superficial uniformity across the volume by dulling the nuances and complexity of the approaches, arguments, and conclusions of each author, we allowed much of the complexity to remain. We realize that the contemporary "story" about rural Canada is a contested one, so a multiplicity of approaches and opinions, including ones that give rise to theoretical and methodological disagreements, are necessary to paint a more complete picture. Inevitably, once that picture has been painted, the dynamics will have shifted yet again.

In closing, we would like to move beyond these academic concerns to briefly highlight what we see as the key takeaways of this volume for the policy-makers, community leaders, and interested residents across rural Canada who share our practical interest in building more inclusive rural communities. From the first section of this book, we would like to highlight the diversity that does exist across rural Canada and invite rural residents to reflect on this diversity (including the trends toward an even more culturally and racially diverse future across rural Canada). We invite them in particular to reflect on the types of diversity that already

exist in their own communities. It has been our experience that most rural residents underestimate how diverse their community actually is—an assumption that can quickly lead many to believe that questions related to diversity and inclusion are solely an "urban" problem. They are not, and we hope that this volume will help to build awareness around that fact.

From the second section of the book, we hope that rural readers will reflect on just what racism can look like, as well as on their own personal views and those of their fellow neighbours towards Indigenous, racialized, and newcomer members of their community. Racism and intolerance can spring from many different sources. It is something that can be far more subtle than the actions of a local hate group or the online ravings of a blatantly anti-Semitic or Islamophobic community member. It can grow in church congregations who are suspicious of, or attempting to save, others. It can emerge out of a resentment that itself is rooted in the economic struggles of a community in decline. It can be present even in supremely well-intentioned individuals, such as the rural citizens eager to sponsor refugees, whom we met in Haugen's chapter. Given these quite varied sources, how might your community begin to chart out a strategy aimed at becoming a more inclusive place?

While that question is, admittedly, big and complicated, we hope that section three of the volume provides at least some guidance in terms of thinking about initial steps. Although written with teachers and university professors in mind, the self-study and reflection approach that Corbett, Tinkham, and Bonner adopt in Chapter 6 is one that community leaders and residents could use to come together in groups to "think critically about issues of equity and social justice." We believe this is an excellent place to start. Lam and Lynch provide even more practical steps in their chapters—steps that, we suspect, could play significant roles in rural communities across Canada. Why not invest in a set of educational board games of the type Lam describes and allow rural residents, young and old, to become exposed to new perspectives together in this way? Similarly, to those rural residents who belong to a Christian church in their community, we would urge you to think carefully about Lynch's words and the power of Contextual Bible Study as a tool for broadening the horizons of participants, leading to new understandings of how

Christians are called to relate to the other—a calling that is all the more important when those others are their neighbours. For non-Christian rural residents, we urge you to think about how this same approach could be adapted for use by interfaith and secular community groups in your area.

From section four, we hope that rural settler readers have accepted the invitation to reflect on their relationships with their neighbours. As Pohler and colleagues note in Chapter 9, one of the best ways to build trust and social cohesion between diverse groups in a community is to work together on a common project to meet shared needs. In what ways could a co-operative organization, ostensibly designed to address a specific economic or social goal in your community, simultaneously draw settler and Indigenous residents and communities together in ways that bridge long-existing divides?

Perhaps most importantly, in the two final chapters of this book, Henderson and Epp invite rural residents to think more critically about an idea about deep equality that is already central to the identity of rural communities throughout the country: that of neighbourliness. It would be difficult to find a rural community in Canada that does not pride itself on its neighbourliness, but as Henderson and Epp both note, the uncritical acceptance of such a sentiment can easily reinforce existing hierarchies and divisions, thereby dampening any serious movement in the direction of deep equality. How can you use the familiar idea of the good neighbour, so powerful in rural communities, to reframe your relations with newer community residents and between your settler community and the Indigenous community or communities down the road? Both Henderson and Epp provide some insightful thoughts on this topic that deserve to be read, deeply absorbed, and acted upon in practical ways by rural community leaders and residents as they consider the current state of their relationships with their neighbours.

Rural residents might also take a moment within their families and faith and community groups to quietly contemplate the fundamental question asked, and simultaneously answered, by Epp (this volume) as he (re)considers the radical lessons in the story of the Good Samaritan: "Who is the neighbour? Not the one you expect, not the one who is like you, and not necessarily the one you have been taught to respect…The neighbour

is the one who acts like a neighbour, and who takes no small risk in doing so." Understanding and learning how to act like a neighbour is the work of everyday anti-racism that will move us closer to our goal of building more inclusive and deeply equal rural communities in Canada.

REFERENCE

Beaman, Lori. 2017. *Deep Equality in an Era of Religious Diversity*. Oxford: Oxford University Press.

CONTRIBUTORS

Clark Banack is the director of the Alberta Centre for Sustainable Rural Communities and an adjunct professor of political studies at the Augustana Campus of the University of Alberta. Clark is the author of *God's Province: Evangelical Christianity, Political Thought, and Conservatism in Alberta* (McGill-Queen's University Press), the co-author of *Faith, Rights, and Choice: The Politics of Religious Schooling in Canada* (University of Toronto Press), and has published numerous articles and book chapters related to Alberta politics, rural issues, religion and politics, education policy, and populism in Canada. He is also a proud rural Albertan who is very active in his home community.

Ray D. Bollman retired from Statistics Canada in 2011. He was the founding editor of Statistics Canada's *Rural and Small Town Canada Analysis Bulletin*, of which there are now 65 available. He is a past chair of the OECD Working Party on Territorial Indicators, and currently a research affiliate at the Rural Development Institute, Brandon University; a professional associate at the Leslie Harris Centre of Regional Policy and Development, Memorial University; and a research associate at the Rural Futures Research Centre, Dalhousie University. He is the author of *Rural Canada 2013: An Update* for the Federation of Canadian Municipalities

(available from the Canadian Rural Revitalization Foundation website) and over 100 fact sheets in *Focus on Rural Ontario* for the Rural Ontario Institute. His recent research contributions have focused on the dimensions of rurality including from the perspective of the right to be rural, COVID-19 impacts on rural employment and rural schooling.

Claudine Bonner is a scholar of African Canadian history and education, and a member of the Department of Sociology and the Women's and Gender Studies program at Acadia University. Her research is grounded in history and broadly applied in analyses of race, gender, education, and identity in contemporary Canada. Her scholarship bridges the gap between studies of the Black Canadian experience and the broader African Diaspora, and crosses generational boundaries through innovative oral histories, community-based research, and published collaborative research with leading Canadian scholars.

Corina Borri-Anadon is a full professor in the Education Department at the Université du Québec à Trois-Rivières. Her academic work and publications are at the intersections of special education and ethnic relations in education fields. Her research focuses on three main axes: ethnocultural, linguistic, and religious diversity in training school personnel; inclusion-exclusion issues in special education; and paramedical personnel practices in schools.

Jen Budney is a professional research associate at the Centre for the Study of Co-operatives and an instructor at Johnson Shoyama Graduate School of Public Policy, University of Saskatchewan, where she has developed and instructed one course on Social Economy and Public Policy and another on Ethical Leadership and Democracy in Public Service. She collaborates with the nonprofit organization Co-operatives First on the course Good Governance Matters, and frequently writes and speaks about diversity and inclusion in co-operatives and nonprofit organizations.

Michael Corbett is a professor in the School of Education at Acadia University and an adjunct professor of rural and regional education in the Faculty of Education at the University of Tasmania. Corbett has studied rural out-migration, the politics of educational assessment, literacies in rural contexts, and the position of rural identities and experience in education. He has published more than 70 scholarly works including books, papers, book chapters, and review essays relating to rural education in Canada. He lives in rural Nova Scotia.

Roger Epp is a professor of political science at the University of Alberta. He is the author of *We Are All Treaty People* (University of Alberta Press 2008), contributing co-editor of *Writing Off the Rural West* (University of Alberta Press 2001), and co-producer of the documentary "The Canadian Clearances: The New Rural Activism" for CBC Radio's *Ideas* (2003). He was an honorary witness at a hearing of the Truth and Reconciliation Commission at Ermineskin Cree Nation and a panelist at the Commission's final national event.

Murray Fulton is a professor in the Johnson Shoyama Graduate School of Public Policy and a fellow in co-operatives and public policy with the Centre for the Study of Co-operatives, University of Saskatchewan. Murray has published widely on co-operatives and industrial organization. His current research is focused on governance in public agencies and co-operatives, and in behavioural economics and its application to business strategy and public policy formation.

Stacey Haugen is a PhD student in the Department of Political Science at the University of Alberta and a research associate at the Prentice Institute for Global Population and Economy. She holds a Master of Arts degree in global governance from the Balsillie School of International Affairs, has worked as a researcher at the Canadian International Development Research Centre, and has extensively studied the attitudes and realities present in rural Canadian communities. Her research particularly focuses on the resettlement and integration of Syrian refugees in rural Canada.

Phil Henderson is a settler and PhD candidate in Political Science and Indigenous Nationhood at the University of Victoria (Lkwungen Territories) and an incoming SSHRC post-doctoral fellow at Carleton University's Institute of Political Economy. His work investigates Canadian Politics through community-based relationships between settlers and Indigenous peoples with an eye to both white backlash politics in an era of rising white identitarianism, and also towards the emerging possibility of land-based alliance-building projects in the face of global climatic change. Future research plans include a detailed study of the interrelations between Indigenous land/water defenders and organized labour.

Sivane Hirsch is a full professor in the Department of Education at the Université du Quebec à Trois-Rivières. Her research lies at the intersection of sociology and educational sciences, focusing on the way religious and cultural diversity is taken into account in both formal and informal education. Recent publications include *Judaïsme et education: Enjeux et défis pédagogiques* (Presses de l'Université Laval, 2016) as well as articles that have appeared in journals such as *McGill Journal of Education*, *Eruostudia*, and the *Revue de didactique des sciences des religions*. She has also authored several pedagogical guides to support teachers in the challenges they meet in their work.

Michelle Lam, PhD, is the director of BU CARES Research Centre, an applied research centre in the Faulty of Education at Brandon University. She lives and works on Treaty 2 territory, land traditionally shared by the Dakota and Ojibway, and home to the Métis people. Michelle is interested in anti-racist educational interventions, human migration, newcomer integration, and the role that education plays in promoting equity in rural areas.

Coleen Lynch BEd, BA, MDiv, MTh, has nearly 50 years of ministry experience in rural settings in western Canada and in Peru in the Anglican and Roman Catholic traditions. As well, her extensive prison and community corrections ministry has proven that lasting change can happen. Through the frequent use of scripture as the catalyst for examining real-life issues today, Coleen has promoted dialogue with individuals and groups that differ, often radically, towards a greater mutual tolerance through reflection and planning for the common good.

Aasa Marshall is Co-operatives First's communications lead. She has a BA in Development Studies from the University of Calgary, and a master's of public policy from the Johnson Shoyama Graduate School of Public Policy at the University of Saskatchewan. While there, she worked as a research assistant for the Centre for the Study of Co-operatives.

Darcy Overland was the research manager at the Centre for the Study of Co-operatives, University of Saskatchewan, from 2015 to 2019. She is strong believer in community and the power of the local and is a passionate community volunteer. She has over 15 years' experience working for the Government of Canada and the Province of Saskatchewan in labour market adjustment programming focused on youth, rural, and Indigenous populations. She holds a master's of public administration from the University of Saskatchewan and a bachelor's of education and arts from the University of Regina.

Trista Pewapisconias is a member of the Little Pine First Nation in Saskatchewan and the Indigenous relations lead for Co-operatives First. In her role with Co-operatives First, Trista works alongside community members to form new businesses based on the co-operative model. Her support with business development and planning helps guide groups through the process of starting a successful business. Trista's professional experience includes various marketing roles, as well as writing business plans for Indigenous start-up companies. A tireless advocate for Indigenous business, Trista was also a founding board member of the Indigenous Chamber of Commerce of Saskatchewan.

Dionne Pohler is an associate professor at the University of Saskatchewan Edwards School of Business and a research fellow at the University of Toronto Rotman Institute for Gender and the Economy. She holds the Co-operative Retailing System Chair in Co-operative Governance at the Canadian Centre for the Study of Co-operatives and the Johnson Shoyama Graduate School of Public Policy. Pohler is the editor of *Reimagining the Governance of Work and Employment* (Cornell University Press) and has several publications related to labour and employment, co-operatives, organizational governance, and public policy. Dionne was a founding board member of Co-operatives First, a business development and community-building organization focused on working with rural settler and Indigenous communities to address the needs identified by these communities through the co-operative model.

Samuel Reimer is Professor of Sociology at Crandall University in Moncton, New Brunswick. He specializes in Protestant Christianity, including congregations in Canada, the United States and Britain. He is the author of *Evangelicals and the Continental Divide* (McGill-Queen's University Press, 2003), *A Culture of Faith: Evangelical Congregations in Canada* (McGill-Queen's University Press, 2015), and many journal articles and book chapters. He is the recipient of the Alan Richardson Fellowship at Durham University, England.

Jennifer Tinkham is an associate professor of social studies education at Acadia University. She holds a doctorate in social studies education from the University of Alberta. Her research program is rooted in social studies and Indigenous education. She is actively focused on making spaces for counternarratives in Canadian history, how to decolonize the field of social studies teaching and learning, how to inspire students to engage with and enjoy social studies, and how to support teachers along this same journey. Jennifer is a former elementary teacher and has been working in social studies teacher education since 2006.

Kyle White is the governance and education lead with Co-operatives First. His work focuses on developing and delivering educational and development services for Co-operatives First. Originally from Newfoundland and Labrador, Kyle has worked his way across Canada focusing on community economic development in rural and Indigenous communities. With degrees in geography and public policy, Kyle's educational background has focused on community development, governance, and organizational policy. Aside from his work with Co-operatives First, Kyle is an active volunteer with several Saskatoon-based nonprofits and serves on a variety of boards.

Other Titles from University of Alberta Press

The Right to Be Rural
Edited by KAREN R. FOSTER & JENNIFER JARMAN

The provocative concept of a "right to be rural" illuminates challenges facing rural communities worldwide.

Sustainability Planning and Collaboration in Rural Canada
Taking the Next Steps

Edited by LARS K. HALLSTRÖM, MARY A. BECKIE, GLEN T. HVENEGAARD & KARSTEN MÜNDEL

Fourteen case studies examine and exemplify academic-community partnerships in sustainability planning across rural Canada.

More information at uap.ualberta.ca

BUILDING INCLUSIVE COMMUNITIES IN RURAL CANADA